Traversing the Fantasy

Traversing the Fantasy

The Dialectic of Desire/Fantasy and the Ethics of Narrative Cinema

Sandra Meiri
and
Odeya Kohen-Raz

BLOOMSBURY ACADEMIC
NEW YORK · LONDON · OXFORD · NEW DELHI · SYDNEY

BLOOMSBURY ACADEMIC
Bloomsbury Publishing Inc
1385 Broadway, New York, NY 10018, USA
50 Bedford Square, London, WC1B 3DP, UK
29 Earlsfort Terrace, Dublin 2, Ireland

BLOOMSBURY, BLOOMSBURY ACADEMIC and the Diana logo are trademarks of
Bloomsbury Publishing Plc

First published in the United States of America 2020
This paperback edition published in 2021

Copyright © Sandra Meiri and Odeya Kohen-Raz, 2020

For legal purposes the Acknowledgments on p. vi constitute an extension
of this copyright page.

Cover design by Ben Anlsow | Image: Kim Novak in a still from Vertigo, 1958.
Directed by Alfred Hitchcock © Alfred J Hitchcock Productions /
RNB / Collection Christophel / ArenaPAL

All rights reserved. No part of this publication may be reproduced or transmitted
in any form or by any means, electronic or mechanical, including photocopying,
recording, or any information storage or retrieval system, without prior
permission in writing from the publishers.

Bloomsbury Publishing Inc does not have any control over, or responsibility for, any
third-party websites referred to or in this book. All internet addresses given in this
book were correct at the time of going to press. The author and publisher regret
any inconvenience caused if addresses have changed or sites have ceased to
exist, but can accept no responsibility for any such changes.

Library of Congress Cataloging-in-Publication Data
Names: Meiri, Sandra, author. | Kohen-Raz, Odeya, author.
Title: Traversing the fantasy: the dialectic of desire/fantasy and the ethics of
narrative cinema / Sandra Meiri and Odeya Kohen-Raz.
Description: New York: Bloomsbury Academic, 2019. | Includes bibliographical
references and index.
Identifiers: LCCN 2019035755 (print) | LCCN 2019035756 (ebook) |
ISBN 9781501328732 (hardback) | ISBN 9781501328701 (pdf) |
ISBN 9781501328718 (epub)
Subjects: LCSH: Psychoanalysis and motion pictures. | Motion pictures–
Psychological aspects.
Classification: LCC PN1995.9.P783 M45 2019 (print) | LCC PN1995.9.P783 (ebook) |
DDC 791.43019–dc23
LC record available at https://lccn.loc.gov/2019035755
LC ebook record available at https://lccn.loc.gov/2019035756

ISBN: HB: 978-1-5013-2873-2
PB: 978-1-5013-8581-0
ePDF: 978-1-5013-2870-1
eBook: 978-1-5013-2871-8

Typeset by Deanta Global Publishing Services, Chennai, India

To find out more about our authors and books visit www.bloomsbury.com
and sign up for our newsletters.

*To the beautiful daughters in our families:
Ruthie, Sharon, Mia, and Annabelle.*

*A special dedication to our mentor and friend,
Régine-Mihal Friedman.*

CONTENTS

Acknowledgments viii

Introduction 1

PART ONE Body-Character-Breach Films 21

1 Desire, Fantasy and the Ontology of Film 23

2 Traversing the Fantasy: Body-Character-Breach Films 59

PART TWO Dreaming-Character Films 85

3 Dreams in Films and Implicit Reflexivity 87

4 Cinematography, Subjectivity, and Guilt 122

PART THREE Gender-Crossing Films 165

5 This Gender That Is Mine: Feminine Enjoyment and Self-Creation 167

6 From "Inherent Transgression" to the Body as "Semiotic *Chōra*" 202

Appendix 251
Notes 260
References 277
Index 297

ACKNOWLEDGMENTS

A special "Thank You" to those who helped make this book possible:

The Israel Science Foundation (ISF) for its unwavering support.

Nir Ferber, our assistant, without whose help this book would have taken much longer.

The Open University of Israel and Sapir Academic College for affording Odeya Kohen-Raz the time to realize this project.

Katie Gallof of Bloomsbury Publishing, who has been a constant source of support.

And special mention to Alon Judkovsky, Helene Landau, and Alex Newgrosh.

Introduction

This book establishes a new and comprehensive psychoanalytic model of spectatorship based on the conjunction of the operation of desire/fantasy in narrative film (classical, mainstream, and classical/mainstream authorial) and film's ontology and aesthetics, especially the nature of the cinematographic image regarding the correspondence between characters and actors. This conjunction consists of the following correlations: Desire, which according to Jacques Lacan is related to lack, taps into the lack of the screen; while fantasy, whose traits are visuality and specularity, taps into the visual fullness projected onto the screen. This constitutes a unique experience of an absent presence. Within this framework we draw an analogy between the ethics of psychoanalysis and the ethics of narrative film by introducing the notion of subjectivization, as defined by Bruce Fink ([1995] 1997: xii–xiii).

Subjectivization refers to a shift in the unconscious fundamental fantasy that organizes the subject's relation to the Other's desire. Fantasy stages the position in which the subject sees itself "with respect to the object that causes, elicits and incites its desire" (xiii) and enjoyment, what Lacan terms "the traversal of the fantasy" and what Fink goes on to describe as "a reconfiguration of fantasy . . . a new subject position" ([1995] 1997). The subject's process of modifying its position with regard to the Other's enigmatic desire thus entails acknowledgment of the desire that is in the subject, re-economization of the enjoyment, and the overcoming of fixations. At the end of this process, the subject is free to make a choice regarding their own fate, and then pursue it, which constitutes the ethics of psychoanalysis—subjectivization. This book, in other words, offers, as well as traces, a journey that is contingent on getting to a point where the subject knows what their own desire is and then realizes it—a process we detect in narrative films. Some films put the emphasis on the first stage of this journey, namely, acknowledging the desire that is in the protagonist; in other films this is the protagonist's starting point.

We demonstrate this journey via three film corpora, all revolving around characters, who are the agents of subjectivity and subjectivization: (1) body-character-breach films; (2) dreaming-character films; and (3) gender-crossing films. These rhetorical devices (breaching, dreaming, and crossing) in compliance with film's unique ontology, tamper with the spectators' engagement with fantasy. This tampering is achieved in relation to the nature of the cinematographic image regarding characters-actors (mostly protagonists): their *corporeality* (real flesh and blood actors), on the one hand, and their physical absence from the screen, on the other. The book demonstrates that tampering with fantasy in order to traverse it can only occur within a careful dynamic of desire/fantasy, the latter being what engages us unconsciously with film. The rhetorical and aesthetic devices and strategies the films use to manipulate the dynamic of desire/fantasy generate a process of subjectivization for both protagonists and spectators. Hence the analogy between the ethics of psychoanalysis and that of *narrative* film.

Desire/Fantasy

Desire, according to Lacan ([1964] 1998: 205), characterizes all human beings, is unconscious, and is manifested as a longing that can never be satisfied. It is related to lack because it derives from a chain of alienating experiences, all related to the Other: at the moment of birth, the subject already loses a portion of itself, and with the entry into the symbolic (the acquisition of language), it has to repress the incestuous desire for the mother (e.g., Lacan [1959–60] 1997: esp. 57–84). But above all, desire is born into a linguistic structure even before children learn how to speak, as they must articulate their needs vocally (e.g., Lacan [1958/1966] 2006): Children address their mother (or another) by crying; the latter can satisfy their needs (which are purely biological instincts, for example, hunger and thirst) but not the unconditional demand for love. However, when she responds to the helpless infant's demand to fulfill a need, her presence comes to acquire an importance in itself, now symbolizing her love, beyond the satisfaction of the need. Therefore, the child's demand takes on a double function: articulation of need and demand for love. Desire is born from the gap between need and demand; it is what is left over, resulting from the subtraction of the appetite for satisfaction (the need) and the demand for love. Desire thus emerges in the field of the Other as a longing; it is related to a lack that can never be filled, encapsulating both the desire for recognition by another and the desire to be the object-cause of another's desire.

To the extent that desire originates from another, it is also the Other's desire, which is always enigmatic. Thus, the subject's *fundamental* question in relation to the Other's desire is, "What does the Other want from me?" (Lacan [1960/1966] 2006: 690). The repressed fantasy of incest with the mother, the fantasy of (re)finding the (already) lost object—the lack in the Other, or "castration"—not only creates the unconscious but also establishes a mechanism by which the subject will never cease to seek a defense against this lack by attempting to provide an answer to the enigma of the Other's desire. This mechanism—namely, the erroneous scenarios the subject imagines the Other wants—is fantasy in Lacanian psychoanalysis.

However, Lacan, while accepting Freud's formulation of fantasy as a visual configuration that stages desire, also emphasizes its protective function against lack because of its satisfying nature. Moreover, in the neurotic "normal" structure, fantasy "is the support of desire; it is not the object that is the support of desire" (Lacan [1964] 1998: 185).

Desire/Fantasy and the Ontology of Film: The Engagement of Spectators, the Primal Scene, and the Actor-Character

In Christian Metz's ([1977] 1982) description of the ontology of film in relation to the appeal of classical narrative film to large audiences, three facts are essential: (1) the absence of actors and objects from the spectators' space; (2) the role of seeing in spectatorship in regard to this absence; (3) and the ability of cinema to embellish its imaginary objects, the latter playing the role of fantasy objects. While the first taps into the experience of lack and desire, the other two are attributed to the world of fantasy as daydream—Freud's term for conscious fantasy.

For Metz, the cinematic object is doubly imaginary because it is both fictional, like in theater, and absent from the screen, unlike in theater (see especially 129–37). Thus, when comparing cinema with Freud's notion of the daydream, he emphasizes its protective function, contending that classical narrative cinema offers spectators an experience whereby we can pretend for an hour and a half that there is no lack. He further argues that although we are absorbed in the sequences of images projected on the screen, we are nevertheless aware of the film being only a daydream. Because of film's imaginary nature, as well as the spectators' awareness, Metz sees no substantial gain in developing the contents and manifestations of the *unconscious* engagement with a film, namely with the dynamic of desire/fantasy. In arguing that the experience of viewing a film is specifically Oedipal, simulating the fantasy of the primal scene, he goes only as far as to make a structural comparison between the physical conditions of the primal scene and the viewing of film in a movie theater (see especially 63–66).

We claim that what enables spectators to be so absorbed in a narrative film is the unconscious engagement with the protagonist's desire (not necessarily *identification* with it), with the anticipation that it be fulfilled in the end, and an unconscious inscription in the primal scene fantasy, enabled by the imaginary nature of film as well as its various techniques. This is narrative film's paradoxical nature: It is precisely the unattainability of the object on the screen, associated by Metz with the imaginary, that makes it possible for spectators to let the camera inscribe us into a fantasmatic space, compatible with an unconscious inscription in the primal scene fantasy.

According to Jean Laplanche and Jean-Bertrand Pontalis ([1967] 1973: 335), the primal scene fantasy is a "scene of sexual intercourse between the parents which the child observes or infers on the basis of certain indications." The primal scene is one of what Freud called primal fantasies (*Urphantasien*), which are also fantasies of origin, and it generates sexual excitation as well as anxiety. It accounts for the origin of the subject as well as the child's wish to be included in the desire of those who created them. As Laplanche and Pontalis ([1964] 1986) show in their reexamination of Freud's theory of fantasy there are three primal fantasies that constitute an Oedipal structure: (1) the primal scene, which, as mentioned above, refers to the origin of the subject; (2) the seduction fantasy, which refers to the emergence of sexuality; and (3) the castration fantasy, which refers to the origin of sexual difference. The truth of these constitutive unconscious fantasies, which Freud regarded as hereditary schemas going back through generations phylogenetically, is reconfirmed by the experience of each individual (child) ontogenetically and is subsequently repressed. Conscious fantasies, or daydreams, they say, are thus a secondary elaboration, "a restoring of minimum of order and coherence to the raw material handed over by the unconscious mechanism" (21). The Oedipal configuration is identifiable in both primal fantasies and daydreams. In the scenario the subject envisions in a waking state (the daydream), the staging is scripted in the first person; the subject is the protagonist. In the unconscious fantasy, the child/subject is one of the characters in the scene and may occupy more than one position/place simultaneously[1]—for example, in the primal scene, they may be both a witness to the parental coitus and a participant in it, as is often apparent in dreams (see Freud [1919] 1955a).

Through its editing techniques and camera movements, cinema uses its temporal and spatial discrepancy (the presence of the actors, who are absent from the spectators' scopic space; conversely, the spectators' absence from the space in which the scenes were shot) to inscribe us into the spatial and scopic space of its characters. It creates an imaginary presence through which the character's body and that of the actor are coalesced into one unity. The absent presence of the actors in conformity with the techniques of film allows us to be where the characters are, as in the theater; but, unlike the theater, we also get to see what they see from the place in space they are positioned. In short, what film "realizes" is our desire not only to see but also to be "physically" included in a space from which as subjects we were and still are excluded. The filmic scene renders the past and the location (the then and there) as here and now (the setting of the daydream). As asserted by phenomenological film theories (mostly Vivian Sobchack), the camera, which imitates the human eye, is present in the space of the scene, transposing our bodies into it as if we were there, allowing us to see what the characters see but, at the same time, preserving our awareness that we are not really "there." The spectators' unconscious inscription into the fantasmatic space/scene, facilitated through its affinity with the primal scene fantasy and enabled by the camera's multiple positioning, is unique to film. It thus transgresses both the prohibited and the impossible.

This unconscious process constitutes, in our view, the appeal of narrative film regardless of cultural and social constructions and identities. It first addresses the spectators' lack, as we are excluded from the space of the actors portraying desiring subjects, as the child is excluded from the setting of the parents' coitus. Second, by minutely showing the spectators how and what/whom the protagonist desires, it positions us in a place that aspires to fill the lack in the Other, regardless of the specific content of the protagonist's desire. To our understanding, narrative cinema thus brings together the Freudian desire to occupy the position of one of the parents in the primal scene (the prohibited) and the Lacanian position of a subjective inscription into the Other's desire (the impossible), with the intention of veiling its lack.

The prohibited and the impossible within the structure of the primal scene are transgressed due to the imaginary unity of body-actor, time and space. This imaginary unity explains why the one thing a plot will almost always refrain from omitting in film is showing its characters, mostly the protagonists, embodied by actors. In Lacanian psychoanalysis the object that sets desire in motion ("the object-cause-of-desire") is called "*objet (petit) a*"—an object that can never be attained, including the four partial objects that define the partial drives (partial because they realize sexuality only partially). As an object designating a pure lack, a nonexistence, we associate the absence of the body of the actor from the screen, signifying cinema's lack, with *objet a*, but its translation to the imaginary (the way it appears on the screen) turns it into a fantasy object, an object that fills the lack of the screen tantamount with the lack in the Other. The filling of *objet a* with a fantasy object that is conceived in the conjunction of the character with the actor's attributes—a conception that guides casting decisions—is the linchpin of cinema covering over the lack of the screen. The actor's body may function as a fantasy object in relation to the spectator, to other characters in the film's diegesis, or both.[2]

Subjectivization and Ethics: Three Cinematic Corpora within a Tripartite Model

The precondition for subjectivization is the dynamic of desire/fantasy. Although desire is what first attracts us to view a film, it is fantasy that sustains the desire to go on viewing it. Therefore, if there is no fantasy to engage with, there is nothing to traverse. We find that subjectivization consists of two major stages: inscribing the spectators in the fantasy of the primal scene (compatible with inscription in the Other's desire) and then casting us out of it through various rhetorical and aesthetic devices. Thus, the first stage in the process of subjectivization is renouncing inscription in the Other's desire. It may (a) pertain to the protagonists, (b) be directed at the spectators, or (c) both. The notion that runs the gamut of the book is that within the economy of desire/fantasy in narrative film, the encounter with, as well as acceptance of, castration is best achieved when the network of fantasy, both in its role of veiling castration and sustaining desire, is not entirely dissolved. The reason for it is that the dialectic of desire/fantasy reverberates with the subject's unconscious struggle with castration (the lack in the Other) in life. This means that a process of subjectivization regarding spectators is only possible in narrative films that maintain a careful dynamic of desire/fantasy; and that such films, including not only counter-cinema or highly artistic authorial films but many popular mainstream films as well, deserve to be included in the discourse of film and ethics.

The book is divided into three parts, in accordance with the three film corpora through which subjectivization is demonstrated: body-character-breach films; dreaming-character films; and gender-crossing films. The first (body-character-breach films) and third (gender-crossing films) corpora each provide a taxonomy (detailed in the appendix) regarding the different ways and forms that upset the relations between actor-character-body in the dynamic of desire/fantasy. These classifications provide the basis for our claim that the traversal of the fantasy is not only prevalent in narrative film but that it must concern the protagonists, the actors who play them, and the fact that their body is absent from the screen. The first corpus (Part One, body-character-breach films) thus comprises films that tamper with the links between actor and character. It encompasses six categories: (1) body switch, (2) reincarnation, (3) body transformation, (4) multiple-body character, (5) body host, and (6) bodiless characters. In the first three categories (1–3), the fantasy of wholeness, of filling the lack in the Other, is configured in the (initial) desire to be the Other and to know what the Other wants; in the last three categories (4–6), the films center on the desire to occupy a place that marks a lack. In all categories the desire to fill the lack in the Other is undermined (therefore, although the characters change bodies, they do not really become the Other) by tampering with casting, like two characters-actors switching bodies, the protagonist transforming physically, the protagonist embodied by many actors, a main character without bodily representation, and so on. Subjectivization, or the process of the traversal of the fantasy, is contingent on the following conditions: identification with the protagonist's fantasy to conceal the lack in the Other (inscription in the primal scene); dissolution of this fantasy, initiated by the body-character breach; and additional rhetorical and aesthetic devices. All these encourage us to adopt a reflective/reflexive position and acknowledge our desire.

In the second corpus (Part Two, dreaming-character films) subjectivization is also connected to the protagonist's inscription in the Other's desire and is related to the intrinsic guilt of cinema. The protagonists' dreams reveal guilt, due to which they are unable to recognize reality for what it is. In all the films of the corpus, the guilt is associated with the prohibited desire for the mother and the repressed fantasy of being the object of her desire in the configuration of the fantasy of the primal scene. Subjectivization is thus allied with renouncing this position. In the explicitly meta-cinematic films of the corpus, the guilt expressed in the dreams is linked to screen tests and audition scenes representing non-diegetic components in the production of a film, that is, the casting process: a situation occurring prior to the actual filmmaking and one that spectators are not aware of because we only see the result—the actor chosen for the leading role (never the rejects). These scenes reveal that casting aims to satisfy a collective desire by providing a fantasy object (the star system depends on this): the physique and persona of actors are meant to fulfill that which in life the subject is guilty of, namely pretending to guess what the m/Other (the audience) wants. The meta-cinematic films thus draw an analogy between the subject's erroneous position vis-à-vis the desire of/for the mother and the spectators' engagement with the fantasy of a film. Therefore, subjectivization here is attributed not only to the protagonist (and the spectators), but to the films themselves in that they reveal why both narrative cinema and counter-cinema should feel guilty.

The third corpus (Part Three, gender-crossing films) comprises a six-category taxonomy of gender-crossing characters in narrative cinema, whose bodily image in terms of spectatorship is always visually ambiguous, uncanny, or multilayered: (1) the cross-dresser, (2) the tomboy, (3) the transvestite, (4) trans protagonists, (5) the trans-body (a fantastic category only possible in fiction), and (6) the drag queen. We explain how the gender-crossing figure cuts through all primal fantasies (the primal scene, castration, and seduction) in terms of both the protagonist and spectators, inexorably yoking together three distinct phenomena—sex (female/male), gender (man/woman, feminine/masculine, transgender), and sexuality (heterosexual, homosexual, bisexual)—in new and versatile configurations, all undermining binary cultural notions regarding these phenomena, in fact, dismantling all connections between them. As mentioned before, subjectivization is not only a process of acknowledging one's desire but also one of re-economizing enjoyment whereby the subject is no longer "fixated, as symptom, as a repetitive, symptomatic way of 'getting off' or obtaining *jouissance*" (Fink [1995] 1997: xii) but overcomes "that fixation, the reconfiguring or traversing the fantasy, and the shifting of the way in which one ... obtains *jouissance*: that is the face of *subjectivization*, a process of making 'one's own' something that was formerly alien" ([1995] 1997, italics in the original), alien because what the subject internalizes through their intersubjective relationships is mostly the undecipherable and enigmatic otherness of the Other, for which Lacan ([1959–60] 1997: 139) coined the term "extimacy"—that which is experienced as the most foreign and exterior to the subject becomes the inmost, intimate core aspect of subjectivity.

The way out of extimacy in the gender-crossing films is "feminine enjoyment" (*la jouissance féminine*) as opposed to "phallic enjoyment," thus completing the notion/process of subjectivization—from acknowledging the desire that is in the protagonist to satisfying it in the real. While feminine enjoyment yields to the drives and affords lasting satisfaction by finding a special signifier in the real (a form of sublimation of the drives), the phallic one, which yields to desire (the symbolic, "castration"), leaves the subject in the realm of unsatisfied desire. We further ally feminine enjoyment with Julia Kristeva's notion of "the semiotic." Subjectivization here is explored through the journey undergone by gender-crossing protagonists, a path beyond neurosis (the "masculine" structure in Lacan), as characterized by the "feminine" structure in Lacan's formula on sexuation.

Thus, our model of subjectivization is developed in these three film corpora in two stages: In the first (Parts One and Two), we describe a transition from being trapped in the Other's desire to acknowledging one's own desire and acting upon it. In the second stage (Part Three) this constitutes the starting point for the protagonists (or most of them), hence the association of subjectivization with feminine enjoyment—a form of satisfaction achieved in *the real*. Underlying this model is the function of the actor's body in relation to the dynamic of desire/fantasy in narrative film and the structure of subjectivity, namely the Lacanian tripartite structure in its entirety, in its "Borromean knot" sense: the imaginary, the symbolic, and the real.

The Book Chapters

Each part comprises two chapters. Chapter 1 lays the theoretical foundation for the relationship between the act of viewing a film and the dynamic of desire/fantasy in terms of film's ontology and aesthetics. While desire (in the narrative, desire is related to what the protagonists lack) is linked to the lack of the screen, namely the absence of the object from the screen, which is what generates the spectators' desire to see *more*, fantasy is linked to the visual richness of the images projected on the screen and how they are rendered (the aesthetics of film—what, where, when, and how they are shown). Fantasy's function thus is to compensate for the lack/absence inherent in the filmic experience and to ensure our libidinal investment in the act of viewing a film. Moreover, the unfolding of the narrative and film's aesthetic devices and techniques not only answer our desire with fantasy but also sustain desire.

As mentioned before, in Lacanian psychoanalysis *objet a* is the object that sets desire in motion—an object that can never be attained, including the four partial objects that define the partial drives, two of which play a vital role in the engagement with film: the scopic and the invocatory. Both can be manipulated in film either in service of desire (evincing the lack of the screen, the traumatic lack, the "split" subject, etc.) or in service of fantasy (evincing fullness, wholeness, veiling the separation between spectator and screen, and so on). Usually, films refrain from omitting to show its characters, mostly the protagonists, thus answering our desire to see the characters embodied by actors. The character, as incorporated by an actor, along with the actor's physical attributes, persona, and their transformation to the cinematographic image, thus constitutes both a desiring subject (what the character we are engaged with wants) and an object of desire/fantasy (*objet a*), that is, not attainable or accessible but owning the capacity to veil lack.

We elaborate on the role of the actor in the engagement of spectators with film, focusing on (a) the spectators' inscription in the filmic space via its affinity with the structure of the primal scene fantasy and (b) the conversion of the body of the actor into its incandescence on the screen (the manipulation of the cinematographic image through *photogénie*) through casting and the use of the close-up. We analyze films that challenge the engagement with fantasy (as related to both casting and the use of the close-up), all of which are exceptions that prove the rule.

Our first example regarding the embodiment of characters by actors are films that impede inscription of spectators into the filmic space via the actor's body by precluding his or her presence in the diegesis, like *Lady in the Lake* (Robert Montgomery 1947), in which we are mostly denied the desire to see the protagonist. We see only what he sees, the camera acting as the body that occupies his place. When the other characters address him, they are in fact addressing the camera—the spectators—so that we do not see his reaction shots. Thus, rather than functioning as an invisible eye/body that allows us to "be" "everywhere," transcending or transgressing the limits and the discrepancies of space and time, the camera reveals them, impeding our engagement with the protagonist's desire via the inscription in the primal scene.

Another example regarding the embodiment of characters by actors is what we call "bodiless-character films" (in Chapter 2 this is a category in our body-character-breach taxonomy). In such films, characters who are crucial to the unfolding of the narrative are not visually rendered, and hence not embodied by actors, thus frustrating our desire to see: In *Rebecca* (Alfred Hitchcock 1940), there are no flashbacks showing the dead Rebecca and in *North by Northwest* (Hitchcock 1959) we participate in a chase after a character ("Kaplan") that does not exist in the reality of the diegesis; in *2001: A Space Odyssey* (Stanley Kubrick 1968) and *Her* (Spike Jonze 2013) we only hear one of the main nonhuman protagonists (a computer and an advanced operating system, respectively, figuring an actor's voice and possessing a point of view). While the scopic drive in connection to characters is generated in cinema through the visualization of a body and the subjectivity of the character is embodied by an actor, the invocatory drive is generated through the voice, experienced as an integral, albeit illusionary, part of the actor/character. The last two films thus expose cinema's lack—its illusionary unity of sound and image. When detached from a body/actor, the voice is emphasized as a partial object that threatens the imaginary unity of the subject/spectator. Although all these bodiless-character films problematize our inscription in the primal scene, three of them—the two Hitchcock films and *Her*—nevertheless demonstrate that if narrative film does not want to lose its spectators, it must create a fantasy with which we can engage, as well as employ devices that satisfy our desire to see.

Chapter 1 then addresses the conversion of the body of the actor into its incandescence on the screen through analysis of films that tackle it through their use of the face in close-up. Contrary to theories suggesting that the close-up is a device that achieves identification with the protagonist, hence with the film's ideology, we claim that the close-up has two main functions: either to further inscribe us into the filmic space or to preclude such inscription. First, the close-up is a synecdoche, a poetic, visual rhetorical device that enables the spectators to identify the character/actor/star and separate them from any other insignificant or less significant characters. Second, if we compare the motion in cinema (the image in flux) with the perpetual motion of desire, we might assume that the function of the face of the protagonist in close-up is to stop the motion of desire momentarily by fixing the face of the protagonist as a fantasy object (not withstanding its vibrancy, the close-up is a two dimensional and, to a large extent, immobile visual image), often in service of fetishism, thus avoiding an encounter with the lack of the screen. To avoid this encounter that might risk disengagement with the filmic space, the face of the protagonist in close-up is usually sewn into the illusionary three-dimensional space of the diegesis by the rendering of long shots of the character to whom the close-up belongs (before or after the close-up), or long shots of other characters suggesting that the close-up was (or is about to be) a POV shot (a face seen by others). This ensures our (re)engagement with the protagonist's desire and subjectivity (a desiring subject) as well as them being an object of desire (for other characters, as well as us). The face in close-up thus is a vital element in the dynamic of desire/fantasy, evincing that without inscription in the protagonist's desire and without the film creating some sort of fantasy that sustains our desire while viewing a film, we are left in the realm of the traumatic.

To demonstrate this, the chapter offers a close analysis of *Les yeux sans visage* (*The Eyes without a Face*, George Franju 1960), in which the close-up of the face is associated with death and decay—what the film also underscores through its portrayal of characters and the narrative. Whereas in films like *Rebecca* and *Her* the dynamic of desire/fantasy is not altogether dissolved (it only tackles inscription in the primal scene, into the Other's desire), here it is shattered altogether by impeding such inscription throughout. The close-up as a synecdoche that stops motion is treated in the film as an element of frustration and menace, a *representation* of a "dismembered" body. It suggests that contrary to the close-up in still photography or painting, in film, the close-up is usually rendered after a *cut* that "severs" the head/face from the long-shot body (of the actor-character). This cut extracts and abstracts the close-up from the scene, from the body, from the spatiotemporal coordinates of the narrative, performing, in effect, its "monstrosity." As an image, the close-up is a poetic device, meant to function/remain in the imaginary, but *Les yeux sans visage* tackles the close-up by linking it to the real: its protagonist (a surgeon) realizes his desire by cutting into the raw flesh of faces, which impedes our engagement with his desire, precisely because it interferes with the mechanism of the imaginary when viewing a film.

Chapter 2 develops the notion of subjectivization. It presents the six-category taxonomy of body-character-breach films (body switch, reincarnation, body transformation, multiple-body character, body host, and bodiless characters). Body-character-breach films tamper with the initial fusion of the actor's body and his or her character or impede the filling out of *objet a* with a fantasy object (which often creates an experience of "the lack of the lack," of "trauma unveiled"). These films manage to jolt the spectators out of the primal scene, that is, to dismantle the engagement with the protagonist's initial fantasy. Jolting us out of the primal scene occurs parallel to the protagonists' realization that being in the Other's skin or desiring to replace another (in both cases it means inscription in the Other's desire) entails horror scenarios or the loss of subjectivity altogether. Consequently, a change in our initial spectatorial/subjective position in relation to the lack in the Other is induced, enhanced through the visualization of various scenarios of unconscious fantasies (mostly incest). These are meant to unsettle the spectators into awareness of how a conscious fantasy conceals another unconscious fundamental fantasy, thereby encouraging the change in spectatorial position. This demonstrates Lacan's notion of the traversal of the fantasy, both on the level of the films' diegesis and that of spectatorship, thus dis-encouraging the various scenarios in which the subject's/spectator's position in relation to the Other's desire is configured as detrimental, diverting the question of fantasy from "What does the Other want from me?" to "What do I want?" Among the films analyzed in this chapter are *Vertigo* (Alfred Hitchcock), *Cet obscure objet du désir* (*That Obscure Object of Desire*, Luis Buñuel 1977), *Big* (Penny Marshall 1988), *Face/Off* (John Woo 1997), *Shallow Hal* (Bobby Farrelly and Peter Farrelly 2001), and *Freaky Friday* (Mark S. Waters 2003).

Chapter 3, the first of two dealing with dreaming characters, explains the rhetorical function of protagonists' dreams as mise-en-abyme by focusing on their *implicit* reflexive function—exposing the theme of guilt, first of the protagonists, then of cinema. As mentioned before, protagonists' dreams point to guilt that causes them to fail to read the reality around them. The dreams reveal that guilt is associated with the prohibited desire for the mother and the repressed fantasy of being the object of her desire in the configuration of the primal scene fantasy. In most cases, the desire for the mother is expressed through the protagonists' attempts to appease female characters whom they view as moral ideals, while they themselves either are asexual or avoid sexual relations. In reality (in the films' diegeses), the female characters are portrayed as sexual beings, incompatible with the ideal projected onto them. The films analyzed equate inscription in the structure of the film's primal scene with false answers pertaining to the inscription in the Other's desire (associated with the m/Other's). They do this not through unnerving scenarios and images (showing how a conscious fantasy conceals another—unconscious—fantasy, or by mobilizing the real through images that resist signification) like in the corpus of Part One, but through evincing the dire consequences of the guilt-ridden protagonist's actions. Chapter 3 discusses at length the nature of this guilt (which, according to Lacan, is inherent in the subject not following the path of her or his desire) as expressed in the protagonists' dreams, all pointing to being entrapped in the mother's desire. The process of subjectivization occurs when the protagonists must recognize their act of projection and reassess their relation to the m/Other. They reevaluate their mistaken interpretation of reality, stemming from their feelings of guilt, which constitutes the implicit reflexivity of the dream.

The implicit reflexive function of the dream as mise-en-abyme occurs when the films problematize the omnipotent flexibility of the camera to be simultaneously in all possible positions, such as in the fantasy of the primal scene. The theme of guilt here is associated with the fantasmatic "success" of the camera in reaching a place that for the subject is not only forbidden (in regard to the Oedipal prohibition) but also ontologically impossible: the subject cannot be "there" during his/her own creation—similar to our absence from the filming set but our imaginary presence within the fantasmatic space of the film. The failure of this fantasy, expressed in the protagonists' failure to correctly identify the desire of the female characters (representing the mother) and to avoid confronting reality (the symbolic), is thus configured as analogous to cinema's own lack. In the latter context, the films associate the traumatic lack/real with the unreliability of optic and aural technologies, due to the intrusion of subjectivity into the act of interpretation of what the characters perceive through these technologies. The dream thus differs from other mise-en-abymes in that it contains an ethical dimension directed at spectators, as the two films we analyze at length demonstrate: *Spellbound* (Alfred Hitchcock 1945) and *The Conversation* (Francis Ford Coppola 1974).

Chapter 4 (the second chapter of Part Two) explores the *explicit* reflexive function of the character's dream (in its reference to guilt) as mise-en-abyme, rendered in meta-cinematic terms in two films that incorporate the making of a film and associate the guilt expressed in the dreams with narrative cinema's fulfillment of fantasies and desires: *8½* (Federico Fellini 1963) and *Mulholland Drive* (David Lynch 2001). The explicit reflexivity is condensed in meta-cinematic scenes referring to the casting of female roles for a film within the film that function as "textual mise-en-abymes," a literary term used by Lucien Dällenbach ([1977] 1989) to determine the basic code of the medium, which we apply to film: the basic code of the cinematographic image, beyond and before cinematic devices such as framing, camera angles, size of shots, and camera movements (i.e., the "language" of film).

We detect this code in screen tests and audition scenes that represent, as mentioned above, non-diegetic components in the production of a film, that is, the casting process through which the production team and the director of the film make the audience believe and feel that the actress chosen is indeed "the one." Through these meta-cinematic scenes, we are meant to realize that casting aims to satisfy a collective desire by providing a fantasy object inherent in the image of the actresses chosen (the "perfect" casting), which fulfills what in life is impossible, namely, knowing or guessing what the m/Other (the audience) wants. The films thus reflect the interrelations of the different layers of the cinematographic image (its basic code) as pertaining to characters in film, especially protagonists: a quartet comprised of (a) a denotative/referential code (the real body of an actor that was present on the set, before the camera); (b) a connotative one (persona, cultural and ideological attributes, stereotypes, and so on); (c) realization of the desire of/for the mother through the image of the actor/actress; and (d) guilt, due to the cinema's success in achieving such a realization.

What the films suggest is that in the dynamic of desire/fantasy, the mother is the key to both: she is the one who instills desire through her absence, and she is the one behind the fantasy to be included in the Other's desire, to be an object of *her* desire. The emptiness/lack of the screen refers to desire, while the richness of images, most of all the fusion of actor-character (it is not mere chance that both films deal with the casting of female characters), projected onto it, to fantasy. This dynamic characterizes the ontology of film.

Subjectivization here is thus aligned with the meta-cinematic, revealing why both narrative cinema and counter-cinema should feel guilty. Although the films promote the *auteur*'s freedom of creation and attempt to resist various production constraints, they nevertheless exhibit awareness of the value of the fusion of actor-character as fantasy object, which not even films of great *auteurs*, or narrative iconoclasts, can afford to bypass. For example, the screen tests and photographs of actresses contending for roles in both films demonstrate the perpetual motion of desire, attesting to the fact that *objet a* may be occupied in film with endless fantasmatic objects. This, however, occurs in the films' diegeses, while the actresses chosen by Fellini to play the roles of the female characters in *his* film (not in the film within the film) and by Lynch to play the role of *his* protagonist (a failing actress in the diegesis) point to the idea that the perpetual motion of desire is halted by the casting choice to make the audience feel that the actress chosen to play the lead *is* the character.

Moreover, we find that the four-layer code of the cinematographic image as evinced in the relationship between the dreams in the films and the textual mise-e-abymes marks the latter, in Dällenbach's ([1977] 1989: 218) terminology, also "transcendental mise-en-abymes" because they discuss the source of the work, "the code of codes." In contrast to literature, where the code of codes is the word (the symbolic/the Name-of-the-Father), in cinema the code of codes of the cinematographic image is associated with the mother, the primary source of creation. The emptiness of the screen marks Mother's absence, her unattainability; therefore, to make up for it, the audience must be inscribed in her desire (which is the function of fantasy through perfect casting of female leads). It thus renders her a metaphor for the source of cinematic creation, certainly that of narrative film.

Chapter 5 (the first chapter of Part Three) presents the six-category taxonomy of gender-crossing protagonists in narrative cinema (the cross-dresser, the tomboy, the transvestite, the trans protagonist, the trans-body, and the drag queen). The gender-crossing protagonist's position in relation to the (m)Other's desire is tackled from the start by bringing to light (mostly in the case of the transgender, tomboy, and transvestite, but also the cross-dresser—through masquerade) all three primal fantasies: castration; seduction, and the primal scene. The castration fantasy, which refers to sexual difference, raises the question, "Who/What am I—man or woman?" For the gender-crossing protagonist, it becomes almost impossible to maintain the distinction between man/woman and its correlatives (femininity/masculinity; gay/straight). The same applies to spectatorship because of the ambiguous and multilayered *image* of the body of the gender-crossing character. In fact, the gender-crossing figure evinces the problematization of the engagement of spectators in respect with the desire of the Other via the primal scene fantasy at the outset by tackling all three primal fantasies at once. Be it by choice or by circumstance, the protagonists are caught in a space in which they enjoy the experience of being set free from the constraints of such categories and the norms that go with them.

Subjectivization here is conflated with the experience of feminine enjoyment, whose function is to fully satisfy the drives, namely realize the protagonists' desire, while juxtaposing it with the phallic enjoyment. By further allying the feminine enjoyment with Kristeva's notion of the semiotic, Chapter 5 demonstrates this path through close readings of several films, focusing on *Yentl* (Barbra Streisand 1983), *Calamity Jane* (David Butler

1953), and *Some Like It Hot* (Billy Wilder 1959). Unlike the body-character-breach films or the dreaming-character films, in which the question of acknowledging desire becomes valid only at the point where inscription in the Other's desire is proven detrimental to the subject/protagonist, in the gender-crossing corpus it is generated from the start by clarifying what the protagonist's desire is. Regarding the primal scene fantasy (the origin of the subject), this corpus provides a unique answer in that the protagonist is a self-creation. How the character looks and behaves—"man," "woman," "trans"—is reflected in the visual image, as well as in acting, whether the body transformation in the diegesis is an outcome of disguise or achieved through full or partial gender readjustment/reassignment (in the trans category the casting very often complicates matters even further, for example, a female actress playing a trans woman—such examples form part of the body-character-breach taxonomy as well). The expression of self-creation through feminine enjoyment goes hand in hand with the ambiguity of the image of the gender-crossing figure; thus for spectators, engaging with the desire of the gender-crossing protagonist means experiencing a non-phallic enjoyment beyond any pre-given category, but all the same occurring in *the body*, as do all the gender-crossing characters.

Thus, the films discussed in this chapter show that in addition to feminine enjoyment being that which realizes the protagonist's desire, the space created by the gender-crossing protagonist is a semiotic space, and it is into this space that spectators are inscribed. This is true even in cases in which the protagonist (e.g., Jerry in *Some Like It Hot*) is oblivious of their own desire but nevertheless experiences feminine enjoyment and moves in a semiotic space. Hence, our comparison of spaces governed by phallic enjoyment with those in which feminine enjoyment reigns supreme, which, as it turns out, becomes a space that also resists fetishism. In view of the argument that the semiotic is a practice that generates a never-ending and unlimited process of growth and change that might alter societal norms from within (in the symbolic)—the question we are left with at the end of Chapter 5 is why so very often it does not.

Chapter 6 thus centers on an attempt to explain this resistance to change. In addition to the idea that social intelligibility, language itself (the symbolic, which is but a fiction that enables human beings to communicate), is still very much contingent on binary norms of sexuality and gender, this chapter demonstrates Slavoj Žižek's (e.g., 1994: 55; 1997: 18–27, 54–60) notion of the inherent transgression that is manifested in obscene forms of enjoyment, practised in secret, which very often sustain "the Law" itself. Therefore, the gender-crossing character who represents a space of feminine enjoyment is always a potential menace threatening to out someone's dark secrets. It certainly threatens brutal codes of masculinity that reign supreme in many communities. In this context, we examine the way the trans phenomenon is experienced as an affront deserving heinous punishment in two films: *Boys*

Don't Cry (Kimberly Peirce 1999) and *Una mujer fantástica* (*A Fantastic Woman*, Sebastián Lelio 2017).

Because the image of the trans protagonists of these films is a polymorphous one, and because we are engaged with their desire, the polysemic and semiotic space occupied by them is one into which we are inscribed. That such a space in the diegesis clashes with other spaces that refuse to contain it ultimately means that the space in which our desire is engaged clashes with these other spaces. Moreover, *Una mujer fantástica* suggests that the polymorphous body of the transgender might serve as a receptacle of feminine enjoyment, a space of the polyvocality and polysemy of the entire film—the semiotic *chōra*, in Kristeva's terms—not only the habitat of the protagonist but also one spectators are drawn into through the body of the actor/camera. In *Una mujer fantástica* we accompany the protagonist in her journey to literally and metaphorically find her own voice.

We conclude the exploration of this kind of journey in which spectators participate with the meta-cinematic fantasy *Being John Malkovich* (Spike Jonze 1999). We include it both in our body-host category of the body-character-breach corpus in Chapter 1 (in which the body-character breach represents the wish of being able to fulfill the fantasy of being the Other) and in the (fantastic) category of trans-body, as part of the gender-crossing corpus in Chapter 5. The uniqueness of *Being John Malkovich* is the way it conflates Malkovich's *body* with a receptacle/space—a semiotic *chōra*—for all the characters who go through its portal, as well as for the spectators. It is a non-gender, or rather, all-inclusive-gender, receptacle, leading to the drives and the unconscious. Its characters experience and use it in different ways, according to their subjective position in relation to the Other, as well as their willingness to change such positions. This occupancy is a metaphor for the interrelations between screen and spectator, referring also to all factors involved in the making of a film and its "consumption" (actors, director, producers, distributors, and so on). *Being John Malkovich* tackles the notion of identity associated with "fifteen minutes of fame" and false appearances; in contrast, it offers an opportunity to reflect on what it is that can make a subject happy. By designing a body-space that can be associated with the semiotic *chōra* it thus completes the Borromean knot, evincing the importance of the real in its relations to the imaginary and symbolic rings. Herein lies the ethics of the films discussed in Chapters 5 and 6. Moreover, there is great value in analyzing meta-films (*The Conversation*, *8 ½*, *Mulholland Drive*, and *Being John Malkovich*) in that they show us how exactly the dialectic of desire/fantasy operates in narrative films, while at the same time they undermine the destructive potential of fantasy. We might thus argue that in these meta-films subjectivization is deemed as an inherent part of the cinematic work.

The Book's Contribution to Psychoanalytic Film Theories

Through the new paradigm presented in this book we hope to make a substantial contribution to the history of psychoanalytic theories of film and spectatorship regarding the classical or mainstream narrative cinema that dominated our field during certain periods of time. These may be traced through three major paradigms, all based on Freudian and Lacanian notions. The first is *the imaginary paradigm* (1970s–1980s). The most elaborated one is Metz's ([1977] 1982). Borrowing Freud's notion of the daydream—a conscious fantasy that, according to Lacan, alleviates the experience of lack—Metz argued regarding classical narrative cinema that although spectators are caught up in the sequences of images projected on the screen, we can nevertheless be so absorbed precisely because of our awareness of the magic of film as daydream. Metz thus translated the Lacanian dynamic of desire/fantasy into an oscillation between distance from and proximity to the images projected on the screen, between the symbolic and the imaginary. As mentioned before, because of the spectators' awareness (which is reflected also in Metz's objection to comparing the experience of spectatorship with dreaming), Metz saw no substantial gain in developing the contents and manifestations of the unconscious' engagement with a film. We owe a great debt to him in that our point of departure is the unique ontology and aesthetics of cinema that he developed, which, in our opinion, still holds true in our era, when viewing a film is no longer restricted to the big screen. In this respect, our project is to complete what Metz began years ago: To develop a comprehensive model of spectatorship, although based on the imaginary nature of film, nevertheless involving the unconscious. Influenced by Marxism and neo-Marxism, mostly Louis Althusser's ([1970] 1971) theory of ideology and state apparatuses, other film theories of spectatorship during the 1970s and 1980s (e.g., Jean-Louis Baudry [1970] 1985; Daniel Dayan 1974) held that the dominant spectatorial position regarding classical narrative cinema was an imaginary one, ignoring the unconscious. Some relied on Lacan's ([1949/1966] 2006) partial notion of "the mirror stage" (from which the order of the imaginary derives—the visual and imaginary trajectory, as well as the formation of the ego) concerning the infants' identification with a misrecognition of an ideal image reflected to them in a mirror or in another. The main argument that reigned supreme revolved around spectators' identification with the camera (primary identification) and with the protagonist and their motives (secondary identification). This process, enabled by the viewing conditions, the cinematic apparatus, and the cinematic devices (darkness, passivity, classical editing, focalization, and so on, all designed to create the illusion of coherence and wholeness) ultimately coerced us into occupying the same position as their object (camera/character). By occupying such a position, any distance between us and the object was eliminated and with it any knowledge effect of reality, the operation of the cinematic apparatus, or possible awareness of the ideology inherent in the film. The only way out of this trap was to encourage iconoclastic filmmaking. The theories that followed, including the first wave of feminism, adopted this paradigm and even when referring to the unconscious or the symbolic at large collapsed it into patriarchal ideology (Raymond Bellour [1975] 2000; Laura Mulvey, 1975; and many others), which led to a deadlock. Notwithstanding feminist and postfeminist film theories that grappled with woman's place in patriarchy and female spectatorship, this book aims to highlight a psychoanalytic mechanism that is involved in viewing a narrative film, which is common to all. While engaging with "counter-cinema" largely depends on personal taste, education, cultural background, and so on, we aim to demonstrate how narrative cinema works at the subjective and unconscious level common to all people, regardless of cultural and social formations. Moreover, we argue that only narrative film, which operates within a careful dynamic of desire/fantasy on which our engagement with film depends, stands to produce an ethical effect that goes hand in hand with the affect produced during the viewing.

The second paradigm (mostly dominant in the 1990s) is that of fantasy. Laplanche and Pontalis's ([1964] 1986) exposé of Freud's fantasy theory generated several studies in the 1990s that compared the viewing of a film with the fantasy scene. Two works stand out in this context: Teresa De Lauretis's *The Practice of Love: Perverse Desire and Lesbian Sexuality* (1994) and Elizabeth Cowie's "Fantasia" in *Representing the Woman: Cinema and Psychoanalysis* (1997: 123–65). Laplanche and Pontalis's article, which deals with the primal (unconscious) fantasies (fantasies of origin), had been extremely influential in theoretical formulations of how cinema could produce public forms of fantasy as well as provide a stage on which any individual spectator could script their own desire. The viewing of a film, it was argued, provided a setting, a mise-en-scène, in which the spectators, like the fantasizing subject, were more or less free to occupy whichever position suited us by scripting a visual scenario of dramatized scenes. In the daydream, the fantasy is scripted in the first person (the subject is the protagonist); in the (unconscious) primal fantasy, the child/subject/spectator is one of the characters in the scene and may occupy more than one position/place simultaneously (e.g., in the primal scene fantasy they may be both a witness to the parental coitus and a participant in it). Therefore, the camera's position, or the protagonist's, does not necessarily overlap with those occupied by the spectators, because the filmic experience is used merely as a setting, analogous to that of primal (unconscious) fantasies. The fantasy paradigm thus brought to light the unconscious and managed to break the deadlock reached by the imaginary paradigm of the 1970s and

1980s, according to which we were coerced into occupying the (ideological) position of the camera. However, in theorizing the spectators' position, the fantasy paradigm again put the emphasis on already socially constructed subjects, eschewing the necessity of exploring which processes are exactly involved in the engagement of the unconscious with the moving image per se, processes that transcend social constructions and power edifices. Our model of spectatorship is based on the premise that in narrative film, desire is the first step in engaging with the (unconscious) dynamic of desire/fantasy, but that without the work of fantasy in its capacity to veil castration (i.e., the lack in the Other), spectators might find it difficult to sustain their engagement with a film. Thus, fantasy is a key component in our model of spectatorship, regardless of any ideology or inclination on the part of spectators or the films—not necessarily a stage in which we script our desire but rather one inscribing us in the Other's desire, regardless of its specific content and based solely on the dynamic of lack (desire) and the need to veil it (fantasy).

The third paradigm is the real (1990s–2010s). The notion of the real was introduced into film analysis by Žižek's *Looking Awry: An Introduction to Jacques Lacan through Popular Culture* (1991). In *Read My Desire: Lacan against the Historicists*, Joan Copjec (1994) makes a strong case against the psychoanalytic theories of spectatorship prevalent in the 1970s, claiming that they followed a model à la Michel Foucault's historicism rather than a true Lacanian one that places desire at the heart of the filmic experience. In the 2000s, the leading figure in Lacanian psychoanalytic film theory adhering to this notion is Todd McGowan. He tackles, to different degrees, the notions of desire and fantasy in cinema and provides in-depth analyses of what he calls in *The Real Gaze: Film Theory after Lacan* (2007b) "the cinema of desire," that is, authorial and "counter-cinema." McGowan rightly contends in *Psychoanalytic Film Theory and "The Rules of the Game"* (2015) that without the engagement of the unconscious in viewing a film, it makes no sense to recruit psychoanalysis to cinema. His premise (as stated in *The Real Gaze*) is that without fantasy (in its role of veiling the lack in the Other) ideology cannot work, and that most narrative films use fantasy to promote capitalist ideology. Consequently, he turns to counter-cinema and films by *auteurs*, as these have the power to disrupt the social order, characterized by desire or unconscious fantasies (e.g., his study of David Lynch [2007a]). Our contribution to McGowan's approach is the argument that fantasy is crucial to the sustaining of desire when viewing a film, hence the value of narrative mainstream films that tackle, undermine, certain unconscious fantasies *after* engaging us with them. We approach the real in classical and mainstream narrative cinema in its capacity of the traumatic, as well as the realization of desire (feminine enjoyment).

Needless to say, conceiving our own theory of spectatorship and the ethics of narrative film would have been impossible without these three paradigms, which prompted us to look further into the relationships between psychoanalysis and film, until reaching the conclusion that the unconscious mechanisms of desire and fantasy have little to do with ideology and much to do with subjectivity, because being white, black, lesbian, woman/man, or of a certain class or social status is not necessarily germane to one's subjective structure in relation to lack. Therefore, the way to escape the grip of ideology and social constructions or norms does not necessarily lie in the recourse to counter-cinema but rather in an understanding of the way in which the economy of desire, fantasy, and enjoyment in narrative film reverberates with the subject's unconscious struggle with castration, a struggle that the subject/spectator will not engage with solely within an economy of desire (which characterizes counter-cinema).

We wholeheartedly believe that the wisdom of film theory is inherent in films, hence our lengthy descriptions and analyses of the ones chosen from the three corpora of this book. As Gilles Deleuze ([1985] 1989: 280) concludes in his second book on cinema, "Cinema itself is a new practice of images and signs, whose theory philosophy must produce as conceptual practice. For no technical determination, whether applied (psychoanalysis, linguistics) . . . is sufficient to constitute the concepts of cinema itself." We hope to show that this is true of films made not only by great *auteurs* (as often noted by Deleuze) but also of mainstream narrative films as we all know them.

PART ONE

Body-Character-Breach Films

1

Desire, Fantasy, and the Ontology of Film

Desire/Fantasy, the Ontology of Film, Characters, Actors, and Spectators

What roles do the body and the physique of actors play in the dynamic of desire/fantasy in narrative film? No narrative medium can do without characters, for they are the agents of subjectivity. Unlike the theater or the opera, in cinema the spectators' engagement with characters via actors depends on the latter's physique, as evinced, for example, by the close-up. More than any other object whose image appears on the screen, the character (mostly the protagonist), as embodied by a specific actor, has become an anchor for engagement with narrative film. Although today's employment of computerized images of extras replacing humans has become common practice, it is, nevertheless, hard to imagine in the near future films in which "flesh and blood" actors embodying the protagonists will be replaced with digitally produced characters, given the uncanniness of the latter.[1] The corporeality of the actor in film inexorably operates within the bounds of a larger mechanism that engages us with the dynamic of desire/fantasy in relation to the structure of the film's narrative, its filmic space, its language (editing, camera positions, the use of sound, mise-en-scène, etc.) and the unique ontology of film (the dynamic of absence/presence).

Desire is what arouses our interest in narrative film, especially when it is enmeshed in that of the characters'. Desire is intrinsic to the cinema at large (the emptiness of the screen—the material absence of actors and objects) and to the narrative in particular, starting with the desire of the protagonists (what they do not have and wish to obtain) and followed by the unfolding of the narrative (what is left off-screen momentarily or throughout the film). It is the entwining of the two (the lack inherent in the medium and narrative) that draws us into the film. Nöel Carroll ([1985] 1996) divides the unfolding of the narrative between "macro" questions (What does the protagonist want? Will they obtain it and if so—how? What will happen in either of the cases?) and "micro" questions related to *how* the narrative unfolds (What is the protagonist seeing? What are they not seeing? Why is an object rendered in close-up? Who is the enunciator of a specific shot and why? What is left off-screen and why?). Underlying all these questions pertaining to the unfolding of the narrative and to the filmic forms through which they are raised is the spectators tapping into the experience of lack. When it comes to the protagonists, whatever they might be after marks a lack that sets the spectators' desire in motion. In the linear classical narrative structure, the intertwining of the macro and micro questions is achieved in a condensed form. It has been characterized as driven by the desire of the protagonist, who engages in action, to overcome various obstacles posed by the antagonist, reaching their goal at the end of the film and leading to definitive closure.

Since the answers supplied to both the macro and micro questions are related to lack/absence, we might have simply argued that they function as pieces of a fantasy veiling lack. But the dynamic of desire/fantasy in narrative cinema is much more complex than that. Answers to the questions posed by spectators (especially macro questions pertaining to the desire of the protagonist, like "Will the protagonist get the boy/girl s/he is secretly in love with? Will s/he manage to avenge the murder of a loved one?") are carefully and gradually supplied until we reach closure. The reason is to *sustain* our desire. On the micro level too, that is, the forms through which the questions are answered, cinema is a medium that has an inherent affinity with desire. As Christian Metz ([1977] 1982: 77) observes, "Both camera movements and framing are in themselves forms of 'suspense.' ... They have an inner affinity with the mechanisms of desire, its postponements, its new impetus." This is true, to various extents, also of nonlinear narrative forms, such as multiple-draft narratives, forking-path plots, and alternate stories. Thus, fantasy in its relation to the narrative plays a double role: It veils the lack in the Other (castration) and sustains desire. For Todd McGowan, as well as previous theorists of film and fantasy, desire emerges in a film through the very fact that film is a public form of fantasy, a way of allowing us to see the impossible:

> Fantasy is not secondary in relation to desire. Fantasy establishes the scenario and the coordinates through which the subject experiences itself as a desiring subject. Without fantasy, there would be no initial impetus for desire, and yet, paradoxically, fantasy compromises the subject's desire, providing a justification or a rationalization for the impossibility that it presents. In other words, despite its supplementary position in the

psychic economy of the subject, fantasy has a phenomenological priority. This is evident nowhere as clearly as in the cinema. Even the film that tries most steadfastly to strip away the dimension of fantasy sustains it at a minimal level. In this sense, a cinema of fantasy is a mode of cinema that merely accentuates a direction that inheres in the medium as such. (2007b: 24)

We argue that leaving too many "holes" in a story (i.e., radically breaking with the tenets of classical narrative) might frustrate spectators to a point where desire is "left out" of the film altogether. In other words, if a film leaves its spectators solely in the domain of desire, some might abandon their seats and leave the movie theater or switch to another channel. The same might occur if we are given the answers too soon or too abundantly.

Engaging with a film thus means engaging with the operation of the mechanism of desire/fantasy. In our view, for this to happen we do not have to identify with the contents of the protagonist's desire nor with their actions to fulfill it. If identification is at all a factor in engagement, what characterizes it is the fundamental common denominator of any subjective structure—the desideratum to deal with castration (the lack in the Other). To sum up this point, the structure of film, in its affinity with the structure of fantasy, reflects the double nature of fantasy: to defend the subject against castration and to sustain desire.

In our lives, "Visually, desire concerns what we don't see, not what we see.... In the visual field ... the subject desires to see precisely what is not visible in the Other, and what results is that the subject continually seeks without ever finding" (McGowan 2007b: 69). Narrative film allows us to *see* more than we see in our everyday lives in relation to the Other by maintaining a "satisfactory" economy of desire/fantasy. This visual economy then is based on what any film chooses to make visible and how it does so as well as what it does not show. In the narrative, this is manifested in the distinction between story and plot.

Given that when viewing a film, our relation to the screen onto which it is projected is one related to lack (because of the screen's emptiness as well as the unattainability of the film's objects), we identify the absence of the cinematic object from the screen, including the human character in film as embodied by an actor with what in Lacanian psychoanalysis is called *objet (petit) a*. This object that can never be attained can exist only in fantasy, like the cinematic object. Gaze and voice, two of the four partial objects, around which the scopic and invocatory drives circulate, respectively, are the two most relevant to cinema—involved in the experience of viewing a film. Indeed, *objet a* is translated in the imaginary as a fantasy object, an object that fills the lack in the Other. This is basically the ontological status of the cinematic object, hence the imperative that a plot should show its characters embodied by actors. This means that the mechanism of desire/fantasy is contingent on the embodiment of characters by actors, in compliance with film's unique ontology and techniques. Unlike literature, in which the reader is free to imagine the corporeality of the protagonist, in film this corporeality is visualized, a visualization that has at its heart the fundamental desire inherent in the experience of viewing a film—the desire to *see* the characters embodied by actors.

It is precisely this desire that a film like the classical noir, Robert Montgomery's *Lady in the Lake* (1947), an adaptation of Raymond Chandler's novel *The Lady in the Lake* (1944), resists. It is a cinematic version aspiring to simulate a first-person narrative style. The protagonist (the narrator), Philip Marlowe (Robert Montgomery), appears only in three frontal shots in which he tells us about story developments and in six shots in which the front of his body is reflected in a mirror. The rest of the film is rendered from his point of view; therefore, we cannot see him (we occasionally see his hands) but only what and how he sees, and, of course, we hear his voice while his body remains off-screen. To the best of our knowledge, such an experiment in classical/mainstream narrative cinema has never been repeated.[2] For what works in literature cannot work in film. In film we desire to *see* the protagonist, or alternately, to see their *subjectivity* visualized.[3] The rendering of point-of-view shots alone, without linking them to a body that appears on the screen or to mental/subjective images, may hardly be expected to work.

To clarify this point, Rouben Mamoulian's *Dr. Jekyll and Mr. Hyde* (1931) is also an adaptation of a novel (*The Strange Case of Dr. Jekyll and Mr. Hyde*, by Robert Louis Stevenson, first published in 1886). Its opening sequence, in which the desire to see the protagonist—the connection between desire/fantasy and the character's body—is suspended, exemplifies not only that the experiment of rendering subjective shots without seeing the protagonist cannot work throughout the viewing of a film but also that such a suspension must be justified in the film's diegesis with which we become engaged. The whole sequence is shot from the protagonist's (Fredric March) point of view, marked by the iris shape of the frame.[4] It begins with a shot showing his hands playing an organ and his shadow on the music sheet. Then it renders a dialogue between the protagonist and his valet. The editing alternates shots showing the valet from the protagonist's point of view, rendered in the iris shape, and shots showing the shadow. This conveys the idea that the dialogue is conducted between the valet and Dr. Jekyll's "shadow"—Mr. Hyde, who will emerge later in the visual field through a physical transformation. But for now, he remains "hidden," represented visually by Jekyll's shadow alone. Then a one-take point-of-view tracking shot commences, sustaining our desire to see the protagonist, which is answered when we see his reflection in a mirror. As he leaves his house, we return to camera movements rendering his POV. This subjective sequence comes to an end with Dr. Jekyll addressing his students about the two sides of the human soul—evil/good. The protagonist is a physician who experiments with splitting between evil and good because he cannot accept his dark side, which he associates with his sexual drive as well as with nineteenth-century social hypocrisy regarding this matter. This split is visualized by two different and distinct physical appearances. While in the part of Dr. Jekyll, a handsome and respected physician, we may easily identify March, in the part of Mr. Hyde, March hides under heavy makeup that conceals his physique, making him look and behave like a Neanderthal (although dressed like Jekyll in a tuxedo, March evinces this animal-like comportment in his acting). The rendering of subjectivity by means of poetic, cinematic devices instructs spectators of the protagonist's insistence to separate his good side from his dark one, an experiment doomed to failure. In contrast, *Lady in the Lake* is a film rendered from the point of view of the protagonist whose desire is to write gore fiction. It seems almost superfluous to point out the disadvantage of a film that neglects the visual in favor of an attempt to render subjectivity solely through simulating a first-person narration in a novel.

Indeed, this comparison raises the question of the relationship between the act of viewing a film, the dynamic of desire/fantasy, and the figuring of the embodiment of characters by actors in this dynamic. In the complex operation related to the very ontology and language of film, namely the dynamic of absence/presence, the desire to see and hear (hearing alone, however, will never suffice in cinema), as Metz ([1977] 1982: 58–66) maintains, is at the heart of cinema. However, the two sexual drives—scopic and invocatory— are characterized by a distance that keeps the object apart: We can neither touch nor smell nor taste the objects on the screen, for these are senses that relate to the tangibility of the object viewed and its materiality.[5] Metz writes: "These two sexual drives are distinguished from the others in that they are more dependent on a lack, or at least dependent on it in a more precise, more unique manner, which marks them from the outset . . . as being on the side of the imaginary" (58). By "imaginary" Metz means the world of fantasy. In other words, although the scopic and the invocatory drives remain unsatisfied (in their relation to desire), maintaining a gulf between the spectator (the "voyeur" in Metz's terms) and the object (one on which the very act of "voyeurism" depends), the imaginary objects on the screen are nevertheless satisfactory precisely because they are not there. Voyeurism is then the act through which the two partial drives (the scopic and the invocatory) aim to be satisfied, the act on which our libidinal investment (engagement with the dynamic of desire/fantasy) depends: Fantasy might be what veils lack, but it only does so in the imaginary, hence the immanence of voyeurism. Indeed, this is why nudity and sex (both involving humans) are so popular in film.

It is also in this light that we may understand Metz's other argument that it is precisely the absence of the object from the screen that necessitates the richness unique to cinema, one that answers the desire to see by compensating for the lack of the screen (and, we might add, for its two-dimensionality[6]):

> What distinguishes the cinema is an extra reduplication, a supplementary and specific turn of the screw bolting desire to lack. First because the spectacles and sounds the cinema "offers" us (offers us at a distance, hence as much *steals* from us) are especially rich and varied: a mere difference of degree, but already one that counts: the screen presents to our apprehension, but absent from our grasp, more "things" (The mechanism of the perceiving drive is identical for the moment but its object is more endowed with matter; this is one of the reasons why the cinema is very suited to handling "erotic scenes" which depend on direct, non-sublimated voyeurism.) In the second place (and more decisively), the specific affinity between the cinematic signifier and the imaginary persists . . . in a primordial *elsewhere*, infinitely desirable (= never possessible [*sic*]), on another scene which is that of absence and which nevertheless represents the absent in detail, thus making it very present, but by a different itinerary. (61, italics in the original)

What Metz seems to be saying is something like this: Film spectators are deprived of an object, say, a cake, that they can neither touch nor possess, but not of the recipe: its ingredients, how it should look, when and how to eat it, how to enjoy its taste, smell, and so on (tactile and haptic theories have amply elaborated on this). Film will show us every aspect of the cake that will make us *desire* it. At the beginning of *The Pervert's Guide to Cinema* (Sophie Fiennes 2006), Žižek states: "The problem for us is not whether our desires are satisfied or not. The problem is how do we know what we desire? . . . We have to be taught to desire. Cinema . . . doesn't give you what you desire, it tells you how to desire." The "how" is indeed achieved through the film's fantasy, by directing it to an object. In minutely *visualizing* a fantasy, it externalizes how a desired object should look and makes it worthy of investing our desire in it.

In his discussion on framing and fetishism (the absence of the object from the screen "elevates" it to the status of a fetish, which by its very definition functions on an erotic level, one that has both a disavowal value and a knowledge value), Metz compares the film's framing of space to an act of striptease:

> The way the cinema, with its wandering framings (wandering like the look, like the caress), finds the means to reveal space has something to do with a kind of permanent undressing . . . a less direct but more perfected strip-tease since it also makes it possible to dress space again, to remove from view what it has previously shown, to *take back* as well as to retain . . . : a strip-tease pierced with "flesh-backs," inverted sequences that

then give new impetus to the forward movement. These veiling-unveiling procedures can also be compared with certain cinematic "punctuations," especially slow ones marked by a concern for control and expectation (slow fade-ins and fade-outs, irises). ([1977] 1982: 77–8; italics in the original)

If we think about this metaphor further, not only in terms of suspending time and space but also in relation to what is revealed, we might say that the veiling-unveiling of the filmic procedures contains "dressing up." This idea is succinctly described by Alfred Hitchcock in one of his interviews with François Truffaut regarding what might be considered the most fetishistic scene of *Vertigo*, namely, the protagonist's (James Stewart) insistence and efforts to turn Judy (Kim Novak) into the dead Madeleine (also played by Novak):

> Cinematically, all of Stewart's efforts to recreate the dead woman are shown in such a way that he seems to be trying to undress her, instead of the other way around. What I liked best is when the girl came back after having had her hair dyed blond. Stewart is disappointed because she hasn't put her hair up in a bun (Figure 1.1). What this really means is that the girl has almost stripped, but she still won't take her knickers off. When he insists, she says, "all right!" and goes into the bathroom while he waits outside. What Stewart is really waiting for is the woman to emerge totally naked this time, and ready for love. (Truffaut [1966] 1984: 244)

The suspension of the "taking-off" of clothes in the act of striptease on the one hand, and on the other, the demand for accuracy of details in a film

FIGURE 1.1 Vertigo *(Alfred Hitchcock 1958).*

(the dressing up), is associated by Hitchcock with the eroticism inherent in the desire to see. Hitchcock points precisely to the way in which the cinema compensates for its lack—by making a fantasy (daydream) as rich and accurate as possible, through its many devices and make-believe strategies. And this compensation is by definition erotic and fetishistic. The framing, for example, which for Metz is the emblem of the veiling-unveiling mechanism in the cinema, always promises us more. Therefore, like the dynamic of the absence/presence (lack/richness), film's framing of space and objects—what, when, and how a film chooses to show—through its unique various techniques and strategies is part and parcel of the work of fantasy. Thus, the setting of fantasy in narrative film must be visualized as accurately as possible.

Moreover, if we put together these two examples (Metz and Hitchcock), we get what we have been trying to theorize so far in relation to the operation of desire/fantasy in narrative film and how it involves spectators: While Metz relates it to the ontology and language of film at large, Hitchcock links it specifically to human characters (the protagonists). In other words, in speaking about narrative films, as well as their erotic appeal (voyeurism), human characters, mostly the protagonists, are essential. Although Hitchcock does not want his spectators to be fetishists like Scottie, who insists on realizing, materializing a fantasy, he recognizes that cinema's spectators are by definition voyeurs, and that voyeurism is contingent on the dialectic of desire/fantasy, the protagonist/s being part and parcel of it: They who are not there must be very appealing.

Objects, spaces, or different occurrences alluded to in the plot thus may be omitted from it; but its protagonists, always embodied by actors, may not. This embodiment marks the filling in (in fantasy) of *objet a*. In the theater, the body of the actor is present in the scopic space of the spectator, but the theater lacks the inherent visual richness of film and its freedom of focalization—film allows us to *see* establishing extreme long shots that familiarize us with the characters' surroundings and the characterization of the protagonists and the antagonists through subjective and close-up shots, multiple points of view, "view-behind" shots, shots rendered from different angles, and so on; literature possesses this freedom, but its presence is not visualized; film combines the presence of characters in the theater with literature's freedom of focalization. Film uses, mainly through its editing techniques and camera movements, its temporal and spatial discrepancies (the actors are physically absent from the spectators' scopic space in the present, namely when the film is being viewed, while the spectators were not included in the space in which the scenes were shot) to inscribe the spectators into the spatial and scopic space of its characters on-screen. Moreover, a shot/reverse-shot scene, for example, might have been shot in different spaces or, in case of a dialogue, in one space in which the actors were not present at the same time. It is the editing that creates the illusion of spatial and temporal coherence into which we are drawn.

The imaginary presence of the actors triggers the desire to be "there," to be where the characters are (like in the theater) but (unlike the theater and because the actors are not there), to also get to see what they see from the place in space they are "positioned" (to get what a detailed paragraph in literature might achieve). In short, what film "realizes" is our desire to be physically included in a space from which we were and still are excluded but only as a form of fantasy.[7] The filmic scene renders the past (the then and there) as presence, experienced as a here and now (the setting of the daydream). Hence, the various strategies in cinema that sustain the desire to be "there" are paradoxically those that veil the screen's lack. As asserted by phenomenological film theories, the camera, which imitates the human eye, is present in the space of the scene, transposing our bodies into it as if we were there, allowing us to see what the characters see but, at the same time, preserving our awareness that we are not really "there":

> As perception-cum-expression that can be perceived by another, as a communication of the experience of existence that is publicly visible, the anonymous but centered "Here, where *eye (I) am*" of the film can be doubly occupied. "Decentered" as it is engaged by an other in the film experience, it becomes the "Here, where *we see*"—a *shared* space of being, of seeing, hearing, and bodily and reflective movement performed and experienced by both film and spectator. However, this "decentering," this double occupancy of cinematic space, does not conflate the film and spectator. The "Here, where eye (I) am" of the film retains its unique situation, even as it cannot maintain its perceptual privacy. Directly perceptible to the spectator as an anonymous "Here, where eye am" simultaneously available as "Here, where we see," the concretely embodied situation of the film's vision also stands *against* the spectator. It is also perceived by the spectator as a "There, where I am not . . ." (Sobchack 1994: 41–42, italics in the original)

Because of the unique ontology of film, in terms of the unconscious the real power of this double positioning—the simultaneous being and not-being of spectators in the filmic space—resides in its engagement with the primal scene. We argue that spectators become unconsciously engaged with the primal scene, active "participants" in it (without being aware of it), through the inscription into the Other's (the protagonist's) desire and through cinema's richness regarding its visual focalization. In other words, as explained above, narrative film first arouses our desire through the protagonist's lack, and then it sustains it by creating a rich fantasy that fills this lack as well as that of the screen. This unconscious process first addresses our lack, as we are excluded from the space of the actors portraying desiring subjects, like the child's exclusion from the setting of the parental coitus. Second, by minutely showing us how and what/whom the protagonist desires, it positions us in a place that aspires to fill the lack in the Other, regardless of the specific content of the protagonist's desire. This is cinema's way of bringing Freud and Lacan together. In Freud, the position occupied by the subject in the Oedipal scenario of the primal scene depends on the particular unconscious desire of every subject, the particular attachment developed for each parent (though in dreams the subject can occupy more than one position); in Lacan, this plays no role, as the formation of fantasy, by its very nature, is rooted in the subject's relation to the lack in the Other, whose gender in this respect is irrelevant, although Lacan relates *objet a*, which is the one instilling desire by its very disappearance/absence, to the first primordial object in the subject's life, namely the mother.[8] The cinema brings together the Freudian desire to occupy one of the parents' position in the primal scene and the Lacanian position of a subjective inscription into the Other's desire, with the intention of veiling its lack. The embodiment of characters by actors, which creates an imaginary unity of time and space (the filling in of *objet a*) is essential in this equation. The motility of the camera, the creation of multiple focalizations in the filmic experience, "realizes" the desire to be present ("included") in the primal scene. This becomes evident when viewing intimate or erotic scenes from which we were excluded (during its filming), like the child in the primal scene, but are made present in the imaginary scene (the fantasy), where the actors-characters are. The prohibition against seeing the intimacy of others, let alone be included in it, can thus be transgressed due to the imaginary unity of body-actor, time, and space: The unique ontology of film together with its sophisticated techniques thus enables an unconscious transgression that never risks surpassing the boundaries of the imaginary. In other words, the secret charm of viewing a film lies not only in voyeurism as related to our awareness of film as fantasy (daydream) but also, and specifically, in being inscribed in a structure that has an affinity with that of the primal scene, which occurs unconsciously.

Lady in the Lake is a frustrating film because it deprives us of the imaginary transgression achieved by this unconscious operation, by depriving us of the freedom of motion that transposes us into the diegetic space of the film, into its fantasy world. A film in which we would only get to see the protagonists facing the camera would be equally frustrating.[9] In both cases we are robbed of the imaginary unity of the film, through which we become engaged with the spatial and temporal coordinates of the diegesis. In *Lady in the Lake*, because we mostly get to see what the protagonist sees during the viewing of the film, the camera is limited to a single diegetic point of view of which we are constantly aware: The camera is the body that occupies the place of the protagonist; when the other characters address him they are in fact addressing the camera—the spectators. Rather than transcending or transgressing the limits and the discrepancies of space and time, the camera reveals them, becoming an impediment in our fantasmatic engagement with the diegesis; rather than functioning as an eye/body (that allows us to "be" "everywhere" and in the present of the diegesis), it functions as an impediment that stands between us and the diegetic space of the film. Namely, it structurally impedes inscription in the primal scene. In contrast, in *Enter the Void* (Gaspar Noé 2009), which is not only shot from the protagonist's point of view but also renders his subjectivity, his unconscious, the camera is free from all constraints of space and time, emphasizing its ambition to enter and conquer the space of the Other's desire in the primal scene, which is in fact the theme of the film.

If in narrative film part of our unconscious engagement with the film's diegesis and the structure of the primal scene resides in the imaginary coalescence/presence of the body of the character and that of the actor into one unity, what can we learn about this engagement, which occurs within a larger dynamic—that of desire/fantasy—when characters are not embodied by actors? The following four examples, all by *auteurs*, are exceptions that prove the rule, namely narrative film's paradoxical nature: That it is precisely the unattainability of the object on the screen, associated with the imaginary, that makes it possible for the spectators to let the camera unconsciously inscribe us into a fantasmatic space compatible with the unconscious inscription in the primal scene fantasy. We have chosen to elaborate on Hitchcock because he adheres to the classical language of film, affirming its relevance to the spectators' engagement with the unconscious aspect of the dynamic of desire/fantasy.

Bodiless Characters

Alfred Hitchcock's *Rebecca* (1940) makes a clear distinction between the protagonist's desire to be loved and seen by her husband (which we engage with and which is sustained all through, until it is finally fulfilled), and the way she pursues it. The latter is conflated with the inevitable failure related to attempts to guess what the Other wants. But this distinction is not made at the outset. Were we to condemn the protagonist (Joan Fontaine), a plain young woman whose name we never learn,[10] for her immature and futile behavior from the start, we would find it hard to engage with the film altogether (of course, the rendering of the protagonist's dream in the opening sequence—the camera movement takes us into the space of the diegesis—is a mise-en-abyme that condenses her story and the main theme of the film, but this we can know only in retrospect). Our inscription in the primal scene structure is achieved through the unfolding of the romantic relationship between her and the aristocrat Maxim de Winter (Lawrence Olivier). All the scenes that take place in Monte Carlo, leading to Maxim's decision to marry her, are edited in a classical way (mostly using the S/RS device) which unswervingly draws us into a structure that affords our inscription in the couple's intimacy and the space in which it occurs. However, after the couple arrives at Manderley, Maxim's mansion, things become more complicated. The protagonist feels inferior to Rebecca, Maxim's dead wife, when she learns that the latter was very beautiful, greatly admired, and extremely successful at her role as mistress of Manderley. In Manderley, Rebecca's monogram (RdeW) appears on objects that belonged to her, which the protagonist repeatedly comes in contact with. The film thus uses objects that metonymically testify to Rebecca's omnipresence, which make up for her absence, and at the same time reflexively point to narrative film's necessity to compensate for the screen's lack. The one character in the film who disavows lack is the perverse Mrs. Danvers, the housekeeper (Judith Anderson), for whom these objects are indeed fetishes.

The sexually inexperienced protagonist assumes (as do spectators when first viewing the film) that Rebecca had been the object of desire for everyone who knew her, men and women alike: Mrs. Danvers; Jack Favell (George Sanders), Rebecca's cousin and lover; and of course, her husband, Maxim. She relentlessly tries to become the object of Maxim's desiring look, a look she imagines Rebecca effortlessly enjoyed. As Raymond Durgnat (1974, in Tania Modleski 2016: 44) suggests, this is the archetypal Oedipal dream of a young girl to marry a father figure who rescues her from a domineering mother whose possession of the father she must confront.

In one of the most mesmerizing scenes in the film, Mrs. Danvers walks the protagonist through Rebecca's and Maxim's bedroom. While she displays the objects that belonged to Rebecca, treating them with care and sexual admiration, she is in fact "visualizing" Rebecca's sensuality for the protagonist; she makes her feel Rebecca's furs, given to her by Maxim; she shows her Rebecca's lush underwear, "laced by hand by the nuns of St. Clare," and marvels at the sight of Rebecca's transparent black nightgown. She thus lures the protagonist into standing in for Rebecca, simulating how she used to brush her hair every night, while a large silver-framed photograph of Maxim is "staring" at them from the top of the dresser.

Danvers's actions are malevolent—her sole purpose is to make the protagonist feel inferior to Rebecca, whom she adored—but by holding on to Rebecca's lingerie and entrancing the protagonist, imbuing them with sexuality and awe, she forcefully inscribes her into the primal scene. Overwhelmed by what the protagonist imagines having been the sexual relationship between her husband and his late wife—like the child watching her parents' lovemaking—which Mrs. Danvers forces her to envision, she tries to leave the room. But Danvers insists, "You wouldn't think she'd been gone for so long ... would you? Sometimes when I walk along the corridor, I fancy I hear her, just behind me. That quick light step, I couldn't mistake it anywhere. Not only in this room, it's in all the rooms in the house. I can almost hear it now."

By replacing Rebecca with the protagonist in the primal scene scenario, Danvers clearly articulates the protagonist's unconscious desire to take Rebecca's place as well as its lethal aspect. Her words express her unconscious fantasy of wholeness, that eternal "bliss" lies in the fantasy of occupying *objet a*, which Rebecca represents. However, their subtext also conveys a different meaning: That such bliss is in effect lethal for both the subject and the object usurped, and that the desire of the m/Other is itself lethal—its imagined overwhelming powers will haunt the subject forever. Modleski writes,

> In *Rebecca* the beautiful, desirable woman is not only never sutured in as object of the look, not only never made a part of the film's field of vision, she is actually poised within the diegesis as all-seeing—as for example when Mrs. Danvers asks the terrified heroine if she thinks the dead come back to watch the living and says she sometimes thinks Rebecca comes back to watch the new couple together. (2016: 50)

As *objet a*, in its capacity of object-cause-of-desire, Rebecca can never materialize. This all-seeing non-embodied character represents the gaze, that which never coincides with the eye (of the subject) that does the looking (this division represents the split subject in the visual field)—the partial object gaze is in the field of the Other (not in that of the subject), namely the object that sets desire in motion. By imagining her husband's desire for the sexually mature beautiful woman ("her mother") and by attempting to occupy that place, the protagonist, in the primal scene fantasy, is in fact attempting to answer the question underlying every fantasy: "What does the Other want?"[11] And, as in every fantasmatic scenario, the answer imagined is erroneous. She thinks that her husband wants her to be like Rebecca; she wrongly conflates her desire to be seen/recognized by her husband with replacing Rebecca, a conflation that points to the impossibility of occupying *objet a* as well as guessing what the Other wants.

As long as the protagonist's desire to be seen and acknowledged is conflated with actions directed at attempts to replace Rebecca, the film draws the spectators more and more into perilous territory in which the protagonist seems to be punished for her various transgressions. Instead of gaining her husband's adoring look, she is reprehended and ridiculed by him. The harder she tries, the more bitterly she fails. This disdainful chain of events culminates in the traumatizing costume ball scene. Not knowing that her costume for the ball is the same one that Rebecca wore the year before—by Mrs. Danvers's malicious design—the protagonist comes down the stairs, radiant with anticipation, positive that she will finally succeed in gaining her husband's admiration. But Maxim reacts violently, insisting that she be out of sight before the guests arrive to see her. In repeated viewings the enhanced spectators' sense of anxiety and pity persists, particularly because we empathize with her desire to be loved by her husband, which is satisfied in the end, as it has nothing to do with guessing what the Other wants. Therefore, any fantasy that the protagonist might have entertained up to the ball scene by thinking that what her husband wanted is for her to be glamorous like Rebecca is miserably shattered. For spectators this generates a split between the desire to be loved (for what we are) and fantasy (believing that we can achieve this through guessing what the Other wants from us or occupying *objet a*).

This becomes clear near the end of the film, when Maxim tells his young wife about the night Rebecca died. While he describes her actions and reiterates her words in minute detail, the camera simulates these actions. As Modleski (2016: 50) notes, a different adaptation of this Daphné Du Maurier novel would have resorted to a flashback, "allaying our anxiety over an empty screen, by filling the 'lack.'" But instead, Hitchcock lets his camera follow a void. We are thus deprived of the satisfaction of seeing Rebecca materializing through the body of a "bigger than life" star (Joan Crawford might have been a "good" choice). As we listen to Rebecca's words and intonation enacted by her husband (his body off-screen), his voice portrays a spiteful character, creating an acousmatic, uncanny presence that contradicts the protagonist's romantic visual fantasy imagined in relation to Rebecca and her husband up to this point. Maxim hated his wife and believes he accidentally killed her. What we have here is an inscription into the primal scene with an *uncanny* twist. By refraining from using a flashback, the scene maintains its temporal and spatial coordinates, which enables the protagonist's inclusion in a space that is not hers. A flashback, occurring in the past, not only would have had an actress impersonating Rebecca but also would have made it impossible to physically include the protagonist. Conversely, it would have included the spectator, possibly stitching the split created earlier between the desire to be loved and the fantasy to know the Other's desire.

The scene starts with showing Maxim speaking, then cuts to the protagonist, who is situated at the other end of the room, her eyes turning from Maxim to a divan placed opposite them, rendering a static shot of the divan from *her* point of view. It thus inscribes her into Maxim's and Rebecca's intimacy—the primal scene—while we remain inscribed in the protagonist's space (her desire to be loved by her husband). But even this inscription is tackled: When Maxim, his body off-screen, utters the words "suddenly she got up, started to walk toward me," the camera tilts up and then pans toward him, simulating Rebecca's movement and thus undermining the illusion previously created by the eyeline match, although what we see is still the protagonist's point of view, as if thrusting us out from an intimacy in the making. We become aware of the camera through its movement, the movement of an absence—the gaze in all its uncanniness. This evinces the presence of the camera in an *elsewhere*; we do not see the camera, which, like the actor, was present on the set, only its movement. The camera reveals here its power/function to inscribe our body into the primal scene fantasy by undermining both the protagonist's inscription in it, created earlier by the editing, and ours, as we are more affected by the movement of the camera simulating a void than by the knowledge that this movement is supposed to be rendering the protagonist's point of view (a POV following a ghost that signifies cinema's lack).

The void that Hitchcock's camera evinces exemplifies how the film protagonists, through their physical absence, draw our desire and, at the same time, impede the "materialization" of a fantasy meant to fill this void. The desire for the lost object, which is absent from the visual field and represented by Rebecca, is achieved via a multitude of objects of fantasy, but the fantasy of filling the void via inscription in the primal scene is later dissolved. This is how Hitchcock disables the probability of occupying a perverse position—represented by Mrs. Danvers, who forces the protagonist's body into the primal scene—but, at the same time, engages the spectator with the protagonist's desire to be loved by her husband, carefully creating a "happy ending." At the end of the scene, the protagonist seems more than happy to be relieved of a childish fantasy and realize that her husband loves her for what she is (the opposite of Rebecca).

This suggests not only that every subject is prone to fantasize a scenario without lack but also, and more importantly, that if narrative cinema wishes to engage spectators with a film, it cannot renounce creating a fantasy altogether. Hitchcock, the master weaver of the dynamic of desire/fantasy, always confronts his spectators with the lack of the screen as well as their own by shattering a fantasy that he is first very meticulous in creating. Unconsciously, we are "allowed" inscription in the primal scene by identifying with the desire to fill the lack, only to be jolted out of it. This two-faced strategy is Hitchcock's way of evincing the role of fantasy in narrative cinema and at the same time finding various narrative, aesthetic, and rhetorical devices that undermine our inscription in the film's fantasy, enabled by its affinity with the structure of the primal scene. Counter-cinema (à la Jean-Luc Godard), for example, impedes such an inscription from the very beginning of the film, an impediment often resulting in nonengagement with the film.

North by Northwest does not differ much in this respect. The character of "Mr. Kaplan" is a non-existent agent. "George Kaplan" is invented by a US government intelligence agency as a decoy for their real agent who has infiltrated an enemy group headed by a man named Vandamm (James Mason). Vandamm's men mistake Roger Thornhill (the protagonist/Cary Grant) for Kaplan as a result of an unfortunate coincidence linked to Thornhill's mother (Jesse Royce Landis). In a hotel lobby, where Thornhill is having a business meeting, Mr. Kaplan is being paged at the same moment that Thornhill, realizing he has forgotten to send a telegram to his mother, waves to the pager. The two men waiting for Kaplan to show up think that Thornhill is answering the page, abduct him, and later try to kill him. The intelligence chief, called "the Professor" (Leo G. Carroll) suggests the agency do nothing to help Thornhill because they do not want to risk exposing their real agent. Furthermore, Thornhill as the "real-life" Kaplan lends credibility to their invented agent. The agency creates a trail of hotel registrations complete with prop clothing and other personal belongings moved in and out of the various hotel rooms by fellow agents. After surviving the first attempt on his life, Thornhill backtracks to one of the hotels with his mother, entering Kaplan's room, only to discover that no one at the hotel has ever actually seen the man. Both the chambermaid and the valet address *him* as "Mr. Kaplan." As his life is constantly threatened by Vandamm's men and having been framed for a murder of a UN official (Mr. Towsend), Thornhill, who is now on the run, believes that should he find Mr. Kaplan his troubles would be over. He becomes romantically involved with the beautiful and mysterious Eve Kendall (Eva Marie Saint), only to discover first that she is Vandamm's mistress and later that she is in fact the undercover agent the agency has been protecting.

Like Rebecca, the character of Mr. Kaplan functions as the object-cause-of-desire during the first half of the film, motivating Thornhill's actions. Our desire consists of the fact that we want to fill the gap of Mr. Kaplan with a body, not unrelated to our desire that Thornhill be exonerated from suspicion of having killed Mr. Townsend. Until Thornhill, as well as the spectators, learn that there is no Mr. Kaplan, desire is conjured by the question "Who is Mr. Kaplan?" In the scene where Thornhill is in Kaplan's hotel room, he and his mother inspect his belongings. Thornhill concludes that he has dandruff and while trying to fit in Kaplan's suit, he says: "Obviously they've mistaken me for a much shorter man." Like the protagonist of *Rebecca*, who fails in all her attempts to occupy Rebecca's place/position, here, in a more humorous manner, Thornhill cannot fit in the suit of another. His mother's mocking regard intensifies his failure to fit in. This impossibility, which marks the failure to fill the Other's lack, is also the fantasized place that the subject ascribes her or himself in the primal scene (in the Other's desire). While in the Oedipal triangle of *Rebecca* the protagonist occupies her mother's place, here it is the father's. With her mocking regard, it is as if the mother were saying, "Ha, you really think you can take your father's place?! Think again!" This is Hitchcock's way of bringing together the Freudian desire to occupy the father's position in the primal scene and the Lacanian position of a subjective inscription into the Other's desire to veil its lack. What matters is that the subject be able to accept the signifier of the symbolic lack, something Thornhill will have to learn (for now he is still trapped in his mother's desire). This notion reverberates later on in the film, when the name of the symbolic father, "the Name-of-the-Father" ("CIA" or "FBI") seems not to matter because it signifies a lack (like the initial "O" in the name "Roger O. Thornhill," signifying "nothing"), a function that imposes "the Law" by regulating desire in the Oedipus complex.[12]

As it turns out, we realize that Eve is in fact the "body" of Mr. Kaplan. While the Professor functions as the one who introduces "the-Name-of-the-Father" into Thornhill's life, symbolizing separation from his mother, Eve is the object entrusted by the film to make sure this separation is successful. Indeed, as soon as she emerges, Thornhill's mother disappears, and we never see her again. Eve is also a character whose evolvement is marked by a transition from entertaining a fantasy of filling *objet a* (being Mr. Kaplan) to a subject that desires to be acknowledged for what she really is—a vulnerable woman. Although her playing a double agent might also be considered part of her subjective flexibility to play a fictional role within the coordinates of the symbolic (unlike Thornhill, whose quest marks the entrance into the symbolic), her willingness to join the secret agency in her capacity as Vandamm's mistress (which in turn, refers to the fantasmatic flexibility of the subject's position/s in the primal scene) does suggest that she might have been too confident, if not presumptuous, in having agreed to play with fire.

This becomes clear in the scene in Eve's hotel room, when we notice she has developed real feelings for Thornhill (who begins to suspect that she might be of the Devil's party) and is intensified in the auction scene that follows, which marks a separation of our desire from Thornhill's (not unlike the difference between the protagonist's desire in *Rebecca* to be loved and appreciated for what she is and her relentless efforts to become *objet a*): The film cautions us against falling into the trap of insisting to fill the lack in the Other (represented by the urge to solve the enigma of Kaplan) by creating a gap between what we see and what he sees. The scene starts by giving us a close-up of Vandamm's hand gripping Eve's nape, which evinces her vulnerability. The camera then dollies out, pans the room, and arrives at Thornhill, showing his reaction. Although this shot is simulating Thornhill's point of view, emphasizing that Eve's intimacy with Vandamm is the very first thing that catches his attention, because he is quite a distance from Eve, he cannot see what the close-up enables us to see: that the hand holding tight connotes not only intimacy but also danger. Herein lies Hitchcock's greatness: Structurally and phenomenologically (as explained above) he includes us in the scene (even more so, through the close-up) but, at the same time, cautions us against occupying Thornhill's position in the primal scene, inscription in the Other's desire. From this point on, our desire, which up to now has been invested in Thornhill's, shifts. Absorbed in his jealousy, Thornhill hurries to where Eve and Vandamm are located and lashes out at them, walking right into an "Oedipal" trap (emphasized by the triangular composition). This trap evolves into another attempt to murder him, and he will need to use every bit of creativity to escape from it. Spectators who view the film for the first time understand from Eve's reactions of hurt and indignation that she is in love with Thornhill; also, the interest in finding out who Kaplan is diminishes after an earlier scene in which Hitchcock releases the information about Kaplan being a fiction of the Secret Service (of which Thornhill is oblivious at this stage). In repeated viewings we *feel* the danger he puts Eve in, and because of his infantile actions our desire shifts to her desire that she be seen by him.

This shift, as in *Rebecca*, in the scene in which Maxim confesses his true feelings for Rebecca, marks an interference with inscription in the primal scene for both the protagonist and the spectators. Watching Vandamm and Eve from a distance and not understanding what is really going on and then, driven by a sense of betrayal and jealousy, rushing in to usurp Vandamm's position in the primal scene, almost costs Thornhill his life. It is well known that Hitchcock often has less significant characters who are assigned the roles of witnesses or passers-by reiterate verbally what he wants us to understand from the visuals. Here it is a woman at the auction. After realizing that his life is in danger, Thornhill creates a commotion by which he hopes to force the intervention of the police: He offers ridiculous prices for the items presented at the auction, claiming that "it is a fake." The woman, sitting in front of Thornhill, turns around and says to him, "One thing is for sure, you're a *genuine idiot*!" Her remark alludes to Thornhill's not seeing what we saw at the beginning of the scene, allowing for his inscription in the Other's desire, while cautioning the spectator against a similar inscription.

Such interferences in Hitchcock's films, whose purpose is to eschew inscription in the primal scene/inscription in the Other's desire, are achieved through various "view-behind" shots (rendered in close-ups, flashbacks, and so on), in which we get to *see* what the protagonist cannot, or does not, want to see. In the two examples addressed here, as in most of Hitchcock's films, they occur within the dynamic of desire/fantasy that follows the basic structure of classical narrative, no matter how far-fetched the story might be. The point is that fantasy is conjured only in relation to characters because of film's affinity with the unconscious primal scene fantasy. An inanimate object will hardly stand in for an occupant in the primal scene scenario, unless the objects represent a subject or a subjective look. The problematization of filling the lack in the Other through a bodiless character is emphasized through the channeling of desire into two different modes, represented also by the division of characters into those embodied by actors versus the bodiless ones. The fantasy of occupying *objet a* is juxtaposed with "growing-up," with occupying a place in the symbolic, a place from which the subject articulates their own desire. In *Rebecca*, this articulation is born when the protagonist is finally freed from her futile attempts to guess what her husband wants from her. After Maxim tells his young wife his truth about Rebecca, he tells her that she has changed and is no longer the innocent young woman he married. This marks for her a double recognition on his part, first that it was the *difference* between her and Rebecca that drew him to her when they first met and, second, that he now recognizes a change in her. He thus assures her that she can finally be "she." In *North by*

Northwest, Thornhill finally succeeds in starting a new, married life, leaving his mother out of the picture.

We may now further understand why cinema must not only show us the characters but also alternate between "objective" shots and subjective point-of-view shots. While the primal scene cannot be conjured without the presence of the character/actor, it is the economy of seeing that either jolts the spectators out of the primal scene or impedes our inscription in it altogether. We have seen an example of this in Hitchcock's use of the close-up at the beginning of the auction scene in *North by Northwest*. The close-up is indeed a paradoxical device, emblematic of the ontology of film. It renders details that the human eye cannot perceive outside the cinema, not even the character/s in the scene to whom the point of view is attributed. The close-up thus belongs to the camera, whose body is never present on the screen. Therefore, when assigned to a character's point of view in the diegesis, we are always skeptical of its subjective nature (all the more so if we consider that the object closely perceived was not even in the scopic field of the actor who plays the perceiver).

The Hitchcock example of the close-up introduces a new element of suspense in addition to empowering us with view-behind information. On the one hand, it functions as the gaze of a recording machine, emphasized by its movement. Rather than cutting from the close-up to Thornhill, who is doing the looking, the camera dollies out and then pans the auction room, which gives us the establishing shot. Only after this long camera movement, visually evincing the existence of the camera body, does it return to Thornhill, whose point of view it has supposedly been rendering. And so, it is the camera that splits our desire from that of Thornhill. On the other hand, by this very splitting, the camera also takes us, the spectators, to see in the diegesis—the fictional/fantasmatic field—more than the character, as if the camera's body and that of the spectator have become one. Paradoxically, while we "are" in the scene, we are not in the primal scene. This trap is saved for Thornhill.

Our analyses of *Rebecca* and *North by Northwest* are meant to demonstrate that narrative film cannot do without fantasy. Desire needs fantasy to stay alive; however, film can employ many strategies that alert spectators to the dangers of succumbing to chasing after the impossible: veiling the lack in the Other. This alert, which is both reflexive and rhetorical, reflects the ontology of film as well as the way the mechanism of desire/fantasy operates in relation to this unique ontology. Herein lies the main fallacy of the 1970s "suture" film theories that considered the alternation of shots, for example (like the S/RS device), as a strategy designed to draw the spectator into the filmic fiction, covering a lack and ultimately accepting the film's ideology (e.g., Dayan 1974). As Thomas Elsaesser and Malte Hagener (2010: 104–5) note, Žižek's reading of the cinematic suture differs substantially in that it introduces the *real* gaze, the object looking at us, into the scopic regime.[13] Our point is that the introduction of the real functions in *North by Northwest* not as an alienating device but rather as one that aspires to impede the spectators' inscription in the primal scene (which it achieves through employing a variation of the S/RS) and to evince the protagonist's entry into the symbolic without overly disturbing the balance necessary for sustaining our engagement with the dynamic of desire/fantasy, which persists in repeated viewings.

The following two examples, which are more overt in their reflexivity, appeal to our invocatory drive and expose cinema's lack—its illusionary unity of sound and image: Kubrick's *2001: A Space Odyssey* (1968) and Jonze's *Her* (2013). While in *2001: A Space Odyssey* this lack taps into the real, in *Her* the unity of body and sound is not entirely dissolved. Put together, these examples illustrate the difference between the scopic and the invocatory drives. The scopic drive, in connection to characters, is generated in cinema through the visualization of a body and the subjectivity of the character, embodied by an actor, the voice of the actor/character being an integral part (albeit illusionary) of it. When detached from a body/actor, the voice becomes a partial object, which, like the gaze as partial object, threatens the imaginary unity of the subject/spectator.

In these examples, the bodiless characters (the first is the film's antagonist; the second is one of two protagonists) are inanimate objects—a computer and an advanced operating system; they are voiced by actors and they have a gaze (shots are rendered from their point of view). In *2001: A Space Odyssey*—an example of authorial counter-cinema—the anthropomorphic HAL 9000 personifies both the fantasy to be flawless, complete, and omnipresent, and the desire to receive recognition. This fusion ultimately leads to his demise. In the Jupiter Mission episode, Dave Bowman (Keir Dullea) and Frank Poole (Gary Lockwood), the two astronauts operating the spaceship, start suspecting HAL of malfunctioning. When queried, HAL insists that the problem, like all previous issues with the HAL 9000 series, is due to "human error." Concerned about Hal's behavior, Dave and Frank enter one of the EVA pods to talk without HAL overhearing them. They agree to disconnect HAL if he is proven to be wrong in his assessment. But, during their conversation, HAL can view the astronauts through the portal of the pod and read their lips as they discuss their plan.

When HAL reads the astronauts' lips without the two being aware of it, the image of the two speaking is rendered from *his* point of view, with the camera panning from Frank to Dave and back again, simulating his eye movement. This conjures up the child, who when excluded from the intimacy of two others and seeing what he is not supposed to becomes enraged, and even lethal. The question here is what happens to the spectators in relation to the economy of desire. Can a machine, an automaton, one simulating human subjectivity, engage us with it? Cinema has ample anthropomorphic robots and extraterrestrial creatures with whom spectators engage, but the condition for such an engagement is the belief or knowledge that underneath the robot costume (indeed, most robots are played by actors wearing costumes) is a human who has a psyche like ours—flawed, desiring, fantasizing. This is even more evident in films in which we can easily identify the actor who plays the role of the robot (e.g., Steven Spielberg's *A. I. Artificial Intelligence*, 2001).

Although HAL is endowed with subjective attributes, his visual and aural portrayal makes him appear inhuman, more like a huge seeing and hearing *machine*. He embodies the two partial objects—gaze and voice in the field of the Other—in all their disintegrated form, two foreign autonomous, externalized entities (indeed, two aliens) threatening to annihilate the subject and its imagined unity. His all-seeing gaze often appears on the screen as a big red eye whose light is blinding, his omnipresent voice somewhat sinister. It seems that HAL's portrayal says something not only about human subjectivity, namely that it may become detrimental when the desire for recognition is fused with insistence on a fantasy to be all-knowing, all-seeing, and endowed with prodigious powers—lacking nothing; it also says something about the cinema, which is a huge visual and aural machine. It makes itself present through a voice and a gaze, located in the field of the Other's desire. Therefore, HAL's portrayal as an autonomous eye and ear is an uncanny experience. Even before we become aware of his plan to murder all the astronauts, he evokes an eerie affect. How may we then relate to *his* subjectivity, his desire, his fantasy?

When viewing a film, our invocatory drive is supposed to be activated by what we hear and our scopic drive by what we see. If what we hear all along is an *acousmêtre* and what we see is a gaze staring at us, we in fact see and hear an aspect of subjectivity without a subject. That most of us are not familiar with Douglas Rain (he only "acted" in two other films, one before *Kubrick's Odyssey* and again, as HAL, in the sequel of the *Odyssey—2010: The Year We Make Contact* [Peter Hyams 1984]) does not help much. Michel Chion describes HAL's demise as follows:

> In the course of this agony, narrated live by Hal's pseudo-consciousness ("Dave, stop. Stop, will you? Stop Dave . . . I'm afraid . . . Dave, my mind is going. . . ."), there is a precise moment of *shifting into automatism*. . . . HAL changes from being a subject to a non-subject, from a living acousmêtre to an acousmachine. . . . he abruptly changes tone and begins to spout, with a perked-up voice of a young computer, the pattern he was taught "at birth" . . . . From then on he is only a recording; he sings "Daisy, Daisy." As soon as he is quiet, another recording takes his place—not Hal—which discloses to Dave the goal of his mission. ([1982] 1999: 45; italics in the original)

In our view, HAL is not a subject to begin with. The breaking down of his voice and the additional substituting recording are pacifying because of his uncanny portrayal throughout the film. That HAL is the antagonist is not the real point here. Rather, the point is that his voice and gaze remain partial, alienating, uncanny objects—the traumatic real taking over the dynamic of desire/fantasy (the symbolic/imaginary). This does not mean that we cannot appreciate the film or enjoy its aesthetics; it only means that our unconscious engagement with it is somewhat blocked.

Her appeals to our invocatory drive and also exposes cinema's lack by undermining the illusionary unity of sound and image.[14] As mentioned above, while the scopic drive in connection to characters is generated in cinema through the visualization of a body and the subjectivity of the character embodied by an actor, the invocatory drive is generated through the voice, experienced as an integral, albeit illusionary, part of the actor/character. The bodiless character in *Her* is one of the film's two protagonists, an inanimate object—an advanced operating system named Samantha, figuring an actress' (Scarlett Johansson) voice and possessing a point of view. When detached from a body/actor, the voice is emphasized as a partial object that threatens the imaginary unity of the subject/spectator (see, for example, Chion [1982] 1999; Mary Ann Doane 1980; Metz 1980). However, our invocatory drive in *Her* is not directed to a partial terrifying on-screen object but to the off-screen body of Johansson. In both *2001: A Space Odyssey* and *Her*, the imaginary unity of body and voice achieved through the technological skills of the cinematic apparatus is deconstructed. But in *Her*, because we know Johansson from other films and media photographs, when hearing Samantha's unique, somewhat throaty, deep, seductive voice, we cannot help but relate it to Johansson's ravishing, non-diegetic body—a fantasy object.

If, as Metz asserts, the objects and sounds of the film always remain out of our reach, *Her*'s achievement lies precisely in associating a diegetic voice with a body that is visually absent from the film's fiction but present in the spectator's imaginary. This is emphasized in the scene with the surrogate. In her desire to simulate an intersubjective relationship with Theo (Joaquin Phoenix), Samantha sends him a young blonde, Izabella (Portia Doubleday). Izabella does not speak to Theo; she receives instructions from Samantha through headphones while trying to act out Samantha's desire for him. A small camera shaped like a beauty mark is glued to the surrogate's cheek, affording Samantha a view of Theo's expressions during "their" lovemaking. We hear Samantha's voice, but the surrogate does not lip-synch her words. This has a double, contradictory effect. On the one hand, it exposes the incoherence of body and sound in cinema—a lack; on the other, it emphasizes that the voice we hear does belong to a body it cannot be separated from. This second effect is later expressed in the film's diegesis. Knowing what the actress we have associated with Samantha's voice so far looks like, the love scene (our inscription in the primal scene) can hardly work for us, except for maybe the few seconds when the surrogate's face is not shown. The task of engaging with the desire between Theo and Izabella's body while hearing Johansson's voice thus becomes very challenging. For Theo, too: At first, when he closes his eyes or when the surrogate is with her back to him, he goes along with it, much like entertaining a private or shared fantasy during the act of lovemaking in order to stimulate desire, but when Samantha demands to hear him say to her "I love you" and to see his face, he opens his eyes. Seeing Izabella's face, he stops the lovemaking, claiming he does not know her. The fact that her lips remain sealed while we hear Johansson's voice precludes *our* entry into this primal scene simulation. This scene exemplifies the role of fantasy, as well as its precision, as the support of desire in that the moment fantasy is realized, desire vanishes. It reflexively states that what spectators love about viewing a film is precisely their detachment from real objects, which are richly visualized.

Disappointed, the surrogate locks herself in the bathroom, crying, her voice sounding surprisingly husky, like Johansson's. She says, off-screen, "The way Samantha described your relationship, and the way you guys love each other, without any judgment, I wanted to be a part of that because it is so pure." Again, this has a double effect: Being thrown out of her primal scene, the surrogate behaves like a little child who is confronted with the impossibility of the unconscious fantasy of indivisibility, coherence, plenitude, as well as the impossibility of participating in one's own creation; for the spectator, Theo's rejection seems justified because of the discrepancy between Johansson's voice, representing Theo's fantasy, his imaginary, and Izabella's body. It could be that Izabella's body contradicts the body of his fantasy (a fantasy that supports his desire), but for the spectators the fantasy object is Johansson as depicted in other films and media photographs.

Her might be considered an ultimate example of an absent presence that both marks the very ontology of cinema and the way it engages spectators.[15] It manages to sustain our desire through a lack and simultaneously create a fantasy by directing us to a body that has been imprinted in our imaginary by other films. Furthermore, it makes clear that without the work of fantasy in its role of both veiling lack and supporting desire, the traumatic voice as a partial object, an autonomous entity introducing the real, would be too uncanny (as in Kubrick's *A Space Odyssey*) and would leave us in the realm of the traumatic.

An encounter with the real of the voice, which is tantamount in its effect to the real of the gaze, occurs near the end of the film. Samantha's voice, which we have attributed to Johansson's body, tells Theo that it has become involved with a series of others (like desire that bounces from object to object), until it announces that it must leave him. This marks the point when Theo must come to terms with no longer being able to entertain his fantasy, with renouncing his virtual love, which he has substituted for the reality of a relationship with another human being. Like in Hitchcock, and like any film spectator, he must learn that he cannot substitute a fantasy with reality. Neither can he succeed in solving the enigma of the Other's desire. This is a painful, almost devastating experience for him. For the spectators as well, it is the moment when the partaking in Theo's fantasy is disabled. However, his desire to be able to maintain a relationship with another human being is not dissolved. In the last scene of the film, Theo takes his neighbor Amy (Amy Adams) to the roof of their building and together they watch the sunrise, much like viewing a film, which suggests that viewing a narrative film teaches us how to use fantasy in order to support our desire. Having given up their operating systems, the two, sitting side by side, must learn now how to use fantasy (leave it in the imaginary, like viewing a film) in a relationship with another human being so that desire does not die.

Rebecca and *Her* reflexively evince the distance between spectators and the objects viewed, that is, the aspect of lack/absence inherent in the cinema, by renouncing the *sine qua non* of embodying characters by actors as well as problematizing inscription in the primal scene. However, as the films' analyses show, if narrative film does not want to lose its spectators, it must create a fantasy with which we can engage as well as employ devices that satisfy the desire to see. Bodiless-character films reveal, to various degrees, the unconscious operation inherent in our engagement with the dynamic of desire/fantasy, one that shows the very importance of this dynamic. In the neurotic structure, although fantasy's role is to veil lack, the subject finds their satisfaction purely in the fantasy, being aware that it cannot be an answer to the enigma of the Other, that the fantasy object plays a main role in an imagined story, never to be realized, which is what happens when viewing a film. Narrative cinema's role is thus to teach spectators how to support desire: by fantasizing. The unique ontology of film, together with its sophisticated techniques, enables, as previously argued, an unconscious transgression that never risks surpassing the boundaries of the imaginary.

The Real Body, the Paradox of the Close-Up (the Face), Characters and Actors

The face in close-up in cinema has been associated with human subjectivity, thus connecting the aesthetics of film with psychoanalysis, endowing it with either a fetishistic or an uncanny quality/function. However, we must remember that it belongs to a character, who, ontologically, is a conjunction of an image projected onto an empty screen with the (real) corporeality of an actor who was present in front of the camera. The close-up thus is inherently paradoxical: On the one hand, as an image that appears on the screen, it is a synecdoche, a poetic visual device, which enables us to identify the character/actor/star and to separate her or him from any other insignificant or less significant characters; in classical and mainstream narrative films, our engagement with the protagonist's desire is often achieved via the close-up, in its function both as a representation of a desiring subject and as an object of desire. On the other hand, again ontologically, the human close-up in film connotes a "dismembered" body: It always entails some sort of movement (contrary to the close-up in still photography or painting); it is a "living-dying" partial organism in that it appears like a head that has just been cut off from its body (which we know is alive). It is usually rendered after a *cut* that severs the head/face from the long-shot body (of the actor-character) that comes before or after it—an incredulity that we are meant to accept as part of the cinematic language as well as its imaginary nature.

Of all the classical film ontologists, Siegfried Kracauer is perhaps the most attentive to the psychoanalytic dimension of the cinematographic image of the character/actor, due to its amalgamation of the body materiality and the unnaturalness of the close-up. When writing about the film actor's functions, Kracauer ([1960] 1997: 97) argues that the actor is no more than "an object among objects," a raw material, linking this materiality to cinema's *photogénie*, "The cinema in this sense is not exclusively human. Its subject matter is the infinite flux of visible phenomena—those ever-changing patterns of physical existence whose flow may include human manifestations but need not climax in them." In comparing the actor in theater with that in film, Kracauer asserts that while the former relies on exaggeration and amplification of speech in order to create an illusion of naturalness and convey a sense of credibility, the latter is characterized by being, casualness, and physique. "What the actor tries to impart—the physical existence of a character—is overwhelmingly present on the screen" (94) through the close-up. But film's *photogénie*, as evinced by the close-up, also entails a quality of the unnatural, as Doane (2003: 90) emphasizes when she starts her essay with Jean Epstein's *photogénie* of the close-up:

> The description [Epstein's] verges on the obscene, perhaps because it transforms the face, usually reserved as the very locus of subjectivity, into a series of harsh and alien objects.... Epstein's prose extracts and abstracts the close-up from the scene, from the body, from the spatiotemporal coordinates of the narrative, performing, in effect, its monstrosity. Any spectator is invited to examine its gigantic detail, its contingencies, its idiosyncrasies. The close-up is always, at some level, an autonomous entity, a fragment, a "for-itself."[16]

As a "for-itself," the close-up is rendered idiosyncratic, prone to revealing that which lies beneath the surface, through motion, simultaneously connoting death and life, as Epstein asserts, "Everything is in movement, imbalance, crisis." Indeed, here is where the cinema departs from still photography. While in the close-up of still photography we only have the "death" of the subject, who is no longer "there," in film, life is connoted through motion. A facial expression is always a gesture, a movement—an eye blink, a tremor, a shedding tear. But, as mentioned before, considering its unnaturalness, as well as the fact that it fills the whole field of vision, it defies spatiotemporal coordinates, evincing thus the flatness of the screen. No wonder film theoreticians have considered it not only as essentially replacing the grand body gestures of acting in the theater but also menacing, bringing together life and death by distorting "ordinary notions about [the face's] social semiotics" (Doane 2003: 95). According to Gilles Deleuze (in Doane, 95), the face functions as "(1) the privileged site of individualization (it embodies each person's uniqueness); (2) the manifestation of social role or social type; (3) the primary tool of intersubjectivity, of relation to or communication with the other (this also refers to an adequate, mimetic relation, within the individual, between face and character or role)."

Doane notes that Deleuze (as Béla Bálasz and Jacques Aumont before him) does not distinguish between the close-up and the face in the cinema; it is an object suspending signification, interfering with the flow of the narrative, its temporality and spatiality. For Deleuze, the close-up and the face are equated—the close-up is the face, stripped of all the three functions mentioned above, a nudity in which Doane discerns a gaze à la Lacan; it is a partial object, staring at the spectator, without expression, devoid of any interiority and feeling (of the desire of a character). In Pascal Bonitzer's (1992: 18) discussion of the introduction of classical editing into films, which he associates with the loss of innocence, the close-up is associated with death, "It was indeed a revolution, like all revolutions, it was based upon death and upon a staging of death, a revolution whose symbol in this case too was a severed head, the close-up."

It is almost impossible to read about the unnaturalness of the close-up and its association with death without thinking of the classical French horror film *Les yeux sans visage* (1960),[17] an adaptation of Jean Redon's novel that demonstrates the notion of the close-up as a representation of a "dismembered" body, a two-dimensional face severed from its body by the cinematic cut. The uniqueness of Franju's film resides not necessarily in its use of the close-up (although it does that as well) but in the way it literalizes the notion regarding the monstrosity of the close-up in the story it tells. The question that it raises is the following: How does a film "attacking" one of the basic elements of engagement with the protagonist's desire—the face of the actor—affect spectators regarding this very engagement?

In *Les yeux sans visage*, Christiane Génessier (Edith Scob) is the daughter of Dr. Génessier (Pierre Brasseur). Her face was horribly disfigured in an automobile accident caused by her father. The latter promises to restore Christiane's face and until then insists she wear a mask to cover her disfigurement. With the aid of his assistant Louise (Alida Valli), he abducts young women with blue eyes and facial characteristics that resemble his daughter's (though we never see her original face) and then performs heterograft surgery, removing the face and grafting the skin onto his

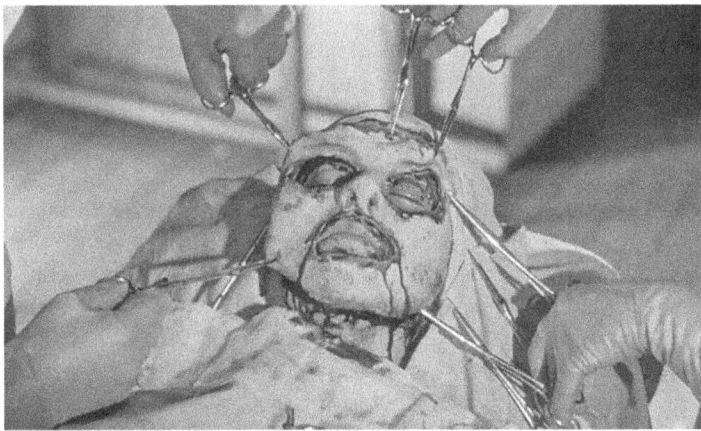

FIGURE 1.2 Les yeux sans visage (The Eyes without a Face, *George Franju, 1960*).

daughter's. This procedure is repeated off-screen, after which the bodies of the abducted women are disposed of, except for one scene. In it the surgery is rendered in medium close-up. It shows Génessier, aided by Louise, carefully cutting into the face of his female prisoner and removing it, after which the cut-out face appears as a mask, without eyes, devoid of subjectivity, leaving the prisoner faceless. The raw flesh connotes a loss of subjectivity, decay, and death (Figure 1.2).

The decision to show the procedure is linked to a diegetic motivation: Génessier believes that this time around the transplant of the face will be successful because he cuts deeper into the flesh of the face, uprooting it in its entirety, whereas before, as he tells Louise, he carried out the procedure in sections. In its gruesomeness, this scene clearly alludes to the use of the close-up as a revealer of that which the subject avoids encountering, namely decay and death. While all the mirrors in the house are removed so that Christiane can avoid encountering her disfigurement, the mask she is forced to wear shields Génessier and Louise, as well as the spectators, from seeing it. But, at the same time, the frozen inanimate mask emphasizes how, in filmic terms, the face disfigurement has hollowed out Christiane's subjectivity.

The mask that Christiane must wear/bear is thus "the eyes without a face." The sole motivation to the action in the plot is her father's mad ambition to restore her face. As a character lacking a beautiful face that sets her father's desire in motion, she can never be identified or recognized by the spectators via a close-up of her own but only by her ghost-like, ethereal characterization—her slim figure dressed in a long white gown and her slow-pacing walk. The only expression of subjectivity is rendered through her eyes, conveying simultaneously her wish to regain a beautiful face and horror from what her father is doing to achieve this goal. Unlike her father,

Christiane does not believe in the procedure ever succeeding. Her despair is already a form of death and the mask she wears is conflated with the face removed from the female prisoner on the operating table, who dies, like all the other victims before her. The horror of both thus derives from their being without human expression.

After the surgery, Génessier notices flaws on Christiane's face. Her face deteriorates within days; the new tissue is being rejected, and she must resume wearing her mask. The only sequence after the surgery showing Edith Scob's beautiful face, rendered in medium close-ups, conveys the notion that it matters who plays the role of Christiane, who for the rest of the film wears a mask. However, that Christiane's face is associated here with that of another unknown, dead character is the film's way of suggesting that alienation and death are inherent in the close-up. When Christiane's face starts decaying, a process rendered in a series of still photographs documenting the disfigurement, is the only time we feel not only horror but also sorrow and regret. The incorporation of the stills in the film evinces the use of the close-up in film as death in the making or rather a living death. Finally, Christiane, who has long been terrorized by her father's experiments and, as a result of guilt and isolation has been slowly losing her sanity, frees the last girl, stabs Louise, and releases the multitude of caged dogs her father has been using for experiments. The dogs maul Génessier to death, disfiguring *his* face in the process. Christiane, unmoved by her father's death, is seen walking slowly into the woods outside Génessier's house, evincing thus her ghost-like characterization throughout as a living doll. Her rejection of the skin of the other girls thus reflects a rejection of her father's desire, one rejected by us as well. What might sustain our desire throughout this film is most certainly not Génessier's psychotic fantasy but the curiosity to find out how it ends.

Les yeux sans visage is a classical narrative horror film, not what we call "counter-cinema," but in its radical problematization of the use of the face/the close-up, it shows its unnaturalness, or uncanniness, as stemming from a condensation of the materiality of the body of an actor and her or his imaginary/fantasmatic appearance on the screen: As an image, the close-up is a poetic device, meant to function/remain in the imaginary, but Génessier cuts into raw flesh (signifying the material body of actors), which impedes our engagement with his desire, precisely because it interferes with the mechanism of the imaginary when viewing a film. We denounce Génessier not because he is mad but because of the way he insists to *realize* his fantasy, to conceal the lack in the Other. Like the bodiless-character films, this is an unusual example that proves the rule, namely, how the close-up, as an emblem of the cinematic language, is used in the dynamic of desire/fantasy regarding both the diegesis and spectatorship. Whereas in films like *Rebecca* and *Her* this dynamic is not altogether dissolved (it only tackles inscription in the primal scene, into the Other's desire), here this dynamic is almost shattered. The film can engage us either in its function as an essay on the monstrosity of the close-up or simply by raising our curiosity regarding the unfolding of the narrative. This obstruction is also evident in the slow rhythm of the film, conveying a surreal effect, as if nothing ever happens, although the events are more than dramatic.

To sum up, what we learn from *Les yeux sans visage* is that in narrative cinema the face/close-up is used to channel our desire into the trajectory of the protagonist's desire—which the film resists. As stated before, in contrast to theories upholding that this channeling creates identification with the characters and their motivations, we argue that such identification is not the key to the engagement with narrative but is rather the activation of our desire through the very fact that the character desires something. In *Les yeux sans visage*, Génessier's desire is constructed so that it fails to engage us, not because he is mad in wanting to restore his daughter's face but because of how this madness is characterized and how he carries out his project. His own face is almost devoid of any other expression but madness, evinced by his unnaturally wide-open eyes from the very first shot in which he appears. In other words, the film suggests from the start that a desire associated with such a form of madness (a psychotic position in relation to the Other's desire, in which castration/the lack in the Other is foreclosed) is bound to lead to catastrophe. Therefore, the surgery fails repeatedly. Like Frankenstein in Mary Shelley's gothic novel, the result of Génessier's efforts to shun the lack in the Other is configured as monstrous. And this monstrosity is related to the materiality of actors when rendering their face in close-up, an unnaturalness that film makes appear "natural" only through the trajectory of the imaginary. *Les yeux sans visage* suggests, although in a roundabout way (as it precludes our engagement with Génessier's desire), that what makes it possible for us to invest our desire in a film is precisely its imaginary nature through which real bodies are transformed into fantasy objects. Not acknowledging this is construed as a form of madness.

Part and parcel of the close-up, and *photogénie* in general, are the physical attributes of actors, especially stars. In cinema, a rendition of Shakespeare's *Romeo and Juliet*, for example, cannot recruit but young and attractive actors, as Franco Zeffirelli very well knew when casting Leonard Whiting and Olivia Hussey in the roles of Romeo and Juliet (1968). Thus, for Kracauer, the physique of the actor, which is the main asset of nonactors (like in the Soviet *typage* or in the Italian neorealism), is what also characterizes the star system:

> The typical Hollywood star resembles the non-actor in that he acts out a standing character identical with his own or at least developed from it, frequently with the aid of make-up and publicity experts. As with any real-life figure on the screen, his presence in a film points beyond the film.

He affects the audience not just because of his fitness for this or that role but for being, or seeming to be, a particular kind of person—a person who exists independently of any part he enacts in a universe outside the cinema which the audience believes to be reality or wishfully substitutes for it. ([1960] 1997: 99–100)

Kracauer does not distinguish between the real body of the actor and his or her persona not merely because the latter is an inherent component of the actor's personality (be it real or fabricated) but also, and more importantly, because both are contingent on a coalescence that is unique to cinema: *physicality* and *photogénie*. For Kracauer then, the stylized image of the star and what it connotes, as well as its credibility, depend on one thing—the actor's physique, which cannot be separated from the materiality of the body, no matter how stylized the latter. We return to this notion and its repercussions in Chapters 3 and 4. For now, it is enough to note that this "being" in film needs to possess certain physical attributes to convince us that this is *our* protagonist, especially when rendered in close-up.

But, as we know, many film theories have argued that the physique of actors has also been used in promoting certain ideologies. As Doane (2003: 97) maintains, theories enamored with the *photogénie* of the close-up failed to recognize that it is not only a menacing gaze looking at the spectators but also a practice of classical cinema, "caught in a network of other gazes." Indeed, such a contention seems difficult to refute, since Hollywood cinema, even before the big studios, learned very quickly how to manipulate the stylized physique of the actor in order to make cinema more accessible and attractive to audiences. And this was achieved through using the close-up to create identification with physical attributes of actors as well as with the protagonists' emotions. It all began with D. W. Griffith's long cooperation with Lillian Gish and his exhaustion of the latter's child-like, fragile, appearance. In *The Birth of a Nation* (1915) Griffith assumed, intentionally or unintentionally, that he could get away with justifying racism by laying the foundations of classical editing—the pillars of narrative—its mainstay being the close-up. He was not totally wrong. Though the film did arouse much controversy among critics, it was an enormous success at the box office. The damning reviews that the film received were addressed by Griffith in his succeeding project—*Intolerance: Love's Struggle throughout the Ages* (1916). However, this film flopped at the box office because it was too abstract for the audiences of that time; it did not have one specific desire, one narrative, and one or two protagonists. In its effort to portray four different stories, through which the theme of in/tolerance was supposed to emerge, achieved by crosscutting between the plots, it baffled audiences.

Bonitzer names Griffith the first filmmaker to be attributed the (Lacanian) gaze due to the introduction of the close-up and editing:

> What, then, is the object that this anxiety or suspense releases, revives and sets going? I would hazard the response that this object, when emerged at the same time as the close-up was discovered, is, because of its characteristic malice, the gaze.
>
> We ought therefore to return to the source, to Griffith's films, for the gaze is a feature of his work. The gaze, as it functions in Griffith, doubtless issued from cinematography to be born of cinema. (Bonitzer 1992: 16)

Bonitzer in fact associates the close-up and the editing with the two devices that introduced desire and fantasy into the filmic experience: "The dirtiness did not disappear but was interiorized and moralized, and passed over into the gaze—that is, into the register of desire. . . . Once focused upon the face or the gaze, the law, desire and perversion made their entrance into the cinema" (18). We may thus assume that in associating Griffith with the loss of innocence in the cinema, Bonitzer does not restrict Griffith's work to the field of ideology. Rather, he is suggesting that the transition from the burlesque and the carnivalesque to editing and close-up marked a transition from entertaining audiences to engaging them with mental processes, such as the mechanism of desire/fantasy.

Is this enough to prevent ideology from getting its hooks on fantasy? After all, it is "fantasy [that] fills in the blank spaces in an ideological edifice" (McGowan 2007b: 36). So, can we really watch *Birth of a Nation*, engage with its mechanism of desire/fantasy, and at the same time reject its racist ideology? We argue that this is precisely what happens. If our views contradict such ideological fantasy to begin with, no close-up of any star will convert us. Similarly, for racist spectators, such a film will only strengthen their views. And these responses are conscious. The ways audiences reacted, respectively, to the two films by Griffith do not reflect any acceptance or rejection of ideology but a difference in each film's mode of engaging spectators with the mechanism of desire/fantasy.[18]

When addressing the notion of actor/acting in the filmic system, especially in relation to stardom, several terms that work on two intertwined levels—diegetic (the portrayal of a fictional character) and extra-diegetic (persona, image, personality, cultural context, etc.)—should be kept in mind. For example, in his discussion of stardom, Barry King argues that an analysis of acting should address, in addition to "character," the definition of which seems to raise no debate, the term "person":

> [The latter] should be taken to include an understanding that the physical presence of the actor is already coded in the general sense of having the

socially recognized attributes of an individual in the host culture . . . , a "personality," and in the specific sense that this "personality" is adapted to the exigencies of acting. Likewise, the term *image* should be restricted to the visual impact of the film "system" on the actor's "personality" off screen, so that the coherence of the actor's image on screen is clearly identified as a technological based construction. [As to the term] *persona*, [it should cover] what Stephen Heath has called "the conversion of the body, of the person, into the luminous sense of its film image"—an articulation of person and image as I have redefined them. (King 1991: 175; italics in the original)

As many studies on stardom show (e.g., Richard Dyer 1986; King 1991; Judith Mayne 1993; and Jackie Stacey 1994), over the years, Hollywood stars have played important and even constitutive roles for different audiences, turning the star system and its relationship with audiences into a rather complex system. The star system became an industry during the era of the big studios, both in Hollywood and in Europe, and lasted until circa 1960, when the era of classical cinema came to its end. After the dissolution of the studio system in Hollywood, and ever since, the power centralized in the hands of studio heads and producers/executives was transposed to actors/stars and their agents and publicists.[19] What this means is that, coupled with the speedy advancement of technology (the internet at large, Facebook, Twitter, etc.), stars have become an indispensable commodity independent of any part they might play in a given film. Moreover, some stars are also known for using their persona and power to advance certain social or political agendas.

The concept of stars as commodity has been addressed both by film scholars and critics, as well as by filmmakers, including in classical Hollywood. Suffice it to mention Billie Wilder's *Sunset Boulevard* (1950), not forgetting Norma Desmond's (Gloria Swanson) ending the film with: "Mr. DeMille, I am ready for my close-up!" Concomitant with the decline of the big studios, in the 1960s, it became a common practice both in filmmaking and in film theories to promote cinemas that subverted classical modes of representation, including the use of stars. For example, in Jean-Luc Godard's *Le Mépris* (*Contempt*, 1963), a specifically meta-film, French sex symbol and star Brigitte Bardot, famous for her long blonde hair, puts on a short black wig (so she resembles actress Anna Karina—at the time Godard's wife), resisting the spectators' expectations to watch the blonde Bardot. In 1972, Godard and Jean-Pierre Gorin made the radically political *Letter to Jane: An Investigation about a Still*, in which the two filmmakers viciously attack (on the soundtrack) the star system by analyzing a still news photograph showing Jane Fonda surrounded by Vietnamese Communists during her visit to Hanoi. When Peter Wollen (1972: 6) developed what he termed "the seven deadly sins" of classical cinema, counterpointing them with "the seven cardinal virtues" of counter-cinema, his emblematic example was thus Godard. Wollen set them out schematically in a table as follows:

Classical Cinema	Counter-Cinema
Narrative transitivity	Narrative intransitivity
Identification	Estrangement
Transparency	Foregrounding
Single diegesis	Multiple diegesis
Closure	Aperture
Pleasure	Un-pleasure
Fiction	Reality

As many film scholars have long recognized, such a binary distinction no longer holds true in the filmmaking of the last three decades, even though the star system, which for Walter Benjamin ([1936] 1968) represented the last remains of aura in the age of mechanical reproduction, still has the power to engage mass audiences. Today, the multitude of stars' images disseminated by mass media and the internet and consumed daily via the screens of our computers and handheld devices, in the comfort of our homes, in the streets, at work, and so on has been gnawing away at our awareness of film as fantasy. In other words, in the past the big screen intensified the mythical dimension of the star, their being affecting spectators precisely because this being was always experienced as larger than life, carving a specific fantasmatic space in our imaginary. The aura of stars that was then predicated on distance thus maintained our awareness of fantasy. But now we carry them in our pockets.

Indeed, Metz's approach when stating that spectators could succumb to the world of the film's fantasy was that we could do so precisely because of the awareness of its power to immerse us in a daydream meant to shield us from the traumatic lack experienced outside the movie theater, even if it was only for ninety minutes. But, considering today's technologies, how might we reconcile such an approach with the tumbling down of the awareness that the viewed actor is part of a fantasy, all the more if we bear in mind Kracauer's conflation of the character on-screen with the actor/his persona off-screen? How are we to interpret his argument that the actor/star affects the audience because of "being," or seeming to be, a particular kind of person—a person who exists independently of any part he enacts in a universe outside the cinema, which the audience believes to be reality or wishfully substitutes for it? Obviously, for Kracauer also, the real body of the actor is not to be confused with its wishful substitutes. "Being" can be conflated with a wishful substitute because the real body is never accessible to the spectator. In this respect, his argument is not unlike Metz's.

However, what distinguishes Kracauer from Metz is his conflation of the cinematographic image (mechanically reproduced in his time) with the human psyche/unconscious. Therefore, according to Kracauer, the film actor does not even have to act, but be, be his character, and it is precisely in this casualness of being that he recognizes the projection of the unconscious. When quoting René Claire's and Vsevolod Pudovkin's work with actors, writing that "both value projections of the unconscious" ([1960] 1997: 95), the function of the actor, through specific cinematic devices (such as the close-up, but not exclusively) is to reveal the unconscious, not the personality of the character or actor but *our* unconscious as such. This is the secret charm of characters as portrayed by actors for Kracauer. Kracauer associates this blurring of boundary to the experience of cinema as devoid of a past in that what makes the fantastic "avowedly imagined or believed to be true to fact" although it "belong[s] to worlds beyond camera-reality proper" (85) is precisely the fact that its characters were present in front of the camera as real persons (actors). However, this presence is not to be confused with the presence of *having-been-there* of the still photograph; it is one of *being-there* (Barthes [1964] 1977: 45). This is hinted at in Kracauer's admission that "history is problematic cinematically because it lacks the character of present-day actuality," whereas the filmic image that fuses with real-life impressions manifests itself "here and now."[20] And since the ontology of the image in narrative cinema is not one that bears witness to historical reality, we might conclude, as all film theories of fantasy have asserted, that narrative cinema at large activates our unconscious, even in its most "realistic" of styles. To sum up this argument, although the ontological status of film is an imaginary one, our engagement—via the dynamic of desire/fantasy—is unconscious. And this dynamic, as all the examples of the films analyzed so far have shown, largely depends on the characters/protagonists, always embodied by actors. Therefore, in narrative film, within the dynamic of desire/fantasy, one of the most effective ways of unsettling the engagement with fantasy, especially the spectators' inscription in the primal scene, is by tampering with the links between body, actor, and character.

Films' experimentation with the links between body-actor-character has always preoccupied narrative cinema. Using costumes and makeup, or even one actor for more than one role, films have demanded that audiences make certain adjustments regarding their expectations, attempting, if not to provoke a traumatic effect, at least to achieve some kind of estrangement in the act of viewing a film. We might mention here the case of different actors playing the same character in film sequels, such as James Bond over a period of over fifty years and the *Harry Potter* characters played by the same actors maturing in front of our eyes. This latter use of actors has been perfected in just one film thus far, *Boyhood* (Richard Linklater 2014), whose production lasted twelve years, showing the life of a character from age 5 to age 18, using the same actors. The physical changes that the characters/actors undergo (the boy growing up and his parents maturing) are thus real changes brought about by real time, condensed into just 165 minutes.

Many films use a rhetorical device that might be termed "the return of the referent": the use of still photographs or documentary footage at the end of the film that reveal what persons on whose life a film is based really looked like. Examples include *The Blind Side* (John Lee Hancock 2009), *American Sniper* (Clint Eastwood 2014), *Loving* (Jeff Nichols 2016), *The Glass Castle* (Destin Daniel Cretton 2017), *Bankier van het Verzet* (*The Resistance Banker*, Joram Lürsen 2018), *Bohemian Rhapsody* (Bryan Singer 2018), and *The 15:17 to Paris* (Clint Eastwood 2018).[21] In *Schindler's List* (Steven Spielberg 1993), at the end of the film, the actors accompany the real persons they played in the film to Schindler's grave in Jerusalem. In all these cases, the imaginary body (that of the actor) portraying the real person is "replaced" here by the latter. Such a replacement always tampers with the fantasy object (the actor embodying the character).

A variation of this are films in which the lives of iconic figures are "resurrected" on the screen, like those of James Dean, Pablo Picasso, Truman Capote, Coco Chanel, Marilyn Monroe, Jacqueline Kennedy, Michael Jackson, and so on. These films reenact or reconstruct famous scenes imprinted in the public memory, what Alison Landsberg (2004: 28) calls "prosthetic memories," memories disseminated by the mass media and culture—radio, film, television, and the internet: "Prosthetic memories are adopted as the result of a person's experience with a mass cultural technology of memory that dramatizes or recreates a history he or she did not live." We might think that the fantasy created around iconic figures and stars is disturbed when the actor playing them does not resemble "the original" enough, but in fact the opposite is true. The greater the resemblance (which in the TV biopic *Michael Jackson: Searching for Neverland* [Dianne Houston 2017] is indeed striking), the more intensified the feeling of uncanniness is—the original always remains out of reach. This teaches us that in cinema the referent is always allusive, unattainable, and that the star/actor can be grasped only as a fantasy object. In *The Life and Death of Peter Sellers* (Stephen Hopkins 2004), which is an unsettling portrayal of Sellers, this notion is underscored by the film's main theme that there was no real Peter Sellers (played by Geoffrey Rush) behind his many masks.

As already noted, casting establishes a bond between the character, the actor's body and persona, and the spectator's fantasy. In classical and thereafter mainstream cinema, especially as practised in the star system, casting has become a vessel through which the image is manipulated to meet our expectations: "Classical Hollywood star system engineered a correspondence between star and role that was archetypally embodied in Clark Gable's casting as Rhett Butler in *Gone with the Wind* (Victor Fleming 1939). At the time of the movie production, and ever since, it has seemed impossible to imagine the part being played by anyone else" (Richard Maltby 1995: 252).

Behind the wish to achieve utmost correspondence between casting and roles is an attempt to guess what the Other—in this case, the audience—wants in relation to the embodiment of characters by actors. It is the answer to the fundamental question of the subject in relation to the Other's enigmatic desire (What does the Other want from me?). The answer given by the subject to this question is a fantasy scene—a defense against castration. When producers or those responsible for casting decisions ask what audiences want from them, the answer is perfect casting. Perfect casting becomes thus an immobile visual image, a fantasy object meant to avoid an encounter with the lack of the screen, to stop the perpetual motion of desire. We have shown how the richness of cinema makes up for the lack of the screen and emphasized that this richness is carefully and minutely crafted to maintain the equilibrium of the dynamic of desire/fantasy. In keeping with Metz's assertion that cinema is doubly imaginary (because it is both fictional and absent from the spectator's space), we argue that casting is its principal mode of covering up for its lack. The creation of a fantasy that meets the spectators' imaginary regarding the embodiment of characters on the screen thus means the filling of *objet a* with a body of an actor. We have no idea who the actors embodying characters really are, but this does not preclude using their "materiality" as a fantasy object, more so because they are not present in front of us. Indeed, when we claim that this or that actor has been miscast, we seem to be implying that the physique and persona of the actor do not comply with how we imagine/d the character *should* look like, that they clash with our fantasy. Good acting, of course, will only strengthen the ties between the operation of fantasy and the physique and persona of an actor chosen to play a certain role (especially that of the protagonist) and will convince us that he or she *is* our fantasy object. As previously mentioned, we return to this subject in Chapter 4. In the following chapter, we begin to explore the process of subjectivization within the dynamic of desire/fantasy in films that tamper with casting. As we shall see, the main strategy of these films in generating such a process is, like in most of the films analyzed so far, thrusting the spectators out of the primal scene.

2

Traversing the Fantasy

Body-Character-Breach Films

Casting, the Return of the Repressed and the Real of the Body

The "body-character-breach" corpus lays bare the connection between characters, actors, the operation of fantasy, and spectatorship precisely by disrupting this connection. Body-character-breach films problematize the bond between actor and character; some of them create a rupture between the actor's body—physiognomy and distinct attributes usually associated with the actor's persona—and the character that she or he initially plays in a film. For example, in John Woo's mainstream action drama *Face/Off* (1997), which, in the taxonomy that we detail below, belongs to the category "body switch," an FBI special agent, the composed Sean Archer (initially played by John Travolta) subjects himself to a face transplant—he takes on the face of the megalomaniac terrorist, Castor Troy (initially played by Nicolas Cage), who is in a coma, in order to gain access to information on a bomb planted by Troy. Archer's (the protagonist's) desire is thus marked by his effort to restore order at any cost. But Troy (the antagonist) regains consciousness and undergoes the same surgical procedure in order to supplant Archer both in his family and job. For most of the film, we see Travolta's physique/body and have to believe that he is in fact Troy, whose personality and mannerisms had been imprinted in our memory by Cage's characterization and acting at the beginning of the film. Furthermore, throughout the film, we must remember and modify our perception accordingly so that when being Troy (in Archer's environment), Travolta tries to simulate Archer's responsible tormented personality in order not to be exposed. The same multi-effort is required from us when viewing Cage as Archer, starting with their first encounter after the swap. In this scene, we see Archer/Cage in prison as Troy. Troy/Travolta enters his cell saying, "You're good-looking, you're hot; it's like looking in the mirror . . . only not." Archer/Cage is shocked when he realizes that his opponent has taken his face, identity, and position, destroying all evidence of their true identities.[1] Troy/Travolta gleefully declares, as he leaves the beleaguered Cage/Archer to rot in prison in his stead, "I got a government job to abuse and a lonely wife to fuck. . . . Oh, did I say that? I'm sorry . . . to make love to!" The scene is shot in circular camera movements, immuring the two in an infrangible mirror positioning, conveying a structure of opposition while evincing the similarity derived from the position switch highlighted by the shot/reverse-shot editing and the close-ups. In terms of spectatorship, the bond between character and actor expected to be maintained is the one established at the beginning of the film: Travolta (as Archer) playing a conscientious FBI agent; Cage (as Troy) playing a psychopath. Breaching this bond forces spectators to imagine the swap in terms of oppositions (Travolta as a sadistic, gleeful psychopath; Cage as responsible and tormented).

The film thus tampers with the links between the actors; their image on the screen; and the characters they embody, an embodiment that is contingent on a merger between the actors' physique and how it is presented on the screen. This tampering first demands that we make a perceptual (cognitive) effort throughout the viewing of the film. Second, it interferes with the spectators' engagement with the dynamic of desire/fantasy when following the unfolding of the narrative, an interference that we explore in detail in this chapter.

We have divided the body-character-breach taxonomy into six categories (see appendix). They comprise only films in which some sort of narrative can be detected: mainstream films, which rely on the linear classical narrative; *auteur* narrative films (including those considered highly artistic) that largely follow the structure of the classical narrative; and *auteur* "counter-cinema" films that subvert the classical narrative structure and the formal conventions of rendering it. All the films in the taxonomy tamper with the fusion of body-character-actor in numerous and unique ways, thus problematizing the dynamic of desire/fantasy. But films that renounce their spectators' engagement with fantasy, leaving us in the blind spot of desire alone, risk losing us altogether.

The challenge of classical and mainstream cinema has always been to find a match between the physiques of the actors, their personae, and the characters they embody that will work for mass audiences. Lacan compares the shielding function of fantasy to a sudden stopping of a rapid cinematic movement, freezing all its characters, fixating them to a place that stops the perpetual motion of desire that never reaches satisfaction (Lacan [1956–7]

1994: 122). The principal visual object in film that fixates fantasy to a place that stops the perpetual motion of desire is the embodiment of characters by actors and protagonists, preferably by stars. Films may tamper with the connection between fantasy and casting but only to the extent that the spectator's desire manages to remain engaged in some way. Again, we emphasize that unsettling this connection to the extreme, excluding thus fantasy from the equation, might present a serious problem in engaging with desire altogether. This is evident in the multiple-body category that comprises experimental films which use two or more actors in the role of the protagonist. The rapid change of actors thwarts the possibility of halting the motion of desire, of providing an anchor for the engagement with either desire or fantasy.

For instance, in *Palindromes* (Todd Solondz 2004, the multiple-body character category in our taxonomy), an example of authorial counter-cinema, desire is dispersed onto so many bodies that we may indeed wonder if it does not leave spectators out of the film altogether. Although the narrative presents one specific desire to us (the thirteen-year-old female character wishes to become pregnant), this desire is embodied by so many actresses of different ages, sizes, and ethnicities that it shifts the question from what the protagonist wants to what the film wants. *I'm Not There* (Todd Haynes 2007) is even more radical than *Palindromes* in that it uses six actors and one actress, some of them stars or rising stars (e.g., Cate Blanchett, Richard Gere, Christian Bale, Heath Ledger), to embody the cultural *spirit* of Bob Dylan, immaterializing his corporeality altogether. Moreover, while *Palindromes* has basically one linear narrative, *I'm Not There*'s multiple narratives, in addition to the multiplicity of characters/ actors, present a massive difficulty in engaging with the film. Not so in *Every Day* (Michael Sucsy 2018), a mainstream drama, in which the protagonist (Angourie Rice) is not the one who changes bodies and, moreover, engages us with her desire to be loved as well as the need to realize that to fulfill this desire she must break up with her insensitive boyfriend.

All the categories in the body-character-breach films taxonomy unmask the operation of the mechanism of desire/fantasy in cinema. In the films' diegeses, the oppositions that run the gamut of Categories 1–5 reflect the fantasy of wholeness, of filling the lack in the Other, through the desire to be the Other, as well as know what the Other wants (in Categories 1, 2, and 3 the characters change bodies but do not really become the Other, thus emphasizing the impossibility of filling the lack in the Other); in Categories 4, 5, and 6 the fantasy of wholeness is reflected in the desire to occupy a place that marks a lack. Films in the first five categories bring to the surface unconscious scenarios (mostly seduction and incest) hiding behind various conscious fantasies whose purpose is veiling the lack in the Other. The characters, as well as spectators, are faced with the horrific eventuality of such scenarios, which generates a major change in respect to the operation of fantasy in its capacity to veil the lack in the Other. This process, which pertains to the protagonists, is equally addressed to spectators. In Category 6, the emphasis is placed on the spectatorial position regarding the ontology of film (the lack of the screen and its imaginary nature). All categories attest to the embodiment of characters by actors as a major anchoring point in engaging us with the film's (as well as the protagonist's) fantasy, linking this embodiment to the unique ontology of cinema, namely the screen's lack, the fact that the actors and objects portrayed are absent from our space.

The fantastic/fantasmatic scenarios of the plots in the body-character-breach films enable the characters to gain access to the Other's desire (to learn what the other character wants from them in their capacity of embodying the Other) and acquire their privileges: The young gets to be older, black gets to be white, female characters get to be male, and vice versa. For example, in the third remake of *Freaky Friday* (2003), when in her daughter's body, the mother (initially played by Jamie Lee Curtis) not only gets to control both her daughter's looks, which she did not like before, and her life while her own body gets to be young in style and manner; she also gets to better understand her daughter's desire to become a musician. The daughter (initially played by Lindsay Lohan) has free access to her mother's credit cards and she learns how to feel more at ease with the boy she is secretly in love with, but she also comes to understand her mother's desire that she get along with her future stepfather. Indeed, if we look at what most characters represent and at the narrative closure in the mainstream body-switch or reincarnation categories, and in some films in the body-transformation category, we may safely contend that they constitute a fantasy that cannot get any more conservative, since it promotes values such as heterosexual relations within an organic family, the restoration of an existing order, and a world in which evil is destroyed and good prevails.

In this respect, the body-character-breach films' power of attraction, if not seduction, lies not in their ideology or haphazard logic but rather in a fantasy shared by all humans—to gain access to the enigmatic desire of the Other, to be the all-knowing, all-enjoying Other, as well as be a participant in the primal scene. These films thus demonstrate, first, our argument that the only thing a spectator cannot escape from identifying with is the fantasy to conceal the lack in the Other. All other forms of identification (as are often expressed in daydreaming) may be attributed to what is prioritized by any particular spectator: personal taste, gender, sexual orientation, ethnicity, social status, and so on. Second, they show that fantasy, like desire, must figure in our engagement with a film. And, in accordance with the very ontology of film, that is, the dynamic of absence/presence, the way film hooks us is by providing a setting in which desire is scripted in a way that veils the lack, thus enabling inscription in the primal scene. While desire, linked to the lack in the Other, arouses our engagement repeatedly, fantasy makes sure that we remain engaged. As we have repeatedly asserted, a film that attempts to operate solely on desire cannot engage spectators. So, what body-character-breach films are saying to begin with is that film operates very much like our subjectivity. And what is common to all human subjects is the fact that desire cannot do without fantasy. For desire to be satisfied in the real it takes a certain personality, or a long process (see Chapters 5 and 6), while fantasy provides instantaneous satisfaction, constantly protecting us from the lack in the Other, and in doing so keeps desire alive.

But body-character-breach films, as we aim to show, do not stop there. The realization of the fantasy to gain access to the enigmatic desire of the Other, to be the all-knowing, all-enjoying Other, is precisely what they undermine when they suggest that such a realization might entail the materialization of incest. This is how these films usher spectators out of the inscription in the primal scene. In *Freaky Friday*, such thoughts and uneasy sensations arise when facing the fact that a marriage is about to materialize between the daughter, while in her mother's body (i.e., Jamie Lee Curtis's), and her future stepfather. Our uneasiness is increased by displaying first her horrified gaze, and later, as the wedding approaches, the mother's dread while in her daughter's body (i.e., Lindsay Lohan's). A variation of this scenario centers on the daughter, still seen in the body of actress Jamie Lee Curtis, having a good time with the boy she is in love with. All the other characters think the fifty-year-old mother, about to remarry, is flirting with a teenager. Her fiancé (Mark Harmon) finds it difficult to follow the reckless behavior of his wife-to-be as well as the unexplained control her teenage daughter suddenly has over her (e.g., when he asks, "Am I supposed to follow this?"). Similarly, the young character of the son and brother (Ryan Malgarini) is not only puzzled by what he believes to be his mother's behavior but also literally repulsed (his reaction is shown in close-up) when he sees her bottom, covered with a thong, sticking out from her pants.

In Marshall's *Big* (1988), we cannot easily dismiss the idea that 12-year-old Josh, in the body of a grown-up (i.e., Tom Hanks's), is having sex with a fellow worker, Susan (Elizabeth Perkins), who could almost be his mother. This eerie feeling is confirmed by Susan's expression in the last scene of the film, when she witnesses Josh's big body shrinking to its adolescent size, going back to his original body and to his mother. In *Chances Are* (Emile Ardolino 1989), Alex's (Robert Downey Jr.), memories of his previous life as Louie (Chris McDonald) return after he becomes romantically involved with Miranda (Mary Stuart Masterson), the daughter whom he never got to meet in his previous life/body. *Birth* (Jonathan Glazer 2004), in which ten-year-old Sean (Cameron Bright) lies about being the reincarnation of Anna's (Nicole Kidman) late husband, evinces what all reincarnation films bring to the surface. For example, in a scene in which Anna is taking a bath, Sean comes in, undresses calmly, and sits in the tub opposite her. Shocked, Anna asks him what he is doing, to which he replies casually, "I am looking at my wife." The image of the two taking a bath together makes us squirm in our chairs because it renders visible the seduction fantasy as well as taps into the primal scene—the spectator is indeed witnessing a taboo scenario.

In *Transamerica* (Duncan Tucker 2005), a week before her sex reassignment surgery, Bree (Felicity Huffman) discovers that she is the father of a seventeen-year-old boy named Toby (Kevin Zegers). *Transamerica* is a road film, which includes a last stop at Bree's unconventional home. Forced by her analyst (Elizabeth Peña) to confront her past, she agrees to meet Toby and the two get acquainted during a long ride to Los Angeles. The latter develops amorous feelings for her. One night as they prepare to turn in, Toby makes a pass at Bree, which forces her to tell him that she is in fact his father. Toby's horrified, violent reaction is connected to the fact that he almost slept with his father, rather than to the fact that Bree is a transsexual, which he has known and sympathized with for some time.[2]

All these examples show the complex structure of fantasy, as explained by Laplanche and Pontalis ([1964] 1986), following Freud, as a two-layered visual configuration: The daydream or the conscious fantasy always hides an unconscious one. Body-character-breach films address this complexity by tackling the relationship between conscious and unconscious fantasies by problematizing the umbilical relation between the body/actor and the character, achieved through casting. The various body-character-breach configurations explain the role of the conscious fantasy, the daydream (to veil the traumatic lack), and bring to the surface unconscious primal scenarios hidden in the daydream, about to be realized in the films and acknowledged by the characters themselves, through reaction shots. These scenarios conjure mostly the unconscious seduction/incest fantasy, as coded in the primal scene. In Chapter 1, we explained film's affinity with the primal scene as related to the ontology of the cinema and to the richness of film. We illustrated, through specific cinematic strategies of focalization (the camera's ability to move between points of view), how a film may inscribe the spectator into a scene or prevent such an inscription when the latter is tantamount to the primal scene.

Inscription into the primal scene is an unconscious process related to an unconscious scenario; occupying *more* than one position in it points to the impossibility of separating between the unconscious (the original) fantasies and the conscious ones (the daydream/the film). Body-character-breach films show us both the Lacanian approach to fantasy as that which veils castration as well as sustains desire, and the Freudian approach concerning the relationship between the two layers of fantasy (conscious/unconscious). Like Freud—who maintained that all daydreams (similar to dreams) conceal sexual unconscious forbidden desires related to the Oedipal triangle, which, in turn, are related to the primal fantasies—by tampering with the specific function of the embodiment of characters by actors, body-character-breach films visualize the primal fantasies that lie beneath what many narrative films conceal through this very embodiment. This visualization, as well as the characters' reactions (horror) to the eventuality of such scenarios, makes it impossible for the spectator to disregard them, equating the characters' attempts to prevent them with the hindering of that which creates an ideal fantasy object whose task is to conceal the lack in the Other—an omnipresence inscription and "active" participation in the primal scene.

The function of the physicality of the body resides, in addition to the exposure of unconscious scenarios, in the exposure of the relation of trauma to "the real of the body." Unlike the real body, which is signified, the real of the body resists signification. Unconscious fantasies, as explored above through the surfacing of primal scenarios, already constitute a first form of symbolization. The real of the body, in Lacanian terms, refers to a traumatic materiality, a rawness that remains outside signification. While the lack related to desire has a signifier (the phallus as symbol of lack—Φ), the lack of the real of the body has no signifier—the real "in general is what lies behind fantasy" (Lacan [1964] 1998: 54), which is trauma "unveiled" (55). The real of the body is thus what is left outside the symbolic/desire, as well as the imaginary/fantasy.

In Lacanian psychoanalysis, trauma begins with the experience of the encounter with our first object of satisfaction that is also our first object of frustration and alienation. In Book VII of his seminar (Lacan [1959–60] 1997), Lacan's point of departure is Freud's distinction between two terms that in German refer to "thing": *die Sache* and *das Ding*. *Die Sache* refers to Freud's thing-presentation in the unconscious—for Lacan, a representation of thing in the symbolic order. *Das Ding* refers to a thing in its dumb reality (55) that remains without representation in the unconscious ("the beyond-of-the signified," 54) and impossible to imagine (125). It is an "X," similar to the Kantian "thing-in-itself" (55). Lacan thus adopts the term *Das Ding* (43)—the Thing[3]—to describe how the real figures in his tripartite scheme of the imaginary, the symbolic, and the real. He connects it to the experience of strangeness (*fremde*, 43–56) characterizing the relation with the first Other in the infant's life, usually the mother, becoming thus the object-cause of desire (*objet petit a*, *objet a*). Here we wish to emphasize Lacan's association of this void with the Thing and how the latter is related to the real of the body in its function as trauma unveiled.

In remaining outside the realm of signification, marking a void that eludes any efforts to fill it with symbols, the real of the body as a brute object left solely in its material dimension is the source of anxiety. Anxiety, according to Lacan ([1962–3] 2014), is the only nondeceptive affect (unlike any other affects or emotions) and is caused by an invasion of the traumatic real into the imaginary (fantasy) when the symbolic ceases to function. In contrast to Freud (e.g., in "Fetishism" [(1927) 1961] or "The Dissolution of the Oedipus Complex" [(1924) 1961]), who considers castration an element of anxiety, for Lacan, castration, albeit dooming the subject to lack, belongs to the symbolic and is in fact what saves the subject from anxiety. Regardless of the anatomical differences of the sexes, it introduces the paternal metaphor that separates the child from the imaginary wholeness with the mother. Hence, for a boy, without renouncing the fantasy of being the imaginary phallus of the mother, the penis, which is the real object made felt in masturbation, will always provoke anxiety. This is not only because of the discrepancy between his position as imaginary phallus (that for which he is loved) and his insignificant real organ (that which he must give) but also, and mainly, because of an inefficacy of the incest interdiction (the symbolic).

The incest interdiction is concomitant with the repression of the fantasy of being the mother' imaginary phallus (the birth of the unconscious and the symbolic); when this fails to occur (the symbolic is cast off), the *real* of the body is experienced as a traumatic invasion into the imaginary. In his seminar on anxiety ([1962–3] 2014) Lacan so interprets *Little Hans*,[4] although it is clear, as stated above, that such an experience is genderless; it does not concern only boys/men but every subject experiencing her body or any part of it or another's as an alien enjoyment (in the case of *Little Hans*, it is the enjoyment of masturbation), in which the horror of the Thing is not protected by desire and the law of the Father. In contrast to desire, which is related to lack (it springs from it), anxiety occurs when this lack is in itself lacking (it is the lack of the lack). In other words, the operation of fantasy in its function of sustaining desire (the filling out of the lack in relation to the Other's desire with an object) ceases to function and *objet a* is experienced as a pure lack "beyond-of-the-signified," namely without the *signifier* of the lack.

Bodies, certainly those of actors, are symbolic and semiotic signs, both on-screen and outside the cinema. To even think of the body in film as "the Thing" in its brute appearance, without the operation of desire and fantasy, is thus unimaginable. Nevertheless, some of the horror expressed in narrative mainstream and *auteur* body-character-breach films derives its power and efficacy from an encounter with the real of the body, one shared by both characters and spectators—as exemplified in our analysis of *Les yeux sans visage*.

In *Face/Off*, this is rendered in the surgery scene. The scene starts with a low-angle, close-up shot of the lighting device (fixed on the ceiling) in the operating room, accompanied by extra-diegetic shuddery music, generating an uneasy affect. The light flash appears then as a white screen, accompanied by a thundering sound, intensifying this affect. The scene cuts to a high-angle shot showing two beds on which Archer (Travolta) and Troy (Cage) are lying, respectively (Archer is under general anesthesia, Troy is in a coma). The beds are pushed toward each other, in opposite directions (left to right/right to left) to attain a mirror position in which the two characters' heads are as close as possible to each other. The shot simultaneously reveals the similarities between the two characters/actors—their naked bodies are covered only with a blue cloth veiling their genitals and both characters have dark brown hair and hairy chests—and the notion of the exchange of faces. This high-angle mirror composition is followed by a shot governed by a semicircular camera movement in which we see a close-up of Troy's face starting to be cut out. The camera moves then to a close-up of Archer's face, showing the same procedure. The rest of the scene is shot in close-ups, from different angles, as the camera is in constant motion, conveying a sense of total hysteria, building up to the shot of the surgeon's hands cutting into Archer's face, lifting it with a transparent plastic vacuum mask, revealing the rawness of flesh and blood underneath, and placing it in a liquid, in which it remains, floating (Figure 2.1). Thereafter, Troy's face is attached to the faceless Archer. When this procedure is completed, the close-up reveals Archer "wearing" Troy's face, followed by a reiteration of the lighting device shot, only this time the light is put out.

The horrified gaze in Archer's colleague's reaction shots to the sight of the faceless face and the disjointed floating face expresses a response to an encounter with the traumatic real of the body, magnified for the spectator in the shot showing the face as a mask without subjectivity—a raw object. In their first encounter after the swap, in the prison scene, this horror is associated with the real of the whole body, suggesting that Archer's decision to assume Troy's position by literally taking his face might be a point of no return. Archer/Cage is terrified when he realizes that the swap might be irreversible. Troy/Travolta does not display such a concern, not because he momentarily has the upper hand in the battle between good and evil but mainly because he is a psychopath, for whom the symbolic law does not really apply. Travolta's acting indeed emphasizes Troy's ebullient "anti"-phallic enjoyment as the archvillain, void of any moral constraints or considerations.

The film thus creates an ongoing affect of anxiety and apprehension, further reinforced when watching Troy/Travolta seductively working his

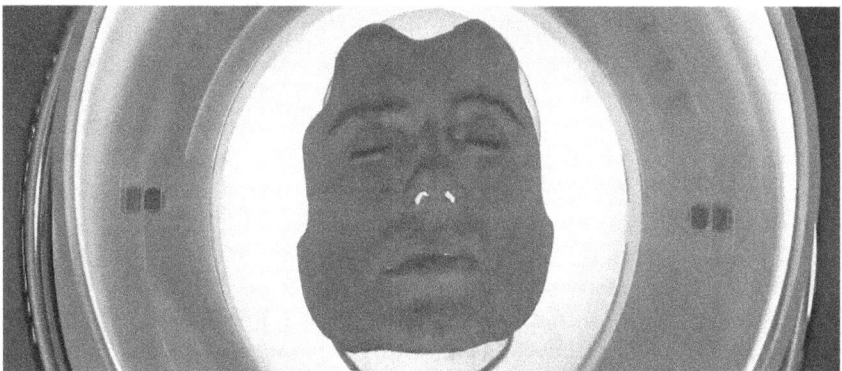

FIGURE 2.1 Face/Off (*John Woo 1997*).

charms on "his" daughter. The onus of the horror of both the traumatic real of the body and the incest in such scenes is on the spectator. Our knowledge of the fact that Travolta's body is occupied by Troy's character (not the real father) does not help preclude the incest scenario conveyed by the image of Travolta's body seductively approaching "his" daughter. This horror is directly related to the swapping of faces as a point of no return, namely to the real of the body taking over the symbolic. In the transplant scene, the soundtrack and the frenetic, ceaseless camera movements intensify the terror and gruesomeness of the images of the real of the body. The floating of the face connotes movement, but this movement is not associated with any subjectivity. Rather, like the camera movements, it expresses the unbearable experience of a face and a body devoid of subjectivity and significance. The close-up too, rather than seaming us into the narrative's flow (that is generally synchronized with the character's desire and motivation), functions as an encounter with the real of the body, generating anxiety.

Our television screens are inundated with streams of blood and raw flesh being cut into, but these recurrent images, rendered in close-up, do not seem to bother us (some of us even enjoy them). In *Face/Off*, like in *Les yeux sand visage*, it is the association of the real of the body with the face that is deeply disturbing, as its removal strips the character/actor of all social, cultural, and semiotic readings and meanings. We are invited to look into a material void, a brute physicality resisting signification, a red blank spot that looks at us, suggestive of an eye socket after its eye has been plucked out (quite like the image of the eyeless man in Hitchcock's *The Birds* [1963] or the eye sockets of the mother's skeleton in *Psycho* [1960]). No wonder Archer's colleague first looks away from this display of horror and then covers his eyes with his palms. As the expression "the material void" infers, what we have here is a void that does not refer to an absence (lack) but to an overburdening presence, that of a part of the material body (the face), in excess (the close-up), a cinematic excess. And this, to the best of our knowledge, is unmatched by any other visual or literary art form or medium. It is very different from the excesses of "body genres," in which the enjoyment of viewing a film is directly linked to the excess of the body, which is always signified, no matter how repulsive or gory it is visualized.[5] In *Face/Off*, there is not much room for enjoyment in the transplant scene. The overpowering affect that it generates presents a threat on both the ego and the body. This is reflected later in Archer's terror when standing to lose his identity and subjectivity as well as his control over his sexual, bodily relations with his wife.

For the spectators, the transplant scene thus functions as a site of anxiety, operating as an excessive segment: In terms of time, its length is not justified by the narrative flow; in terms of mise-en-scène and sound, it is highly exaggerated. As noted above, Lacan asserts in his seminar on anxiety that it is characterized by an invasion of the real into the imaginary, an experience overburdening the subject with the presence of the object, affecting both the body and the ego, an experience that characterizes *Les yeux sans visage* in its entirety. Christiane's faceless face impedes the very mechanism of engagement with the fantasy to veil the lack in the Other, because there is no object onto which we can project this fantasy. In a sense, her body, albeit its ethereal characterization, functions for us as an encounter with the real of the body, like the one in the shot revealing the raw flesh underneath the young woman's face skin. As to Génessier, as mentioned before, along Lacanian terms, he represents a psychotic position in relation to the Other's desire, whose fantasy is carried out in the real, leaving the spectator in this realm, without the protection of the symbolic.

In narrative cinema, the dynamic of lack and presence, immanent in the dynamic of desire/fantasy, characterizes both the narrative flow and the spectators' engagement with it, sustaining the ratification of the signifier of the lack. The encounter with the real of the body casts desire aside and thus becomes, for both the characters (provided they are not psychotic) and for us, an overwhelming experience. The real of the body bursts forth in many other body-character-breach films, although not as forcefully as in *Les yeux sans visage* and *Face/Off*, but all the same, the excessive configurations of imagery and situations draw us into the territory of the uncanny, generating anxiety (rather than desire). However, in contrast to *Les yeux sans visage*, whose domain is the traumatic real, or many counter-cinema films (see below, *Cet obscure objet du désir*) that resist the operation of the mechanism of the dynamic of desire/fantasy, leaving us in the realm of desire alone, mainstream films like *Face/Off* incorporate anxiety within the dynamic of desire/fantasy, thus allowing the encounter with the real of the body to take its effect where subjectivization—the traversal of the fantasy—is concerned.

Narrative Cinema, Subjectivity, and Subjectivization

In her discussion of fantasy and spectatorship, Teresa De Lauretis (1994) addresses the question of a particular film's failure to engage certain spectators in its fantasy, making a significant distinction between *subjectivity* and *subjecthood*. While the former term refers to the realm of psychoanalysis and the unconscious (fantasy, desire, identification, etc.), the latter relates to the subjects' social locations, those attributes they are conscious and aware of (sexual orientation, race, class, gender, etc.). In De Lauretis' view, it is the latter "complex subject processes [that] have more weight in a spectator acceptance of a film as ready-made fantasy" (129). As we have already established, when dealing with fantasy we deal with an impossible separation between conscious and unconscious, and simultaneously, with early symbolization. Symbolization in Lacanian psychoanalysis is first and foremost linked to the efficacy of the operation of the unconscious—the repression of the fantasy incest with the mother and acceptance of the paternal metaphor. Social constructions come later. Therefore, the unconscious mechanisms of desire and fantasy have little to do with subjecthood and much to do with subjectivity: Being white, black, lesbian, woman/man/trans, or of a certain class or social status does not bear a necessary relevance to one's subjective structure in relation to the lack in the Other—whether neurotic (obsessional or hysterical), perverse, or psychotic.[6] Hence, spectators might engage with a character and their motives even though resisting the film's overt ideology. As asserted in Chapter 1, in this case engagement does not mean that we condone the film's ideology but that we unconsciously condone the character's actions because all subjective structures have a common denominator (veiling castration) in relation to the dynamic of desire/fantasy (subjectivity).

Engaging with the dynamic of desire/fantasy in viewing a film means engaging with an elasticity that enables the spectator to move along the axis of this dynamic, especially when confronted with unnerving images. However, a fetishistic position in cinema cannot and does not refer solely to a distinctly perverse spectator/subject but to all of us spectators (a concept underlying all body-character-breach films), prone to the same defense mechanisms that govern the pervert's organization vis-à-vis castration. Our argument regarding subjectivization and the viewing experience is based on this premise. Theories of cinema discussing classical and mainstream films in relation to fetishism are in fact arguing for the predominance of a perverse structure, which is not the case. Fetishism in cinema cannot and does not refer solely to a distinctly perverse spectator/subject but to one who is prone to a defense mechanism vis-à-vis castration. This is why we may engage with the operation of desire/fantasy not only as pertaining to "normal," but also to perverse and psychotic ones—we may like them, understand their motives, sympathize with their actions, want them to succeed, and so on.[7] It is this diffluence that enables narrative film (mainly classical/mainstream and authorial cinema that largely adheres to the principles of classical/mainstream) to set in motion a process of traversing the fantasy.

To induce such a process, the spectators' imaginary (the realm of fantasy) must be joggled. Although Lacanian early psychoanalysis puts the emphasis on the symbolic and, like all other psychoanalyses, relies on speech, if we understand correctly, the process of traversing the fantasy starts when something is rattled in the subject's imaginary, which is then reflected in their discourse. We maintain that the advantage of cinema is that it uses images and sounds that activate the scopic and the invocatory drives to engage its spectators with desire as well as to generate a traumatic gaze that jolts our imaginary. The process of subjectivization is contingent upon this activation. We have seen how such a process works in body-character-breach films, where the traversal of the fantasy (subjectivization) is achieved via various strategies, such as focalization and disablement of the engagement with the primal scene (in Hitchcock—the bodiless category); via the intrusion of the voice (as partial object) on the imaginary (fantasy) in *Her* (the bodiless category); and via the visual surfacing of forbidden unconscious scenarios and images tied to the real of the body (in body-switch, body-transformation, and reincarnation films). In all these cases, the process undergone by the protagonists (e.g., the protagonist in *Rebecca* [1940]; Thornhill in *North by Northwest* [1959], and Theo in *Her*) is what we regard as subjectivization or the traversal of the fantasy—a process entailing subjectivity (a change in the subject's position in relation to the Other's desire) not subjecthood.

Subjectivity involves a tripartite structure: symbolic-imaginary-real. Therefore, subjectivization must occur within the dynamic of this structure. So far, we have shown how subjectivation operates regarding the dynamic of desire/fantasy (symbolic/imaginary)[8] because it is the most relevant to narrative film and spectatorship. An affective-reflective position cannot be achieved without it. Subjectivization thus entails an initial engagement with the desire of the protagonist (what they want/lack), a fantasy that is meant to realize this desire (tantamount to concealing the lack in the Other) and then dissolution of this fantasy (through the body-character-breach devices), employing additional rhetorical and aesthetic strategies, like the use of the close-up; view-behinds; reaction shots evincing horror; unfavorable (in the way they harm other characters) characterization of perverse/fetishistic or psychotic protagonists, exposure of the unsymbolized body (the real of the body); and so on. All these devices evince the ethical dimension—why, rather than veiling castration, the subject acting in conformity with their desire is the right path of subjectivization. Not all mainstream body-character-breach films follow this path to the same extent, in the sense that they make unconscious scenarios (mostly incest) visible or traumatize spectators with images relating to the real of the body. However, they do display a high awareness of the imminent dangers of maintaining fantasy at all costs with the sole purpose of masking the lack in the Other, functioning thus as a warning directed at spectators.

Such is *Shallow Hal*, which belongs to the body-transformation category in our taxonomy. Hal (Jack Black), an "undesirable" (to use his best friend's terminology) young man, is hypnotized into seeing all undesirable women as desirable. He meets Rosemary—Gwyneth Paltrow in a fat suit—a grossly obese woman whom only *he* can see as a vision of physical perfection— Gwyneth Paltrow as we all know her from other films and photographs. In contrast to Hal, throughout the film we are visually confronted with the discrepancy between the two bodies. This view-behind assigned to us is a device against assuming a fetishist position because it tampers with possible identification with Hal's fantasy.

This is further reinforced by Hal's process of subjectivization. One day his friend undoes the spell while Hal and Rosemary are having dinner in a restaurant. Hal is first confronted with the gap between his fantasy and the real body of the women surrounding him when he turns to the hostess, whom he previously believed to be a delightful brunette. As it turns out, this hostess is a particularly tall, not very pretty, manly looking transvestite wearing a black wig (identical to the pretty brunette's hairdo) and the same cute uniform as the fantasmatic character in Hal's mind. The image of the transvestite hostess (unsettling in itself because of the blurring of the man/woman division and its campiness) is Hal's first encounter with the radical strangeness of the Other's body.

Hal's horror is intensified when he returns to his table and his eyes meet Rosemary's obese body, shot from behind, devouring the food on the plates. Avoiding a frontal confrontation, a panicky Hal flees the restaurant. Later, when Rosemary arrives at his apartment, still terrified of a confrontation, Hal smears his eyes with Vaseline and pretends to have some kind of congestive eye infection. When he finally opens the door for her, we get a close-up of his Vaseline-smeared eyes, then a blurred static shot (from Hal's point of view) of Rosemary. The shot/reverse-shot editing repeats this pattern, only this time Rosemary's shot is not static. The camera tilts down on her silhouette, conveying both Hal's desire to see her body for what it is and his horror of it.

After recovering from these encounters, Hal realizes that he is in fact in love with Rosemary's inner beauty and goes to her house to declare his love. Upon entering, he sees a big woman and starts kissing her passionately on the lips, not realizing that she is the maid. This instance exemplifies how a fixed fantasy—here, a male fantasy in relation to women—may blind a perverse subject to the point of being unable to recognize the very fact that there is an Other (in the body of another), precluding thus the role of the symbolic through which bodies must be symbolized.[9] For Hal, in compliance with his fantasy, up to this point all "desirable" women looked like models, therefore now all fat women can be "Rosemary" (i.e., all fat women are alike). It is only when Hal is able to associate his own desire with the specific body and personality of Rosemary, namely to signify it, that he finally assumes responsibility for his desire, renouncing the infantile fantasy of being the imaginary phallus—the object of desire of ideal women, representing the phallic mother. This marks Hal's acceptance of castration, his process of subjectivization, assuming responsibility for the fact that he is in love with a fat woman.

Shallow Hal specifically deals with a male fantasy. Here too it is not hard to identify with the protagonist's fantasy—what straight man or gay woman would not like to be the object of desire of women looking like Gwyneth Paltrow? This identification is broken by Hal's traumatic experience when encountering the real body of the Other/Woman (which, *for Hal*, is an encounter with the real of the body[10]) before he can symbolize it. This encounter is then followed by its ethical dimension, a lesson to be learned. In body-switch films such a process is sealed by the characters' return to their own bodies, assuming responsibility for their own desire and fate.

Hitchcock's *Vertigo*, which also belongs to the body-transformation category in our taxonomy, is an artistic reflexive film that does exactly what all mainstream body-character-breach films do—it explains how being able to face and acknowledge the lack in the Other generates subjectivization by engaging the spectator with such a process while cinematically explaining its mechanism. In *Vertigo*, we have one actress (Kim Novack) playing "two" characters, the blonde "Madeleine" and the brunette Judy. The female character's transformation is achieved by makeup and clothes. As in *Shallow Hal*, this transformation is related to a male character's fantasy.

Scottie (James Stewart) is a retired detective who suffers from acrophobia, which thwarts him from preventing the fall of a fellow policeman to his death. An acquaintance, Gavin Elster (Tom Helmore), asks Scottie to follow his wife, Madeleine, a mysterious and elusive ideal blonde object of desire, for whose life he fears, claiming that she is obsessed with her grandmother's suicide. Scottie falls in love with Madeleine and Hitchcock lures us through various romantic devices—her mysterious, fragile, elusive, ethereal characterization as well as Scottie's fascination with this object—to engage with this love story. Scottie is eventually forced to witness Madeleine falling to her death, unable to prevent her "suicide" due to his vertigo. This ends the first part of the film, in which the romance fantasy is cinematically conveyed as a reverie. We experience loss, enhanced by Scottie's mental breakdown as well as by his frequenting the places Madeleine visited, often imagining that he sees her when he does not.

One day, Scottie notices a woman resembling Madeleine, despite her vulgar appearance. He follows her and she identifies herself as Judy Barton. The traumatizing uncanny fusion of the fantasy/real body provoking anxiety surfaces as soon as we meet Judy. She is photographed in profile, in the same way that Madeleine was in many of the scenes Scottie was looking at her. The camera is fixed on her profile for quite a while, evincing thus her resemblance to Madeleine. At the same time, it emphasizes her coarse physique: her auburn hair, unrefined hairdo, green outfit, and heavy makeup, all of which present a rough contrast to the refined and ethereal Madeleine. We have seen how this mixture is brought about in other body-character-breach films through the encounter with the real of the body. In *Vertigo*, Hitchcock manages to turn one character, Madeleine/Judy, into an object of anxiety *par excellence*. The uncanny, the horror, resides in Judy's first bodily appearance, for which Madeleine can no longer act as a veil. It does not matter whether or not we know that the two characters own the same body (that of Kim Novack). Either way, we experience Judy's appearance as the Freudian "uncanny" ([1919] 1955b) with a Lacanian twist, because it also evokes the real of the body.

Perhaps we should mention here, briefly, Freud's definition of the uncanny. Its horrifying characteristic is that it derives its strangeness and menacing force from its double nature, the unfamiliar being or becoming an inherent aspect of the familiar. The eerie feeling or sensation provoked in the reader of fictional literature (aesthetics) centers precisely on these two opposites (*Heimlich/Unheimlich*—familiar/unfamiliar) that contain each other's qualities, depending on the circumstances. In realist fiction, it is a fantastic element that disrupts the believable aspect created by the coordinates of the narrative. In the body-switch category, the real of the body is specifically related to a fantastic phenomenon that unsettles the soundness of the diegesis, or at least to some implausibility, such as the one in *Face/Off*. In *Vertigo*, Hitchcock's recourse is neither the fantastic nor the implausible (notwithstanding the far-fetched plot). In E. T. A. Hoffmann's short story "The Sandman" ([1816] 1969), which Freud analyzes, there are many manifestations of the double: the splitting of one character into two, the one reflecting the other; reality/the fantastic; human/inhuman, robot-puppet; life/death; normalcy/madness; science/mysticism. All these oppositions are represented by respective bodies or objects. Hitchcock manages to maintain the oppositions inherent in the uncanny solely by using the body of one actress. In most body-character-breach films, the horror of the real of the body derives from the fact that the character is displaced to another body. In *Vertigo*, it is one and the same body that conjures the double: the splitting of one body into two characters, one reflecting the other, connoting life/death and fantasy/the traumatic real.[11]

For Freud, the crux of the uncanny as something repressed that resurfaces is linked to the fear of castration, exemplified in "The Sandman" by the face-without-eyes motif. What is repressed (especially of a sexual nature) and must be regulated through hiding it from consciousness as well as from the public eye returns in a threatening form, ridden with Oedipal guilt and fearing symbolic castration as punishment for deviating from societal norms. Certain images, objects, or individuals onto which we project our own repressed impulses thus become uncanny. In contrast, as explained before in our discussion of the intrusion of the real (of the body) into fantasy, Lacan maintains that it is precisely the lack of castration that is experienced as the uncanny: a blend of fantasy and the real without the protection of the symbolic, in Scottie's case—the protection of fantasy, as what he disavows is the lack in the Other. This is what Scottie cannot endure in his first encounter with Judy.

Soon enough, in a flashback of Judy, we learn that Madeleine Elster is in fact Judy, who impersonated Gavin's wife as part of a murder plot. Gavin had deliberately taken advantage of Scottie's acrophobia to substitute his wife's recently killed body in the apparent suicide jump. Here, as in *Shallow Hal*, it is our view-behind that creates a gap between our spectatorial position and the protagonist's, assigned to the spectators as a device against assuming a fetishistic position, a strategy used by Hitchcock often, as in *North by Northwest*. Hitchcock shatters our fantasy of (re)finding the ideal object and forces us to look into the traumatic void through the encounter with the real body of Judy, as opposed to Madeleine's fantasmatic one, long before Scottie is able to do so. In terms of spectatorship, this marks a beginning of subjectivization. This horror we are faced with before Scottie learns that Madeleine and Judy are one and the same ends our fascination with her.[12] Needless to say, viewing the film over, Madeleine, the object of fantasy, is simply not there to begin with. For some of us this might present a reason why not to see the film again. For others, we would argue, the film's luring power resides in the process of the traversal of fantasy that compensates for the experience of being in limbo or overwhelmed with anxiety. The uncanny experience is further (visually) reinforced in the scene in which Judy comes out of the hair salon looking almost like Madeleine: She is wearing Madeleine's outfit and has her hair color but still maintains *her* own hairdo and mannerisms.[13] The strange image of two characters united in one body reflects simultaneously (like in Judy's first appearance) the traumatic gap and its veiling but without the effect of the latter.

Oblivious of the information with which the spectators are entrusted, Scottie, obsessed with Madeleine, coerces Judy into a makeover. Here two positions become viable in terms of spectatorship, answering the question, "What do *I* want?" This question starts the process of subjectivization, in contrast to the question, "What does the Other want from me?" In the case of *Vertigo*, "What do *I* want?" overlaps with the question "What does the film want from me?" The point is thus how the film answers the question, "Do I want Scottie to succeed or fail in his endeavors to resuscitate Madeleine?" Scottie's obsession marks a fetishistic position, a perverse one, regarding the lack in the Other. In the opening sequence, he is already characterized by a fear of castration (in the Lacanian sense), expressed in his acrophobia. This is enhanced by the trauma of his slipping down a roof during a chase, causing the death of a fellow policeman. When looking down, the abyss whose sight Scottie cannot endure (hence the vertigo) represents an encounter with the real: "Dangling helplessly in space from a gutter, Scottie comes face to face with a deadly void, the incarnation of the Lacanian real" (Manlove 2007: 92). Madeleine becomes a fetish for Scottie, a veil to castration. The loss of this object enhances his trauma. And so, when he meets Judy, he cannot stand the sight of her and compulsively makes her over into Madeleine.

"I want Scottie to succeed" would thus mean occupying a fetishistic/perverse position, equally maintained by identifying with Judy's desire to be the Other's object of desire. But spectators might revolt against Scottie's somewhat sadistic treatment of Judy. The latter position would be a more critical one, beginning with the knowledge of who Madeleine really is. For both Scottie and us, Madeleine's death is an experience of loss. However, as soon as we learn that Madeleine is Judy, although we move into the realm of trauma, nevertheless, occupying here Scottie's position in his insistence (fantasy) to make Judy over would run the risk of experiencing the inert aspect of fetishism/perversion. Scottie's violent reaction (expressing his traumatic encounter) upon realizing what we have known and experienced for some time intensifies the wake-up call directed at us. The "second" death of Madelaine/Judy for Scottie thus means the death of fetishism, namely the transition from a pervert disavowing the lack in the Other to one who accepts it. It marks, for both Scottie and us, another traumatic encounter with the void. But, this experience, traumatic as it may be, is a necessary one for becoming a "subject."

Another rhetorical device that pulls us in the direction of a position that accepts the lack in the Other is Scottie's devoted female friend, Midge (Barbara Bel Geddes), of whose love he (unlike the spectators) remains oblivious throughout the film. She is tragically aware of his obsession and one day shows him a painting she did. Scottie is deeply hurt and horrified when he discovers it is a reproduction in which Midge has substituted Madeleine's grandmother's face as a young woman with her own plain-looking face, wearing a heavy pair of spectacles. This uncanny reproduction deeply upsets him, like the dream he has in which his head appears severed from his body. But for us, the portrait functions as a "tutor code" guiding us to see what Midge sees, that Scottie's enchantment with Madeleine is a form of illness, no different than his vertigo, which he cannot control. Furthermore, like the desire of the protagonist in *Rebecca*, the portrait reflects Midge's desire to be seen for what she is, a flesh-and-blood woman, to force/help Scottie into renouncing his obsession with a fantasy object—accept the lack in the Other.

Vertigo teaches us that classical/mainstream cinema has the advantage of engaging the spectator with a subjectivization process in relation to cinema's innate uncanniness, one gravitating toward the real, by tapping into a trauma that any subject shares with Scottie and into the endless efforts of avoiding an encounter with it. At the same time, it demonstrates the high price that the subject risks to pay when adopting a fetishistic/perverse economy. *Vertigo* maintains the conditions of subjectivization (identification with the fantasy to do away with lack and then its dissolution through rhetorical strategies that explain the subjectivization process). However, in associating male fantasy with fetishism (representing not only male spectatorship but also Hitchcock's own fantasies regarding female actresses), incorporating the ethical dimension in the dire repercussions of insisting to maintain a fetishistic position, the film dissolves fantasy altogether. *Vertigo* thus operates within the tripartite schema of the symbolic-imaginary-real, favoring the acknowledgment that the subject's desire be detached from the protagonist's desire (like in the other Hitchcock films mentioned in Chapter 1) but without the protecting network of fantasy, which in the other films offers us love and a happy ending. This might be the reason why *Vertigo* baffled audiences and received mixed reviews when it was first released, taking decades to be cited as one of the defining works of Hitchcock's career (attracting significant scholarly criticism, it replaced *Citizen Kane* as the greatest film ever made in the 2012 British Film Institute's *Sight and Sound* critics' poll). That said, the point is that the film emphasizes awareness of the fact that subjectivization cannot occur without engagement with the fantasy to conceal the lack in the Other—this is what the first part of the plot is all about (the "love" story). Hitchcock's greatness consists precisely in this awareness.

We may better understand this point by counterpointing *Vertigo* (as well as the other examples analyzed so far) with a narrative body-character-breach film that belongs to counter-cinema and that bars any engagement with the characters' desire or identification with their fantasy, leaving the spectator emotionally detached. *Cet obscure objet du désir* (which belongs to the multiple-body character category in our taxonomy), like *Shallow Hal* and *Vertigo*, centers on the mechanisms of male desire and fantasy. The film is notable for being the first to use two actresses (Carole Bouquet and Angela Molina) in the single role of Conchita. An aging wealthy Frenchman, Mateo/Mathieu[14] Faber (Fernando Rey), pursues an impoverished elusive young woman who keeps frustrating his romantic and sexual desires. Without any narrative justification, the two actresses, who differ slightly physically, but greatly temperamentally (Bouquet's persona is aloof and elegant while Molina is sensual and vivacious), play Conchita in separate scenes and sometimes, unpredictably, even in one scene. Robert Stam writes,

> More important than Mathieu's desire *per se* is Buñuel's playful foiling of *our* desire. The title itself designates our own position as desiring (largely male) spectators. The film is a protracted joke on the spectator, a narrative striptease that refuses to strip. The film never delivers on the abstract erotic promise of the title. We too are cruelly locked out of the spectacle, subjected to an infinite regress of spectatorial frustration. . . . Buñuel holds the mirror to our own psychic fix on films themselves. He analyzes, as if on a Steenbeck, the most mystified moment in our culture—the moment of sexual surrender—and scrutinizes our phantasmatic relation to the spectacle. (1983: 20; italics in the original)

If the film never delivers what it promises, how can a spectator engage with it? Recalling Metz's striptease metaphor and our "inversion" of it, a narrative striptease that refuses to "strip" is a precise description of a film that precludes engagement with the dynamic of desire/fantasy. According to Peter Evans (1995), the hybrid Molina/Bouquet marks the difference between how Mateo experiences Conchita (which in colloquial Spanish means "cunt"), namely as "an exchangeable sexual property," and how the spectators do. The latter, in Evan's view, become complicit with Conchita's refusal to be an object of Mateo's unsatisfied desire and with her revengeful conduct as a reaction to his treatment of her (126–8). In our view, this kind of complicity depends on the spectators' subjecthood/ideology. Some men, for example, might find Conchita's resistance annoying. In psychoanalytic terms, a full engagement with the film or with either character would be difficult, as Conchita *is* precisely the object (cause) of desire, like the Lady of "courtly love": "The Lady is never characterized for any of her real, concrete virtues.... On the contrary; she is as arbitrary as possible in the tests that she imposes on her servant" (Lacan [1959–60] 1997: 150). As to Mateo, he is the epitome of man's demand "to be deprived of something real" ([1959–60] 1997: 150). Hence, why should we even care what happens to the characters? Some of us may experience in the last scene, when a bomb explodes, possibly causing Conchita's and Mateo's annihilation, a feeling of relief. The film is a flashback told by Mateo to a group of strangers he meets in a train compartment. The way he begins to tell it, ignoring the presence of the young boy (this is Buñuel's way of suggesting that childhood is everything but innocence in terms of psychoanalysis) arouses our desire and curiosity. We wait in anticipation for something extraordinary to happen, as Mateo has promised us. But then nothing happens in terms of sustaining our desire, which Buñuel pulverizes, as the explosions in the film suggest.

Cet obscure objet du désir belongs to a modernist tradition of European cinema that reflexively problematizes character portrayal in film via the body and persona of actors and stars, as shown by the examples in the first chapter. But, unlike mainstream body-character-breach films, which on the level of spectatorship enable subjectivization, by centering on the mechanism of desire per se, this film succeeds only in frustrating the spectator. Linda Williams writes,

> Surrealist film exposes the fundamental illusion of the film image itself to focus on its role in creating the fictive unity of the human subject.... The term desire ... refer[s] ... to the visual figures of the text that elaborate a structure of opposition which expresses not so much the desire *for an object as* the psychic process of desire itself. (1981: xvi–xvii; italics in the original)

Indeed, in terms of spectatorship, the problem with films like *Cet obscure objet du désir* is that they present us with an abstract intellectual commentary on desire and fantasy without engaging us in this dynamic, "killing" the spectator's desire altogether. This commentary might be accurate, but in failing to involve us with the films' characters it also precludes a process of subjectivization. In other words, *Cet obscure objet du désir* is a meta-film explaining how the mechanism of desire/fantasy works (desire in particular), while carefully resisting following the tenets of classical narrative cinema that engage the spectator with such a mechanism.

Pedro Almodóvar, another Spanish *auteur* who is incessantly preoccupied with desire, fantasy, and the traumatic, displays a high awareness of this in all his films. This may account for their success at the box office. *La piel que habito* (*The Skin I live In* 2011), which belongs to the body-transformation category in our taxonomy, lies somewhere in the middle of mainstream and classical (Hitchcock) body-character-breach films and *Cet obscure objet du désir*. Almodóvar is known for his formal hybridity (here, a blend of melodrama, horror, and thriller), one that is also reflected in his use of gender, the body, casting, and abundant intertextuality. All these render his cinema highly reflexive. No matter what the films' stories are about, they are always related in some way to cinema, the act of creation (filmmaking), and how desire and fantasy figure in them—for both the filmmaker and spectators.

However, *La piel que habito* was not well received by either critics or spectators, like *Vertigo* at the time, it baffled audiences; and moreover, it lacks the lighthearted humor typical of Almodóvar's scripts. What the film seems to convey is that there is something in the subject that is untouchable and genderless, no matter how definitive the Other's fantasy is, which is the subject's own desire and the determination to act in conformity with it. This is marked by "Vera Cruz" (Elena Anaya) killing Ledgard (Antonio Banderas) to return to "her" mother and pursue her artistic inclination. In this sense, it may be regarded as a film essay on both subjectivity and subjectivization in that it associates them with inner/mental, psychoanalytic positions and a process undergone by the protagonist, Vicente (Jan Cornet), although not necessarily involving spectators: Ledgard manages to change, even "steal" Vicente's gender but not his or her desire, which is genderless. We suspect the reason for its failure to engage audiences was not its nonlinear narrative but its seeming vagueness where desire is concerned. Ledgard, like Génessier in *Les yeux sans visage*, is a cold, ambitious, master-manipulator surgeon who will stop at nothing to alleviate his guilt for his wife's death and his daughter's loss of sanity—thus occupying a psychotic subjective position. In this sense he is very different from other perverse characters in Almodóvar's previous films, certainly from those who undergo subjectivization but also from those with whom we identify because of their conviction that they can veil the lack in the Other. Engaging with Ledgar's desire (to do away with the lack in the Other) or fantasy (carrying it out in the real) is thus as difficult as engaging with Génessier's desire. As to Vera's desire, we are not sure what she wants until the end of the film: Is she accepting her enforced gender transition and falling in love with Ledgard? Is she becoming a friend of Marilia (Marisa Paredes), Ledgard's servant and his real mother? In other words, does she become an active participant in Ledgard's mad fantasy? All these questions are answered only at the end of the film (and hinted at through Vera's turning her captivity room into an art "studio" in Ledgard's huge mansion in the Spanish city of Toledo, which with all the art hanging on its walls connotes a museum), leaving us less baffled than in *Cet obscure objet du désir* or in *Les yeux sans visage* (in which we are left in the territory of the uncanny throughout): Vera's desire is to be an artist/fashion designer, which her captivity, cruel as it may be, forces her to fully acknowledge, regardless of her gender transition. At the end of the film, Vera returns to her mother's dress shop for the first time since being kidnapped (as Vicente). She tearfully tells her lesbian friend (who works in the shop and whom Vicente had loved six years prior—a love Vera can now hope to realize) of his kidnapping, forced sex change, and the murders she committed. Then, as Vera's mother enters the room, Vera says, "I am Vicente," which is the final line of the film, implying that although she has physically changed, her desire is left untouched.

Another example of body transformation, or rather, a variation of it, which might be baffling for audiences (only in the first viewing), but nevertheless describes a process of subjectivization, is *Fight Club* (David Fincher 1999). This film seems to draw an analogy between the way film maintains our fantasmatic engagement with a film through a perfect match between the body/persona and the character (the narrator [Edward Norton] and "Tyler Durden" [Brad Pitt], his imaginary alter ego) and the way the fantasy of endless consumerism is maintained through the inculcation of images related to it that inundate our brain. Its protagonist is a depressed young man who loathes his work and the world he lives in. He develops an imaginary violent friend, Tyler Durden, and an equally violent world. We become aware of the fact that we have been watching a fantasy at the end of the film, when the Edward Norton character himself acknowledges his split personality.

Hints are spread out through the film, such as remarks made by Marla (Helena Bonham Carter), the female character in the film, who falls in love with Tyler/the narrator, or the scene in which the Edward Norton character punches himself. Notwithstanding the strangeness of this incident, it does not present a real impediment to our viewing and experiencing of Tyler Durden as a "real" character in the plot, existing in a universe created in the outer world of the narrator. This occurs mainly because of that unique "materiality" presented by the body/persona of the actor. Upon becoming aware of the fact that Tyler Durden and the narrator are one and the same character, the protagonist/Edward Norton has short flashes that basically must have initiated the emergence of Tyler. All these flashes are related to aggression. Thereafter, he collapses on the bed, while on the soundtrack we hear his voice, "It's called a change-over: the movie goes on and nobody in the audience has any idea." We suggest that this moment in the film is a liberating moment for the protagonist, his breaking free from the desire of Others—"Buy me!" "Consume me!"

In terms of spectatorship, it is at this point that the film engages our imagination actively; we realize now that our perception has been tampered with and we go back in time, forced to reconstruct the plot from the beginning.[15] This going back in time recreates disturbing images and situations that relate to primal fantasies (such as the primal scene). Such images as well as whole scenes constitute stimuli for the reconsideration of our own fantasies, our own fixations—through the trajectory of the visual and specular. This crisis in spectatorship unveils the unique way in which films engage our fantasy. This engagement relies on the twofold, rather paradoxical, nature of films. On the one hand, films inundate our brain with stereotypical images that resonate with our own appeasing fantasies. On the other, they stimulate us to create our own imagery, using our imagination beyond what is present on the screen—in *Fight Club* through a double reconstruction of the film's "past" and our own (much like in the therapeutic process of psychoanalysis). In this light, it may be said that *Fight Club*, like many narrative films, carries the task of the imaginary, which not only shields us against our worst fears but also provokes new scenarios, sometimes creating a new consciousness.

The protagonist undergoes a similar process of emancipation. The creation of an alternate personality, totally divorced from his other personality, enables him to set himself free from all the different "masters" in his life, beginning with his job and boss and ending with his consumerism compulsion. The scene that best exemplifies this is the one in which he hits himself as if he were punching another person. Although he acts out his aggression against his abusive boss, his fist takes on a life of its own, exactly like that of Tyler Durden, whose function is to free the character from the compelling life of consumerism. Seen in this light, Tyler Durden and the fist have the same function, the fist becoming an object that is supposed to give the character a wake-up call. Herein is the complexity of *Fight Club*: It criticizes the American way of life that "sells" fantasy as reality by doing precisely this—up to a point in the film, when it forces the viewer to undergo a similar process to that of the character, it engages us with a fantasy of violence. Only later in the film, are we thrust out from this fantasy (representing so many films in which violence is used as a mode of false liberation, made for mass consumerism): We understand that the process of recognizing our own desire in today's world is a difficult process, one demanding that we "punch" ourselves. The protagonist punching himself thus is correlative with the way the film punches us.

In analysis, subjectivization is a long, unconscious process. Viewing a film cannot match this process, which is why mainstream cinema needs its own unique special strategies. Julia Kristeva's reflections on fantasy and cinema could not be more relevant here:

> Since its inception cinema has not only projected the specular (imagination/fantasy) by making itself the bold revealer of our psychical lives, more seductively and more frighteningly than other arts, but it has

also assumed the power of thinking the specular. Thinking it in a way that is itself specular: using the visible, not evacuating fantasy but being protected from it while demonstrating it; not necessarily displaying it in its oneiric naïveté but exhibiting its main themes, its skeleton, its logic. (Kristeva [1997–8] 2002: 75)

We have shown that the thinking of the specular in classical and mainstream body-character-breach films is achieved in a process of subjectivization, which marks the ethical aspect of cinema, no different from Lacan's ([1959–60] 1997: 314) ethics of psychoanalysis: "And it is because we know better ... how to recognize the nature of desire ... that a reconsideration of ethics is possible, that a form of ethical judgment is possible, of a kind that gives this question the force of a Last Judgment: Have you acted in conformity with the desire *that is in you?*" (our italics).

Indeed, the power of thinking the specular may resonate with us long after a film has ended. Today's technology enables us to view films repeatedly and in various formats, thinking and rethinking the specular.

In conclusion, body-character breach films infer, on the one hand, that we do not have to be "perverts" to condone or even identify with the desire to veil the lack in the Other—a struggle common to all subjects. On the other hand, they encourage us to follow the path of our own desire by dismantling fantasies whose purpose is either the veiling of castration, its disavowal, or foreclosure altogether. In condoning the desire to veil the lack (which is what narrative film does), these films rather display what might be called a "Hamlet position." For Ernest Jones ([1949] 1976), following Freud, Hamlet's hesitation to revenge his father's death at the hands of his uncle is caused by the repressed desire for his mother, displaced onto Hamlet's uncle. He *sees* his uncle *realizing* his desire, his own "film" being acted out—same role, different actor. According to Lacan ([1959] 1977: 50), Hamlet's hesitation is related to his mother "having filled herself with it [Claudius' phallus]." Hamlet's mother, having replaced the lost object with a new one (by remarrying shortly after her husband's murder), impedes Hamlet's own subjectivization, causing him to repeat, over and over again, a confrontation with the object of desire as an impossible object (an encounter with the object of desire as a signifier of impossibility). Lacan draws an analogy between the mourning of the phallus (during the dissolution of the Oedipus complex, as recounted by Freud) and symbolic mourning rites, whose function is to fill the gap in the real caused by the death of someone close. Due to unsuccessful castration, to insufficient mourning of the phallus—a failure in the cutting of the imaginary bond between mother and child and the symbolization of this radical loss by words—Hamlet (an obsessional neurotic) is trapped within his mother's desire as well as within the desire of other characters, "Hamlet is always at the hour of the Other" (25), unable to follow the path of his own desire.

In body-character-breach films, the characters are trapped in the Other's body/desire, realizing later (like Hamlet, at the end of the play) the dangers entailed. The spectators witness the many potentially transgressive, sometimes taboo-breaking, incestuous situations and feel troubled or horrified at the character's futile attempts to veil the lack in the Other. Many of these films disguise some of this horror in the mode of comedy. Like the play-within-the-play in *Hamlet*, these transgressive scenes function as rhetorical *mise-en-abymes*. By explaining film's unique ontology as a visual and specular form by first appeasing castration and then bringing to the surface that which is barred from consciousness, as well as the traumatic real, body-character-breach films compel us to (re)examine our position in relation to our fundamental unconscious fantasy; they guide us into modifying this position. In fact, they infer that in mainstream cinema, casting is the principal locus to which a cinematic image and the spectator's reaction are anchored in one shared fantasmatic image, whose purpose is to veil the lack in the Other—the lack of the screen.

PART TWO

Dreaming-Character Films

3

Dreams in Films and Implicit Reflexivity

Dreams and Guilt

The corpus of Part Two consists of films in which the protagonist has one or more dreams. Our analyses of these dreams show that the primal unconscious desire of the protagonist is to be the mother's sole object of desire, also entailing the desire to dispose of such rivals as a brother or the father, all of which generate guilt feelings. According to Lacan ([1959–60] 1997: 321), guilt is associated with the disavowal of the subject's desire: "From an analytic point of view, the only thing one can be guilty of is having given ground relative to one's desire." As Žižek emphasizes,

> Lacan takes seriously and literally the Freudian "economical paradox" of the superego—that is, the vicious cycle that characterizes the superego: the more we submit ourselves to the superego imperative, the greater its pressure, the more we feel guilty. According to Lacan, this "feeling of guilt" is not a self-deception to be dispelled . . . we really *are* guilty: superego draws the energy of the pressure it exerts upon the subject from the fact that the subject was not faithful to his desire, that he gave it up. Our sacrificing to the superego, our paying tribute to it, only corroborates our guilt. (1994: 67–8; italics in the original)

This chapter, as well as the next one, complies with Lacan's notion in that the protagonists of the films analyzed cannot recognize their own desire because they are trapped in those of their mothers. For most of them, extrication from this entanglement marks their process of subjectivization, a process in which spectators partake.

Guilt feelings, or the sense of guilt, are connected by Freud to the relation between ego and superego: "an actual splitting of the ego between accuser (the superego) and accused—a split which is itself the outcome, through a process of internalization, of an inter-subjective relationship" (Laplanche and Pontalis [1967] 1973: 415). Furthermore, "One may . . . venture the hypothesis that the great part of the sense of guilt must normally remain unconscious, because the origin of conscience is intimately connected with the Oedipus complex, which belongs to the unconscious" (Freud [1923] 1961: 52 in Laplanche and Pontalis [1967] 1973: 415). The characterization of the protagonists in the films suggests that they position the mother in their fantasy as an accuser (superego) demanding they remain sexually chaste and pure and, in many cases, also desexualize the women in their lives, who must be moral ideals (caring, nurturing ideal mothers; innocent little girls). However, the various relationships they maintain with women also arouse feelings of anxiety, panic, and shutting down, as the female characters are incompatible with the ideal projected onto them. This discrepancy points, inter alia, to how the protagonists' guilt colors their subjectivity, rendering them unreliable in the way they think or act. What in fact we are dealing with here is a fixation that blocks identification with the castrating father in the Lacanian sense, a fantasy whose purpose is to sustain the imaginary misconception about the wholeness of the mother.

In cases of traumatic tragic events the protagonists were involved in and feel responsible for, interpreting them as a realization of their primal unconscious desire (to dispose of a rival contending for the mother's attention), the guilt feelings develop into an actual guilt complex (Hitchcock's *Spellbound* 1945; Coppola's *The Conversation* 1974). The complex is evinced by the fact that the characters are not punished by the law (*The Conversation*), and if they are, it is for a crime they have not committed (*Spellbound*). In other words, the superego here has become an imaginary judgmental accuser that has no relevance either to the law or to ethics. In fact, the harder the protagonists attempt to correct real or imagined injustices, the more the superego toughens, thus paradoxically increasing rather than decreasing feelings of guilt. The fantasy of moral and sexual purity incapacitates the protagonists from reading the reality around them (function in the symbolic), for example, distinguishing between victim/perpetrator. This renders them unable to assume responsibility for their actions, consequently causing more harm to themselves and to the people they are involved with. The inability to distinguish between victim ("innocent") and any other kind of criminal offense is ingrained in the nature of the guilt feelings, which may

> designate emotional states (varying from the remorse of the criminal to apparently ridiculous self-reproaches) which follow acts that the subject deems reprehensible, though the reasons he gives for doing so may or

may not be adequate ones. Or again, it may refer to a vague sense of personal unworthiness unconnected with any particular act for which the subject blames himself. At the same time the sense of guilt is postulated by psychoanalysis as a system of unconscious motivations that accounts for "failure syndromes," delinquent behavior, self-inflicted suffering, etc. The words "feeling" and "sense" should be employed with caution in this connection; since the subject may not feel guilty at the level of conscious experience. (Laplanche and Pontalis [1967] 1973: 414)

For example, in *Der Krieger und die Kaiserin* (*The Princess and the Warrior*, Tom Tykwer 2000), Bodo's (Benno Fürmann) self-inflicted suffering is expressed when dreaming about his dead wife's forgiveness (she burned herself to death in a gas station after they quarreled, hence his guilt): While the two embrace in his dream, Bodo, sleepwalking, puts his arms around a burning stove. In *Felicia's Journey* (Atom Egoyan 1999), Felicia's (Elaine Cassidy) dream expresses her self-reproach over her abortion, feeling guilty because she could not find the father; in both Ingmar Bergman's *Smultronstallet* (*Wild Strawberries* 1957) and Fellini's *8½* (1963), the protagonists, Dr. Borg (Victor Sjöström) and Guido (Marcello Mastroianni), respectively, reproach themselves for mistreating their wives; in *Geheimnisse Einer Seele* (*Secrets of a Soul*, G. W. Pabst 1926), *Giulietta degli Spiriti* (*Juliet of the Spirits*, Federico Fellini 1965), and *Cop Land* (James Mangold 1997), it is the personal unworthiness of the protagonists that is the origin of their guilt feelings. In the following films, the protagonists have a direct responsibility for the death of others: *Spellbound*; *The Conversation*; *The Man Who Wasn't There* (Joel and Ethan Coen 2001); *Lalechet al hamayim* (*Walk on Water*, Eytan Fox 2004); as well as the murder intended and planned by the protagonist in Lynch's *Mulholland Drive* (2001).

In early films in which the dream is interpreted by a psychoanalyst, Freud's method, a complex interpretive language undergoes schematization into simpler patterns of interpretation with the intention of popularizing it. The prototypical example is *Geheimnisse Einer Seele*: "The film embodies the structure of dream analysis as Freud intended it to be performed" (Friedberg 1990: 51). Furthermore,

Secrets of the Soul is a film narrative with the structure of a detective film, the psychoanalyst as a sort of Sherlock Jr. who witnesses each image as the analysand retells the events leading up to his nightmare and his resulting phobia. The analyst must then deduce and decode the origins of the client's phobia. *Geheimnisse* uses dream analysis as the central hermeneutical tool of its narrative; the dream is a cinematic attempt at direct pictorial transcription of psychic mechanisms, a key to the locked room of unconscious. (Friedberg 1990: 46)

Spellbound adopts the ploy of popularizing the talking cure through the structure of a detective film. However, as we shall see, the "talking cure" in *Spellbound* almost verges on parody.[1] The film, as all other films containing a protagonist's dream, goes way beyond it. This is already evident in *Geheimnisse*, which is a silent film: "Yet the 'talking cure' is successfully reduced to silent images. An analysis is conducted, not on the speech of the analysand but on the images that Pabst provides" (1990: 51). In later films following *Spellbound*, the investigation of a crime within a detective plot in combination with a dream symbolically replaces the traditional role of the psychoanalyst investigating the patient's past (e.g., *The Conversation*).

Narrative films depicting dreams are vital to the understanding of the ways cinema relates to or engages with the mechanism of the unconscious.[2] As Freud asserts, dreams are the royal road to the unconscious. They are universal, and as Metz ([1975] 1976: 89) notes, "[The dream] has a further privilege in that it is the only one that is neither neurotic, like the symptom or acting out, nor excessively minor, like slips and bungled acts." The dream in the films is clearly marked as such in the diegesis by showing the protagonist falling asleep before the dream is depicted, awakening after its depiction, or sometimes both, in keeping with Freud's ([1899] 1997: 6) basic definition: "The dream is defined as the psychic activity of the sleeper, inasmuch as he is asleep." It thus constitutes a cinematic device that enables representation of abstract mental processes similar to the individual's dream in life[3]—to be distinguished from all other depictions of human subjectivities in a waking state, such as memories, conscious fantasies (daydreams), hallucinations, and images/shots rendered from a character's point of view or imbued with human subjectivity. Moreover, in films rendered in a dreamlike style, the central characteristic of the dream—the ability to identify the mental sources from which the dream is derived—is lacking. In contrast, in films in which the dream is directly connected to the protagonist's inner world, the symbolic organization of the dream semantically distinguishes its images from other subjective activity such as memory, fantasy, and hallucinations.

In our interpretation of the dream segment we broadly adopt Freud's terminology, such as representation through symbolic images, condensation, displacement, and affect as well as his assumption that the dream's main function is to express unconscious Oedipal wishes.[4] However, we mostly relate to the mode in which the dream gives away the basic (Lacanian) fantasy question, "What does the M/Other want from me?" In most films, the dream's symbols derive from events in the protagonist's personal history, the traces of which can be followed throughout the film by means of recurrent images and cinematic devices pointing to the protagonist's affect. Thus, interpretation of the symbolic imagery of the dream relies on the imagery of the entire film, while the interpretation of the film is shaped by the symbols in the dream. Films that present a dreaming character are thus inevitably transformed into texts organized around an unconscious symbolic subjectivity.

Because of its symbolic organization and the semantic distinction between the dream and the narrative as a whole, we consider the function of a character's dream in the film similar to that of the mise-en-abyme: It is a rhetorical device as well as a reflexive one. The mise-en-abyme refers to a work of art enclosed within a work of art and reflecting it, such as, for example, the play within a play in Shakespeare's *Hamlet*. Lucien Dällenbach ([1977] 1989: 36) refers to it as "the mirror in the text": "A 'mise en abyme' is any internal mirror that reflects the whole of the narrative by simple, repeated or 'specious' (or paradoxical duplication)." The similarity between these two rhetorical and reflexive devices (dream and mise-en-abyme) can be attributed to both determining the relations between them and the work of art as a whole and having an important rhetorical function in that they guide the interpretation of the text. However, contrary to the dream, the mise-en-abyme, although a rhetorical device, does not necessarily derive from the individual character. Moreover, it does not necessarily entail an ethical function like the dream which, by pointing to guilt, reflects the protagonists' refusal to acknowledge their own desire (the real reason for their guilt feelings). We, the spectators, do not become aware of it while viewing the dream sequence; such awareness is generated only through the actions of the protagonists, specifically when they realize their mistakes.

Subjectivization (involving spectators) thus occurs when the protagonists become aware of their mistaken interpretation of reality. The dissolution of their fantasy, their fixation, leads them to comprehend that the basis of ethics (to do right) is contingent on the complexity of intersubjectivity, which enables them to assume responsibility for their actions rather than adhere to strict systems of morality such as the church, the police, the courts, or supposedly objective ones like science and technology. This enables the protagonists to change their position in relation to the mother's desire and spectators to become aware of working through the interrelations of certain aspects of subjectivity—desire, fantasy, and trauma. Gaining insight into the origin of the characters' guilt (the guilt being inherent in the dream) thus has an ethical dimension, not only regarding the protagonist but also regarding spectatorship.

The dream as mise-en-abyme reflects both the protagonist's subjectivity and the medium itself. The films discussed in this chapter tackle the medium through subtle references to the filmic apparatus, such as the human eye, the camera, and optic instruments. We refer to these references as implicit reflexivity: "implicit" because the dream as mise-en-abyme is incorporated in films that are not properly meta-films such as those discussed in Chapter 4, which deal with filmmaking, hence, their explicit reflexivity. The meta-films discussed in Chapter 4 tackle the basic code of film, which we term "the cinematographic code." In both cases, the questions the dream inexorably evokes are what does narrative cinema have to feel guilty about, and what does the process of subjectivization involving the filmic apparatus tell us about the ethics of narrative cinema? This chapter addresses these questions by looking at two films that figure perhaps the most guilt-ridden of dreaming cinematic protagonists: *Spellbound* and *The Conversation*.

Spellbound

Dr. Anthony Edwardes (Gregory Peck) arrives at Green Manors, a mental hospital, where he is to replace the director of the hospital, Dr. Murchinson (Leo G. Carroll), forced into retirement because of nervous exhaustion. Dr. Constance Petersen (Ingrid Bergman) is a young psychoanalyst at Green Manors, the only woman on the medical staff, deemed by her colleagues to be analytical and cold. When the young and handsome Dr. Edwardes introduces himself to her, she is enthralled but also notices that he has a phobia about sets of parallel lines against a white background that cause him to have an aggressive reaction (mostly toward Constance, who is always by his side when the attacks occur) and dizzy spells. They fall in love, but coming across the signature of the real Dr. Edwardes in a copy of his book, she compares it with that of the young doctor and realizes that the disturbed man she has fallen in love with is an impostor. He confides to her that he killed the real Edwardes and has taken his place but due to massive amnesia cannot remember who he is. Constance believes he is innocent and that he suffers from a guilt complex. The young doctor flees, his impersonation of Edwardes, as well as the real Edwardes's disappearance and possible murder, becomes public knowledge.

Constance manages to track the impostor down and begins to use her psychoanalytic training to break his amnesia and find out the truth. He assumes the name of John Brown. She takes him to the house of her former mentor, Dr. Brulov (Michael Chekhov), with the police in pursuit. They introduce themselves as newlyweds, but Dr. Brulov suspects John is Constance's patient, and further, that he is a schizophrenic, not to be trusted, and is afraid John might harm Constance. The chain of events that follows indeed substantiates this apprehension: John wakes up in the middle of the night and decides he needs to shave. He exits the bathroom with a straight razor in his hand, which is designed to resemble a lethal weapon ready for attack. Dr. Brulov, who is awake at his desk, offers him a glass of milk containing a sedative because he would rather have him sleep. John falls asleep and has a dream that the two doctors analyze.

John recounts his dream to the doctors: He is in a sort of a gambling house where odd people are playing with blank cards and a half-naked girl is kissing everyone; he is playing cards with a bearded man. He deals him a seven of clubs and the man says, "That's twenty-one." The proprietor (whose face is covered with a white cloth mask) enters and accuses the bearded man of cheating; the latter then threatens the bearded man. A man is falling off the steep sloping roof of a high building and the proprietor is hiding behind a chimney; he drops an oddly shaped spoked wheel from the roof. John is running down a steep slope, pursued by the shadow of a pair of large wings. Constance and Brulov deduce that John was a patient of the real Dr. Edwardes, who took him on a ski trip as part of his treatment (the slope of the roof in the dream resembles a ski slope). They assume that Edwardes had an accident and fell from a precipice (the man falling from the high building in the dream) and died there. The pattern of dark lines on white symbolizes ski tracks, which explains why every time John sees this pattern he reacts in horror. Constance and John go to the Gabriel Valley ski resort (the imagery of the wings chasing the man in the dream provides the clue to the name of the resort) to reenact the event and find Dr. Edwardes' body.

While skiing, they are about to approach the bottom of a hill when, heading toward a precipice, John's memory returns to him. He recalls not the death of Edwardes but a traumatic event from his childhood—his younger brother was sitting outside at the bottom of a banister when John swiftly slid down it, accidentally knocking him onto the sharply pointed pickets of the metal fence surrounding the house, impaling and killing him. John then remembers that his real name is John Ballantyne and that he suffers from post-trauma (the result of active service as a doctor in the Second World War). He used to be a patient of Dr. Edwardes, who indeed took him to the ski resort to treat him. Ballantyne remembers seeing Edwardes fall over the precipice to his death and now realizes that he did not murder him—it must have been an accident. Thus, his childhood trauma was the incident that induced him to develop a guilt complex and believe that he had killed Dr. Edwardes. Upon the return of Constance and Ballantyne (expecting that Ballantyne would be exonerated), they are told that Dr. Edwardes's body has indeed been found at the ski resort (in keeping with the information Constance and Ballantyne gave to the police) but with a bullet in it. Ballantyne is convicted of murder and sent to prison. A heartbroken Constance resumes her position at Green Manors, where Dr. Murchinson is once again the director. In conversation, he casually mentions that he had known Edwardes slightly and did not like him, thus contradicting his earlier statement that they had never met. This arouses Constance's suspicions because if indeed he knew Edwardes, he should have told everyone from the beginning that Ballantyne was an impostor.

She asks Murchinson's help in analyzing Ballantyne's dream. They follow her notes and agree that the bearded man, as an authority figure, represents Edwardes and that both he and Ballantyne where dining at a place called the 21 Club, where Ballantyne witnessed the proprietor with the covered face threatening Edwardes. They further deduce that the gambling house with the odd people surrounded by eyes and playing blank cards refers to two places: Green Manors—where odd patients play cards (the eyes representing those of the guards) and where at the beginning of the film, one of Constance's patients, Miss Carmichael (Rhonda Fleming), is seen playing cards and then being taken by a guard to a session with Constance—and the 21 Club, an actual restaurant in New York.

Murchinson suggests that the proprietor with the covered face threatening Edwardes was himself. Constance adds that the wheel symbolizes a revolver, and that the proprietor with the covered face hiding behind the chimney and dropping the wheel was in reality Murchinson shooting Edwardes in the back, hiding behind a tree, and then dropping the gun. Constance says she believes the gun with his fingerprints is still there in the snow, but Murchinson corrects her, saying that the gun is not there. He takes it out and aims it at her. In what follows, he tries to shake her belief that she can prove her hypothesis by analyzing Ballantyne's dream, that is, that Murchinson accused Edwardes of stealing his job and then threatened and later shot him. He calls Constance "a love-smitten analyst playing a dream detective," however, she insists that "there will be no dreams for the police," expressing her conviction that the police will find witnesses at the 21 Club as well as at the ski resort. She walks away, telling Murchinson that, while his first murder was committed under extenuating circumstances (his fragile mental state), for which he would receive a prison sentence but would still be able to continue reading and researching, murdering her would certainly lead him to the electric chair. She leaves the room on her way to call the police, whereupon Murchinson turns the gun on himself and shoots. The film ends with Constance and Ballantyne leaving for their honeymoon.

Dreaming and Guilt in *Spellbound*

The theme of guilt in *Spellbound* is overt. First, the guilt complex is explained by Constance to one of her patients, Garmes (Norman Lloyd), who believes he has killed his father, while Ballantyne, who is impersonating Edwardes (the latter is an expert on the subject, having written a book titled *The Labyrinth of Guilt*) is present in the room. Garmes' guilt complex resonates with and doubles Ballantyne's. Constance says to Garmes,

> No, you didn't kill him, that's a misconception that has taken hold of you.... People often feel guilty over something they never did, it usually goes back to their childhood, a child often wishes something terrible would happen to someone, and if something does happen to that person, the child believes that he has caused it, and he grows up with a guilt complex over a sin that was only a bad dream.

Although the scene starts with a dialogue between Constance and Garmes, it then cuts to a reaction shot of Ballantyne looking somewhat perplexed.

At first this seems to be a sign that Ballantyne is feeling that in some way Constance's words might be relevant to him, giving credence to the interpretation of the dream later in the film: Ballantyne was willing to take the blame for Edwardes' murder because he felt guilty about causing the accidental death of his brother. But the reaction shot, showing Ballantyne's face rather than the patient's, who keeps insisting that he did kill his father, points to a displacement of another sort. The subtext of Constance's words suggests that the patient thinks he is responsible for his father's death because it constitutes a fulfillment of an unconscious wish he had as a child—to do away with the father, to remain the sole object of his mother's desire.

In this film, as in other narrative films portraying dreams of protagonists, the primal guilt associated with this desire is displaced to a guilt related to an *actual* occurrence caused by them that exacerbates the primal guilt. Ballantyne's childish fantasy, which was supposed to remain in the unconscious but was "fulfilled" through the actual death of his rival/ brother, resulted in a guilt complex, interfering with the symbolic function. The unbearable experience of his brother's death is a result of the real intruding upon the imaginary, the guilt complex explaining Ballantyne's willingness to be punished for a crime he did not commit. Every time he experiences something remotely alluding to the scene of Edwardes' murder, a traumatic affect related to his brother's death is generated and he becomes panic-stricken. He was a witness to both events, seeing both victims sliding down to their deaths. As Richard Rushton (2004: 382), in discussing the "afterwardsness" of trauma in *Spellbound*, claims, the dream essentially "diverts attention from the status of the events as key moments in the understanding of Ballantine's trauma (the death of his brother, the death of Edwardes) and instead allows the film to focus on the unconscious fantasy structures . . . [that point to] the tendency of Ballantine to 'take the blame,' or his 'desire to be punished.'" The connection between the two events is made through the explanation of the psychoanalysts in the film: Dr. Edwardes' murder triggered the repressed memory of his brother's fatal accident, causing Ballantyne to take the blame for the former—thus augmenting his experience of being a killer.

However, the symbols in the dream referring to the childhood traumatic incident that shaped Ballantine's guilt complex, and in fact the whole of his subjectivity, are never interpreted in the film beyond Edwardes' murder. Our interpretation shows that every image triggering his affect of anxiety not only shows the displacement of his guilt from one event (the death of the brother) to the other (Edwardes' murder) but is also related to his sexual attraction to Constance and his acute fear of sex; namely, in his guilt complex, sex is associated with death. Any sharp object penetrating another's body (recalling the way his brother died) becomes a lethal object killing his partner.[5] Remaining asexual thus becomes a way of coping with his guilt complex, of being cleansed of any traces of ever fulfilling his unconscious desire to remove his rival in order to remain his mother's only object of desire. Moreover, Ballantyne must turn the woman he desires into an asexual object as well so that he can remain frozen in latency. He lets Constance take care of him, nursing him the way a mother is supposed to nurse her child (Brulov tells her, "You're not his mother!"). The threat that Constance poses thus evinces the fear of conceiving the mother as a sexual object lest the fantasy materialize.[6] Herein lies the reason for the guilt associated with his resistance to acknowledging his own desire. Both the images triggering Ballantyne's affect of anxiety and some of the symbols in the dream (including portions of the dream that were planned, and some even shot, but later cut out of the final version of the film) condense the following: Ballantyne's primal guilt (stemming from his primal desire) prior to the death of his brother, his childish interpretation of his guilt (the belief that his brother's accident was a fulfillment of this desire, resulting in his taking blame for Edwardes's murder), and the halting of his sexual maturation and his fear of sex. These explain his remaining trapped in his mother's desire (not unlike Hamlet). For spectators, all the scenes in which Ballantyne expresses his fear of sex evoke an eerie feeling.

We should follow the guilt labyrinth to its fullest complexity, first in the film and then in the dream. Every time Ballantyne sees dark lines on white triggering the memory of the recent murder of Edwardes and the memory of the death of his brother in the distant past (fulfilling his unconscious wish), his reaction (panic, violence toward Constance, dizziness, and fainting) is related to his sexual attraction to Constance in the present, lest the sexual act with her result in her death. At Green Manors, at the beginning of the film, while sitting at the dinner table with the hospital staff, Constance's colleagues tell Ballantyne about their plans to build a swimming pool. Constance tries to concretize its shape by "drawing" with her fork a slightly pear-shaped oval on the white tablecloth (Figure 3.1), the marks of which alarm Ballantyne (his affect is always evinced by cinematic means, for example, a medium close-up showing his facial expression, ominous music, and other amplified sounds), leading to a verbal aggressive reaction directed at Constance: "I take it that the supply of linen in this institute is inexorable!"

We cannot but wonder at this aggressive reaction, as she is his friend, not foe. We ask: What is it in Constance's scribble on the tablecloth that is so upsetting? While the stripes made by the fork are associated in Ballantyne's mind with the site of Edwardes's murder and the fork itself with how his brother died, the shape marked on the tablecloth clearly connotes a woman's womb. On the night Ballantyne kisses Constance for the first time, the panic affect related to the dark stripes he perceives on Constance's white robe (recalling the marks made by his skis in the snow) comes *after* she and John have already kissed and embraced. Sexually aroused, he suddenly becomes aware of the stripes, pushing her away in an abrupt gesture, apologizing that it is not her but her robe.

FIGURE 3.1 Spellbound (*Alfred Hitchcock 1945*).

Soon after, the two are called to a hospital operating room to attend to Garmes, who attacked a doctor and then attempted suicide by slashing his own throat. Ballantyne's panicky reaction to the white surgery room is augmented by the proximity of this scene to the kissing scene. We thus learn that Garmes's act (slashing his throat) as well as the surgeons operating on his body in Constance's presence, all point to Ballantyne's fear of sex with her. After these two incidents, Constance tries to help Ballantyne remember who he is and cure him of his guilt complex. As long as Ballantyne is treated and cared for by Constance the two cannot have sex because of their doctor-patient relationship, which secures Ballantyne's fixation in regard to his latency. But the more Constance declares her intention to become feminine and expresses her love for him, and the quicker she advances in solving the mystery of Ballantyne's guilt complex, the more anxious he becomes. This is evident in the dining car scene when the two are traveling to Gabriel Valley: When Constance describes the change she is going through as a woman,[7] the "feminine" clothes and funny hats she intends to buy, clearly referring to her sexual arousal, Ballantyne suddenly becomes aware of her knife cutting the meat. Constance notices his horrified expression (and so do spectators) and puts the knife down.

In the privacy of their bedroom when they are pretending to be a married couple at Dr. Brulov's house, they declare their love and mutual physical attraction. But after they kiss, Constance decides they should not share a bed because they need to maintain the doctor-patient relationship. When she turns the light on, Ballantyne has a terrified reaction to the lines on the bedspread and becomes hostile to her attempt to find out what in the room he is reacting to ("I am sick of your double talk!"). Realizing that his reaction is connected to dark lines on white, she tries to evoke his memories, whereupon he collapses.

In the scene that follows, Ballantyne wakes up in the middle of the night and goes to the bathroom to have a glass of water. He stares at his reflection in the mirror, feels the whiskers on his face with his hands, and decides to shave. Seeing the bristles of the shaving brush under the white shaving foam, the sink, and chair (again dark lines on white), his panic intensifies, and he cannot continue shaving. The act of shaving symbolizes a moment of realization that he is no longer a child and therefore he must consummate his love, which again terrifies him. What follows thus represents a culmination of his sexual conflict. When he exits the bathroom without shaving to return to the room he and Constance share, holding the straight razor in his hand, he looks menacing. The camera simulates his eyes glaring at the stripes of Constance's bedspread, ending at her beautiful peaceful face, fast asleep. He leaves the room and goes downstairs, as if in a daze. If we read these symbols only as pertaining to the murder on the ski slope, the conclusion at this stage must be that Ballantyne is about to attack Constance because he is a disturbed person reacting violently to black stripes on white objects. This is certainly the effect Hitchcock is interested in creating, one enhanced later when Brulov and Ballantyne meet. Downstairs, Ballantyne sees Brulov sitting at his desk in his office, which is opposite the stairs. Brulov offers him a glass of milk, coming toward him on his way to the kitchen. Although it is clear Ballantyne has not killed Constance, the apprehension that he is dangerous, a potential killer in a trance holding an open razor in his hand as a lethal weapon about to murder Brulov still persists, intensified by his earlier descent down the stairs: The camera is located at the bottom of the stairs, showing him in a long shot from a low angle, back-lighted, emphasizing him as a threatening silhouette. The scene is accompanied by ominous music.

While Brulov is in the kitchen preparing the milk, his voice is heard off-screen. The kitchen door wide open; Ballantyne, razor in hand, remains outside of it. He is in profile in the foreground, closest to the camera at the left side of the frame, filling half of it. His body is cut from the waist up and the knees down. The dark trousers contrast with the brightness of his hand holding the shining razor (located at the top of the frame), which evinces the threat to Brulov, but the pointed object (the open razor) adjacent to Ballantyne's crotch also connotes male erection. For spectators the eerie feelings accompanying the viewing of the scene (certainly in repeated viewings) thus acquire justification, as it is hard to miss the image of a male erection as well as relate Ballantyne's horror to the fear of sex. This becomes even more evident when we notice that in contrast to the spectators, Brulov seems to be oblivious of this threat: The shot that follows is rendered in one take, the camera following Brulov getting up from his desk, going to the kitchen, and coming back holding a glass of milk. Twice he passes by Ballantyne, the camera movement enabling the rendering of the same mise-en-scène as in the previous shot (the lethal erection). Ballantyne drinking his milk is rendered from his own point of view (Brulov is seen through the half-empty glass), the white liquid filling the screen, leading us to wrongly assume (a device that clearly cannot work in repeated viewings) that at the sight of it Ballantyne will snap and kill Brulov. This impression is heightened in the morning when Constance goes down the stairs and finds Brulov sleeping in an armchair, looking as if he is dead. Alarmed, she hurries to him, making sure he is all right.

Indeed, the mise-en-scène of Ballantyne holding the open razor outside the kitchen suggests that what is at stake here is not a murder to be committed, and that Brulov really had nothing to be afraid of. As Ballantyne does not attack either Constance or Brulov, we must deduce that he is sexually attracted to Constance but experiences his sexuality (rendered by the open razor) as lethal and is afraid he might kill her—his threatening behavior resides solely in his own unconscious fear of sex. At this point (when first viewing the film) we understand that Ballantyne is no killer and thus corroborate the understanding that what terrifies him is his sexuality. In repeated viewings, we connect our affect accompanying the looming danger in the scene strictly to the way the razor is associated with a male erection, which is what terrifies Ballantyne. When Brulov gives him the glass of milk, it suggests a regression to childhood—for us, it represents his fixation; for Ballantyne himself, it represents not only a consoling element but also a threatening one.[8] This is when the bromide in the milk takes effect and he falls asleep and has the dream.

In the morning, Ballantyne recounts his dream to Constance and Brulov. A dissolve takes us to its visualization.[9] When he says, "I can't make out what sort of a place it was," we see flickering lights, then individual eyes floating in the dark accompanied by alarming music, the camera zooming in to one eye, then more eyes appearing, dissolving into one another and becoming painted eyes on an elevated curtain (except for two eyes that still look real), disclosing a stage on which people are playing cards. Ballantyne's voice-over tells us that it seemed to be a gambling house but with no walls, just a lot of curtains with eyes painted on them. He describes a man walking around with a large pair of scissors cutting all the drapes in half—however, the visuals show only one specific eye being cut in half, which is a clear allusion to the beginning of *Un Chien Andalou* (*An Andalusian Dog*, Luis Buñuel with Salvador Dalí 1929). The cutting of the eye symbolizes castration, especially the divided subject as expressed in the field of vision—precisely what Ballantyne is trying to avoid by clinging to his primal fantasy, something he can no longer escape. The scissors are also a (large) sharp object, an emblem of his fear that his sexuality might be lethal.[10] The allusion to

Un Chien Andalou further emphasizes the connection between psychoanalysis, dreams in general (the whole of the short surrealist film simulates a dream, however, lacking a dreamer and a narrative, it remains totally open to extra-diegetic interpretations), and castrated sexuality/subjectivity in particular.

Un Chien Andalou starts with a man (Luis Buñuel) as he sharpens his razor at his balcony door and tests it on his thumb. He then opens the door and glares at the moon, which is about to be engulfed by a thin cloud. A close-up of a young woman (Simone Mareuil) appears, held by the man. She looks into the camera while he brings the razor close to her eye, opens the razor, and then holds it open. The moon is then shown covered by a thin cloud horizontally passing over, followed by a match-cut of a close-up of a hand (probably the man's) slitting the eye with the razor, the vitreous spilling out from it (which happens so quickly the viewer is led to believe it is the woman's eye, though it is the eye of a cow). The razor is like Ballantyne's (a straight razor in common use at the time), and the fact that it is a woman's eye that is being slashed is connected to Ballantyne's fear of killing a woman by just penetrating her; the moon also connotes femininity, while the thin cloud covering it suggests heterosexual intercourse.

Going back to *Spellbound*, we see the painted eye in extreme close-up superimposed on an extreme long shot of the gambling house (in the background are traces of the curtain with eyes). Ballantyne and the bearded man are seated at a table in the foreground on the right, playing cards. A girl described by Ballantyne as having hardly anything on walks around the gambling room kissing everybody, first coming to their table. When asked by Brulov if he recognizes the girl, Ballantyne says, "I'm afraid she looked a little like Constance," although she looks more like Miss Carmichael (a similarity that cannot escape us, contrary to Brulov, who cannot know what we know, as he has never seen Miss Carmichael), one of Constance's patients, a man-hater who tries to seduce every man she comes in contact with. That Ballantyne confuses her with Constance suggests not only that he is afraid of Constance's sexuality but also that he experiences it as a threat to his own well-being.[11]

Ballantyne recounts the incident with the card game. He says, "The bearded man says, 'That makes twenty-one. I win.' But when he turned up his cards, they were blank. Just then, the proprietor came in and accused him of cheating. The proprietor yelled 'This is my place. If I catch you again, I'll fix you.'" The camera zooms in to a close-up of the proprietor's covered profile, dissolving into Ballantyne's profile. The visuals show the proprietor with his head covered by a piece of white cloth, alluding to the covered face of the man (as well as that of his female lover) in René Magritte's *Duo* (1928), figuring a kiss.[12] The dissolve between the proprietor's profile and Ballantine's (as well as the phrase "this is my place") creates an analogy between Edwardes's killer (the proprietor/Murchinson) and Ballantine, pointing to the displacement of guilt. The proprietor yelling

"This is my place, if I catch you again, I'll fix you!" symbolizes the threat of the castrating father against Ballantyne's desire to take the place of the father/brother. The allusion to the painting symbolizes Ballantyne's fear of eroticism evoked by his feelings for Constance as well as his "blindness" (the covered face).

The rest of the dream segment continues to show details recounted by Ballantyne. We see the décor in Salvador Dalí's surrealist style: In the background on the left is a huge male statue in profile, recalling a witch's profile, as if sprouting from a cubist stone assemblage and hovering over the site (which might be interpreted both as Ballantyne's superego and his fear of female sexuality); in the mid-ground on the right is a high building, a chimney on its top growing roots. When he recounts seeing the masked proprietor again, hiding behind the tall chimney and holding a wheel in his hand, the camera zooms in and then focuses on the wheel he has dropped from the roof, the wheel now the sole object on the screen while the camera keeps zooming in to its hub. At this point another dissolve brings us to the next segment in which Ballantyne, seen from afar and from a high angle, flees the scene and is running down a slope with a great pair of wings chasing him. The symbol of the wheel condenses, again, the gun Murchinson killed Edwardes with, as interpreted by Constance in the end; the traumatic accident (the wheel spokes symbolizing the sharp pickets that killed Ballantyne's brother); and the danger of sex: The wheel is not round but pear-shaped, recalling the shape of the pool Constance drew on the white tablecloth, connoting a womb.[13] Thus, when the camera zooms in on the wheel hub, it clearly suggests penetration into a woman's sexual organ, precisely what Ballantyne dreads. His fear of having sex is tantamount to his fear of castration, mentioned above. Still, the part of the dream that tells us the most about Ballantyne's guilt in relation to his brother's death and its outcome—his fear of sex—was cut out of the film.

The original dream sequence as designed by Dalí and Hitchcock proved to be too lengthy and complicated, so the vast majority of what was filmed was cut during editing, leaving only about two minutes of visualization. Ingrid Bergman was heard saying that the sequence had been almost twenty minutes long prior to being cut by the producer, David Selznick.[14] The portions of the dream that were cut were intended to come after the image on the roof and before Ballantyne's escape from the slope. Ballantyne recounts that he does not remember how he got there, but in the original design of the dream he is in a ballroom. The dancers, all dressed in white, are pretending to be dancing, but they remain motionless. Dr. Brulov is the conductor of an orchestra that is playing Rimsky Korsakov's "The Snow Maiden." Ballantyne approaches Constance and asks her to dance but refuses to put down his name on her dance card. Forcefully grabbing her, they dance passionately outside the ballroom and he kisses her. Later, she turns into a sculpture. It is then that Ballantyne runs for his life, the wings belonging to the sculpture/Constance chasing him, their shadow mercilessly hitting him, the sculpture holding a book.

The only symbols representing Ballantyne's attraction to Constance that remained in the dream portrayed in the film are the design of the legs of the gambling tables, which look like those of women wearing high heels; the girl kissing the gamblers; and the shadow of the wings. The rest of the dream in its full version relating to the ski symbols—mostly the white—also represent Ballantyne's relation to Constance: "The Snow Maiden," the orchestra players dressed in white and wearing white fur hats, and Constance's white gown and blond hair all connote virginity, if not frigidity, pointing to his childhood fixation. While the white dress connotes purity, the design of the metal collar with a pointed arrow on Constance's neck represents the unconscious obstacle between the two lovers. It condenses two images: The first symbolizes the sharp pickets that killed Ballantyne's brother; the second is a phallic symbol, connoting sexual penetration. This explains Ballantyne's violent reaction to Constance in the dream—first, he refuses to put his name down in her dance card, and then he grabs her forcefully to dance with him. As previously mentioned, this is not a realization of his love for Constance (as Brulov suggests in relation to the kiss of the girl in the dream) but rather a violent reaction to it, emphasizing his horror of sex. What Ballantyne wishes is precisely to dodge the sexual act with Constance, which culminates in turning her into a statue, one that nevertheless persecutes him (the chasing wings beating down on him). The persecution imagery suggests Constance's constant presence in Ballantyne's life (even alluded to in her name, Constance[15]): She is there to stay, forcing Ballantyne to resolve his guilt complex, which means they will have sex.

Although most of the incidents showing Ballantyne's affect of horror and the symbols in the dream are associated with Edwardes's murder, the murder itself is never rendered in a flashback. In contrast, the guilt regarding the death of Ballantyne's brother is visualized in a flashback rendering his memory of the tragic event. This has to do with Ballantyne's process of subjectivization. When he and Constance are skiing, just before reaching the abyss, Ballantyne suddenly recalls the traumatic incident, which is rendered in flashback; he screams, "Now I remember, I killed my brother!" He then stops Constance from falling and while embracing her says, "I didn't kill my brother, it was an accident!" As long as Ballantyne is blinded by guilt, he is incapable of being a reliable witness in relation to Edwardes's murder. The moment he can express his traumatic memory in words—thus transposing it from the real into the symbolic—he can also identify how his unconscious misinterpreted his brother's death. As Andrew Britton ([1986] 2008: 176) suggests, this is reparation not only on the psychological level but also on a social level—the real murderer has been exposed. Saving Constance from falling over the abyss constitutes reparation for his involvement in his brother's death, now enabling a sexual relationship with her—Ballantyne's process of subjectivization is sealed and so is our awareness of it.

The Dream and Implicit Reflexivity in *Spellbound*: Subjectivization of the Apparatus

As mentioned above, when Ballantyne starts recounting his dream to Constance and Brulov, the dream imagery depicts eyes (Figure 3.2). The fact that these images appear at the beginning of the dream sequence suggests a clear analogy with the cinematic apparatus.[16] The dark space with flickering lights in it connotes a projection room, the image of the individual eye floating in the dark symbolizes the film as a gaze in that it undermines the fantasy of wholeness, the human eye symbolizes that of spectators, while the painted eyes on the curtain symbolize those of the ones creating the film's fantasy. The curtain also stands in for a "wall" that separates spectators from the screen (it also recalls movie theaters in the early days of cinema, when a curtain would rise and the film would begin), but at the same time, the camera knocks it down: The repeated dissolves and the zoom-ins seem to endlessly penetrate the space, leading us into the site of the action—the

FIGURE 3.2 Spellbound (*Alfred Hitchcock 1945*).

gambling room. This symbolizes how our eye and "body," with the help of the camera, are present in the imaginary space of the scene. However, the blank cards suggest the emptiness of the screen, its lack.

Moreover, as the eye is cut in half and another painted eye in extreme close-up is revealed (an eye inside an eye), it is superimposed on an extreme long shot of the gambling room, shown again on the background curtain with eyes being cut, the gambling room seen now in a mirror image. The superimposition creating the image of the gazing eye (looking at us) through which we see the action performed in the dream, as if the eye were transparent, or rather perforated, is designed as a mise-en-abyme within a mise-en-abyme, since the dream itself is a mis-en-abyme. The painted eyes are shown—in the distance—as pertaining to a different level of reality than the real photographed eye. This mise-en-abyme contained within the larger one (the dream) duplicates and reflects the dream as well as the cinematic apparatus. And, as the dream is about a guilt complex, the question is: What does the camera feel guilty about?

We argue that guilt has something to do with the imaginary realization of subjective fantasies (conscious but particularly unconscious) regarding different positions of the subject in relation to the desire of the Other, in particular that of the mother. The eye imagery and guilt feelings stem from the re-enactment of the primal scene, as explained in the previous chapters—allowing the viewer to see/be in different positions. This suggests that the eye of the camera is always subjective, imbued with human desire and sexuality (the camera zooming in on the wheel hub, revealing a black hole, suggesting sexua). The dream thus problematizes the omnipotent flexibility of the camera not only to be simultaneously in all possible positions but also and particularly to inscribe spectators in a space that reenacts inscription in the primal scene. The theme of guilt here is associated with the desire of the camera, as well as its fantasmatic "success," to do just that. The protagonists' failure to correctly identify the desire of the female characters (representing the mother) and the reality around them, to "read" it in the symbolic sense, as well as their inability to be reliable witnesses, thus signify not only the guilt of the camera but also the way *Spellbound* undermines the power of film as fantasy to conceal cinema's own lack. Ballantyne may finally be cured and exonerated from his guilt, but the film ends with a hand holding a revolver pointed at the camera and shooting it (we do not see Murchinson when he shoots himself, only a close-up of the revolver pointed at the camera—as well as at the spectators).

In many films featuring one or more dreams of the protagonist, there are different variations of what we term "the flawed eye": lacrimation, wounds, blindness, and so on. Thus, what in Lacanian terms symbolizes castration, which *is* the condition for entry into the symbolic, entailing renouncing the fantasy of wholeness and incest with the mother, in these films it is the flawed or blemished eye/s that suggest the films undermining their own capacity to provide a regressive fantasy. Furthermore, the films thus suggest that this capacity is a scam, represented in *Spellbound* by the empty cards and the gambling house. The eyes being cut suggests a kind of impossibility to really see, namely, to represent reality for what it is through the camera's eyes, what we refer to as "the crisis of testimony": Metaphors or metonyms of the cinematic apparatus, such as eyes, mirrors, lenses, windows, frames, glasses, microscope, and so on, all symbolize limited optical instruments. All these manifestations symbolize "castration," both of the cinematic apparatus (the eye of the camera) and of the subject/spectator. Keeping in mind that the dream is Ballantyne's testimony about Edwardes's murder, which he witnessed (an idea ridiculed by Murchinson) but cannot remember, we cannot ignore the desire of the eye of the camera to witness the murder, to reach a place that our body or eye cannot be, undermined by Ballantyne's amnesia. Also, the camera cannot really penetrate the human mind, film the unconscious; it can only shoot from the outside. The film thus challenges its own ability to render a dream. In many films with dreams, there are references to religion (especially Catholicism). In the religious Judeo-Catholic discourse, God is omnipresent and omnipotent, the subject never being able to escape his Almighty ability to see into the human soul. The fact that in *Spellbound* there is no flashback of the murder emphasizes the failure of the camera to witness, which taps into its guilt in desiring the godlike ability that no human has and creating an illusionistic fantasmatic experience for spectators. The allusion to *Un Chien Andalou* as well emphasizes the implicit reflexivity of the dream in relation to the cinematic apparatus by evincing its conflation with the eye of the camera/subject being "castrated." The woman's close-up gazing directly into the camera in *Un Chien Andalou*, her eye then being slashed, makes us aware of the camera's existence; both the eye of the camera and ours, rather than being aligned in a fantasmatic space, signify a gaze (in the Lacanian sense): the gaze of the Other, split from the eye of the subject/spectator. Here the gaze of the Other is clearly associated with an anonymous woman representing the mother. The value of this meta-aspect of the film, which might remain inaccessible to spectators at large in terms of consciousness, consists in that it emphasizes subjectivization, namely how narrative film can both engage us with its fantasy and affect our unconscious regarding being free from the clutches of the Other's desire. The guilt associated with the cinematic apparatus thus points to its power of doing just the opposite. Like in the other Hitchcock films of this period, he is very particular in dismantling the fantasy of remaining trapped in the Other's desire, on the one hand; on the other, he maintains a careful economy of desire/fantasy, linking his protagonist's desire to consuming his love for a woman as an adult. It thus involves us in a process that, although we remain partly unconscious of, we nevertheless understand the dire consequences of our protagonist's fixation and the value of being released from it.

The Conversation

Harry Caul (Gene Hackman) is a surveillance expert, a loner who runs his own company in San Francisco. He is obsessed with his own privacy: His almost bare apartment behind its triple-locked door has a burglar alarm. He uses pay phones to make calls, claims to have no home telephone, and his office is enclosed in wire mesh in a corner of a much larger warehouse. His only relationship is with his girlfriend Amy (Teri Garr), who knows nothing about him. He has one hobby—playing a tenor saxophone to jazz recordings. Harry insists he is not interested in or responsible for the actual content of the conversations he records or the use to which his clients put them; however, he is tormented by guilt over a past wiretap job that resulted in the murder of three people. His sense of guilt is augmented by his devout Catholicism.

Harry, his colleague Stan (John Cazale), and some freelance associates have taken on the task of bugging the conversation of a couple—Marc (Frederic Forrest) and Ann (Cindy Williams). As the couple walks through crowded Union Square in San Francisco surrounded by a cacophony of background noise, they discuss fears that they are being watched and mention a discreet meeting in a hotel (room 773) in a few days. The challenging task of recording this conversation is accomplished by multiple surveillance operatives located in different positions around Union Square. After Harry has merged and filtered the different tapes, the result is a sound recording in which the young man says to the woman, "He'd kill us if he got the chance." Harry feels increasingly uneasy about what may happen to the couple once his client, the woman's husband, "The Director" (Robert Duvall), hears the tape. Would he kill them if he had a chance? Harry goes to confession and tells the priest he fears a young couple might be hurt because of him. He further tells him that a similar event happened to him in the past but insists he was not responsible.

During a party held in Harry's warehouse, Bernie (Allen Garfield), a fellow professional who claims to have known Harry in New York, says Harry was famous there and everyone was impressed with the job he did. He recounts that Harry used to work in the attorney general's office and managed to bug conversations between the president of a phony welfare fund and his accountant on a fishing boat (all that time wondering how Harry did it). The accountant and his family (wife and child) were murdered as a result because the fund president was convinced the accountant had betrayed him. Harry does not reveal how he managed to do the job and, again, insists he was not responsible for the unfolding of the tragic event. However, it is clear that he left New York shortly after to move to San Francisco. Bernie, who wants to become Harry's partner, tapes a private conversation Harry had earlier in the evening with Meredith (Elizabeth MacRae), who seeks his company to gain his trust. Harry feels his privacy has been violated and kicks everyone out except for Meredith, who insists on staying. She takes him to bed, undresses both of them, and tries to make love to him. But all this time Harry keeps listening to the tapes, finally synchronizing with his own voice the sentence, "*He'd* kill us if he got the chance," and then saying, "Oh God, what have I done?" He tells Meredith that the woman sounds frightened and he must destroy the tapes; he cannot let this happen again. He then falls asleep and we view his dream, often interrupted to show us his nightmarish affect.

The dream starts with undecipherable metallic sounds, seemingly from a bugged conversation, and Ann in constant motion in medium close-up, recalling the beginning of the film. The imagery is covered in fog and stairs appear in what seems to be a park. Ann flees up the stairs, realizing she has been followed. Harry appears with his back to the camera, looking at Ann. He follows her, reaches the stairs, and calls to her ("Can you hear me?"). He introduces himself and begs her to listen to him. She turns around and he reassures her she need not be afraid. He tells her that she does not know him, but he knows her and "there isn't much to say" about him. He stops for a minute and she starts to walk again, looking at him. He tells her that when he was a young child his left hand and foot were paralyzed, and his mother used to put him in a hot soaking tub. One time the doorbell rang, and she went to open the door. He slid down the bathtub until the water reached his chin and nose. When he "woke up" he says his body was all greasy from the holy oil his mother had applied to it, and that he remembered being disappointed that he had survived. He goes on to tell her that when he was five his father introduced him to a friend of his and for no reason, Harry started hitting him with all his strength. The friend died a year later. Then he says, "He'll kill you if he gets a chance," adding that he is not afraid of death but of murder.

Another segment of the dream starts. Harry is standing in front of a hotel door numbered 773. Daunting music accompanies the visuals. He opens the door, goes in, and a series of very short consecutive shots show Ann standing by the wall, her husband running toward her, attacking her, while she screams and tries to defend herself. The hotel room is photographed from the balcony door, its thin curtain splashed with blood. On the wall of the bathroom are also traces of blood.

Harry wakes up and discovers that Meredith has stolen his tapes. He is angry, but "The Director," who commissioned the bugging, sends him a message to come get his payment and forget all about it. Harry decides to go to the hotel where Marc and Ann arranged to meet and takes a room adjacent to 773. He drills a hole in the bathroom wall (under the sink, near the toilet) and inserts a listening device. The voices are a little blurred, but he manages to hear the husband playing the tapes to his wife and her saying, "I can't stand it." Angry and frustrated, Harry takes his headphones off. Agitated and helpless, he goes out to the balcony and looks through the rather opaque window separating the two balconies. He sees the silhouette of Ann's husband attacking her, his blood-smeared left hand leaving marks on the glass. Harry panics. He swiftly enters his room, forcefully shutting the door and curtain. He turns on the television and tries to cover his eyes and ears. But that is not enough—he dives under the bedclothes and covers his head with a pillow. Too agitated, he jumps up and wallows in the corner, again covering his ears. After a while he breaks into room 773 looking for signs of the violent event he has witnessed but finds nothing. The room appears spotless, and so does the bathroom. He glares at the toilet seat, lifts the lid, flushes the water, and is horrified to discover streams of blood gushing from it, covering the toilet seat and the floor. Harry flees the room and later tries to see the husband but is blocked off. However, he sees Ann surrounded by journalists. As he looks at her from afar, he passes a newsstand, his eye catching a headline reporting her husband has died in an accident. He recreates in his mind the murder in the hotel: the husband playing the tapes for his wife, she consoling him, and then her lover killing him. They cleaned the room and staged the accident. This means that when the couple were in Union Square they were talking about killing the woman's husband—Harry's client (meaning "He'd kill *us* if he got the chance"). The last scene of the film shows Harry playing his saxophone. He is interrupted by a phone call from his client's assistant (Harrison Ford), who tells him that Ann and Marc know that he knows and not to look any further into the matter, concluding, "We'll be listening." Harry goes on a frantic search for a bugging device, tearing up his apartment but finding nothing. He sits amid the wreckage, playing the only thing in his apartment left intact: his saxophone.

Dreaming and Guilt in *The Conversation*

In referring to Freud's conclusion regarding the primal scene, Ned Lukacher writes,

> Psychoanalysis begins with the recognition that the recollected image is not the repetition of the same, that recollection is not a mode of self-presence. Whether the scene actually happened or not is immaterial, for what analysis has access to is the way unconscious phantasy structures the scene, not its "exact repetition." Freud no longer presupposes that what-is can be represented before a subject. Freud turns from the univocal perspective of the subject *of* the scene to the structure of the subject's displacement *in* the scene. (1986: 56–57; italics in the original)

The dream sequence in *The Conversation*, which appears toward the last third of the plot, attests to Harry's behavior being dictated by the structure of his fundamental unconscious fantasy regarding the primal scene and his inscription in his mother's desire. Hence, the misinterpretation of what he sees and hears: the wish to be constantly looked after by his mother, to be her sole object of desire: It fixes him in the position of a helpless and needy child (that he might have been a paralytic for a while only augmented this experience), unable to recognize the reality around him and act in accordance with it.[17] His involvement in the welfare fund affair that resulted in the murder of the accountant's family generated a guilt complex, exacerbating both his feelings of helplessness and his inability to interpret the reality around him. The first segment of the dream connects his experience as a child—when he tells Ann about two memories (of almost drowning in the bathroom and of hitting his father's friend. The former alludes to his neediness, the latter to a displacement of the father to his friend, expressing his anger and frustration)—and his guilt complex; the guilt complex is expressed in the paraphrasing of Marc's sentence ("He'd kill us if he got a chance") as "He'll kill you if he gets a chance," adding that he is not afraid of dying but of murder. The paraphrase points to his inability to interpret reality (he thinks Ann's husband is planning to kill her, while the reality is that Ann and her lover plan to kill her husband), while his fear of murder suggests not only his wish to caution Ann but also his own affect in relation to the murder of the accountant's family—he feels like a murderer. This last sentence leads to the next segment of the dream, rendered in consecutive images showing Harry's "foretelling" of the future (the misinterpretation of reality): Ann seems defenseless in view of her husband's violence toward her in the hotel, thus affirming Harry's apprehensions.

The structure of Harry's fundamental unconscious fantasy in both parts of the dream is rendered in terms of space. He is either at a considerable distance from the other characters (symbolizing his fear of separation from his mother) or closed in, separated from the action (excluded from the range of her desire, directed at a third party), his vision partly blocked. In the first segment, Ann keeps distancing herself from him—the closer he gets to her, the further she detaches herself from him. In the second segment, seen from the inside of the hotel room, the door opens, and Harry enters the room; the next shot shows the husband running toward Ann, standing frightened with her back to the sliding balcony door. Then, seen from the balcony, a transparent curtain with traces of blood on it appears separating the balcony from the room; through the curtain, two beds can be discerned. Then Ann, fleeing toward the door, her husband chasing her, and a third character are all struggling with each other. The dream ends with an image of a toilet, traces of blood smeared on the wall above it. Again, Harry is being positioned as an outsider—he is not in the bathroom but sees the image through the open door.

This structuring of Harry's fundamental fantasy (although not an "exact repetition") characterizes him all through the film, until the end.[18] He must remain his mother's sole object of desire, fearing abandonment, separation. If he was indeed half paralyzed, he was helpless to begin with, which made him more dependent on her presence. The fear of being abandoned by his mother (separated from her) thus constituted the traumatic (expressed in his mother leaving the bathroom and leaving him to "drown" as she went to answer the door, directing her attention at someone else). Whether his near-drowning in the bathtub happened or not is beside the point; his desire to be included in her desire by always caring for him and staying by his side is expressed by experiencing her leaving as traumatic as well as by the memory of her spreading oil on his body, meaning that she followed the sacrament—anointment of the sick in the Catholic Church. Thus, the traumatic separation, as well as the gap in his memory (when he lost consciousness in the bathtub), is counterpointed by the soothing memory that she was a good and caring mother—upon returning to the bathroom, she did not neglect to apply oil to his body and was by his side when he "woke up."

Later in Harry's life, bathing and anointment as a testament of unification with the mother was translated into a fantasy of cleanliness and chasteness (turning every woman he meets into a caring mother). In the Union Square opening sequence, he is touched by Ann's caring and compassionate words when she notices a homeless person lying on a public bench, her tone filled with grief, saying, "Look, it's terrible." When Marc tells her he is not hurting anyone, she replies "Neither are we," then continues,

> Oh god, every time I see one of these old guys, I think the same thing.... I always think that it was once someone's baby boy and he had a mother and father who loved him and now there he is, half dead on a park bench and where are his mother and father and all his uncles now, anyway that what I always think.

At this point, we no longer see the homeless person or the couple but Harry walking toward the surveillance van. Then we hear Marc saying that many homeless people died during the newspaper strike because they lacked the paper to keep them warm and safe.

The couple's reaction to the homeless person makes them look innocent (they are "not hurting anyone") and caring. Moreover, when Ann says she imagines the homeless man as a baby being cared for, the camera focuses on Harry so that her words resonate with Harry's own condition. A visual analogy with the homeless person on the bench is created when Harry is seen stretched on a camp bed in his warehouse while listening to the recording of the couple's conversation before the dream (after Meredith tucks him in like a mother) as well as in that his apartment is without furniture. In Harry's mind, her words conform with his conception of the ideal mother as conceived by the Christian iconography of Madonna and Child. Indeed,

Harry's private associative world derives from his Catholic upbringing. In it the Madonna and Child represent not only the good and righteous but also an ideal relationship of mother and child, never to be separated. In his imaginary, Harry interprets Ann's words in accordance with this ideal (again, it must be noted that spatially she remains far away from him), Ann being a displacement of his mother. His own displacement in the fantasy scene provokes a continuous experience of a helpless child in need of care and attention, while his present situation of "homelessness" (expressed in his identification with the homeless person on the bench) symbolizes his mother's desertion or rather his fear of separation.

Harry's desire to be his mother's sole object of desire is linked to a wish to dispose of any third party interfering between them—hence his "confession" to Ann in the dream that he hit his father's friend (a displacement of his father) who died a year later, expressing his wish to eliminate any rival in his life.[19] The fact that the father's friend die implies that Harry believes, as a child does, that he has some sort of superpower that might harm people. The fear of materializing the wish that his rival be dead evoked primal guilt feelings that after his involvement in the welfare fund affair developed into a guilt complex. The traumatic (fear of being abandoned by his mother, separated from her) is expressed in the dream not only by Harry's inability to unite with Ann, who keeps distancing herself from him, but also through his disillusion with the women in his life. At first, he experiences them as caring mothers (regardless of what they really are) and later as deserting (his girlfriend, Amy, and Meredith), treacherous (Meredith), and murderous (Ann).

Harry's fundamental subjective structure mostly involves a relation between the traumatic real (the lack) and the imaginary (erroneous scenarios whose function is to veil any experience involving lack). It includes a twofold manifestation: On the one hand, he experiences himself as victim, paralyzed (expressed in the second segment of the dream, when he positions himself as a helpless and unreliable witness, unable to act). Toward the end of the film, when he imagines the murdered husband wrapped in transparent plastic, the imagery associates Harry with the victim, rendered by his wearing a transparent raincoat during most of the film. On the other hand, he imagines himself being able to overcome all separating obstacles (originally the walls of the bathroom in his childhood). This fantasy is manifested in both his profession as a surveillance professional and as a listener uninterested in the content of the conversations he bugs because in his unconscious fundamental fantasy all he wants is to bridge the gap, the separation from his mother. Thus, all the situations/scenes in which he finds himself in his adult life, with assorted variations, are reenactments of his double position in his primal scene. The first segment of the dream visually reflects his inability to bridge the distance from his mother. The second segment visually reflects his wish to separate between his parents, who are displaced to the couple (the wish to come between them is symbolized by the separate beds in the room), as well as being helpless to protect his mother. However, the curtain with blood is a symbol of separation and the blood one of castration and potential murder. They express both his guilt (afraid of murder because he feels responsible for the murder of the accountant's family) and his fear of castration. Therefore, the transparent raincoat he wears might also be interpreted as an analogy between him and Marc the murderer, whom Harry imagines must wear plastic to avoid being covered in blood and to cover his traces. Also, this is the reason why Harry is horrified at the sight of blood on the murderer's hands—it taps into his experience as a murderer.

Thus, the dream reveals that despite his confession to the priest, Harry does feel responsible for the murder of the accountant and his family, which also explains his reluctance to tell his fellow professionals where he was while listening in on the conversation. It reflects uneasiness on Harry's part related to his experience in the affair as an actual fulfillment of his fantasy of being omnipotent and ubiquitous in relation to his inclusion in his mother's desire (in terms of space) at all cost—although not physically present, nevertheless able to hear what is being said. At the party, Harry seems very pleased when Bernie lets everyone know that he, Harry, managed to do the impossible when he bugged the boat in the middle of a big lake and was able to tape the conversation between the president of the welfare fund and his accountant. Although Harry does mention several times in the film that people were murdered because of him (though he is unwilling to assume any responsibility), the more Bernie pressures him to recount the details of the affair, the stronger his refusal to provide details. This is not because he does not want to divulge his professional secrets—he boasts about other techniques he uses, like a big telescope (an object enabling *seeing* that was not used in the welfare fund affair)—but because the "realization" of his fantasy ended in murder, hence his guilt feelings turning into a guilt complex. When the possibility of another murder surfaces (in the couple's conversation), it constitutes for Harry the surfacing of his traumatic experience in the welfare fund affair. His paraphrasing the sentence to Ann ("He'll kill you if he gets a chance") reflects his fear of repeating the same mistake, actualizing his unconscious fantasy once more, that he will again end up with "blood on his hands"; he thus tries to redeem himself by warning Ann. However, the guilt complex together with adherence to his infantile fantasy are the cause of his misinterpretation of the couple's conversation in Union Square. His ambiguous position in his unconscious—as both victim and murderer—precipitates him confusing the murderer with the victim when interpreting the conversation.

His guilt complex thus becomes an absolute impediment in his reading of reality, exacerbating the element of paralysis and helplessness (the traumatic). And, it is this dynamic that constitutes the spectators' resistance to partake in his infantile fantasy: We might not be aware of what exactly this fantasy consists of, but we are aware of its consequences (Harry's misreading of the reality around him). This awareness increases as the film progresses, which is its way of keeping us out of Harry's primal scene as well as the film's. Unlike other narrative films that first inscribe us into its primal scene structure only to later thrust us out of it, *The Conversation* blocks our way into such a structure to begin with. This is evident in the way it uses space as well as other cinematic devices. For example, the doors, windows, and walls of the hotel do not function as elements to be overcome but as barriers rendering Harry totally incapacitated, while keeping us at a distance. The second segment of Harry's dream depicting a murder about to happen seems to signify his wish to be able to foretell the future so that he can be exonerated from guilt. But the editing of his entrance into the interior of the room symbolizes Harry's position as both insider and outsider as well as both victim and murderer, not being able to recognize his actual position in reality—that he is about to witness a murder committed by the people he thinks are the victims. At the same time, it blocks our entrance into the filmic space. We first see Harry standing outside the room, then the scene strangely jump-cuts to its interior, showing the door from an insider's POV (although physically Harry is still on the exterior side of the door); only later is Harry shown opening the door and entering the room (similarly, there is a jump-cut from his location outside the window to the bathroom at the time of the murder in the hotel room). His position in the dream as both outsider and insider thus foretells not his ability to prevent a murder but rather the opposite. The jump-cuts and the complication of the POV, as well as the overall treatment of space, thus hinder our being complicit in Harry's unrealistic fantasy of preventing a murder. Being completely unaware of what is at work in his unconscious, Harry treats the dream as a prophecy, which the films make sure we do not go along with. When he finally understands that he has misrecognized the identities of the victim and the murderer, it is too late.[20] During Ann's husband's murder, he remains an outsider, "uninvolved," like in the murder of the accountant's family and, what is more, a helpless child unable to deal with the reality around him. Megan Ratner (2001) too notes that Harry's position in the murder scene recalls that of the Wolf Man[21]—outside the scene, as a paralyzed viewer, or a listener that no one is aware of, interpreting the scene according to his own fantasy: "Harry's final bugging of the hotel room resembles a primal scene; he tries to shrink himself—huddling fetus—like under the bathroom sink, directly next to the toilet—just like a child would." Harry's comportment during the actual murder scene indeed attests to the fact that his intention is not to prevent the murder (Why does he not interfere? Why wait until it is all over to inspect the murder scene?) but to spatially reenact his position in the primal scene as well as in the traumatic past event for which he feels responsible (his location when he was bugging the boat, which led to the murder of the accountant's family); in both cases, he is "trapped" as listener, not able to do anything. Spectators, on the other hand, are led to resist this entrapment. In addition to the treatment of space and the editing, which hinder our entrence into the filmic space, the fact that Harry does not act in accordance with his overt desire to prevent the murder disengages us from this desire. Another challenge for the spectators is that, "Harry, a character Coppola himself feared would be impossible for viewers to sympathize with, is the film's central figure, a man so obsessed with making himself unavailable to others that he almost completely eradicated his own personality" (Johnson 1977: 134). Unlike *Spellbound*, which offers us a desire with which we engage throughout (being able to fulfill mature love and sexuality), here, contrary to other thrillers, the desire of the protagonist to prevent a murder is gradually undermined until it is shattered in the end. Moreover, although the film makes it hard for us to accept Harry's reclusiveness and secrecy, nevertheless, we do want to be given the reason behind them. But as the film progresses, it becomes clear that it is we, the spectators, who are entrusted with the task of solving this riddle. And it is only through analyzing Harry's dreams, as well as his comportment, that we understand that his reclusiveness and secrecy are connected to guilt, that, in fact, how he feels about his involvement in the murder of the accountant's family renders him incapable of speaking about his life (which he does only in his dream) and thus makes him a recluse.

Harry's guilt as a witness concealing how he managed to bug the boat and listen to the conversation in the welfare fund affair renders him unable to use language as a vehicle of testifying and assuming responsibility. We begin to suspect that his avoidance of social life (the party in his warehouse is his only social event, and it ends in conflict when he feels his privacy is violated) might have something to do with this past event. Indeed, his reclusiveness attests to his difficulty with the transition into the symbolic order, his affect exposing his inner life, mostly his imaginary and traumatic through the blurred noises and the cacophony of sounds and voices he listens to (which are obvious to spectators). Spectators might not consciously understand the different layers of Harry' guilt (stemming from his wish to dispose of all rivals contending for his mother's attention and his involvement in the welfare fund affair, all boiling down to the guilt regarding the disavowal of the desire that is in him), but we do feel and later understand that he *is* guilty. And if we want to fully understand these layers of guilt, we must interpret Harry's dream and his affect in it (as well as ours)—as we have done—which is the only key to the interpretation of his inner life that helps us understand that by closing himself off from the symbolic, Harry in fact blocks any ethical or credible dimension of being a witness to events happening in reality. In his dream, when he tells Ann about the two childhood incidents as he remembers them, she remains silent, like a priest in confession (rather than in a real conversation). Harry's habit of going to confession is another way of avoiding communication (the symbolic), creating the structure of a scene in which only he is heard so that he can be cleansed from guilt. In fact, the act of confession allows him to ward off responsibility. Robert K. Johnson (1977: 136) rightly notes that religion is not the path to vindication for Harry. In fact, "Harry suffers from an extreme *desolation of the spirit*, a nearly pathological loneliness and *guilt*" (Denby 1974: 131; italics in the original).

Harry becomes aware of his misinterpretation of reality when he discovers that the husband is the victim, and not the couple, which for spectators constitutes a clarification of his guilt. Along with Harry, we realize that the way he listened to the couple's words stemmed from his desire to find one definite meaning in the paradigmatic structure of the sentence, due to his guilt. If he had considered the likelihood that there was more than one possibility in the paradigmatic, his ethical position would have been that of a psychoanalyst, whose attention focuses on the paradigmatic: "The analyst who *really listens* is not interested in syntax, in the way the words are linked together in order to produce meaning, but in the words themselves, in their respective positions—the proximity, the distance, the intervals which constitute the fundamental relations that syntax most often veils" (Roustang 1983: 21–2, quoted in Lukacher 1986: 188, our italics). While the sentence, "He'd kill us if he got the chance," cannot be changed in terms of syntax, it is the way it is listened to that makes the difference, one achieved by its paradigmatic aspect in a wider context. When the context is only what is being said in the couple's conversation, Harry interprets the sentence as "He'd *kill* us if he got the chance" (meaning "we are in danger of being killed"), as a threat to the couple. Though she is unfaithful to her husband, Ann and her lover say they are not harming anyone; moreover, Harry's desire dictates the way he listens to Ann: Projecting his feelings for his mother onto her, he cannot bear that she be harmed. In the wider context of the whole film, we learn more about the couple and realize, with Harry, the difference in reading the paradigmatic, namely that "*He*'d kill *us* if he got the chance" means "We have to kill him first."

Harry's subjectivization thus resides in a different kind of listening, which for spectators becomes a "tutor code" for "listening" to a film as well as listening to our inner voice. At the end of the film, when he realizes that he is being listened to, he wrecks his apartment trying in vain to find a bugging device, suspecting it might even be hidden in a figurine of the Madonna. After a short hesitation, he finally breaks the holy figurine, the romantic ideal of the mother in Catholicism, only to find that it is hollow. Having found no device, he returns to playing his saxophone, this time sitting in a corner, his apartment almost empty, his walls stripped of wallpaper and plaster, the wooden floor ripped up, and the little furniture he had torn apart, all turned into a pile of debris. He plays to himself without a record, which signifies that he is finally ready to really listen to himself, his inner self, rather than to other people's conversations. He seems to understand that he has been persecuted by his own subjectivity. The fact that Harry reconstructs the events that happened, including the murder, in his imagination leads us to believe that his imaginary has been shaken, which constitutes a first step in repositioning himself in the symbolic, an ethical position in contrast to his position as a surveillance expert.

The Dream and Implicit Reflexivity in *The Conversation*: The Ethics of the Apparatus

Until the end of the film, because of Harry's advanced technological devices we are led by his interpretation of events, which is a subjective, distorted organization posing as reality; the only clues pointing to this reality as being distorted by his fantasy are provided in the dream. Harry's relationship with the Other is mediated through technical and inanimate devices for the purpose of surveillance, in which he places all his professional confidence. These devices help Harry simultaneously bridge the distance between him and the Other and keep people at bay, thus maintaining his illusion of omnipotence. The distance between the surveillant and the surveilled is overcome by a telescope that can get so close to someone as to show their lips while speaking; interference in sound and vision is overcome by amplification and isolation of the relevant voices, the mixing process. Together they are meant to provide the perfect surveillance. However, as the opening sequence already suggests, such an achievement is only technically possible. Just the parts of the conversation recorded in proximity can be made out. The bits of the couple's conversation when listened to and recorded from afar (like those of the man holding the telescope) sound like a cacophony of electronic interference; when Harry finally manages to "clear" the tapes, especially the drumming noise that interferes with what was being said, he gets the sentence, "He'd kill us if he got the chance"; we are thus trapped in the illusion that he has managed to isolate the core of the conversation. We go along with his ambition as he declares that during the surveillance process what is important to him is the *quality of sound* and not the content (he never tries to connect what he hears to what he sees or listens to).[22] But as we have explained, this sentence carries both the subjectivity of the couple and of Harry; the technical isolation process therefore can be read as a metaphor of how Harry isolates and disconnects all elements interfering with his own fixation/fantasy.

The difference between the syntactical and the paradigmatic referred to above also reflects the gap between the fragmentary nature of film and its syntactical, coherent organization: The limited, imperfect, fragmentary relationship between image and sound (the two different trajectories—visual and auditory), the split between them, as well as the ambiguity of the image that interprets the sound, or vice versa, are all united in classical narrative into cohesive meaning.[23] Furthermore, the telescope connotes the camera's ability to get as close as it wishes to its object (the close-up or the extreme CU), uprooting it from its context, rendering it as either fetish or (traumatic) gaze, thus suggesting the scopic drive. The lips that the telescope can reach suggest the erogenous zone of the oral drive; the interruptions in the voices being bugged and recorded seem to render the invocatory drive. But, as we have repeatedly argued, this fragmentary apparatus has the power to phenomenologically situate spectators in an imaginary position that "includes" us, correlative to the primal scene fantasy, in a way that makes all gaps between its various links disappear, which the film tries to avoid from the outset.

The fragmentary relationship between image and sound suggests not so much cinema's limited technical abilities (we know what cinema can achieve technically and technologically) as its limited ability to render reality, because it is always infused with subjectivity (unconscious desires and fantasies) as well as the complexity of subjectivity. Hence the meaningful symbols in Harry's dream regarding his guilt (in connection with his position in space): They are expressed in the relationship between sound and image, pointing to the gap between the advancement of technology and the human experience. Harry thinks the couple is in danger of being killed, when in fact the conversation forebodes the killing of the husband. As we have shown, this misinterpretation is based on his misreading of the relationship between sound and image (the homeless example). And because of it, Harry also misinterprets the prophetic portion of his dream. Johnson (1977: 138) notes that the argument regarding the interpretation of the whole film through Harry's limited point of view is tantamount to one about his limited ability to listen.[24] Hence the film's style: It expresses his subjectivity, which distorts the events happening in reality, like in other meta-films.

Two main cinematic sources are evident in this respect: Hitchcock's authorship and European modernism. Harry's character is a mixture of two famous still photographers in cinema, L. B. Jeffries (James Stewart) in Hitchcock's *Rear Window* (1954) and Thomas (David Hemmings) in Michelangelo Antonioni's *Blow-Up* (1966).[25] In *Rear Window*, the protagonist and his technical equipment (alluded to by Harry's telescopic device in *The Conversation*) are limited in terms of space but can still get to the truth and solve a murder that has no witnesses. Coppola was obviously more influenced by Thomas's character. As Johnson (1977: 143) notes, *Blow-Up* was an important inspiration for *The Conversation*, particularly the scene with the blowups expressing the protagonist's conviction that his camera inadvertently witnessed a murder, one that Antonioni undermines. What Thomas realizes at the end of the film through his participation in the mime tennis game is that photography is an art form pertaining to human imagination and desire; similarly, cinema is an art form, not a representation of reality. In *The Conversation*, there are a few allusions in the Union Square surveillance scene to this topic in *Blow-Up*: the mime performed by a young man; the homeless man (social awareness documentary vs. entertainment fiction); two girls fixing their makeup (fashion), not noticing Harry's assistant taking their photo with erotic instructions. *The Conversation* adds to *Blow-Up* the art of sound, with the vocal jazz music performed at the square and the African drumming.

In terms of the relationship between "objective" reality and the filmic apparatus, *The Conversation* falls somewhere between *Rear Window* and *Blow-Up*. In *Rear Window*, what the protagonist, a photojournalist (who would take any risk to "get the shot"), thinks he has seen through his telescopic camera lens is correlative to a murder being committed; in *Blow-Up*, the protagonist is a fashion still photographer whose ambition is to produce a book of documentary stills, but no such correlative exists because there is no body to be found and hence there is no proof of any murder; in *The Conversation*, we are led to believe there was a real murder but no one to witness it and no devices to record it. Harry's reconstruction at the end of the film of the events as they might have happened remains in the imaginary. The ethical therefore resides not in the ability or inability to record reality by eliminating subjectivity from the operation of the camera and other devices but solely in the decisions made by their operator, subjective in nature but owing an ethical dimension:

> [Coppola] points out that no matter what they may try to tell themselves, people who deal primarily with technological equipment, whether they be surveillance men, scientists, or filmmakers, have definite moral responsibilities. He also points out that although modern man has made awesome technological progress, he is still—even with his inventions—pathetically unable to understand the human experience, or himself. (Johnson 1977: 144)

Thus, *The Conversation* does not restrict itself to the idea of the shortcomings of the cinematic apparatus, it being only a subjective art form reflected in style (Bazin vs. Pasolini). The protagonist cannot get to the truth because of his *fixation* in relation to the desire of the Other, engrained in a strict religious indoctrination regarding good and evil resulting in guilt (as we shall see in Chapter 4, this notion underlies *Fellini 8½*). This blocks any ability to see reality for what it is, from being a witness to events occurring in the subject's proximity. The technological apparatus cannot scientifically mediate between the human spirit and the world, or God, to know the truth (as religion pretends to), but it can mediate between subjectivities, which constitutes the ethical aspect of film: the subjectivity of the characters, of the filmmaker, and of the spectators. Neither can it represent reality or be a testimonial vehicle in its brute sense ("the real"). "Reality" in *The Conversation* is thus more of a Lacanian one in the sense that testimony can be achieved only through a symbolic grid (language as well as other forms of communication and expression), at the heart of which there is lack. In other words, testimonial inability like the one in *The Conversation* is tied up with the fixed position of the protagonist/subject in the primal scene; realizing this connection also means that it must be dissolved—the subject must accept castration and move on to a different kind of "listening." In terms of using the filmic apparatus, this means that the filmmaker must recognize his or her desire, that is, use the apparatus ethically.

Using the apparatus ethically means not being trapped in the Other's desire. We might recall Hamlet again, who, trapped in his mother's desire, needs the players in the mise-en-abyme to be his mediators, to "reenact" his father's murder that had no witnesses. This re-enactment functions as a testimonial vehicle, causing the murderer of his father to expose himself. The silence surrounding an event that has no witnesses to testify about it remains without accountability. The fact that Hamlet himself cannot *speak* the truth in public, weaving around himself an endless web of words, has to do with his Oedipal guilt, with being a prisoner of his mother's desire, which is what happens to Harry in *The Conversation*. Although Harry is not much of a speaker, certainly not a rhetor like Hamlet, he *is* trapped in a web of words and voices of others he cannot make out because of his guilt feelings and his fixation. The difference between the two protagonists is that Hamlet knows the truth but cannot bring himself to be an "accuser," while Harry, who only thinks he knows the truth, a priori cannot be a reliable witness. Hamlet uses the players and the medium to expose the truth that only he and the audience are aware of. Conversely, by letting Hamlet direct them, the players bring him face to face with his Oedipal guilt. In *The Conversation*, the truth remains somewhat evasive (all we have is the newspaper headline). What is important is that Harry can at this point imagine a different course of action; he recognizes that he was misled by his fixation, which may count as a first step toward acknowledging his desire—a beginning of subjectivization. Using the filmic apparatus, therefore, involves first, recognizing the filmmaker's desire, and second, using the apparatus ethically. The filmmaker's command over the organization and design of his film is evinced in *The Conversation* by the fact that we hear the recording of the conversation in numerous scenes that do not feature the couple but other activities; this reflects the gap between sound and image, creating awareness of the manipulation of the apparatus by the filmmaker in general—that he is the one calling the shots in accordance with his desire. Indeed, in *The Conversation*, tackling the primal scene and the testimonial crisis reflects the ethical aspect of the complex relationship between image and sound, how it is used and manipulated.

The key to the interpretation of the film, as well as of Harry's characterization, is provided in the dream, but we can interpret the dream as well as the possible unfolding of the plot, its denouement, only retroactively, which emphasizes the act of manipulation in film. The dream as mise-en-abyme thus has a double function as a rhetorical device: the key to interpretation (which remains open, inconclusive) and implicit reflexivity.[26] In both cases, it owns an ethical dimension. As Ann Jefferson (1983: 204) argues in relation to the reflexive function of the mise-en-abyme—no matter if placed at the beginning,[27] middle, or end of a film—it always reflects the act of interpretation itself, rectifying misreadings pertaining to the reality of the film by both the protagonist and spectators, although such misreadings do not necessarily coincide. In *The Conversation* they do. The "prophetic" dream/mise-en-abyme appears at the middle of the film and the viewer has no choice but to go along with the protagonist's wrong interpretation. All we know is what Harry knows, what he tells in confession, and that he is afraid of murder. As mentioned before, it is only at the end of the film, when we see the newspaper headlines about "The Director" being killed in a car accident that we become aware, along with Harry, of his mistaken interpretation of the dream. As mentioned before, that the film blocks the spectators' inscription in the primal scene does not preclude us from attempting to follow the threads of the detective plot (engaging with Harry's desire to prevent a murder). This is how *The Conversation* differs from counter-cinema in which the plot is devoid of any motivation: It arouses *our* curiosity (desire) by engaging us with its riddle; that this riddle is solved in Harry's imagination ("where" the flashback occurs) makes us investigate our own imaginary, if not our unconscious. The "prophetic" at this point is transformed into an ability to look into and listen to our soul, possibly understand the value of breaking free from the clutches of a romantic, compulsory religious ideal. In the end, Harry does not seem to care anymore if he is bugged or being listened to. He plays his musical instrument for everyone to hear, probably feeling that he has nothing to hide anymore, listening to his own sound/voice. Hence the ethical aspect of the dream that always deals with human subjectivity, as distinct from any other mise-en-abyme (in *Hamlet* it is endowed with a subjective and ethical aspect, though most mise-en-abymes do not have to be). But this retroactivity is also an invitation to examine the functioning of the apparatus.

The protagonist's process of subjectivization in *The Conversation* is therefore more difficult for us to partake in (unlike in the body-character-breach corpus that confronts spectators with the question, "Is this really what *you* want?") because it reflects the guilt of cinema—herein lies the true reflexive aspect of the dream as mise-en-abyme. Cinema is found guilty because of its ability to recreate the primal scene, to phenomenologically situate the spectator (Harry, as Jeffries, in *Rear Window* also represents the spectator, not only the technological apparatus) in an imaginary position that no other art form can do. The fact that the reenactment of unconscious primal fantasies is achieved through a technological, so-called "objective" apparatus renders cinema even guiltier (as elaborated on in the next chapter). This is why the film precludes our inscription in the primal scene structure all through. Should we remain engaged with Harry's desire (the basic condition of narrative film) to prevent a murder, finding out the truth in the end constitutes a devastating event not only for him but also for us, which marks our involvment in Harry's beginning of subjectivization. We at least realize that in this film, as in *Spellbound*, it is a fatal event (the death of others) that caused a guilt complex that rendered the protagonist unable to read the reality around him. Analyzing his dreams, as we have done, tells us that the protagonist unconsciously experienced the tragic death of others as a materialization of his unconscious Oedipal wish to remain his mother's sole object of desire. The meta aspect of the film points to the guilt inherent in narrative cinema's (imaginary) ability to structurally enact such fantasies.

4

Cinematography, Subjectivity, and Guilt

The Cinematographic Image

This chapter analyzes two meta-cinematic films that focus on the filmmaking process: Fellini's *8½* (1963) and Lynch's *Mulholland Drive* (2001). Although neither of them complies with a classical narrative structure, thus avoiding engagement with the dynamic of desire/fantasy as laid out so far, they nevertheless recognize the importance not only of the role of fantasy in narrative film (the support of desire) but also and specifically of the role of casting regarding the engagement of audiences with film.[1] Both films indicate that the making of the films-within-the-films are of a mainstream nature attempting to satisfy the desire of audiences, as well as directors and producers. The reason we have chosen Fellini and Lynch is their incessant preoccupation with dream and fantasy, turning their authorship into a mastery of both. Because of their deep understanding of the relationship between the ontology of film and fantasy, dream, and the unconscious in general, we regard them as the pundits of this field.

As observed in Chapters 1 and 2, spectators engage with the desire of the protagonist who, through casting, becomes a fantasy object. This is why the reflexivity of both *8½* and *Mulholland Drive* concentrates on the difficulties involved in the *process* of choosing an actress by tackling the question of fantasy—What does the Other want?—in relation to the collective desire of the audience, which can be answered by film in general, but in particular through perfect casting. This reflexivity is also demonstrated by evincing the perpetual motion of desire in relation to fantasy through the use of photographs, screen tests, and auditions of actresses. They attest to the way desire bounces from object to object, suggesting that the object itself is replaceable and forcing the film industry to continuously look for new actresses/fantasy objects. We thus become aware of what remains hidden from our eyes when viewing a narrative film, which shows us only the result, that is, the actress chosen for the lead, never the ones not chosen. If the casting is successful, we feel that she is indeed "the one."[2]

In both films, the protagonists' dreams express guilt involving fixation with the mother's desire or a character representing her. Key scenes depicting auditions, screen tests, and the coaching of actors reveal the notion of female stars/actresses designed to conform to a fixed fantasy image. In *8½*, these scenes are not part of the protagonist's dream; in *Mulholland Drive*, most of them are. The relationship between guilt as expressed in the protagonists' dreams and that of the key scenes points to the fact that answering desire through casting entails a kind of transgression that surpasses the boundaries of the imaginary because it involves an actor who is a real human being, a referent. In other words, configuring a cinematographic image of a leading character is conceived as a *realization*, materialization, of collective desire.

Casting in these films revolves around female leads and the question the protagonists ask themselves still revolves around the mother's desire (or those representing her, like in the films discussed in Chapter 3). This means the mother is part and parcel of any discussion relating to either desire or fantasy in film. In *8½*, it is the guilt of the protagonist (a filmmaker) in relation to his fixation on what he thinks is his mother's desire that prevents him from deciding which actresses to cast; in *Mulholland Drive*, the frustration of the protagonist (an unsuccessful actress) from being excluded from the desire of the one representing the mother, not giving up her fixation on both having the object of her desire and being herself the object of desire, causes devastating consequences, hence her guilt.

So far, we maintained that all the transgressions (inscription in the primal scene being the principal one) of narrative film remain in the imaginary, but these films seem to suggest that the fantasy achieved through casting goes beyond it and pertains to the basic code of the cinematographic image regarding character-actors. Therefore, subjectivization is achieved through a meta-cinematic exposure of the guilt inherent in the *success* of realizing a transgression which is specifically based on this code. In knowing what the Other wants/desires (audiences), directors and producers are found guilty of using the uniqueness of the medium—doubly imaginary, and yet referential—for ensuring not just the success of their film but also that of the industry. In addition, subjectivization includes finding a solution for the freedom of expression, creation, and imagination, both on the part of the filmmaker (the one entrusted with the success of his film by choosing the "right" lead) and that of spectators.

The key scenes depicting auditions and screen tests, particularly when emphasizing the limitation of imagination by restricting it to a specific actress, all explain the guilt inherent in the cinematographic image. We thus argue that the relationship between guilt as expressed in the protagonists' dreams and these scenes reflects cinema's guilt as part of the code of the cinematographic image—inseparable from the uniqueness of the film ontology as doubly imaginary (Metz [1977] 1982), that is, fictional and unattainable (the actor is absent from the screen), and yet referential (the actor was present on the set)—whose purpose is to veil the screen's lack. We thus deem the screen tests or auditions to be what Lucien Dällenbach ([1977] 1989) refers to as "textual mise-en-abymes" because they function as a reflection of the code of the medium in its entirety. In literature, the textual mise-en-abyme, "the reflection of the entire language code" (94)—to be distinguished from other mise-en-abymes that only reflect narrative and thematic elements—mirrors the basic code that organizes meaning in language, which is its *common* arbitrary set of symbols. The cinematographic image, which is based on perceptual analogy, lacks a basic common code and has no arbitrary set of symbols, as Christian Metz and many other film semioticians have argued. Metz's ([1968] 1991: 226) following observation still holds true regarding perceptual analogy as an inherent part of the basic code of cinema:

> For it is indeed true that filmic denotation . . . could always be guaranteed outside of any codification thanks to perceptual analogy alone. . . . One can imagine an hour-and-a-half-long film composed of a single shot whose angle would be constantly horizontal and frontal, with no camera movement at all, and no optical effect . . . with no temporal ellipsis, no lighting . . . and no voices besides those that would be strictly diegetic. . . . But the point is that such a film is possible, whereas nothing similar is imaginable . . . in a book. . . . Even . . . a zero-degree of "writing"—if such a thing exists—would still retain the code of its language (whose function in the cinema is guaranteed by perceptual analogy that allows one if necessary to economize on any language-like codification).

To illuminate this point, we might think of animation and computer-generated images as well, where all elements of the cinematic language (framing, distance, organization of the elements in the frame, camera movements, lighting, color, editing, narrative, etc.) are present in the film, except for the guarantee of filmic denotation (the recorded objects in motion), that is, its reliance on a referent.[3] The cinematographic image of the character entails perceptual analogy based on the notion that the character appearing in a film is a real human body that was placed in front of the camera. But this body on the screen also has a cultural codification (imbued with ideology) present in the image itself, "that is to say, within the 'analogy,'" or at a point that in relationship to the total economy of the filmic significations, *is distinct* from that occupied by the codifications that constitute what one calls 'cinematographic language'" (215, our italics).

Thus, for our own purposes and without getting into semiotic debates, what we call here "the cinematographic image" must include the condition that its reproduction be composed of a denotative code (a referent—the actor before the camera) and a connotative code (cultural, including film iconography, and ideological), which take precedence in a film before any other kind of elements in the total economy of the filmic significations come into play. Furthermore, we argue that, as this basic but complex code entails the realization of desire through a fantasy object, guilt is an inherent part of the cinematographic image. The following reflexive example demonstrates this.

In the last sequence of *Smoke* (Wayne Wang 1995), Paul (William Hurt), a writer, is commissioned to write a Christmas story but suffers writer's block. His good friend Auggie (Harvey Keitel) volunteers to tell him a true story, one that happened to him, and he does so in extreme detail. The story goes like this: While unsuccessfully pursuing a young man who stole a magazine from his store, Auggie finds the man's wallet, which fell during the chase. On Christmas Eve, Auggie, lonely and forlorn, decides in a moment of grace to return the wallet to the young man, Roger (Walter T. Meade). When he arrives at the address found in the wallet, Roger's blind grandmother (Clarice Taylor)—who is also lonely—mistakes him for her grandson. Auggie goes along with it. He pretends to be her grandson and spends the whole day with her, which ends in a festive Christmas Eve dinner. Before leaving, he goes into the bathroom and notices a stack of cameras in unopen boxes (probably stolen). He decides to steal one, a deed he says he has never forgiven himself for. When Auggie starts recounting the incident with the stash of cameras, the filmic camera slowly starts zooming in to Auggie's face until it reaches an extreme-close-up of his mouth, then cuts to an extreme-close-up of Paul's eyes when Auggie finishes the story. The use of cinematographic language here emphasizes the transition from the oral recounting to the visual one that is about to follow. The scene then returns to a medium-shot dialogue rendered in a shot/reverse-shot series, Auggie telling his friend that he has his story for Christmas and Paul concluding that it is a good one.

The scene that follows starts with a black and white close-up showing a sheet of paper in Paul's typing machine that reads "Auggie Wren's Christmas Story by Paul Benjamin," immediately dissolving into a (black and white) retelling of the whole story, this time around by the filmic camera. There is no dialogue, only visuals accompanied by Tom Waits' "Innocent When You Dream" on the soundtrack, and later, credits superimposed on the visuals. In the very first shot of the visualized story, we find out that Roger is African-American, and, of course, later, that his grandmother is as well. Albeit all the plentiful details in Auggie's recount, he does not mention this one detail (pertaining to the cultural codification). All he says is that the young man and his grandmother live "in the projects." A resident of New York would know that this indicates their African American origin, but the fact is, the visual appearance of the two not only renders the unequivocalness of their ethnic origin but also freezes imagination by providing certain actors. This example thus illustrates the difference between the two types of descriptions: the verbal description may leave more room to the imagination and therefore also opens up the possibility for error or deception; in contrast, the realization of the cinematographic image (the visual description) depends on a more precise sensory perception. It gives us, in Metz's ([1977] 1982) terms (borrowed from J. P. Sartre), a *visée*, or a *visée de conscience*, as opposed to the content of consciousness: the content of seeing an apple does not change in comparison to the content of having to imagine one when mentioned verbally, in both cases it is an apple.[4] But the *visée de conscience* renders the apple present and particular as a perception evoking numerous sensations, the enactment of unconscious primal fantasies included.

Unlike verbal expression of thought, and with certain differences from mental states such as dream, memory, and fantasy, cinema creates sensory impressions through images; it imitates these mental states, evoking experiences similar to them in life.[5] Although they exist on an imaginary level and do not materialize in reality, a certain choice of image is a form of realization that attests to subjective choices. Furthermore, in the human fantasy, the image chosen is accurate because it derives from the desire of the fantasizing subject. However, a film is a product of collective endeavor designed for mass audiences. The two aspects characteristic of the production and consumption of a film as a collective product show how accurate the cinematic image must be. One explanation for the failure of a certain cinematic adaptation of a literary work is that it does not match the collective imagination of its readers, especially when it comes to those who play the characters. For an actor who plays a character—whether literary in origin or developed from an original script—the necessary condition for success at the consumption end of the process is that he or she must a priori match the character imagined by the audience, as we have repeatedly argued. An extreme example of this is the character of James Bond, played by numerous actors over the years. The audience judges each choice of actor and either approves or rejects the current one, like the failure of George Lazenby against the success of Pierce Brosnan, as well as others.

The example from *Smoke* is clearly reflexive. Auggie does not mention the difference in ethnicity between him and the grandmother, only her blindness and their economic inequality, which suggests that, as opposed to cinematography, the oral or written account is always "blind" to some extent—because the characters are not visually portrayed, in literature anybody can "play" a character, that is, occupy the place of a fantasy object. Significantly, when Auggie tells Paul about some still photographs he had found in Roger's wallet, he describes in detail their content, but it is only when the camera reveals them visually that the ethnic origin of Roger's family is realized through specific casting, attesting to the desire to realize human imagination through fantasy. The difference between Auggie's stills and the cinematic visualization of Auggie's story is that in the latter it has come to life, it has become a present presence, irreplaceable with another. This is suggested also in the theft of the camera in the story: In narrative film, the cinematography "steals" the object and the moment in reality and situates them in an array of fiction, while at the same time according the imagination a dimension of realization. Interestingly enough, Auggie stresses that he feels guilty about the theft and cannot stop thinking about it. Indeed, the reflexivity in the film enables "thinking about film," and thinking about film entails guilt because of its ability to realize human imagination, similar to what a fantasy does in minute detail in accordance with the subject's desire. Paul tells him that he did a good thing (referring to making the grandmother, who had been hoping to spend the day with Roger, happy), but Auggie insists on elaborating on his guilt. Narrative cinema that tells a story in images is a good thing, but replete with guilt. When Auggie finishes his story, saying "Now you've got your Christmas story," Paul compliments him, emphasizing that it is a good one, implying that it might be fictional (though Auggie would not admit it). Thus, Auggie's Christmas present to Paul is not just an offering of a story (about an actual event, answering Paul's desire), but also signifies the effort involved in imagining characters and situations that will "push all the right buttons." In telling Auggie that "to make up a good story you have to know how to push all the right buttons" (which is precisely what leads him to believe that the story is fictional), Paul suggests that a story has to do with answering the desire of listeners/spectators.

Auggie's story also clarifies that cinematography in narrative film is an inseparable part of the fiction. Metz ([1968] 1991: 226–27) describes it as follows: "Now, *from the moment that the cinema encountered narrativity* ... it appears that it has superimposed over the analogical message a second complex of codified constructions, something 'beyond' the image" (italics in the original). However, the reason the story is rendered twice is to show the difference between the two modes of answering desire.

We have shown in Chapters 1 and 2 that without fantasy sustaining desire in a film becomes difficult; that the main fantasy object is the actor embodying the leading role; and that, therefore, destabilizing the image in its capacity of fantasy object is achieved through the problematization of casting. Now, we argue that all devices employed in this kind of destabilization constitute attempts to absolve cinema from its guilt, from seeking to ensure the fixing of the imaginary through the reproduction of the cinematographic image because it wants to appeal to as many spectators as possible.

André Bazin ([1945] 2005: 9), who looks at cinema as a direct technological advancement of still photography fulfilling mimesis, starts his famous essay on its ontology stating that if ever plastic arts were to undergo psychoanalysis, we would find at their origin the "mummy complex," namely the need to alleviate the fear of death, conquer the passage of time, through fixating the material. The use of the term "complex" suggests a deeper meaning, namely a reference to subjectivity, more precisely to the Oedipal complex, which Bazin tries to circumvent.[6] He associates the psychological factor with a religious aspect, claiming that the photographic reproduction, due to its "objective" nature, is without guilt or sin. This suggests that guilt has been an inherent part in debates about the mechanical reproduction of cinema from the start, although what Bazin considers an exoneration of guilt, meta-cinematic filmmaking deems its source. Guilt stems from the desire to alleviate castration and from precisely the wish to triumph over death through fixating the material by mechanical reproduction, addressing collective desire.

Hence, the screen tests and audition in *8½* and *Mulholland Drive*, which present a situation *prior* to the articulation of the cinematic language. The selection of the actors for the different roles occurs before the filming, at a point preceding the coding pertaining to the cinematic language (editing, camera movement, composition, and so on). The director, or producer, is aware of the characterization and design of the protagonist in the script and searches for an actress to suit a specific vision. Before evaluating the actress' acting skills, she is evaluated according to whether she is photogenic, meaning her ability to successfully "pass the screen." Therefore, the choice of actress takes into consideration the analogical, the iconographic (for example, stereotypes like the glamorous blonde and the seductive brunette), as well as her assimilation into the overall meaning of the story, as her character and appearance are part of the whole fictional narrative. Guilt thus is associated with the actress having to serve as a "receptacle" for the realization of collective desires deriving not only from the structure and content of the narrative but from the very image of the actress as a fantasy object. As previously mentioned, the guilt expressed in the protagonists' dreams as pertaining to the fear of realizing or actualizing their fantasy is correlative to the realization of fantasy through casting in the textual mise-en-abymes of the two films analyzed here.

Dreaming and Guilt in *8½*

The film features two dreams near its beginning, while the textual mise-en-abyme (the screening of the screen tests) appears near its end. *8½* is a film about Guido (Marcello Mastroianni), a director, and a film he wants to make. As Metz ([1968] 1991: 232) and others have noted, the audience never gets to see Guido's film, only his passing thoughts and fantasies prior to its production. What we do see is the screen tests (for the film he intends to make) of the actresses contending for the roles of the women in

Guido's life—his wife, his mistress, and the prostitute La Saraghina, who are duplications of the actresses already chosen to play these roles in Fellini's *8½* (Anouk Aimée, Sandra Milo, and Eddra Gale respectively)—as well as the roles of the clerics. La Saraghina is not only the object of Guido's fantasies as a young boy but also the source of his guilt, as expressed in his dreams. By examining the relationship between the guilt in the dreams and the screen tests scene (the textual mise-en-abyme), we show how this guilt is connected to casting. The screen tests scene reveals that Guido's film is about his life, thus, not only reflecting the medium but also duplicating the film in which it appears (*8½*).[7] That Guido cannot decide which actresses will play the roles of the characters *duplicating* the women in his life (as opposed to the actresses Fellini has already chosen to play the roles of the women in Guido's life) means a failure to work through his guilt up to this point.

Guido's two dreams express the guilt he suffers because of misinterpreting his mother's desire, which impedes his living in peace with his choices regarding the women in his life and his ability to make choices regarding his film. Although he must overcome his personal guilt to be able to be the director he wants to be, a great auteur, free to express his vision without taking into consideration the desire of others, he is (as is Fellini, Guido being his alter ego[8]) part of the motion picture industry aiming constantly to satisfy collective desires. As mentioned before, although *8½* does not comply with a classical narrative structure,[9] the textual mise-en-abyme reveals that it does recognize the importance of casting regarding the engagement of audiences with the film's fantasy. Guido's personal guilt reflects the guilt inherent in the motion picture industry, not bypassing great auteurs. In Guido's dreams, the question of fantasy ("What does the Other want?") is addressed specifically to the/his mother ("What does *she* want from me?"). Collectively, this question is diverted (by filmmakers, producers, and so on) to "What does the audience want?" resonating the first object of desire (the mother). Therefore, the screen tests reflexively concentrate mostly on female casting (replacements of the mother). The success of configuring a cinematographic image of a leading character as a realization of collective desire, therefore, constitutes a transgression; it is an impossibility accomplished only in cinema—as is the configuration of the structure of the primal scene. Guilt thus, as mentioned before, is a result of cinema's *success* in precisely realizing a transgression not possible in life. This becomes evident in the juxtaposition of Guido's failure with Fellini's triumph regarding casting—having worked through his own guilt. To understand the origin of this guilt we first need to examine Guido's dreams and memories.

Guido's first dream appears at the beginning of the film. We see a close-up of Guido sitting in his car stuck in a traffic jam with his back to the camera. He looks at the motionless cars around him while most of the people in those cars stare at him. In one of the cars an older man is caressing a voluptuous young woman (played by Sandra Milo, who also plays Guido's mistress, Carla, in the film). A disquieting drumming conveys heavy heart beating and a menacing affect, which intensifies when Guido's car gradually fills with smoke and he begins to suffocate. He tries to clear the smoke out, but unsuccessful, he bangs on all the windows with his fists and feet trying in vain to break through. Suddenly, he appears on top of his car, his arms stretched out as he smoothly drifts above the cars. A soft sound of the wind replaces that of the drums while he hovers gracefully in the air, surrounded by clouds. He then realizes that one of his legs is tied to a rope held by a young man on a beach who is accompanied by an older man on a horse (Guido Alberti, who also plays Guido's producer). The young man holds the rope, as though Guido were a kite. He says to the old man "I got him!" pulling Guido down, and the old man replies "Down for good!" In the shot that follows we see Guido falling rapidly, his head toward the sea. He then wakes up; the soundtrack renders his grasping for air while he raises one of his arms in the dark, as if trying to escape from his rapid fall in the nightmare.

The first part of the dream, until he appears on top of his car, renders Guido's feelings of suffocation, his sense of being closed in, entrapped without being able to break free—surrounded by a crowd of motionless characters gazing at him. The second part of the dream (occurring on the beach) is the key to understanding the whole dream and his essential guilt, as well as the whole film. It alludes to a childhood memory of Guido's that constitutes one of the primary sources of joy in his childhood, as well as of pain and guilt in his adult life. As an eight-year-old pupil at a strict Catholic school, he skips classes and runs to the beach (the same place where Guido is being pulled down in the dream) with his friends to watch La Saraghina the prostitute dancing the rhumba; she invites only Guido to join her. This experience is depicted as a delightful mixture of childish innocence and the beginning of sexual excitement until two priests arrive. They interrupt the party and chase the children away but continue to pursue Guido (as he was the only one dancing with La Saraghina); they catch him by his ear (Figure 4.1) and drag him back to school along a corridor decorated with somber portraits of judgmental men. The reprimanding priests, most of whom are played by elderly women with short hair, place Guido in front of his sobbing aged mother (Giuditta Rissone) after having summoned her to the school. While sobbing, she keeps reiterating the word "shame." Guido's punishment is indeed severe: In addition to having to face his distressed mother, he is humiliated in front of all the other children. He must move around wearing a dunce cap on his head and a sheet of paper stuck to his back with SHAME inscribed on it. He is forced to kneel on gravel while listening to a sermon about how "the pious Luigi abhorred most of all any contact with women, whose presence he so avoided that everyone thought he had a natural antipathy towards them." During confession, one of the priests commands him to renounce La Saraghina, "the Devil." At the end of

FIGURE 4.1 8½ (Federico Fellini 1963).

FIGURE 4.2 8½ (Federico Fellini 1963).

this memory sequence, Guido looks at two marble statues, one representing the Madonna and the other a female martyr. Later he returns to the beach and searches for La Saraghina. She is seen sitting on a chair, facing the sea, looking back at him smiling and softly saying, "Ciao."

The second part of Guido's dream, on the beach, during which he is pulled down violently from the sky by the two men (one of them is his "reproaching producer" in his adult life) is thus a displacement of the traumatic incident of being caught by the two priests on the beach (Figure 4.2), his fall from a blissful, joyous heaven to severe punishment (the fall resonates with the command to "get down" on his knees when he hesitates to kneel on the gravel). Guido, who associates his mother's sense of shame with the priests' and the other children's humiliations of him, assumes that this is also his mother's desire—that he renounce La Saraghina "the Devil" and the enjoyment of dancing with her, as well as perhaps any enjoyment of women, as the pious Luigi did. Guido's fixation on this belief is expressed in the way he envisions his mother in this childhood memory, not like she looked when he was a schoolboy, but as an elderly woman, like she appears in his dreams and fantasies.

Moreover, the fact that the priests are played by old women evinces the magnitude of the presence of the mother, Guido's ongoing fixation. Thus, more than the reproaching attitude of his teachers-priests, it is mostly his mother's tears (Figure 4.3) and her numerous reiterations of the word shame that point to his fixation on what he thinks she still wants from him in his adult life (which is why it is La Saraghina he must say goodbye to).

However, unlike the pious Luigi, Guido does not abstain from sex with women; on the contrary, he has multiple relationships with them (as expressed in the harem fantasy, in which all the women get along with each other). Neither does he alienate himself from La Saraghina's memory and the joy he derived from her—he still longs for it. Therefore, he will always feel guilty and believe that he deserves to be punished for his transgression. This is what the first part of the dream shows: Guido's anxiety (his fear of being "punished" for his desire to be free—to go wherever he wants, to look at whomever he wants), his sense of feeling trapped and gazed at in a petrifying reprimanding manner, like the priests in his childhood memory. His desire to look at La Saraghina without feeling guilty is rendered in the choice of Sandra Milo to play the voluptuous woman in the car in his dream, her blatant sexuality resembling that of La Saraghina, unlike his monastic intellectual-looking wife. This becomes clearer in the scene before the second dream, when Guido "directs" Carla to "play" the role of La Saraghina (without Carla being aware of it) by instructing her how to paint her eyebrows (to resemble La Saraghina's "demonic" expression). We do not

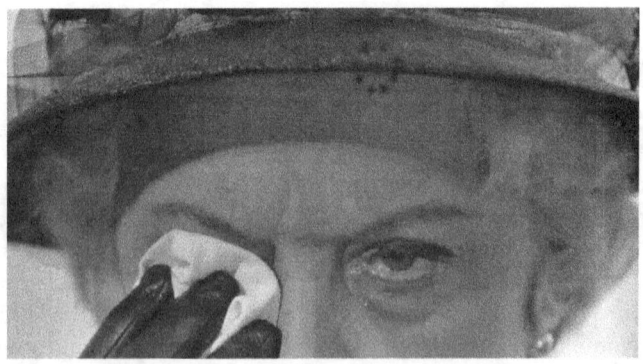

FIGURE 4.3 8½ (*Federico Fellini 1963*).

see Guido's face all through the first part of the dream, only his back and what he sees, without any reaction shots. This expresses his sense of shame (reminiscent of his mother covering her face with her palms in the childhood memory, a gesture Guido himself often repeats). For the spectators, the fact that we do not get to see Guido's face constitutes an anxiety-producing lack, in keeping with Guido's anxiety as expressed in the suffocation sounds, the smoke imagery, his sense of entrapment, and helplessness.

The guilt inherent in the childhood memory of La Saraghina is also present in the second dream, thus pointing to the same source. The sequence starts with Guido in a hotel room with his mistress, Carla, about to make love to her. He paints heavy witch-like eyebrows on her, and the connection to La Saraghina can hardly be missed when he directs her actions and gestures (not just her makeup) in an attempt to recreate his childhood object of desire, as well as revive his own pleasure when watching her (Figure 4.4). This is where we understand that not only is the memory of La Saraghina the trigger of this dream, but also the key to interpreting the two dreams as expressions of guilt.

The dream commences with Carla reading in bed next to a sleeping Guido. They have obviously just finished making love. Suddenly we see his mother in the bedroom, her back is to Guido and she is facing one of the walls, trying to clean it with her handkerchief (she is again portrayed as old and dressed in black, as she was in the childhood memory). As melancholic music begins, the space changes and the bedroom wall becomes a glass wall in a place that later turns out to be his father's burial site. His mother is cleaning the glass (her back to the camera, Guido behind her), her gestures recalling Guido's futile attempts to remove the smoke from his car in the first dream. Her image and that of Guido are reflected in the glass, as though they were facing each other. She stops, shrugs her shoulders, waves her handkerchief, and leaves, her gestures expressing powerlessness in her attempt to clean Guido's and her reflections. He asks her: "Is that you, mama?" She nods

FIGURE 4.4 8½ (*Federico Fellini 1963*).

and says: "So many tears, my son," using her handkerchief to wipe her eyes. Guido then calls to his father, pleads for him not to go, longing for his company, suggesting he is about to leave. The father seems helpless and complains about "the low ceiling" (alluding to his grave), while trying to find out from Guido's producer and set manager if Guido is doing well, as if Guido were a schoolboy. The producer and set manager leave without answering and his father says: "It's so hard, realizing that one has been so mistaken." He then drapes a black cloak around Guido's shoulders, identical to what he used to wear to his childhood Catholic school. Before parting, his father inquires about Guido's wife, Luisa, concluding, "You two have been my joy, goodbye, son." Guido then helps him descend to his grave (neither recognizing what it is) and turns to his mother, who once more expresses her disappointment and helplessness: "Guido, I do my best. What more can I do?" She then opens her arms to console him, embracing him by the head. What began as an innocent kiss on his elderly mother's cheek now becomes an erotic kiss on her mouth, from which he cannot extricate himself. The image of his mother is then replaced with that of his wife (in his mother's attire), who says: "Don't you recognize me? I am Luisa, your wife." These words recall Guido's doubt at the beginning of the dream sequence, when he asks his mother if she is indeed his mother. Guido disappears from the place, leaving his wife alone.

At first the shame and guilt expressed in the dream appear to stem from the classical Freudian Oedipal scenario, meticulously dramatized by the displacement of the mother with the wife during the kiss on the mouth, as well as by "helping" his father into his grave; however, his futile attempts to cleanse his shame and guilt are in keeping with his childish fixation on his mother and his futile attempts to satisfy her desire, which is more of a Lacanian scenario of fantasy. It is in this sense that he betrays both his parents: not only does he betray the promise he thinks he made to his mother, but he also disappoints his father by not remaining true to his wife. Rejecting his mother's kiss and not recognizing the site of his father's grave points to confusion in his mind, as though his unconscious is unsure of his desire: How is it possible to want to sleep with the mother and kill the father, and at the same time long for his company and solace? The answer lies in his guilt toward his mother, which is evident first in her appearance (the same attire and handkerchief she had in Guido's childhood memory), recalling the "trial" scene in his school, and then in her words, "So many tears my son," tears shed because of the shame and agony he thinks he caused her. This can never be cleansed, hence her apology when she tries to clean the bedroom wall but fails. Her failure is correlative to Guido's, whose attempt to atone for guilt in the bedroom is significant because that is where he betrays his wife/mother with his mistress. Guido's guilt and shame in the dream become evident when he covers his face with his hands after his father expresses his disappointment in him. The confusion of identities (mother/wife) too, suggests the difficulty in breaking free from the mother's influence. In life, Guido reenacts these guilt feelings toward his mother with his wife, whom he betrays; but maintaining Carla as mistress also means reenacting the enjoyment with La Saraghina, which, again, is a betrayal of the mother in Guido's mind, not only of his wife. Thus, the splitting of his sexual life (La Saraghina-Carla/mother-wife)[10] is in fact a constant reenactment of the childhood memory: enjoyment of sex will always be accompanied by a sense of betrayal and shame resulting in guilt. This constitutes Guido's fixation.

His desire to clean his guilt finds imaginary "solutions" in two of his fantasies. The first is about uniting all women into one pure ideal woman. The sensual Claudia Cardinale, who is meant to play "Claudia" in Guido's film, embodies in his fantasies a virginal young female figure, always dressed in white, barefoot, taking care of him and keeping everything clean and tidy.[11] Her demeanor is contrasted with earthly sweaty women in two hallucinations. In the first he sees her in slow motion, as a caregiving angelic nurse offering him fresh water (in Catholicism, water symbolizes baptism and the cleansing of guilt) from the spring at the sanitarium where he is staying, replacing the real nurse—tired, sweating under the burning sun, impatiently handing him a glass of water. In the second hallucination, she is again dressed in white, declaring that she wants to clean (her wish expresses Guido's wish to be expiated of guilt). Guido looks at her with tenderness while she lies in bed on a white pillow covered with a white sheet. This hallucination is interrupted by a call to take care of Carla, who is sick in bed, recalling Claudia (white pillow and sheet), which rather than pointing to a similarity, evinces Claudia's pure idyllic image as opposed to Carla's earthly one (her face is feverish, sweaty, and still heavily made-up).

His second (typically male) fantasy is of a harem. It depicts a diversity of stereotypical women (strip dancer, stewardess, young African exotic dancer, and so on), living in peace with each other, their sole purpose to please him. Even his wife, Luisa, dressed as a country housewife and looking like his young mother (portrayed in a childhood memory of her putting him to bed) gets along with the sensual and beautiful women surrounding Guido. There is no conflict and no judgment (the women only reproach him for his rule not to let anyone over sixty stay in the harem). As Clodagh Brook (2007: 122) claims, the harem fantasy is a symptom *par excellence* of undecidedness, thus the ultimate fantasy for Guido, for in it "selection does not incur the dismissal of other possibilities."

Guido's split in his life (characteristic of Catholicism) between his relationship with his monastic intellectual wife and with his strident, common-looking mistress could be a solution to his conflict were it not for his constant fixation to be free of guilt (expressed in the harem fantasy). He carries this guilt onto the film he wants to make, which is about his life. When facing his split strategy "on the screen" in the screen tests scene, he realizes that duplicating the women in his life in his film ultimately means duplicating guilt. That Guido faces the source of his guilt on-screen is indicative: John C. Stubbs, a leading figure on Fellini's auteurism, who discusses at length his creative process (as part of Fellini's self-promulgated "legend"[12]), begins his study with an epigraph that quotes Fellini: "It is really like seeing far away in the night a spark of light, and as you approach you find that it is a light in the window of a house in a street, where people live . . . and as the string unravels you slowly lay bare a whole map of places, characters, sentiments, and situations" (Stubbs 2002: 116).[13] Associates Fellini's spark of light metaphor with *either* "an image" *or* "an idea" from which Fellini develops a whole film. But as Gianfranco Angelucci and Liliana Betti (1974: 95) emphasize, Fellini's films have to do with images and "only images." Furthermore, it is well known that Fellini valued his dreams highly as a source of inspiration, as *The Book of Dreams* (2008)[14] attest and many have noted, because of their reliance on *images*. This ability might be deduced also from Stubbs (2002: 120), who notes, "Many of Fellini's best ideas came to him when he was dreaming and daydreaming." He further quotes Fellini: "In my sleep I have some of my best thoughts, because they are images rather than thoughts."

Translating an image from a dream into film thus becomes an artistic form through which the unconscious is mediated. For example, William Van Watson (2002: 70) rightly quotes Edward Murray who defines Fellini's inspiration specifically as "the artist's ability to make direct contact between the conscious and unconscious mind." Stubbs (2002: 118) recounts that "he [Fellini] maintained a file of head shots of potential actors for his films, and when he began a project, he sent out a casting call for non-actors so he could examine their faces." These quotes show that Fellini was constantly preoccupied with casting, a process that for him entailed two stages, at least: the transition from the unconscious (images that appeared in his dreams) to the imaginary (fantasy)—as the drawings in *The Book of Dreams* demonstrate, the latter being the first expression of Fellini's artistic creation; and the transition from fantasy to the real (casting, which entails the translation from one medium—drawing—to another—cinematography). As the casting of women in the roles of male priests suggests, *8½* shows a deep concern with both stages, tackling/problematizing the second.

Guilt and Cinema: The Textual Mise-en-Abyme in *8½*

Guilt in relation to filmmaking is already present in Guido's dreams—both include his producer as a haunting disapproving figure echoing the priests in his childhood memory. The conflict between Guido and his producer escalates near the end of the film when the latter forces him to view all the screen tests he has conducted over the past five months so they can begin production. But Guido cannot make up his mind about the cast. At one point during this scene one of his wife's girlfriends, watching the screenings with her, whispers: "This is his life!" realizing that he is duplicating the figures of the women in his life in his film. The subject of choosing actresses for Guido's film is first brought to our attention in the scene following the first dream. A doctor comes to examine Guido in his room at the sanitarium. He sees the abundance of photographs of actresses on Guido's bed, and, totally oblivious of his mental distress, picks one and says: "Nice looking girl. American, right? You've got some fine merchandise there." During the medical examination, Guido's face remains out of sight (as in the first dream). First, he hides it with his palms (connoting shame and guilt) while lying on his belly, and then, after he gets up and walks toward the camera, the backlighting renders him as a dark silhouette. When he enters his bathroom, the bright shot showing his face reflected in a mirror clearly expresses his depression and desperation, for which there is no physical cure. The few photographs spread on the floor evince his continual indecisiveness. What appears here as just one of the many problems Guido must contend with during the preproduction process is described in the screen tests scene as the main source of his inner conflict.

The scene creates an ongoing tension between Fellini's 8½ and Guido's want-to-be film. In Fellini's film, Luisa, who is also present in the screening room, is thus forced to watch the screen tests of the three actresses contending for the part of "Olympia," the mistress in Guido's film. When watching this, Luisa understands how short she falls of her husband's mistress as an object of desire—the actresses on the screen contending for the part are all duplications of Carla (in their gesticulation, attire, makeup, and so on). When Guido's voice-off is heard in the screen test guiding the actress auditioning for the part, Luisa seems to understand that she will never be able to play a similar part in her husband's life. Moreover, watching the actress contending to play the part of the wife in Guido's film, Luisa realizes that the former receives more attention and information about Guido's and her marriage than she ever will. She then confronts him with the fact that he can only speak the truth through his films, and decides to leave him.

For us, the tension consists of Guido's indecision regarding the casting of his film juxtaposed against Fellini's cast: Sandra Milo *is* Carla (Figure 4.5), according to whose characterization all the contenders for the role of the mistress in Guido's film are designed (Figures 4.6 and 4.7) but, we feel, do not really compare to Sandra Milo/Carla; Anouk Aimé *is* Luisa (Figure 4.8), unmatched by her duplication (Figure 4.9); and Eddra Gale *is* La Saraghina (Figure 4.10), unmatched by any of the other contenders for her role in Guido's film (Figures 4.11 and 4.12). The way Guido is persecuted by guilt is also evident in his hesitancy regarding the casting of Claudia Cardinale (who *is* Fellini's angelic figure) and in Madeleine Lebeau's confusion as to what her character or role might be in his film (as opposed to the French star/actresses Anouk Aimé who was chosen by Fellini to play Luisa). Although his producer

FIGURE 4.5 8½ (*Federico Fellini 1963*).

FIGURE 4.6 8½ (*Federico Fellini 1963*).

FIGURE 4.7 8½ (*Federico Fellini 1963*).

FIGURE 4.8 8½ (*Federico Fellini 1963*).

FIGURE 4.9 8½ (*Federico Fellini 1963*).

FIGURE 4.10 8½ (*Federico Fellini 1963*).

FIGURE 4.11 8½ (*Federico Fellini 1963*).

FIGURE 4.12 8½ (*Federico Fellini 1963*).

keeps pressuring Guido about the casting process, reminding him that both actresses have other commitments and tight schedules, he remains indecisive. Fellini's choice of actresses clearly suggests that they are not only part of his fantasy world, but also designed to meet extra-diegetic expectations.[15] What Guido is unable to achieve because of his guilt, Fellini seems to master: He has reconciled his fantasy world (stemming from the way he interprets his visions in dreams), his artistic vision, with production demands, including those of the Catholic Church and its indoctrination. In Italy of the 1960s (and even today, albeit to a lesser degree), the involvement of the Catholic Censorship Commission in the film industry, its production, distribution, and exhibition was considerable: "Catholic Church intervened on commercial productions and influenced artistic autonomy thanks to a widespread network of parish cinemas" (Daniela Treveri Gennari 2013: 255).

If the accuracy of the casting process must take into consideration the multitude of expectations (from the audience, producers, and the actors' agents) to address collective fantasies, then the question of fantasy, "What does the Other want from me?" inextricably involves the basic code of the cinematographic image, namely the denotative and the connotative, the latter being part of the former. Therefore, a director is not entirely free to choose an actress without taking into consideration both the actor's physique and his or her cultural value; these are evident not only in Fellini's choice of actresses but also in the stereotypical iconography and characterization of "the prostitute," "the mistress," "the wife," and so on. Thus, working through guilt in relation to the filmmaker's own psyche means also understanding or acknowledging that perfect casting consists of a realization of a collective fantasy through the cinematographic image, which fixes imagination. The audience is not supposed to be aware of the casting process when feeling that an actress is right for the role she plays, but the final choice is always an answer to what the director wants, in compliance with what the audience might expect. Fellini knows that Claudia Cardinale *is* his fantasy for the role of Guido's angelic figure in charge of cleansing the latter's guilt, but he also shows her as "Claudia Cardinale" in the encounter with Guido (after the screenings) as a complex, sensual, multifaceted woman (dressed in black) who criticizes him, telling him that "he doesn't know how to love." The idea behind this is not to depict her as a "real" person—Fellini might know her but the spectators watching the film do not—but rather what she, both as a real woman (beautiful and sensual, photogenic, hoarse voice, and so on) and a film icon, has to offer. As a star, she possesses physical qualities and attributes, all manageable in Fellini's depiction of her as a purifying angel (which is why she does not need a screen test).[16]

The textual mise-en-abyme thus makes us aware of what remains hidden from our eyes when viewing a narrative film, in which we see only the end result, that is, the actress chosen for the lead, never the ones not chosen, feeling that she is indeed "the one," as Fellini makes us feel in relation to his cast of actresses in his film. What for Fellini is a done deal, for Guido, because of his guilt, remains unsolvable. It is precisely where Guido fails that Fellini achieves a masterpiece, but the first condition is to know who the actors in this masterpiece will be before starting production. This is the reason why the star system is so important to the success of the industry.

However, the kind of transgression inherent in answering desire through casting entails *guilt* because it surpasses the boundaries of the imaginary: it involves a real human being (whose presence is reproduced on film for eternity). Unlike theater, the code of the cinematographic image regarding characters-actors secures their immortality, as well as "freezes" them for spectators as fantasy objects. Directors and producers are thus supposed to hold the secret key to solving a riddle that is either impossible to resolve or involves a faulty resolution.[17] The commercial success of a film depends on it, proving that cinema can "correctly" and "accurately" foresee the desires of its audiences. Here is where guilt comes into play—film can *materialize* fantasy through casting; this is why in Fellini's *8½* the filmmaker must work through his guilt.

Where Fellini is concerned, this applies to casting only, as the form of his film—rendering a stream of consciousness, disclosing the unconscious of its creator—is very far from a classical narrative.[18] However, the textual mise-en-abyme does reveal the secret charm of narrative and authorial film that pleases audiences and secures the fame of its directors and stars by hooking the unconscious of its audience. Notwithstanding Fellini's style of directing a film (the characters and the camera are always in motion, the director resembling an orchestra conductor who instructs the coming and goings of every character as if they were musical instruments, as evinced by one of Guido's fantasies), the textual mise-en-abyme makes clear that the cinematographic image of a lead always halts the motion inherent in film because it entails a referent that cannot be doubted, one whose appearance cancels out all other possible appearances. This appearance, together with how the director enacts the character of the script (in authorial cinema, the director is often also the scriptwriter or a co-writer) and the interpretation of the actor fixes, or freezes, our imagination with respect to the fictional character. No film can bypass this. This might be one reason why Fellini will go to great lengths to evince the characterization of women in his future films as figments of *his* imagination, limiting them to a personal vision rather than a collective one.

Guido's process of subjectivization consists of diverting the question of fantasy—"What does my/the m/Other want from me?"—to "What do I, the director of the film, want?" In his talks with the archbishop, Guido attempts to deal with his guilt, which he feels stems from his Catholic education. Two screen tests for the character of the cleric are also shown in the projection room. The connection between the images of actresses and those of the actors contending for the role of the cleric reinforces the connection between guilt, the mother of his childhood memory, and the cinematographic image. In a meeting in the bathhouse, the cleric, who appears as a distorted silhouette behind a sheet, believes that redemption can be found only in the church. But Guido will find it in his imagination (like Fellini has).

Significantly, the film ends with a fantasy, not with the decision to begin production; but this time the fantasy portrays a change in the imaginary, a renunciation of fixation in favor of imagination. Rather than feeling guilty about his fantasies, Catholic education, and memories, he embraces them as an inherent part of his creativity. This means that fantasy sustains desire not only regarding our engagement with a film but also in the process of creation—without fantasy there is no desire to create. But fantasy in this sense must include the freedom of imagination. The transgression inherent in the human photographic image in relation to casting leads, for which the cinema is found guilty, is thus mitigated in 8½ by two components: the freedom of (Fellini's) imagination and the explicit reflexivity of the screen tests—the textual mise-en-abyme—revealing that despite what audiences may feel about casting ("she is the one"), the possibilities are in fact endless. At the end of the film Guido seems to reach a point that for Fellini is his starting point: everything and everyone is in motion.

Thus, the "death" of Guido's film signifies the death of his guilt, not of his fantasy world—in short, his subjectivization. Guido's film might be dead, but the desire to create is reborn as an answer to what *his* desire is, rendered now by a fantasy (the final scene) depicting Guido and all the characters in his life. Encouraged by the magician to let go of his sadness, he imagines them dressed in white: Claudia, his young mother, La Saraghina, his elderly parents, his mistress, the clergymen, his wife, and many more. He tells them that he loves and accepts them and asks for their forgiveness. He says to Luisa what in our view might qualify as a description of the process of subjectivization:

> I feel like I've been *set free*. Everything seems so good, so meaningful; everything is *true* . . . now everything's all confused again, like it was before. *But this confusion is me*, as I am, not as I'd liked to be, what I'm *looking for*. . . . I'm *no longer afraid of telling the truth*. . . . *Only this way I feel alive*. Only this way can I look into your faithful eyes without shame. Life is a celebration.

He then asks her to accept him as he is, and she agrees. He desires truth, freedom, life. A small orchestra of clowns appears on the deserted film set, connoting a circus, a young boy in white plays a flute in the background. Guido's parents and other characters are met by the magician, welcoming them on their return. Then Guido starts to direct a crowd of characters (most of them the inhabitants of the sanitarium, some from the production crew) after descending a scaffold of stairs. Guido is happy to greet them, kisses the hand of a cleric (signifying assuming responsibility over his guilt, as well as Fellini's having his way with the church). A couple of his friends pass him by and then his parents reappear dressed in white. He turns to them while their backs are to the camera; he calls to his mother and she turns to him; he waves his hand to her and she raises one of her shoulders as a sign of approval. He goes on to integrate his mistress into the dancing crowd with the help of the magician. He approaches his wife, takes her by the hand, and they both join the circle in which everyone dances together in harmony and joy. Then, night falls and we see the small orchestra conducted by the young boy in white playing the flute. The encircling crowd has disappeared by now and the boy with the flute dismisses the other players, remaining alone on the set, spotlighted, exiting the frame.

The final scene depicting Guido's last fantasy shows that he is finally able to integrate everyone in his life without feeling guilty because he accepts himself as he is. He can now relate to the young boy in him not as a source of shame and guilt, but rather as the source of imagination, thus gaining his freedom as a film director. Unlike the black cloak the young boy wore as a child, the white one here suggests breaking free of his past traumatic experience, renouncing guilt, and embracing his creative faculties (he "dresses" almost all the characters in white and directs them in the same way Fellini dressed Claudia in white and directed her as an angelic figure), symbolized by the flute—the power of imagination. The ethics of the film lies in depicting the way imagination becomes a prisoner of a rigid and strict fantasy (in compliance with a false assertion regarding the desire of the Other) and then showing how it can be set free by breaking the shackles of this structure.

In conclusion, the textual mise-en-abyme in 8½ reflects the interrelations of the different codes of the cinematographic image: the denotative/referential (the relation of the image to the object in reality, the actor) and the connotative (the cultural aspect, diachronically as well as synchronically), both addressing the question "What does the Other want?" that the film links to the mother. Being able to positively answer this question through fantasy, as the casting process sequence in the film reflexively demonstrates, inexorably entails guilt. It is this quartet (denotation/referent, connotation, the desire of the mother, guilt) that the textual mise-en-abyme reflects, and is why the latter also functions, in Dällenbach's ([1977] 1989) terminology, as a "transcendental" (218) mise-en-abyme "because of its ability to reveal something in the text that apparently transcends the text, and to reflect, within the narrative, what simultaneously originates, motivates, institutes, and unifies it, and fixes in advance what makes it possible" (101). And because the transcendental mise-en-abyme in fact discusses the *source* of the work, which Dällenbach terms "a metaphor of origin," "[It] is a metaphor of the primary instance that constitutes the meaning of meaning and enables signs to communicate . . . it reflects the *code of codes* . . . governs the form of those which are exploited by the narrative and ensures that they form one type rather than another" (106, italics in the original), like God and mimesis (in the past). The example Dällenbach chooses to demonstrate the metaphor of origin in literature is one from Samuel Beckett (102–3), whose use of transcendental mise-en-abyme condenses both the great Western metaphysical and literary tradition and the deconstruction of all principles of the novel. Similarly, Fellini deconstructs the principles of narrative film, except for the basic code on which he must rely. For Beckett it is the word, the utterance. For Fellini, as the Beckett of narrative film (or rather, the James Joyce, as he is the master of "the stream of consciousness" in cinema), it is the cinematographic image as related to casting, which he can design according to his own vision but not do without: any real objects in his films can be replaced by artificial ones (which he will do in future films), except for the actors, whose artificiality must be kitted out on real bodies. Moreover, what the transcendental mise-en-abyme reflects in *8½* in our view is that in the code of codes of the cinematographic image the "metaphor of origin" is the desire of/for the mother, which is also one of the main themes in *Mulholland Drive*. Like Fellini, Lynch exposes the two stages of filmmaking (transition from the unconscious to the imaginary, and then to the real) through casting (the realization of fantasy through a real object), and problematizes the latter.

Dreaming and Guilt in Lynch's *Mulholland Drive*

Most of *Mulholland Drive* consists of the protagonist's dream, revealed as such only toward its end, when she wakes up; the last thirty minutes of the film depict her reality, composed of the "remains of the day" (i.e., her pre-dream memories), past memories, and post-dream experiences. This part of the film is the key for interpreting and understanding the dream. As Jay Lentzner and Donald Ross (2005: 106) note, this is a film about a young woman, Diane Selwyn (Naomi Watts) descending into despair when the bitter taste of rejection reveals her desire to be an object of professional and personal admiration (a film star) nothing but an illusion.[19] Our interpretation of the dream is largely based on Lentzner and Ross' Freudian method of interpretation, guilt being a major component. We further connect the notion of guilt to the reflexivity of the film. As we shall see, *Mulholland Drive* employs the same devices or strategies in relation to the exposure of guilt as *8½*: fixation, splitting, and merger with the mother's replacement.

The film begins with bright flashes of color that appear to be a teenage dance competition, superimposed with an image of the protagonist smiling victoriously and an elderly couple smiling back at her in validation. The camera then reveals an unkempt bed and disappears into the darkness of the pillow. The lights go out, and the dream starts with a plot centered on the adventures of "Betty" (Naomi Watts). The dream opens with a young brunette (Laura Elena Harring) and two men driving down Mulholland

Drive in Los Angeles. Suddenly the men try to kill her, but a traffic accident interrupts the attempt on her life. Although she survives the accident, she loses her memory and wanders around as if being followed until she sneaks into an apartment and finds refuge there. She falls asleep and dreams about two men meeting on Sunset Boulevard in a diner called Winkie's.[20] In the dream, Dan (Patrick Fischler) tells his companion, Herb (Michael Cooke), about a recurring nightmare that took place there, and that he is afraid of a man "at the back of the place." Herb replies that that must have been the reason why Dan came to Winkie's, to see if this man is indeed out there—"to get rid of this God awful feeling," as Dan puts it. The two men go outside to check the back of the place, and suddenly, a homeless-looking man emerges from behind the wall. His face, clothing, and shaggy hair make him look like a wild demon. He appears only for some two seconds, whereupon Dan collapses—either fainting or dead—into Herb's arms.

Later, the young blonde woman named Betty, an aspiring actress who has just arrived in Hollywood dreaming to be a star, reaches her Aunt Ruth's (Maya Bond) apartment and is surprised to discover the brunette taking a shower there. When she asks the woman for her name, the latter glances briefly at her reflection in the mirror alongside a poster of the movie *Gilda* (Charles Vidor 1946) showing Rita Hayworth, and says "Rita." Betty tries to help Rita discover her identity, not an easy task because their only clues are the large amount of cash and a silvery blue triangular-shaped key in Rita's purse, and she can't remember where either of them came from. She only remembers that her accident occurred on Mulholland Drive. After anonymously making a call to the police from a pay phone they find out that, indeed, there was a car accident on Mulholland Drive that night and a woman is missing. Feeling victorious, they go into the closest diner, Winkie's. There, when a waitress named Diane (Missy Crider) serves them, Rita suddenly remembers the name Diane Selwyn and thinks it might be her name. They find out her address and phone number, but the voice on the answering machine is not Rita's, so they decide to go there after Betty's audition.

Betty and Rita's quest and the evolvement of their relationship are alternately interrupted by two secondary plots. In the first, Joe (Mark Pellegrino), a very clumsy blond hitman with one blue eye and one brown, first shoots Ed (Vincent Castellanos), a friend he is conversing with, in order to get his hands on Ed's "famous" address book. Ed apparently knew about Rita's accident (Joe is seen in another episode asking a prostitute about a brunette, as if looking to kill Rita). He then kills an innocent worker in the adjacent office by mistake, whereupon he is forced to eliminate a witness to this blunder, a cleaning employee, causing a fire while doing so. This clumsiness, pointing to the desire to be absolved from guilt, resonates with Claudia's frivolous attempts to clean Guido's bed in 8½. In the second subplot, pressure is being exerted on the opinionated director Adam Kesher

(Justin Theroux) by the Castigliane brothers (Angelo Badalamenti and Dan Hedaya), emissaries of a mysterious mobster named Mr. Roque (Michael Anderson), to cast a blonde actress named Camilla Rhodes (Melissa George) in his upcoming film. Adam is shown Camilla Rhodes' photograph and told: "This is the girl." At first, he tries to resist, but as a result he loses everything: control over the film, his wife, and his fortune. His troubles culminate when he meets another of Mr. Roque's emissaries, the venomous cowboy (Lafayette Montgomery), who instructs him to audition many girls for the lead, but upon seeing Camilla Rhodes, to affirm that "this is the girl."

Back in Ruth's apartment, Rita helps Betty practice for an audition for the director Bob Brooks (Wayne Grace) that turns out to be extremely successful, though the film she auditions for is not likely to be made. However, present at the audition is a casting agent named Linney James (Rita Taggart) who takes her to meet a director "a head above the rest," promising her that "He's got a project you will kill for." When Betty arrives with the agent at the set where Adam is conducting screen tests for the lead part in a 1950s-like musical, she witnesses two tests, the second and last one is Camilla Rhodes's. Betty's appearance catches Adam's attention and they exchange meaningful glances overshadowing Camilla. However, Adam has no choice but to follow the cowboy's instructions regarding Camilla and says: "This is the girl." His producer, who has already been advised by Mr. Roque what needs to be done, tells Adam: "An excellent choice." Adam and Betty exchange glances again, Adam looking very unhappy. Having promised Rita to meet her at a certain hour, Betty runs out of the studio, followed by Adam's yearning gaze. This seems to suggest that he would have cast Betty in the lead role had he not given in to the threats.

After leaving the set, Betty joins Rita and they go to Diane Selwyn's home, hoping this will shed light on Rita's identity. They arrive only to discover what seems to be Diane Selwyn's rotting body, and horrified, they leave in a hurry. The event brings the two women closer, both physically and emotionally. Betty helps Rita disguise herself using a blonde wig, thus giving her a look like her own. Later that night, the two make passionate love. They wake up because Rita keeps repeating the word "Silencio" (silence in Italian and Spanish). Rita brings Betty to the Club Silencio, where a blue-haired woman (Cori Glazer) is seen sitting in a gallery. On the stage, a magician (Richard Green) declares that there is no band, though the playing of a band is clearly heard. The same recurs with a trumpet player and a singer, Rebekah Del Rio (Rebekah Del Rio), who collapses on the stage during her a cappella performance of "Llorando" (a Spanish version of Roy Orbison's "Crying"). While her body is being carried off the stage, the song continues to be heard. Betty and Rita shed heavy tears during the performance of the song, their weeping intensifying when Rebekah collapses. Betty opens her handbag and discovers the blue box with a silvery triangular-shaped keyhole. The two women return to the apartment and while Rita is taking out the key to the box, Betty disappears. Rita opens the box, which is empty. The camera zooms in into the darkness of its emptiness and the screen turns black. The next shot shows the box falling to the floor. Then a camera movement begins, leaving the box and advancing to the entrance of the room where Betty's Aunt Ruth is entering. The shot that follows is rendered from Ruth's POV, showing an empty room: no trace of Rita or the blue box. She leaves and as the camera lingers on the wall, the screen becomes darker and the camera leads us into Diane Selwyn's bedroom. A brown-haired woman wearing a black satin slip is seen from her back, lying in the bed (on pink bed sheets and a green blanket). An off-screen sound of the door opening is heard, and the cowboy appears at the doorstep, investigates the room, smiles and says: "Hey pretty girl, it's time to wake up."

The shot fades out to black once more and when fading-in, shows her again, this time as a decomposing body, the bedsheet cluttered. In the next shot, the cowboy, not smiling, closes the door and the shot fades out to show a black screen again for quite a while. Ominous music begins and knocking on the door is heard. The fade-in reveals a mise-en-scène identical to the one of the woman in bed (same bed; same bedsheets, body of a woman in the same posture; image rendered from the same angle), but this time it is a blonde wearing a gray slip and the sheets this time are in order. We see Diane now (played by Naomi Watts—Betty in the dream) waking to reality from the knock on the door, hinting that the police might be looking for her. But it is a former roommate or lover who has come to collect the remains of her things from the apartment. As they talk, Diane discovers a normally shaped silvery blue key on the coffee table. Then a series of flashbacks (not in chronological order) tells the story of Diane.

Diane, like Betty in the dream, is an aspiring actress who has a romantic relationship with an actress named Camilla Rhodes (played by Laura Elena Harring—Rita in the dream). Camilla breaks up with Diane when the promising director Adam Kesher (played by Justin Theroux—Adam, the director in the dream) casts Camilla in the lead role in his 1950s-like style film, like Adam in the dream. In honor of Camilla and the film's success, Camilla insists that Diane come to a festive dinner party at Adam's home on Mulholland Drive, sending a limousine to bring her. Diane experiences the pain of being rejected when she witnesses a public kiss between Camilla and an unidentified blonde (played by Melissa George—Camilla Rhodes in the dream) and is forced to congratulate Adam on his wedding plans with Camilla. Diane involuntary watches her former lover expressing her desire for others; she also admits her own professional failure to Adam's mother at the dinner table. Diane tells her how she and Camilla met when auditioning for Bob Brook's film. Camilla was the one who got the part and since then her career has been evolving and she has helped Diane get bit parts in her films. After this humiliating and painful experience, Diane meets the hitman at Winkie's (the source of the name "Betty"—the waitress who serves them) in order to contract Camilla's murder. She shows him Camilla's photo (designed like the one of the blonde "Camilla" shown to Adam in the dream) saying: "This is the girl." After she displays a bag of cash, the hitman tells her that the signal confirming the murder would be a silvery blue key. He asks if this is really what she wants because the moment the money is handed over there will be no turning back. Diane answers: "More than anything in this world." After she wakes from her dream, she sees the blue key on her coffee table and realizes Camilla has been murdered. As a result, her depression worsens, and she commits suicide in her bed. In the scenes that follow, the terrifying man from Dan's dream (who appeared in Rita's dream within Diane's dream) reappears. Then Diane and Camilla (the latter wearing the blonde wig) are shown smiling in the spotlight. The epilogue ends with a scene in the empty Club Silencio featuring only the blue-haired woman sitting in the gallery, twice reiterating the word "Silencio."

Diane's dream originates in the responsibility she feels for Camilla Rhodes' murder. When she says to the hitman that the killing of Camilla is what she wants more than anything in the world, it is because she believes that this way she will put an end to her suffering. It expresses her desire to make it in Hollywood as well as remain her lover's object of desire. In this sense, it is a "compensatory fantasy" dream: it makes up for her inferiority, sense of failure, and humiliation. However, the dream reveals and expresses her guilt and conflicts resulting from her decision: her murderous affect and possible remorse, even the wish to prevent the murder. This duality is correlative to the fact that chronologically, Diane has the dream after she contracts the murder and before she discovers that the murder has been committed, that is, Camilla is killed during the time she sleeps and dreams.

Diane's guilt is expressed in her dream first and foremost in the two scenes at Winkie's (where in the reality segment she contracts Camilla's murder): the first, in Dan's dream (within-Rita's-dream-within-Diane's), after the attempt on Rita's life; the second, when Betty and Rita go there. In Dan's dream, as recounted by Dan to Herb, Herb was in it—standing by the cashier paying the bill. Dan's coming to Winkie's symbolizes a return to the scene of the crime. Throughout Dan and Herb's conversation, the camera gently floats up and down and from side to side, creating an affect of sea sickness, rendering Dan's distress, which in turn expresses Diane's affect while dreaming. Before leaving, Herb gets up to pay and stands at the cashier, in compliance with Dan's earlier description of him in his dream. The conversation between Dan and Herb thus is a displacement of Diane's meeting with the hitman at Winkie's; it takes place at the same table. In the reality segment, after handing over her money, Diane glances at the cashier, her eyes meeting those of a customer (Patrick Fischler, who also plays Dan in the dream) standing there paying his bill. Thus, the symbolization of Diane's feelings of horror and remorse, or wish to avert the murder, is a mixture of "remains of the day" and an expression of her revulsion at what she did at

Winkie's, wishing she could go back and stop her nightmarish experience (get rid of "the dreadful feeling"). The customer's appearance in Diane's dream is not altogether inadvertent, as in Diane's experience he has become a witness (unknowingly) to the contracting of the murder.

If so, Dan's dream reflects Diane's guilt and desire to cancel the hit (Lentzner and Ross 2005: 110). Dan's putting his dream to the test—going out to see if the scary man is there or not—symbolizes Diane's desire to find out if the murder has been executed; the fear of her own murderous nature (of resorting to actions characteristic of "primitive"/primary drives), as well as of the punishment she deserves, is symbolized by the scary man. Contrasted with "Betty," a glamorous, beautiful, kind, good-natured, innocent, young actress and devoted friend (attributes that deny or make up for Diane's monstrosity), this terrifying man at the back of Winkie's (the back "alluding" to the unconscious) symbolizes Diane's "rotting" self:[21]

> Thus, while the "dream-within-a-dream" sequence at Winkie's represents Diane's wish to undo Camilla's murder; it also conveys her dread that this is impossible. The male dreamer-within fervently hopes that he might never again look upon the face that he knows is staring at him behind the wall at the back of the diner. Overwhelmed by guilt, however, he treks compulsively to behold that fearsome specter, and the scene ends in his collapse and death. (117)

Diane's sense of guilt is twice symbolized by the paying of the bill (Dan's recounting of his dream to Herb and before Dan and Herb exit Winkie's), meaning that she must pay for what she did (she commits suicide in the end). In Dan's dream, he looks at Herb in terror as Herb (a displacement of the customer at the cashier who "becomes" Dan in the dream) pays the bill. This is the major indication that the price to be paid is connected to the materialization of a fantasy. Dan in the dream is "paying the price" for trying to find out whether the man in his dream is there or not, for "materializing" his dream word-for-word; hence, his collapse after seeing the monster-man. Dan's dream thus also forebodes Diane's suicide. The return to the scene of the crime is also symbolized by the decomposing corpse Betty and Rita discover in Diane Selwyn's apartment.

The second scene at Winkie's in the dream takes place after Betty calls the police from a pay phone nearby to ask if there was an accident on Mulholland Drive. She tells Rita, "We'll call anonymously, like in the movies, and pretend we're someone else." This points to Diane's acknowledgment that she is in fact dreaming, feeling even guiltier because of her powerlessness to undo the murder. When they both sit at Winkie's, they notice that the name of the waitress is "Diane," and Rita, who borrowed the name Rita from Rita Hayworth, recalls that this is probably her own forgotten name. As mentioned before, in the reality segment, Winkie's is where Diane sits with the hitman and hires him to kill Camilla. During her conversation with him, she sees that the waitress's name is "Betty" and adopts it in the dream. That is, she takes the name of the waitress who was present when she hired the hitman, which expresses the ongoing affect of guilt in her dream. Rita's amnesia recalls that of Ballantyne in *Spellbound*, whose amnesia is a protective mechanism for his guilt complex. Because Rita in *Mulholland Drive* has no reason to suffer from amnesia as she is not guilty of anything she needs to forget, the allusion to *Spellbound* works only if we relate it to a displacement of Diane's guilt to Rita's character.

Similar to the mirroring structure in *8½*—in which all the elements are duplicated one-to-one in the film within the film—in *Mulholland Drive*, all the elements of what is understood to be reality are duplicated one-to-one in the dream, but reversed and/or displaced in such a way as to suit Diane's wish to be exonerated from guilt and become a desired star and lover: Rather than being the culprit, she is the rescuer; rather than being a failed actress and Camilla a successful one, she is a promising talent and Camilla a "nobody" who needs her help; rather than being rejected she shines as an object of desire, both professionally and personally; rather than being humiliated by both Adam and Camilla, the crime organization humiliates the director and is responsible for trying to find and kill Rita/Camilla, as well as for "Camilla Rhodes" getting the lead in Adam's film rather than Betty. These reversals, as well as interchanges of identities and splits in the dream, are all meant to blur the boundaries between murderer-failure/victim-success. However, as explained above, Diane's guilt seems to have the upper hand in the dream. All her attempts to get a meaningful part in a film are met with impediments: Bob Brooks' film, Betty is told, will never come to fruition and Adam in the dream is forced to cast "Camilla Rhodes." Not only is this an expression of Diane's fantasy being punctured by the reality of her life, it is mostly an expression of her feeling that she deserves to be punished (guilt).

In fact, all the occurrences in the dream expressing the polar opposite of how Diane experiences reality and herself are tainted by her sense of guilt.[22] That Rita manages to evade constant threats (the attempt on her life is fended off by the accident, in which she is the sole survivor) symbolizes Diane's regret regarding the contract and her wish that she could prevent the murder (also symbolized by the oddly shaped blue key, in Rita's possession throughout the dream, meaning that as long as she holds it, the indication that the murder has taken place is postponed); however, "keeping" Rita alive (in the dream) is an unwavering condition for the dream.[23] Diane's regret and wish to be exonerated from guilt by attributing to Joe the hitman a connection to the criminal cartel hunting Rita down, as well as professional clumsiness (a refutation of the straightforward professionalism of Joe in the reality segment) are futile in the face of the very first thing that Joe does in the dream: he shoots his friend in the head.

Similarly, when Betty first discovers Rita in the shower, her friendly impulse to come to her rescue is counterpointed by the allusion to the shower scene in *Psycho* (Alfred Hitchcock 1960). Betty surprising the naked Rita in the shower at their first encounter implies that Betty is the equivalent of Norman Bates (Anthony Perkins), who murders Marion (Janet Leigh) in the shower. Diane's split, between her naïve, almost childish side and her murderous one recalls Norman's, who is unaware of the split in his personality. Moreover, there is a certain similarity between Rita and Marion, both of whom have purses full of cash. Marion's purse is full of money she stole, for which she feels guilty, and her fatal meeting with Norman puts an end to her attempt to return the money. The allusion to Marion thus reinforces the displacement of Diane's guilt to Rita: it is Diane who has a stack of bills she pays the hitman with.

The audition for Bob Brooks, which leaves everyone present speechless, and Adam's seeming preference of her over "Camilla Rhodes" are counterpointed by symbols pointing to the fact that she is the one who poses a threat to Camilla, that she cannot undo the murder or be exonerated from her guilt. The text of the female character that Betty is rehearsing in the kitchen with Rita and the audition for Bob Brooks,[24] its different interpretations by Betty proving how good an actress she is, alludes to a possible murder. The character warns her lover, a close friend of her father's, that she will murder him if he does not leave her alone, the latter threat being a reversal of Diane's death threat to Camilla in the reality segment: Diane wants to kill her precisely because she left her. During the rehearsal she threatens Rita with a kitchen knife when she utters the words from the script: "I hate you, I hate both of us." The reason that Adam does not cast Betty is not related to her talent, but to threats from a mysterious crime syndicate pressuring him to cast "Camilla Rhodes." This fulfills a secondary wish, to punish Adam, Diane's competitor for Camilla in the reality segment. But even this revengeful wish, which can be traced via several displacements of characters and affects from the dinner party at Adam's home to the criminal cartel, symbolizes her feelings of revulsion at herself. When Diane admits to her unsuccessful career as compared to Camilla's and is forced to watch Camilla's happiness, she feels bitter and hurt and drinks her espresso—we can almost feel the bitter taste of failure as we watch her expression as she tastes the coffee. When she looks up, her eyes meet those of an elderly gentleman (Angelo Badalamenti) sitting on the far side of the room. He becomes one of the Castigliane brothers in the dream who during the production meeting contemptuously spits out the espresso the waiter serves with great trepidation, whereupon he demands Adam cast the blonde actress "Camilla Rhodes" to star in his film. The bitter taste of betrayal and rejection thus turns into an affect of self-contempt, not just of self-loathing, but one associated with the actions of a criminal disregarding anyone and anything not complying with his will. Still, at the dinner party Camilla kisses a nameless blonde before Diane's eyes, betraying Diane with both a man and another woman. After the kiss, when Diane feels the full extent of Camilla's betrayal, she sees a cowboy briefly passing, onto whom she displaces her guilt in the dream by turning him into one of the gangster's emissaries.

Diane's character has no way (except in death—where she can finally be united with her lover) to absolve herself from guilt because she is responsible for carrying out a fantasy in the real. This means that guilt is ultimately and intimately connected to trying to realize the impossible unification with the m/Other, to always be included in her desire—disavowing separation. This fantasy is rendered in the dream through the way Betty molds Rita to look like her, the way the two merge into one personality. After they discover the mysterious body, Betty is quick to disguise Rita's identity by putting a blonde wig on her—like her own hairdo—thinking she might be responsible for the murder or accused of it. There is an allusion here to another Hitchcock's film, *Vertigo* (1958), in which, as we may recall, a character who dreams (Scottie, played by James Stewart) is burdened with guilt. The contrast between the blonde (Madeleine) and the brunette (Judy) in *Vertigo* is disclaimed by the fact that they are one and the same character, played by the same actress (Kim Novak), thus forcing Scottie to look into the abyss—see in a woman the earthy Judy and not the empyreal Madelaine. But Scottie insists on making over Judy to look like Madeleine because he cannot renounce his fantasy of an ideal woman, that which veils the lack in the Other, which becomes even more rigid due to guilt.[25]

Lentzner and Ross (2005: 108) see in Diane and Camilla's lovemaking scene the epitomization of their whole relationship and in Rita's image in the scene a synthesis with the character of Diane's mother, a relationship of childish dependency, seduction, and competition that becomes apparent. They deem it an expression of an internal conflict—"a statement of hatred and a confession of love. The desire to remove her glamorous rival by merging with her in a transcendent union" (111).[26] There is no reference in the film to the kind of person Diane's mother was, but the disavowal of separation through the merging of the two characters does point to a fixation with the desire for/of the mother, the wish to be absorbed in it. This kind of merging recalls the psychiatrist's explanation in *Psycho* at the end of the film, stating that matricide is accompanied by such extensive guilt Norman could not bear it and merged with his mother's image by wearing her clothes and speaking and reacting like her until he completely disappeared into her personality. Norman has already murdered his mother and merges with her over and over again each time he kills. Diane has "not yet murdered" Camilla; therefore, she does not adopt Camilla's (the victim's) appearance, but displaces her longing for merger to Camilla, who adopts that of Diane the murderer. Thus, the act of murder itself is denied and their friendship and love in the dream appear to be strong and stable in the face of external threats; yet the allusion to *Vertigo*, again, points to guilt due to a fixation.

Both allusions refer to cinema's transgression for which it is deemed guilty of materializing a fantasy. Norman is psychotic (psychosis in Lacanian psychoanalysis means the foreclosure of the paternal metaphor, the Name-of-the-Father), embodying the fantasy of ultimate merger with the mother; Scottie is a fetishist, one disavowing the Name-of-the-Father (a pervert). Both Norman and Scottie thus have a problem with the incest taboo in relation to the mother. It might be that the reason for comprising an actual murder (a fantasy realized in the real because of the foreclosure of the symbolic) in *Mulholland Drive* is meant to emphasize cinema's transgressive nature in that it creates the illusion of a possibility to merge with the mother. This illusion is directed at spectators, and we may recall the last scene of *Psycho*, in which Norman, who has now totally merged with his mother, looks directly into the camera and speaking in her voice declares that she couldn't hurt a fly. Namely, the scene reflexively shows how narrative film helps spectators not feel guilty (because they only "sit and stare") in their complicity with an industry that works to satisfy their desire by enacting fantasies.

Guilt and Cinema: The Textual Mise-en-Abyme in *Mulholland Drive*

Two scenes in the film refer to the trauma of being excluded from the primal scene. The first, a textual mise-en-abyme, occurs (in the reality segment) during rehearsal for a love scene in Adam's film. He orders everyone to leave the sound stage, but Camilla insists Diane stay, forcing her to follow Adam coaching his male actor by replacing him: he gets in a car, sits by Camilla, and kisses her passionately while Diane watches in envy. The second takes place at the dinner party at Adam's house on Mulholland Drive when she is forced first to watch Camilla and Adam showing off their happiness and then Camilla kissing a blonde woman on her lips. In the lovemaking scene on the set, Diane can still tell herself Adam is only coaching his actor, part of his job; at the dinner party she might still maintain the illusion that Camilla is marrying Adam to advance her career; but after she sees Camilla passionately kissing the blonde who replaces her she can no longer deceive herself into thinking that she remains the object of Camilla's desire.[27] In all these scenes[28] Diane feels excluded; in other words, the scenes render the traumatic experience of being excluded from the Other's desire. In Diane's case, after witnessing the killing of her fantasy world she feels she has no choice but to murder the object of her desire.

Diane is reluctant to go to the dinner party, but Camilla insists. We see Diane in her apartment wearing an evening dress, ready for an event she does not want to attend. The phone rings and at first, she does not answer.

The answering machine picks up the call and the recording says, "This is me, leave a message." Diane stands next to the answering machine and listens to Camilla's voice begging her to answer the phone. She asks Diane to go to the limousine waiting for her downstairs, giving her the address 60 Mulholland Dr. As she rides in the limousine, it suddenly stops. She tells the driver, "We don't stop here," but the reason for the stop is Camilla, who unexpectedly appears and accompanies Diane to the dinner, using a secret path up the hill. This incident is portrayed in the dream, again, through reversal of identities and roles, whose function is to refute the brutal separation: Betty and Rita try to call "Diane," who is meant to be Rita's true identity in the dream.[29] They dial, and Betty says: "It's strange to call yourself." Rita answers her, "Maybe it's not me." When the answering machine picks up the call, it says "This is me, leave a message." Rita says, "That's not my voice. But I recognize it." Betty replies: "Maybe it's not you, maybe it's your roommate." "Diane's" voice on the answering machine in the dream is Diane's real voice—hence, the beginning of the dream with a trip to Mulholland Drive. The dinner there symbolizes for Diane her deepest wound, one she must make up for. This scene describes how in the dream (fantasy) her "good" side splits from her murderous one in order to free herself from guilt and merge her identity with Camilla's to veil the trauma of separation.

For Todd McGowan (2004: 68), the two parts of the film (dream/reality[30]) represent the cinema of fantasy in contrast to the cinema of desire, and that by separating the two parts, Lynch is criticizing Hollywood inasmuch as this separation implies that the film industry creates fantasy as a way out of the impasse that desire leads to: "The intersection of fantasy and desire is always a point of trauma because it is a point at which signification breaks down. We construct fantasy to cover a gap in the symbolic structure, a place where there is no signifier" (80). It is indeed the role of fantasy to cover up cinema's lack, as well as lack in general, and splitting the two might very well be Lynch's way of criticizing the cinema of fantasy—hence the emphasis on the traumatic aspect of the primal scene, when it is not veiled by fantasy.

Herein lies Lynch's ethics—he reveals how engaging with fantasy is achieved in narrative film (Adam's coaching of his actors), while emphasizing the impossibility of inscription in the primal scene by evincing its traumatic aspect. In contrast to the way Lynch inscribes us in Betty's desire in the dream (we want her to succeed, to flourish in her relationship with Rita, to discover her identity, etc.), in the coaching scene in the reality segment he not only reveals how inscription in the primal scene is achieved—cinema's investment in the illusion that one can be inscribed in the m/Other's desire—but also evinces its impossibility, the traumatic aspect of being left out. When Adam shows his actor how to play the love scene in the car, he accentuates every romantic move. Camilla responds with absolute devotion while Diane watches in despair (like Luisa being excluded from the primal scene in Guido's screen tests)—contrary to the enjoyment of spectators when watching a love scene. Diane's exclusion from the primal scene (the desire of the Other) is how the film makes sure to let us know that inclusion in it occurs only in fantasy, that film as fantasy must be distinguished from reality, in which this cannot happen.

The cinematic reflexivity in relation to the failure to realize the desire for the mother or be her object of desire, merge with her, becomes more evident when Betty and Rita go to the Club Silencio after their attempt to become one. The scene demonstrates the incoherence of sound and image in cinema, the gap/lack at the heart of the apparatus, both with the musical instruments and the singer: the music goes on even when they stop performing. When Rebekah Del Rio sings her *female* Spanish version of the original male rendition of Roy Orbison's "Crying," Rita and Betty weep at what is revealed to be an illusion: "Del Rio, a seemingly sensual, full-bodied presence, at one point collapses like a hollow doll, while her rich voice continues to intone. The issue here may seem to some to be about life and death, but it is actually about fullness and void, as the entire film. Confronted by the hollowed-out image Betty goes into heaving convulsions" (Nochimson 2002: 43). We interpret the void that Martha Nochimson refers to here as cinema's inherent lack, tantamount to an encounter with the failure to be immersed in the desire of the mother. It is not mere chance that this scene occurs right after Betty has made Rita look like her: the two women, desiring to be one, are forced to look into the abyss, hence the heavy tears covering their faces. According to Graham Fuller (2001), the schizoid personality of the protagonist corresponds to the split that underlies the cinematic apparatus. In his opinion, the emphasis placed on how *Mulholland Drive* exposes hidden anxiety is deceptive and trying to match the image to the sound and to the desire of the audience is a sham. The delusion created in films is condensed by loss or fragmentation of the synchronization of sound and image in Del Rio's act when her singing continues after she collapses. The loss of synchronicity turns out to be a menace in the Club Silencio: "When Del Rio swoons unconscious to the floor, her theatrical croon continues unchecked, and Betty—perhaps because this act of violence threatens her romantic epiphany and her ability to suspend disbelief—is deeply disturbed . . . Lynch is breaking through the dream fabric of the film, reminding us of the fragility of cinema's hallucinatory power" (16).[31] Directly after the nightclub scene, Rita opens the blue box. It turns out to be empty, containing nothing. This is the darkness lurking from the very beginning of the film, ever since the mysterious key was found in Rita's purse—the desire accompanying the viewing of a film, but also a corroboration of the lack in the Other, the end of fantasy.[32] And so, once the blue box is opened, the dream ends and Diane wakes up.[33] She discovers the hitman's key on the table, confirming that the murder has been committed. After the memory of her relationship with Camilla and the realization that she caused her death seeps into her consciousness, Diane sits in the living room, staring at the key. Her teary eye is seen in extreme-close-up, reminiscent of the tears of Betty and Diane in the Silencio Club and the end of the fantasy. The film ends with the woman with the blue hair (perhaps alluding to the color of the key/box, a symbol of the death of the object of desire, as well as fantasy in the nightclub)[34] saying, "Silencio,"[35] whereupon the screen darkens, thus evincing cinema's lack, rather than its fullness.

Moreover, the perpetual motion of desire, like in 8½, is emphasized by the screen tests and the photographs of different actresses, one of Camilla Rhodes in Diane's dream and the other of the real Camilla Rhodes, thus suggesting that the "right" choice for a lead is to a large extent also a sham, that, in fact, the process filmmakers go through when choosing an actress attests to the way desire bounces from object to object, that the object itself is replaceable: It is the screen that makes them look irreplaceable and immortal (actors, as opposed to the characters they play in film, do age, die, and rot). In fact, the use of photographs in the film points to an inevitable disaster. In the reality segment, Diane gives the hitman Camilla's photograph and says: "This is the girl, Camilla Rhodes," so he can identify her. Contracting the murder at Winkie's, duplicated in the dream-within-the-dream, takes on the significance of a disaster that has already occurred, recalling what Roland Barthes ([1980] 1981: 96) writes about an 1865 photograph of a boy (Louis Fein) taken before his execution. In it, Barthes finds the "punctum," "*He is going to die*," but also reads it as "*this will be* and *this has been*." That is, whether the subject of the photograph is still alive or not—each photograph is a disaster that has already occurred. The same with Camilla's photograph that Diane shows the hitman, as Nochimson (2002: 44)[36] notes in relation to Adam and Camilla's engagement:

> The announcement of what appears to be their engagement aborts, as Adam, with a malign laugh, leaves off the word "married" from his initial "we are going to be" prefiguring the fact that they are not "going to be" anything. Being has been supplanted by nothingness through Adam's fatal capitulation; Betty will kill both Rita and herself. They are already dead, in some way, anyhow.

We could sum up and say that the reality segment of the narrative deconstructs every bit of fantasy the film constructs in the dream segment, thus constituting the ethical ground of the film, its process of subjectivization, one which the spectators undergo as well. Like in Hitchcock's films, we are inscribed in the heroine's desire, only to be thrust out of it. So, why still feel guilty about it? Why does *Mulholland Drive* not end in a celebration of imagination, as does 8½? To answer this question, we need to examine what the film says about the code of the cinematographic image.

As we have repeatedly seen, choosing and molding an actress for a lead means paving the way for the audience to be implicated in the protagonist's desire. In other words, in narrative film fantasy is an inherent part of the cinematographic image. In addition to our recurring argument that without fantasy, desire cannot be sustained when viewing a film, the reflexivity of the film demonstrates the guilt of cinema in general, and in particular that of the director, in relation to the cinematographic image regarding casting, of which fantasy is an integral part: Like in *8½*, in which Fellini triumphs precisely where Guido fails, what Diane cannot achieve in her life Naomi Watts masters brilliantly when playing both Betty and Diane: She "*is* the girl." The gap between the diegetic director, Bob, his passivity and ineptness at the audition (in the dream sequence) and the way Lynch must have coached Watts to play the scene cannot be missed: "When Lynch selects a medium-shot vantage point to frame Betty's audition (one that allows actors and space, finally in proper attunement, to blend properly), he is subtly displacing 'Bob' as the directorial presence" (Toles 2004: 5). During the rehearsal in the kitchen, Rita tells Betty how good she is, but it is at the audition that Betty/Watts leaves everyone speechless when she performs a different interpretation of the role. Doing the scene twice at the audition means that the physical appearance of an actress is not enough, there must be good acting as well, and, moreover, that the actress' interpretation of her role, in compliance with the director's, insures our engagement with a film.[37]

But above all, it is the director who must possess a "killer instinct" as to whom must be "the girl." In terms of the diegesis,

> Watts not only appropriates Rita's "danger and darkness" (and theft is exactly the right word for it, calling to mind the old acting phrases, "scene stealing" and "stealing the show"), she enhances their interest by making fully conscious use of them, as far as the audition circumstances permit. She appears to know everything that is at issue, at least for the time being, and by turning up the sexual heat while announcing her involvement in masquerade and her intention to murder, she trumps Harring's more passive possession of mystery. (2004: 9)

In terms of spectatorship, "Such enthrallment is obviously sustained by a total, innocent acceptance of whatever happens as happening 'for keeps,' however absurd or overblown the events appear to us in retrospect" (3). In our words, the choice of the actress ("the girl"), the fantasy object projected on the screen in compliance with her acting skills, is both what makes us believe her character ("the one," and no other) and what draws us into her fantasy world (the film), no matter how far-fetched or incredulous it is.

Therefore, when Betty arrives at Adam's set during the screen tests, it is to be expected that she is indeed "the girl," as validated by the way she catches his attention as soon as she arrives, overshadowing with her appearance the two other actresses on the set (a young talent auditioning for the part and Camilla Rhodes). The control Roque/the cowboy/the Castiglianes have over the casting that forces Adam to capitulate and precludes Betty from getting the part in his film alludes to the fall of the director if he is not allowed to choose: the name Adam refers to the fall of man; unlike Adam in Genesis, this Adam falls because he does not choose. As Nochimson (2002: 40) notes, "Adam's compliance with their demands about the casting of Camilla Rhodes is the irrevocable turning point in all their lives. Ironically, the most important link among them is the connection that is pointedly not made, that between Adam and Betty."

What all this means is that the director is responsible for the halting of desire in film first and foremost by how he chooses and characterizes/directs his lead, especially a female one, with whose desire the audience engages. No auteur can bypass such a decision. Moreover, the process it entails means "killing" all those who are not chosen for the part. In the dream, Camilla's photograph is displaced to one of her lovers, the blonde at the dinner party who kisses her, the one who has the main "role" in the primal scene Camilla forces Diane to watch. This displacement has two purposes. The first is related to Diane's guilt over Camilla's murder: It disguises the original contracting of the murder, but at the same time maintains Diane's affect of jealousy. The second is connected to the guilt inherent in the analogy between cinema and dream/fantasy. While in the reality segment Camilla's photograph corroborates her murder, which means that Diane prefers killing the object of her desire to jealously watching her with other lovers, in meta-cinematic terms it means that only *in reality* (or in films dealing exclusively with reality—that is, documentary films) can the object of desire be eliminated (i.e., not in narrative films); the writer/director can kill the protagonist (and Lynch kills both his protagonists), but the actress chosen for the film must remain an object of desire/fantasy as part of the cinematographic image. Narrative film cannot do without it any more than dream can—hence, the guilt. That "Camilla Rhodes" in the dream belongs to a murderous syndicate that associates her with the Devil's party shows that guilt is an inherent component of the casting process that determines the object of desire.

Following this line of thought, we might argue that the constant wavering of the camera when Dan recounts his dream to his friend, emphasizing its own movement rather than expressing a definite purpose, symbolizes its looking for an object of desire and not finding one. Winkie's symbolizes a return to the scene of the crime: In Dan's dream, Winkie's points to Diane's awareness that Camilla is being murdered during her sleep, that she must already be dead; the dialogue between Dan and Herb is rendered in shot/reverse shot, like a classical dialogue, therefore, there is no obvious explanation for the camera movement, except that it expresses Dan's/Diane's affect. As Camilla represents the ultimate object of desire in the film, her murder in meta-cinematic terms means that killing the object of desire in a film, that is, renouncing the right "girl," might end in the collapse of the whole film project. This collapse is evinced not only by Dan's probable death but also by the appearance of the frightening bum (the horror of the empty screen, of not finding the object, or choosing wrongly). Winkie's thus is not only the site of guilt, both Diane's and the filmmaker's, but also symbolizes the disappearance of a female lead (Camilla has already been murdered). As the rotting corpses in Diane's bed suggest, the appearance of the bum implies that when/where there is no body (no embodiment through casting) in film there is nobody (horror, a dead body), no anchor for fantasy. Hence, the bum's appearance only for a split second, making it impossible to recognize the actress (Bonnie Aarons).

Similarly, the espresso symbol that we mentioned in relation to Diane's dream as reflective of her self-disgust affect regarding her decision to have Camilla killed (we know this because the person she sees after drinking the espresso in the reality sequence is a man who is displaced to Angelo Castigliane in the dream—same actor) appears in fact in a mise-en-abyme within a mise-en-abyme (the dream), reflexive of the code of the cinematographic image: It describes a meeting of the production group (Adam, his agent, and the producers) with the Castigliane brothers, Angelo and Vincenzo. The espresso symbol reflects the impossibility of guessing what the Other wants: no matter how hard Mr. Darby (Marcus Graham) tries to please the Castigliane brothers by choosing the right brand of coffee (after researching it), he fails miserably. Vincenzo will not have any and Angelo, after tasting it, spits it out in disgust. Mr. Darby's hand starts shaking with terror as Angelo shouts: "Shit!" Whereupon, Adam's producer appeals to him to keep an open mind in relation to Camilla Rhodes' photograph that the Castigliane brothers have brought with them and Angelo announces categorically that "This is the girl!" But Adam can hardly grasp what the fuss is all about.

In between Adam's verbal protests, before Angelo is handed the espresso, a "duel" of extreme close-ups is shown of him and Vincenzo, an allusion to the protagonist/antagonist in the Western before they engage in a gun fight. The protagonist here is represented by Adam, who wears glasses alluding to those of Guido and his wife in 8½, which is to say, unlike the protagonist in the Western, the director is associated with an intellectual, ironically armed only with a golf club, but also heavily invested in and influenced by the Hollywood tradition (Adam's film is a classical musical, not a film à la 8½). Adam has not chosen a lead yet; his protests stem from the mere fact that as a director he is the one who must choose his lead because he possesses what the Castigliane brothers lack: professionality. This necessarily entails knowing who "the girl" is. Angelo keeps repeating during the meeting, to its end, "This is the girl" (after Adam declares, "That girl is not in my film," to which Vincenzo, looking at Adam, replies, "It is no longer your film"), thus emphasizing that Camilla Rhodes is an arbitrary choice expressing power and has nothing to do with ensuring the success of the film. It is the director (in classical Hollywood, also producers) who must ensure the success of a film by deciding who the girl is, and this means addressing the audience's desire through supplying a fantasy object. But, "This is the girl" also attests to the real Camilla's identity in relation to the photograph Diane shows Joe when she commissions the hit after realizing she no longer holds the key to Camilla's desire—no more than Mr. Darby holds the key to the Castigliane brothers' desire in relation to what brand of espresso they might like, or how to prepare it to their satisfaction. The tension between the two meanings of "This is the girl" points to the guilt inherent in the ability of the director to be the only one who can manage the dialectic of desire/fantasy through casting.

Therefore, subjectivization here, unlike in 8½, does not consist of getting rid of guilt, but rather of acknowledging it and finding ways to cope with it in order to free the filmmaker's imagination. Because of the impossibility of totally severing fantasy from its seeming realization through the cinematographic image of the actor-character, the filmmaker is doomed to feel guilty, as well as to do his utmost to expose the apparatus, the ontology of this image, like the emptiness of the screen (darkness). Nochimson (2002) too, associates darkness with ethics—not a morally negative space, but rather an unknown space of the unconscious from which anything can arise, the wondrous as well as the horrendous, a space between fullness and emptiness; however, she does not fail to mention Lynch's complex relationship with the dream industry, which ultimately means that fullness is associated with fantasy (Hollywood) and emptiness with desire—the dialectic of the two:

> This is a mesmerizing representation of the condition of film production . . . [which] by nature mandate[s] illusion not substance. And yet the breathtaking, indeterminate presentation . . . suggests, as have Lynch's previous films, that popular culture can provide a fullness of meaning even though or perhaps because it is an imaginary signifier (to borrow a term from Christian Metz). . . . The question for Lynch is always whether the imaginary connects with something beyond itself or languishes in the void of solipsism. (43)

We translate this "void of solipsism" into the kind of cinema based solely on desire. As mentioned at the beginning of this chapter, the cinematographic image is composed, inter alia, of a connotative code (e.g., the blonde/brunette as objects of desire) based on our knowledge and ability to recognize iconographic and cultural signs, usually recruited by narrative cinema and genres to the world of fantasy, as evinced by Lynch both in the meta-cinematic scenes in the reality segment and in all the iconography of the dream. Although the iconic cowboy is associated with the demonic side of Hollywood, the film nevertheless acknowledges the undying mythology of Hollywood (e.g., genres like the Western, gangster films, and the musical, especially of the 1950s), which enhance the meta-cinematic aspect in relation to the cinematographic image.[38] The abundant allusions to Hollywood, albeit their semantic meaning, reflect the tension between fantasy and desire. Thus, our argument here is that this is the function of the textual mise-en-abymes, in *Mulholland Drive* as in *8½*: to reveal the dependency of desire on fantasy, especially when it comes to casting.

There are several textual mise-en-abymes in *Mulholland Drive* (five altogether), all relating to filmmaking, most (either explicitly or inexplicitly) pertaining to the casting process: Dan's dream within Rita's dream-within-Diane's-dream, symbolizing contracting the murder where/when Diane gives the hitman Camilla's photo saying "This is the girl"; Adam's meeting with the Castigliane brothers in Diane's dream in relation to their choice concerning the lead ("This is the girl"); Betty's audition scene in Diane's dream; the screen tests on Adam's set in Diane's dream; and, finally, the scene in which Adam coaches his actor in the reality segment. The latter functions as a kind of mirror to the others in that it dissolves the fantasmatic aspect of the film, and yet, the fact that the other mise-en-abymes appear in a dream constituting Diane's fantasy ally them with the role of fantasy in narrative film, in particular with the code of the cinematographic image. In addition, as Diane's fantasy revolves around guilt, this code involves the director's guilt. Because its denotative code contains a measure of materiality in that we can trust that the lead on the screen is a material body, that of an actress (and we must not forget that Naomi Watts is Lynch's "girl"), one that cannot be separated from the connotative code, the latter being part of fantasy, guilt thus becomes part of an actual fraud through the illusion that fantasy can actually be materialized.[39] More so if the filmmaker's unconscious, as well as consciousness, is replete with Hollywood iconography.

Indeed, the dream consists of a pastiche of Hollywood films that alludes to a game of free associations to popular culture.[40] As a result, Diane's fantasy to be a star is not only inspired by cinema but is itself a reflection on films themselves (Lentzner and Ross 2005: 108). Thus, for Lynch, it becomes a discussion about the relationship between creative imagination and the film tradition he *imbibes* from. We thus can sum up to say that in *Mulholland Drive*, the role of the dream segment can be seen to correspond to that of the mise-en-abyme (although it is unique in that it is not a small unit in a larger text, like it should be), because it reflects the similarity between film and dream, evincing the tension between Hollywood as a dream factory and creative imagination. As Nochimson (2002: 37–8) attests, the film constitutes a

> visionary epic about the cosmic degeneration that originate[s] in the thwarting of the creative act by the mechanistic forces of commercialism, and an affirmation of Lynch's belief in the abundance of robust creative potential in mass culture. . . . [A] malignant oppression of "dream" by "factory" . . . represented in the film by a criminal cartel that controls

Hollywood production and thereby brings on the catastrophe that is Lynch's subject, as he, predictably, weighs in on the side of dreams.

Unlike *Sunset Boulevard* (1950), "Billy Wilder's remarkable saga of the dark side of the movies," as well as Lynch's own reference to Hollywood as "human putrefaction [a term Lynch used several times during his press conference at the New York Film Festival 2001] in a city of lethal illusions," Lynch "adds another dimension to his journey: his hard-won optimism about making movies. Unlike the pessimistic Wilder, Lynch believes the culture industry has options for producing authentic public dreams" (2002: 39). And the inspiration to produce "authentic public dreams" is, to a large extent, Hollywood. If for Fellini imagination is replete with Italian art and his own private fantasies, for Lynch, imagination is brimming with Hollywood references, which, as Ruth Perlmutter (2005: 132) notes, are endless: rehearsals and screen tests, demonic casting tactics, allusions to Hollywood hills and road signs, backdrops in the style of the 1940s and 1950s with clichés referring to the genres and aesthetic styles of the time (e.g., film noir), conspirators, a purse with stolen money, a femme fatale behaving like an amnesiac, as well as numerous references to performances and films: theater stages, screens, and characters who are both actors and spectators. Fuller (2001: 14–16) defines *Mulholland Drive* as a (schizoid) fantasy in which a hybrid between neo-noir and 1950s pop film is formed in a postmodern Hollywood gothic style.[41]

Like *8½*, *Mulholland Drive* supports the notion of the freedom of imagination; unlike *8½*, it does not seem to succeed in disposing of guilt because the connotative code is dependent on a radically different artistic and cultural tradition on which the *auteur*, despite his freedom of imagination, must rely. Hence the association of guilt in the film not only with specific casting, as in *8½*, but also with a long tradition of cinematic iconography as we know it from Hollywood history. If for Guido/Fellini getting rid of guilt means doing away with Catholic indoctrination, for Lynch, getting rid of guilt becomes more difficult because of a certain fascination with Hollywood tradition, history, and iconography, no matter how critical he is of its industrial aspect. We might argue that the criminal cartel is analogous to the Catholic Church in *8½*, and that associating it only with the capitalistic/commercial side of Hollywood might make getting rid of guilt a relatively easy task, not unlike getting rid of Catholic doctrines. However, the problem for Lynch seems to be not only the funding of a film, but rather its unavoidable reliance on classical Hollywood's richness (genres, iconography, stars, and so on). Moreover, although Lynch's film emphasizes lack through the traumatic aspect of being excluded from the primal scene, disillusion, and death, his lead, Naomi Watts, "is the girl," the one who mesmerizes us even with her pathetic Diane, couched by Lynch in such a way that we cannot imagine anyone else in the double role she plays, one inspired by a long tradition of Hollywood female stars and iconography. Freedom of imagination thus means deconstructing the classical narrative and exposing the apparatus.

To recapitulate, the textual mise-en-abymes in *8½* and *Mulholland Drive* reflect the interrelations of the different codes of the cinematographic image regarding characters in film, especially protagonists: a quartet comprised of a denotative/referential code, a connotative one, the desire of/for the mother, and guilt. We found that this quartet, as evinced in the relationship between the dreams in the films and the textual mise-e-abymes, marks the latter, in Dällenbach's ([1977] 1989: 218) terminology, as "transcendental mise-en-abymes," because "of [their] ability to reveal something in the text that apparently transcends the text, and to reflect, within the narrative, what simultaneously originates, motivates, institutes and unifies it, and fixes in advance what makes it possible." The transcendental mise-en-abyme discusses the *source* of the work, which Dällenbach also terms "a metaphor of origin" (e.g., "God," "truth"), "a metaphor of the primary instance that constitutes the meaning of meaning and enables signs to communicate" thus reflecting "the *code of codes.*" In contrast to literature, where the code of codes is the word (the symbolic/the Name-of-the-Father), in cinema it is associated with the mother, the primary source of creation. What the films suggest is that in the dialectic of desire/fantasy, in relation to the ontology of film, the mother is the key to both: she is the one who instills desire through her absence and she is the one behind the fantasy to be included in the Other's desire, to be an object of *her* desire. The emptiness/lack of the screen (evinced by Lynch inter alia through the recurring darkness covering it) refers to desire (marking mother's absence, her unattainability), while the richness of images, most of all the fusion of actor-character (it is not mere chance that both films deal with the casting of female characters), marks the filling of lack with fantasy objects (with whose desire spectators must engage to make up for the lack). Hence, the female singer in *Mulholland Drive* representing the deconstruction of the cinematic apparatus. Her death on the stage is lamented: She might be dead (not present on the screen), but her singing, through the very apparatus the filmmaker is trying to dissolve, goes on, sending chills down our spines.[42]

PART THREE

Gender-Crossing Films

5

This Gender That Is Mine

Feminine Enjoyment and Self-Creation

Disconcerting Bodies and "Feminine Enjoyment"

This chapter presents a six-category taxonomy (detailed in the appendix) of gender-crossing characters in narrative cinema, defined by their specificity: the cross-dresser, the tomboy, the transvestite, the trans protagonist, the trans-body (a fantastic category possible only in fiction), and the drag queen. Between the 1930s and the 1990s, cross-dressing was the most popular category in classical and mainstream cinema;[1] however, in keeping with social and cultural changes brought on by feminist and LGBTQ movements, it has lost its appeal (except for third-world cinema, in whose male-dominated societies women are considered inferior to men and LGBTQ persons an aberration of nature). This has paved the way, especially in the last decade, to more contemporary heroes, such as trans people (including trans actors).

Thus far in this book we have been concerned mostly with the dynamic of desire/fantasy in narrative film: We have shown how this dynamic is influenced by a process of subjectivization in relation to both diegetic characters and spectatorship through tackling the relations between the body of the actor, their character, and casting, while keeping in mind the unique ontology and aesthetics of film. Our discussion of the gender-crossing corpus in the following two chapters still deals with these relations, but introduces an additional dimension pertaining to the protagonists as well as to spectatorship: "feminine enjoyment" (*la jouissance féminine*), what in Lacanian psychoanalysis is also referred to as "the Other enjoyment," or "the enjoyment of t/he Woman." In Chapters 1–4 we aligned subjectivization with getting to a point where the protagonists set themselves free from the Other's desire and acknowledge the desire that is in them, a process involving the spectators, either by thrusting us from the primal fantasy scene or by preventing our inscription in it altogether. In the films discussed in Chapters 5–6 this is the starting point for most of the protagonists, whose desire is clear at the outset. Therefore, the obvious question is how to realize it. We find that the notion answering this question is feminine enjoyment, which underlies here the process of subjectivization. Spectators first become involved with this process through their engagement with the desire of the protagonists (to realize it). Second, the films explored in the preceding chapters assigned the inscription in the primal scene (the filmic space) to the disastrous fantasy of being inscribed in the Other's desire; in contrast, the uniqueness, or rather achievement, of the gender-crossing corpus is that by inscribing the spectators in a structure that bears an affinity with that of the primal scene, the films in fact inscribe the spectators in a space of feminine enjoyment, in which desire is fulfilled in the real. Thus, they provoke an *experience* of it—herein consists our partaking in the protagonists' subjectivization process.

What is feminine enjoyment and why attribute it to subjectivization in the gender-crossing corpus? Unlike desire, which can never be satisfied, and fantasy, which is doomed to remain in the imaginary, enjoyment (*la jouissance* in the original French) is a substance, not unlike Freud's notion of the libido, which achieves satisfaction in the body, functioning as a defense mechanism against desire. The term *jouissance* in French denotes erotic pleasure, climax, and orgasm. It was adopted by Lacan to describe the kind of enjoyment exceeding Freud's pleasure principle in which the subject aspires to homeostasis. The suppressed fantasy of re-finding the (already-lost) object of desire, the mother—of being the imaginary phallus that completes her—goes hand in hand with the fantasy of absolute enjoyment, hence the prohibition, which creates the desire to transgress the pleasure principle. The prohibition of the symbolic father thus allows the subject to obtain, or sustain, only a limited amount of this bodily substance, what Lacan refers to as "phallic" (symbolic) enjoyment resulting from castration. This means that the phallus becomes the *signifier* of desire (the sexual pleasure of desiring), hence of *lack*, lack of being (it is what the child is lacking, the fact that not all its needs and demands are satisfied, which impels them to speak). This nonfulfillment allows the subject to come into being as a desiring one; over-closeness to the parent, like abundance of enjoyment, creates anxiety (the lack of the lack, of the phallic function). Beyond that, enjoyment involves pain (the subject cannot endure too much of it). The phallic enjoyment is also related to sexual intercourse.

However, there is another form of enjoyment, also experienced in the body but unrelated to specific sexual organs and unlimited by the phallic signifier. In book XX of his seminar, Lacan's ([1972-3] 1999: 64–77) attention regarding radical otherness shifts from the concept of desire to that of the enjoyment of t/he Woman—"the Other enjoyment," what we refer to here throughout as "feminine enjoyment." In lieu of situating the subject in relation to the signifier (the field of language, the symbolic), linking the concept of castration to giving up the desire for the mother and to the phallic enjoyment, radical alterity is now conflated with Woman, but not in any essential or constructionist way, nor in the sense of wholeness, but rather in terms of psychoanalytic classification—hence the crossed-out definite article (t/he). Although this type of enjoyment is not restricted to women, Lacan nevertheless suggests that it is not very likely men would experience it. The phallic enjoyment pertaining to castration belongs to categories (e.g., "all men . . .");[2] feminine enjoyment transcends any definition (women, men, feminine, masculine, and so on) that places the subject in a preordained category, endowing her or him with an identity; there is no phallic signifier restricting the enjoyment. The feminine enjoyment is therefore associated with "being," and it is unique and unlimited, much like mystical enjoyment. Interestingly enough, Book XX of the Seminar is titled "Encore" ("more" in French, which is phonetically identical to "en corps"—"in the body"). One of Lacan's examples is Bernini's statue of Saint Teresa: "It's like for Saint Teresa—you need but to go to Rome and see the statue by Bernini, to immediately understand that she's coming. There's no doubt about it. What is she getting off on?" ([1972-3] 1999: 76).[3] This example shows that feminine enjoyment is experienced in the body, albeit its spirituality. It is also associated with the core aspect of poetics, that which transcends language as a way of attaining intelligibility or communication.

Because feminine enjoyment is not associated with proper sexual activity (in the gender-crossing films, it is often associated with some sort of artistic activity) it is regarded as a special form of sublimation. This is how Bruce Fink ([1995] 1997: 115) interprets Lacan's notion of feminine jouissance:

> [It] designates a kind of Freudian sublimation of the drives in which the drives are fully satisfied (this *other* kind of satisfaction is what is behind Lacan's expression "Other juissance"), and a kind of Lacanian sublimation whereby an ordinary object is elevated to the status of the Thing. . . . The Freudian thing[4] finds a signifier, simple examples of which may include "God," . . . "the Virgin," "art," "music," and so on, and the *finding* of the signifier must be understood as an encounter . . . , that is, as fortuitous in some sense. (italics in the original)

What this means is that in sublimation, the subject finds a real and lasting experience of (feminine) enjoyment out of the deadlock of desire (and fantasy) that "provides full satisfaction of the drives . . . and Lacan relates it to . . . a kind of bodily, corporal jouissance that is not localized in the genitals the way phallic jouissance is . . . and yet it is *of* and *in* the body" (120, italics in the original). The process of subjectivization as we present it in the gender-crossing corpus consists in the real, finding a special signifier that brings lasting satisfaction to the subject, a path beyond neurosis (the "masculine" structure in Lacan).

The concept of feminine enjoyment in its function to satisfy the drives is linked in most of the gender-crossing corpus to the notion that assuming responsibility for one's desire is a precondition for the experience of feminine enjoyment. For some protagonists, it constitutes the starting point of their unique journey through which they broaden and deepen their experience of self-creation/autogenesis, which means a realization of a specific desire; for others, the encounter with feminine enjoyment (the satisfaction of the drives) is what frees them from various constraints (mostly related to the dependence on love objects), paving the way to a better and more accommodating way of life.

The gender-crossing protagonist's position in relation to the (m)Other is tackled from the start by bringing to light all three primal fantasies: castration (sex/gender), seduction (sexuality), and the primal scene (being). The castration fantasy, which refers to sexual difference, raises the question "Who/What am I—man or woman?" For the gender-crossing protagonists, it becomes almost impossible to maintain the distinction between man/woman and its correlatives (femininity/masculinity; gay/straight): Be it by choice or by circumstance, they are caught in a space in which they enjoy the experience of being set free from the constraints of such categories and the norms that go with them. Thus, in terms of the seduction fantasy, which refers to the origin of sexuality and entails the notion that "my enjoyment is not mine," the space in which the cross-gender protagonists function, that of feminine enjoyment, is not the Other's, but their own. In terms of the primal scene fantasy, which refers to the origin of the subject ("Whose desire is it that caused my being?"), the gender-crossing protagonist can safely assert, certainly at the end of the subjectivization process, "I am my own creation, it was my desire that brought me here, where I enjoy my life!" What this means for many protagonists (whose desire and enjoyment are wholly theirs, not their parents') is that they might have been born as "boy" or "girl," but that does not mean they have to behave like one, desire an object of the opposite sex, or be one, and so on. This tackling of primal fantasies at the outset clarifies the distinction between ego identifications (identity) and subjective positions regarding desire and enjoyment (the positions occupied by the subject in relation to the Other's enjoyment are not different from those occupied in relation to the Other's desire):

> Sexual identity, in Lacanian terms, is constituted on at least two different levels: (1) the successive identifications that constitute the ego (usually

identifications with one or both parents), accounting for an *imaginary* level of sexual identity, a rigid level which very often comes into . . . conflict with (2) masculine or feminine structure . . . as related to the different sides of Lacan's formula on sexuation, any given *subject* being able to situate herself on either side. (Fink [1995] 1997: 116, italics in the original)

Broadly speaking, Lacan's formula has nothing to do with biological men and women; it is a difference between being situated, in terms of enjoyment, under the phallic signifier (that of desire—"men") and a specific signifier that relates to the real because it cannot be represented in the language of communication and comprehension. This kind of enjoyment, as previously emphasized, wholly satisfies the subject and is referred to as "feminine."[5] All the gender-crossing categories relate to these two subjective structures, as well as to the processes involved in the traversal from the phallic to the feminine one. For example, a trans man (also the tomboy and the crossdresser man are salient examples) points to a certain identity, but all the same might be able to show or develop a subjective capacity for enjoyment that places him on the side of the feminine structure. This is the position gender-crossing protagonists occupy, some at the beginning of their process, others transitioning from a space governed by the phallic economy to one in which feminine enjoyment reigns supreme.

Regarding spectatorship, the *image* of the gender-crossing character is always visually ambiguous or multilayered. Its polymorphous appearance thus also cuts through all three primal fantasies as soon as the protagonist appears on the screen. For spectators, the questions often generated (both consciously and unconsciously) by the gender-crossing characters are: What am I seeing—man/woman? What does this mean for me? Who is this object of desire that my enjoyment is directed at and invested in? Such questions (pertaining to the castration and the seduction fantasies) might provoke a crisis in our reading of gender and sexuality—not in our inscription in the filmic space (the protagonist's desire/the primal scene structure). Therefore, to engage with the desire of the gender-crossing figure who seems to be asserting "I am what I am"; and "My desire and enjoyment are my own!" means engaging also with an experience that basically defies gender or any other identity. That most spectators do engage with such protagonists and films indicates that subjectivity operates in unfamiliar ways in a fluid space beyond strict categories and norms, which is exactly what the gender-crossing films take advantage of. Moreover, the polymorphous image of the gender-crossing protagonist challenges the image as fetish, which becomes a unique device for dismantling fantasy as fixation, again, without dissolving the spectator's engagement with the protagonist's desire.

We might thus argue that the ethics of subjectivization in terms of the diegesis as well as spectatorship inexorably yoke together three distinct phenomena—sex (female/male), gender (man/woman; feminine/masculine, or transgender), and sexuality (heterosexual, homosexual, bisexual)—in new and versatile configurations, all undermining binary cultural notions regarding these phenomena, in fact, dismantling all normative connections between them. Unlike the body-character-breach films, or the dreaming-character films, in which the question of engagement with the primal scene becomes valid only at the point where inscription in the Other's desire is proven detrimental to the subject, in the gender-crossing corpus it is generated from the start. Regarding the primal scene fantasy (the origin of the subject), this corpus provides a unique answer in that the protagonist is a self-creation. How the protagonist looks and behaves—"man"; "woman"; "trans"—is reflected in the visual image as well as in acting, whether the body transformation in the diegesis is an outcome of disguise or achieved through full or partial gender readjustment/reassignment (in the transgender category the casting very often complicates matters even further, for example, a female actress—a cisgender—playing a trans man). That the expression and experience of feminine enjoyment is the main source of self-creation, in so far as we as spectators accept the ambiguity of the gender-crossing figure, we experience a non-phallic enjoyment beyond any preordained category, but all the same occurring *in the body*, as do all the gender-crossing characters, as outlined in our six-category taxonomy (see appendix).

"The Semiotic"

We ask: What are the elements that would generate or sustain a space of feminine enjoyment?

In our view, Julia Kristeva's ([1974] 1984) notion of "the semiotic" in oscillation with "the symbolic" function seems an adequate one. While the symbolic includes all discursive practices adhering to the logical and grammatical rules of language (regulated by the phallic economy), the semiotic is a nonverbal drive-related and affective modality, thus belonging to the "signifying" (a term used also by Lacan, as opposed to "signification") practice that generates what Kristeva (e.g., 102; 126) calls "the subject in process"—a never ending and unlimited process of growth and change. The drive-related, affective, and organized according to primary processes semiotic contains nonverbal elements: sound, rhythm, music, kinetics, color, odors, and so on. This distinction between the symbolic and the semiotic, borrowed from Lacan, is applied by Kristeva to a "signifying practice" (in literature), composed of both "genotext," which contains semiotic elements, and "phenotext," which serves to communicate (86–89). Kristeva helps us not only understand how subjective processes and structures may be applicable to artistic creation/practice and *its experience*, but also clarifies for us that the experience of the semiotic, which we conflate with feminine enjoyment, although non-phallic, is not divorced from the symbolic, or else it would be a "psychotic" one. This relates to our above quotation from Fink on the real finding a signifier (only the symbolic has signifiers!), what at first sounds like a paradox. Feminine enjoyment, or the semiotic, can be experienced or practiced by a subject in the real precisely because they have not lost their grip on reality (the symbolic). Moreover, from this, it stems that what sustains the young child in its experience of primordial loss, the semiotic, functions also as a form of satisfaction (of the drives) sustaining the subject of desire: We can so explain the love of music, art, poetry, and so on—the way the semiotic, or genotext, is integrated into the symbolic.

In terms of gender, in the dialectic between the semiotic and the symbolic as an open system, the semiotic is the force that subverts gender norms. It is repressed by patriarchy, but has the power to disrupt it through the versatility of the affect and the semiotic *chōra*. Kristeva ([1974] 1984: 25–30) borrows this last term from Plato's *Timaeus* to denote the articulation of the drives constituted by vocal or kinetic rhythm, independent from representation. The ordering (as distinct from the "law," which pertains to the symbolic) principle of the semiotic, prelinguistic, sensorimotor organization—the *chōra*—is a functional state governing the relationships between the body, objects, and the protagonists of the family structure. The ambivalence of the drives—simultaneously assimilating and destructive—makes the semioticized body a place of constant scission. Thus, what we call subjectivization here becomes in Kristeva's terms a heterogeneous process, a practice of deconstruction and construction.

Such is the gender-crossing figure, a subject in process, who always goes against the grain, whose appearance on-screen is heterogeneous, and whose journey constitutes a practice of deconstruction and construction. Protagonists in gender-crossing films assert that both desire and enjoyment are theirs and not the Other's, that they are their own creation, very often achieved through elements of the semiotic, expressed in different modes of creation/creativity, supported by various performing arts (playing music, singing, acting, dancing, and so on).

Blended Voices: *Yentl*

Unlike the cross-dressing comedies, dramas are rather influenced by a long history of women who passed as men in pursuit of economic independence, avoidance of sexual harassment, the wish to practice a career reserved only for men, and so on. Many of them even married women who kept their secret until they died, when their true sex was discovered upon preparing the body for burial.[6] Salient examples of such dramas are *Yentl* (1983), *The Ballad of Little Jo* (Maggie Greenwald 1993), and *Albert Nobbs* (Rodrigo García 2011).

We consider the protagonist of *Yentl* an emblem of all gender-crossing characters who acknowledge their own desire from the start. In her case, it is the love of the Talmud[7]—its study and practice in everyday life providing her with the experience of feminine enjoyment; it is her signifier for the real, creating a semiotic space for herself, her friends, and spectators as well. Because women are forbidden to practice the Talmud in public, she can do so only as a man, hence the disguise. Yentl's journey consists of the awakening of sexual desires leading to an assimilation of womanhood, through which she comes to fully own what she feels from the beginning is *hers*. At the end of her journey, she can practice the study of the Talmud as a woman, without a man's attire. The acknowledgment of womanhood and sexuality are meant here, as well as elsewhere, to suggest that the experience of feminine enjoyment is not a one-time mystical one, but rather the creation of a space that is or becomes a permanent habitat of the protagonist as an adult in possession of her sexuality and gender. Barbra Streisand's larger-than-life voice and the music (composed by Michel Legrand) and lyrics (by Alan and Marilyn Bergman) through which Yentl (played by Streisand) expresses what she feels during her unique journey are the main elements of the semiotic concerning spectatorship, in addition to the engagement with her desire to study the Talmud. Indeed, many gender-crossing films employ the musical genre or resort to musical numbers through which the semiotic is heightened, thus sustaining the in-between space shared by the protagonists and the spectators. In this sense, *Yentl* is a prototypical film that offers an ideal model that blends spirituality and eroticism, both fully satisfactorily experienced in the body though not through any actual physical interchange (sexual intercourse), empowering both genders to find a kind of transcendental love, the only one that can sustain a lasting relationship by adhering to a common signifier for the real—here, the love of Talmud.

Adapted from Isaac Bashevis Singer's "Yentl the Yeshiva Boy" (1962), the film is Barbra Streisand's directorial debut. *Yentl* tells the story of a young Jewish Orthodox motherless woman in Eastern Europe of the beginning of the twentieth century, who, encouraged (in secret) by her father, Rebbe Mendel (Nehemiah Persoff), has come under the spell of the Talmud—an occupation reserved for men alone. Upon the death of her father, Yentl faces the life of an Orthodox wife—to bear children and serve her husband. Determined to pursue the study of Talmud, she leaves her home disguised as a yeshiva[8] boy, taking the name of her deceased brother, Anshel. It is important to note that she takes this name not because she wants to fulfill her father's unconscious desire that she take her brother's place (if this had been the case, she would have had to face the consequences of the impossibility to guess or know what the Other wants), but because she feels she is *destined* for an occupation reserved only for men.

Yentl joins a yeshiva where she becomes very close to Avigdor (Mandy Patinkin), a fellow student and her study partner for whom she develops feelings without being able to reveal her real gender. Avigdor is promised to Hadass (Amy Irving) and the two clearly like each other, but when it is discovered that Avigdor's brother has committed suicide (which is forbidden in Judaism), Hadass's parents forbid the marriage, lest his brothers' probable mental illness inflict the couple's future children. To remain close to Hadass, Avigdor tries to persuade Anshel to marry her. Unable to resist Avigdor's "crazy plan," afraid that he might leave, which means Yentl would lose her study partner as well as the one she is in love with, she agrees to marry Hadass. Knowing "he" cannot consummate the marriage, Anshel finds another way to sustain Hadass's desire and enjoyment: he teaches her the Talmud and the two develop a special friendship. This leads Hadass to fall in love with her gentle and considerate husband. When Yentl realizes she cannot continue not being herself she decides to reveal her secret to Avigdor and confesses to him that she loves him. Though Avigdor admits he loves her too and expresses his wish to marry her, Yentl declines his proposal knowing that as a woman she would no longer be able to study the Talmud with him as they used to when he thought she was a man. She embarks on a ship in search of a place where she can openly practice the Talmud without masquerading.

In "Choreographies,"[9] Jacques Derrida poses the following question, "What if we were to approach . . . the area of a relationship to the other where the code of sexual marks would no longer be discriminating?" (Derrida and McDonald 1982: 76). Aware of the utopian nature of the answer he is seeking, Derrida answers:

> The relationship would not be a-sexual, far from it, but would be sexual otherwise: beyond the binary difference that governs the decorum of all codes, beyond the opposition feminine/masculine, beyond bi-sexuality as well, beyond homosexuality and heterosexuality, which come to the same thing. As I dream of saving the chance that this question offers, I would like to believe in the masses, this indeterminable number of blended voices. (1982: 76)

Derrida's vision of "blended voices" resonates with the ideal model offered in *Yentl*, and in fact characterizes all the gender-crossing corpus, in that it strives to dissolve sex, gender, and sexual categories based on binarism (male/female; men/women-masculine/feminine; straight/gay/bisexual). It depicts a model reverberating with significant changes the gender-crossing protagonists manage to bring about in relation to other characters close to them. Such changes occur in the midstream of a conventional society/milieu governed by strict norms. In *Yentl*'s case—an Orthodox Jewish community.[10]

Yentl/Anshel also complies with the model of masculinity described by Daniel Boyarin (1997) as the ideal Orthodox Jewish "sissy" male whose life revolves around the study of religious scriptures. Although Boyarin argues that the construction of this ideal man does not necessarily work in women's favor in Judaism because women are excluded from the world of studying the scriptures, he nevertheless contends that it can be recruited for a process of emancipation within a project that negates the male ideal in Western culture that endorses perfection and unity. The Talmud scholar is idyllically by and large a product of the text he studies. Judaism, like desire, is conditioned by lack. It is in this sense that circumcision (castration) attains its full symbolic meaning in Judaism: the substitution of thing with word, through the disappearance of the thing and acceptance of the Law (the Decalogue, as well as 613 other commandments). Indeed, one of the most significant religious innovations regarding sacrificial rituals in the early centuries of the first millennium was the substitution of prayers and verbal rituals for bloody sacrifices.[11] This is the core of Jewish spirituality—learning how to live in the abstract (the symbolic), never reaching satisfaction in the real. However, Judaism also found a way out of the deadlock of desire/lack through the many facets of the Talmud. Studying it and interpreting it thus adds a meaningful aspect to spirituality: the creation of as many as possible interpretations and meanings of the law, in fact, of the nature of God and life. What this means is that rather than live in the domain of desire alone, or a phallic economy, the yeshiva student can participate in and enjoy the constant play and shift of meaning, thus creating a space of feminine enjoyment—the semiotic. In other words, recognizing lack is a condition of (paves the way to) re-economizing enjoyment (a passage from the phallic to the feminine one) to achieve a life of satisfaction. The Talmud understands this, and so does Yentl/Anshel.

Talmudic culture, as elaborated by Boyarin, means a series of different cultural entities that are in large part and in constantly changing ways crucially informed by the centrality of the reading of the Talmud in their practice, a reading that means extracting as many different interpretations of the texts as possible. The Talmud is considered the centerpiece of Jewish cultural life, foundational to all Jewish thought and aspirations. It deals with laws in a way that should provide a guide for the daily life ("Talmud" in Hebrew translates literally as "instruction," which means not just instructions for others but also that which requires constant studying and interpretation). It is rooted in oral Jewish scholarship and generated over the course of hundreds of years diverse schools of thought stemming from unresolved debates. Indeed, rarely are debates formally closed; in some instances, the final word determines the practical law, but in many others the issue is left unresolved. In general, all valid opinions, even the nonnormative ones, were recorded in the Talmud. This polysemic and polyvocal experience, conflated by us with feminine enjoyment/the semiotic and the possibilities it opens up, is ingeniously termed by Boyarin (1997: xvi), who describes the Talmud as "jumbled, carnivalesque, raucous, bawdy, vital, exciting ... almost Rabelaisian," as "*Jewissance*" (xxiii).

But women in Judaism are excluded from such a life of *Jewisssance*, from finding a way back to the drives in sublimated ways that the Talmudic experience provides. In Judaism feminine enjoyment is reserved only for men to experience. It is almost impossible to write about *Yentl* without mentioning Freud's essay on sexual morality and modern nervous illness (originally published in 1908, the period in which *Yentl* takes place). Freud ([1908] 1959: 198) describes the process of draining of the drives in modern society as the sucking of blood by a vampire, damaging people beyond repair. He particularly expresses concern about the double standard women are subjected to, stating that although not all people are inclined to have the same sexual economy, nevertheless, "I do not believe that women's 'physiological feeble-mindedness' is to be explained by a biological opposition between intellectual work and sexual activity. . . . I think that the undoubted intellectual inferiority of so many women can rather be traced back to the inhibition of thought necessitated by sexual suppression." It is in this sense that *Yentl* is no less relevant today (for Rabbinic Judaism even more so) than it might have been at the turn of the twentieth century. By creating a space of feminine enjoyment for her, in which the semiotic provides the way to change, not just for the protagonist, but also for her two other friends, *Yentl* aspires to pave the way to the studying of Talmud for Orthodox women, much like Streisand herself paved the way for women filmmakers.[12]

What excites Yentl most about Talmudic study is its variety, *signifiance*, and color. Like Boyarin's aspirations, *Yentl* makes the distinction between the actual practice of Rabbinic Judaism and a possible reconstruction of it, one that is, nevertheless, rooted in the tradition of the Orthodox rabbis. For Yentl, her love of Talmud marks her starting point, not the end of a process. Part of this process has to do with her sexuality. She seems to still be in "latency." Because she grew up without a mother, sheltered by her father with whom she shared love of the Talmud, she has not met anyone who aroused her sexuality (which relates to the fantasy of seduction) and has no clue what gender difference means (which relates to the castration fantasy). This is one of the reasons she cannot fathom why she is being banned from studying the scriptures; all she knows about her being a woman is that she cannot study. However, the strange thing is that her desire, as well as her experience of feminine enjoyment, are clear to her from the start, as though she has skipped a whole process in relation to the Other. This, on the one hand, is precisely what empowers her to transgress the law that forbids women to wear men's clothes so that she be able to continue learning from books (it does not matter to her if she passes as a man what the implications might be). On the other hand, her falling in love with Avigdor, and Hadass's falling in love with Anshel while Yentl learns what it means to be a grown woman and have a female friend (replacing a sister or a mother), paradoxically enabled by Yentl's disguise, makes her realize that she does not fully own (only "nine-tenth of the law") what she believes is rightfully hers from the start. To fully own it she needs to divulge her secret and assert herself as a woman scholar of the Talmud in the open, thus completing the process of self-creation (which relates to the primal scene fantasy).

The way the film works with sound and space, in compliance with the ambivalent image of the cross-dresser, makes it virtually impossible to pin down any definite sense of either gender or sexuality—an emblematic example of how gender-crossing films engage us with the protagonist's desire, and the subversive way in which they realize it. As the film progresses, it builds up the experience of feminine enjoyment as well as the notion that characters like Yentl/Anshel must become part of any community, namely the semiotic *chōra* must be allowed to be part of a normative space, allowed to create changes from within even if through elements unrecognizable or that do not make sense. Through the cross-dressing, it becomes clear that the wall of sexual and gender discrimination, between gay/straight, women/men, as well as that between the private/public spheres, is knocked down. We should reiterate here: The value of these films is that by adhering to the classical language of film, they maintain their ability to draw us into their space (the primal scene structure), as well as engage us with the Other's (the protagonist's) desire, but they use this inscription/engagement to enhance the worth of realizing our *own* desire. For Yentl, it is a journey of learning and accepting the contradictions and conflicts relating to sexuality and gender in herself, one she cannot learn from books. When Avigdor is about to leave and Anshel tries to persuade him that Hadass is worth fighting for, claiming that they can talk to the Rabbi, that "maybe there is a law," Avigdor explodes: "There are no laws, not for this [referring to his feelings for Hadass], maybe if you took your nose out of the books once in a while you'd know more about life, about men and women, about love, how can I expect you to understand?"

According to Orthodox Jewish practice, the spaces of women and men must be separated lest women arouse sexual desires in men, distracting them from their studies. The first scene of the film shows this separation by associating women with livestock and cooking (buying geese and fish), while men are ardently discussing the Talmud (women are earthly; men, spiritual); when Yentl tries to buy a book designed only for men from a book peddler driving a cart full of books (the books are separated in the cart, "for men/for women"), he refuses to sell it to her; she is not allowed to own such books, least of all to read them. He tells her to go to the back of his cart where there are books for women, with pictures. Only when she lies, saying that she is buying it for her father, does he agree to sell her the book. A similar transgression on Yentl's part is next evident after she comes home: While burning the food on the stove in the kitchen (women's space), she listens to her father teaching the Talmud to a young boy in the study (men's space). When the student does not know the right answer, she hollers it impatiently, so that it is heard. The student, stupefied, asks: "Yentl knows Talmud?" further arguing that women who study are devils. This reaction makes clear that as a woman she is banned from the knowledge of Talmud, especially from voicing it. After the student leaves, her father pulls the curtains over the windows to hide their learning as he declares that God will understand, but he is not sure about the neighbors. He creates a special space for them of secret feminine enjoyment as they both transgress the Orthodox laws, rules, and norms. After her father's passing, it is the manly disguise that enables Yentl to continue this transgression.

In addition, Yentl's *songs* (voice, melody, lyrics) express her sexual awakening in a semioticized body that, combined with the uniquely cinematic design of spaces, offers the spectators a body-mind-space of constant scission. Engaging with the film thus means that together with Yentl, we go through a heterogeneous process, a practice of deconstruction and construction—as Kristeva might put it—enhanced by Yentl's singing. In fact, the relationship between sound and image create an extra/special, semiotic space for spectators, shared only by us and Yentl. Whenever she sings, occupying a space in which she is by herself regardless of the songs' association with either men or women in the diegesis, the lyrics are coordinated with the movement of her lips. However, the minute she is in the company of other people she seals her lips, *but* the songs continue to be played on the soundtrack, thus creating a (sound) bridge between two separate spaces, or scenes. This rhetorical device attracts attention to two contradictory spaces: On the one hand, it complies with the Jewish dictum forbidding women to sing in public (since women's singing in a men's or mixed space is bound to arouse even greater sexual desires in men than just women occupying a gender-mixed space). On the other hand, what Yentl conceals from characters in the diegesis is shared by Streisand with the *spectators*, thus transgressing the law, as well as bridging spaces (private/public; men's/women's) that otherwise never mix. This device, splitting the body from the voice (which, of course, also attracts attention to the fact that the unity of voice and body in cinema is illusionary), ends only at the end of her process and the beginning of a new journey when in the final scene of the film she decides that voicing her love for the Talmud in public is part of her bodily experience. Moreover, the songs, which express Yentl's most inner thoughts, render Streisand's own capacity for inducing an experience of feminine enjoyment/the semiotic through her unique voice. Here it is mostly ballads, which Streisand is famous for, that, through her disguise, allude also to Jewish cantorial singing or chanting, performed only by men (*hazzanut*).[13] Thus, Streisand's astounding voice aspires to achieve for the audience what Yentl's disguise achieves for her.

During the rendering of the first song ("Where Is It Written"), we see Yentl at her father's house lip-syncing the words, the song then proceeds to be heard on the soundtrack in the next scene taking place at the synagogue,

Yentl situated in the women's section (*ezrat nashim*), her lips sealed, the song thus sound-bridging the two scenes; she watches her father in the company of men. When she realizes he is unwell, alarmed, she calls out to him, whereupon everybody reproaches her, including her father, as women are not allowed to voice their feelings in the company of men. Indeed, Yentl's first songs express her bewilderment at the fact that, if she is destined only for bringing children into the world, taking care of them and her husband, and learning how to tell a herring from a carp, how is it that she has such an aptitude for learning—the source of her boundless imagination and enjoyment? Why is she banned from gaining knowledge from the holy books (about life, the universe, God)? In the spirit of the Talmud, she argues with God that if she has a mind, then it must function like any other bodily organ, "Where is it written what it is/ I'm meant to be, that I can't dare/ . . . or have my share of every sweet-imagined possibility?"

After her father's passing, having left home dressed as a yeshiva boy, Yentl turns to the spirit of her father in the second song ("Papa, Can You Hear Me?"). It is the middle of the night and she lights a memorial candle. The light shed by the candle against the background of utter darkness symbolizes Yentl's journey of study as one of light amid the darkness (the discrimination of women) surrounding her. It is important to bear in mind that Yentl's biological father is also her spiritual mentor; she thus allies him with the Father in Heaven, underscored here by the blending of *hazzanic* tones into the song, in keeping with Streisand's colossal protean voice. The transgression of the disguise stems from an inner dictum, believing she has no choice but to follow her free will, hence the apologetic address: "Papa, please forgive me/ Try to understand me/ Papa, don't you know I had no choice?"

After she is accepted to a prestigious yeshiva, in the third song ("This Is One of Those Moments"), the image shows a montage of her initiation into the community of yeshiva students (their exaltation in discussing the Talmud, happy about the new addition to the yeshiva; Yentl's love for books, which she holds and caresses; and Avigdor being paired with her, taking her under his protective wing), while the lyrics refer to an experience she will never forget through what is imprinted in her body—smell, color, light. This leads to her conviction that what she is experiencing now—referring to her access to books and studying—no one can ever take away from her. The montage shows that what Yentl has been able to experience so far only by herself or in her father's company is now shared by a whole community in a space (characterized by motion—the students are seen coming and going, ascending and descending stairs, moving in groups, and so on, while discussing the scriptures) wholly permeated with *Jewissance*. As the song on the soundtrack describes Yentl's enormous sense of freedom the books give her, an experience "no man can take away," toward the end of this montage, the Rabbi, standing at the top of the stairs surrounded by students hollers out a question: "Where in the Talmud is it written that possession is nine-tenths of the law?" Yentl, who is downstairs among a crowd of students, is the only one who knows the right answer. What this means is that Yentl, though in full possession of the knowledge of the Talmud, feeling that no man can take away the enjoyment she derives from it, is embarking on a journey, her initiation into the yeshiva marking only the beginning of a process that what she *feels* is hers must be *fully owned* by her, that is, legally or publicly acknowledged. Spectators may overlook this, perceive it as just another incident showing her erudition; what does not escape us is the experience of *Jewissance,* which permeates the entire film.

Jewissance is clearly what characterizes Avigdor's relationship with Anshel, in contrast to the characterization of his relationships with women (mostly Hadass), which are phallic ones. The film thus draws an analogy between Yentl/Anshel's bodily experience and appearance and the Talmudic text, which is full of contradictions, paradoxes, and a multiplicity of meanings, not unlike Kristeva's analogy of body-subject and text. Boyarin (1997) contends that the model of the yeshiva boy (*yeshiva-bokhur*) does not entail the deep fear and suspicion of meanings that might arise from dependence on other men and is therefore free of homophobia or fear of feminization. Although the Talmud prefers heterosexual relations and deems men superior, it does not prefer masculinity over femininity as we know them in Western culture: the feminine and femininity are not stigmas in Talmudic culture. Since according to the Talmudic spirit nothing can achieve perfection and unity, the text being under constant erasure and deconstruction, Boyarin, who rightly makes the connection between homophobia and misogyny, claims that this connection does not exist in the Talmud, despite its strong presence in Orthodox Judaism, because the Talmud recognizes the existence of homosexual desire resulting from intimate friendship between men. In such a relationship, everything is open, from mundane conversation to discussing the Torah. There is a shared space of study, emotions are expressed through touch, and students even occasionally share a bed. In Anshel and Avigdor's conversations we find exaltation, sharing, friendship, and an intimacy that even facilitates discussions about sex. Thus, in addition of our partaking in a transgressive space created by the unique rendition of Yentl's songs, we also partake in a homoerotic space.

For example, upon Yentl's arrival at the yeshiva, Avigdor invites Anshel to his lodgings. As the landlady's niece has come for a visit and is occupying the spare room, Avigdor offers to share his bed with Anshel. Despite Yentl's attempts at resisting the invitation, Avigdor seems more than pleased about this idea, but at her insistence they go to sleep back to back. In a later scene, Avigdor and Anshel are seen arguing fervently, as is their wont, about the significance of the rib in the creation of Woman. Anshel argues for a double meaning of the Hebrew word *tzela* (both "rib" and "side"). By insisting that *tzela* means "side," Anshel maintains that Adam was created both male and female, rendering the sexes equal and with the same masculine and feminine traits because they come from the same source. The argument takes place outdoors where there are two women. One is pregnant and the other is nursing her baby. Avigdor points Anshel toward the women and says: "Look, can you do that? . . . Create life, give birth to sons? When you can, tell me that we're the same." Although these words are naturally meant to convey irony, what happens next is particularly engaging. At this supposedly instance of essentialism, the text refrains from elaborating its statement on sexual difference; instead, it develops a homoerotic current. As the scene continues, Avigdor keeps grabbing Anshel, fondling and teasing him, while they go on with the argument about rib/side in a playful and completely erotic ambiance.

Hereafter, Avigdor hurls Anshel to the ground, leans over him and the close-up of the two leaves no doubt about their feelings for each other—they look deeply into each other's eyes. Avigdor is clearly not startled by this and shows no signs of homophobia (on the contrary!), as Allison Fernley and Paula Maloof (1985: 43) also note. In fact, Avigdor lets his feelings run free, so much so that (in the scene that follows) he leads Anshel to a lake where, to Yentl's mortification, yeshiva boys bathe in the nude. He takes off his clothes, enters the water, starts swimming, and invites Anshel to join in. When Anshel declines, Avigdor gets out of the water stark naked and lies down next to Anshel, who makes all kinds of excuses for not taking off his clothes. That these homoerotic dips are common practice we also understand from the only explanation Avigdor attributes to Anshel's refusal: he can't swim. And of course, he is more than eager to help remove this impediment. Upon Anshel's categorical refusal, Avigdor says, "I won't force you . . . When you're ready." The double entendre of these words can hardly be missed.

The unique beauty of the scene lies not in its homoeroticism alone, but also in the fact that the lake setting is designed as a heterogenic space containing all sorts of desires—and it is in this space that Yentl's sexual awakening occurs, while the spectators, inscribed in the filmic space, might remain somewhat confused: Avigdor's attraction to Anshel is clearly homoerotic while Yentl's attraction to Avigdor is clearly heterosexual, but they are rendered in one space that does not distinguish between gay and straight desires. Overwhelmed by both her sexual attraction to Avigdor and the homoerotic ambiance, Yentl flees the site as fast as she can. Indeed, *Jewissance* here is experienced as a strange enjoyment that permeates the entire setting with wonderful, albeit a bit scary, emotions that set the drives free. The song begun while Yentl runs away from the lake ("The Way He Makes Me Feel"), her lips sealed, continues in the scene that follows, when she is alone in her room, the lyrics reinforcing the sense of intense bewilderment and wonder: "There's no chill and yet I shiver/ There's no flame and yet I burn/ I'm not sure what I'm afraid of/ And yet I'm trembling." It is clear that Yentl is expressing here her sexual awakening as a woman (she looks in the mirror as she unbinds her breasts, and goes on to caress herself), but the fact that it is generated in a homoerotic space, Avigdor approaching her as a young man, constructs, surely for spectators, an "in-between space," "beyond the binary difference that governs the decorum of all codes"—to use Derrida's phrasing regarding sexuality quoted above. In the scene that follows, on their way to the yeshiva, Anshel, who now seems very much reserved, asks Avigdor, who keeps fondling him, why he is always grabbing him, to which Avigdor responses, as befits a yeshiva boy, with another question: "Must everything have a reason?!"

We might read in the same spirit Avigdor's insistence that Anshel marry Hadass in accord with the *Yabamuth*.[14] Not only is Avigdor not jealous when he hears that Hadass's parents are interested in Anshel as a son-in-law, but rather he is pleased to have found the perfect solution: Anshel will marry Hadass, who likes him, thus she will remain in town and Avigdor will be able to see her. Anshel is not a real sexual rival because he admits he cannot love her, and Avigdor does not wonder why—probably because he assumes Anshel can share with no woman what he shares with him. As he puts it, Anshel marrying her will be "the nearest thing to me marrying her." At the end of a bitter argument between them, when Anshel is still reluctant to marry Hadass, Avigdor's concluding words are: "And another question: Do you feel anything for me?" This might be read/experienced as an emotional manipulation (if you are my friend, you will do this for me), but also as an exposure of homoerotic desire. Moreover, when Anshel says to him that he might meet someone else, "perhaps not so pretty, and with brown hair," naturally referring to herself, as opposed to Hadass's red hair, Avigdor replies "I won't notice her at all." Yentl's disappointment is obvious, wishing that she be desired as a *woman*, but Avigdor's response is ambivalent: Is it because in his eyes any woman falls short of Hadass, or is it (considering his question addressed to Anshel) because of his overwhelming homoerotic experience with Anshel?

The experience of *Jewissance* is juxtaposed with the phallic economy all through the film. Yentl's journey begins with a scornful attitude (on her part) toward the phallic, advances through its acknowledgment as an inherent part of the division of gender (through her relationships with Avigdor and Hadass), societal laws, and so on, and returns to the non-phallic/feminine enjoyment ("more!") as a way of life. In the first song relating to Hadass (the fourth song in the film, "No Wonder"), when Avigdor first takes Anshel to meet his fiancée and her parents, the lyrics ridicule the place that women occupy in Jewish tradition—to know and satisfy their husbands' desires—whereas the last song relating to Hadass (the tenth one in the film, "No Wonder" [reprise]), when Yentl decides to put an end to her masquerade, expresses immense love and admiration for what Hadass has taught her.

The lyrics of the sixth song ("No Wonder, Part 2") accompany Hadass and Anshel when the latter considers marrying the former. It reflects a double position on Yentl's part in regard to Hadass as both a man and a woman: a homoerotic one, stemming from what she earlier imagined Avigdor must feel for Hadass (now it is actually what Yentl herself experiences in Hadass's presence that she attributes to Avigdor's desire for Hadass), and an awakening of her own womanhood while wondering what makes a woman, one that Hadass personifies. ("Is it the smell of lilacs and roses, her silky hair and milky complexion that Avigdor desires? Her softness? Her sweetness?") It is clear that Yentl's senses are at work here, generating a sensual experience, an awakening of her sexual body: "How could he resist her/ And why would he try?/ No wonder he wants her/ He needs her/ He loves her,/ No wonder . . . So would I!" Yentl's attraction to Hadass is conveyed in the image as well. When Hadass places a cushion behind Anshel's back to make him more comfortable, her bosom nearly touches his face, while the lyrics on the soundtrack reconfirm Yentl's attraction to Hadass, who has it all, "in all the right places." The homoerotic space, created by Avigdor's attitude toward Anshel, is now displaced to that of Hadass and Yentl/Anshel. After their marriage, it becomes clear that Hadass is starting to fall in love with her gentle and understanding husband, wishing that they would consummate the marriage. As to Yentl, her "rejection" of Hadass stems from her fear that her secret be found out, not because she is homophobic (she does find Hadass attractive). Thus, she channels this mutual attraction to the study of Talmud.

This fluidity of spaces cannot be more evident than in the crosscutting between the scene at the tailor's (the day before the marriage), when Anshel is being fitted for his wedding suit, and the marriage scene. The song (the seventh, "Tomorrow Night") expresses Yentl's panic, lest her secret be found out (thinking Anshel is a man, the tailor and his assistant ask him to take off his pants and try to touch his crotch to make sure the suit is not too tight, not understanding why he makes such a fuss about it), but also her *ability* to *transgress* boundaries, which terrifies her: "Look how easily I fool them/ They may have eyes but they don't see/ . . . It might be interesting to know/ Just how much further I can go." She is about to marry a woman (an unforgivable transgression in Orthodox Judaism) because she wants to keep enjoying the company of Avigdor who is her study partner and the one she has developed feelings for, fearful of the dire consequences of her actions.

Realizing that to stand the next day under the marriage canopy with Hadass is her greatest transgression, she turns to the mirror as she tries the wedding hat on, her eyes almost fully covered by it, looking at her image as the groom-to-be and sings: "Tomorrow night, tomorrow night/ . . . I can't believe what I'll presume to be/ Tomorrow night/ I'm not the bride but I'm the groom to be . . . ." The camera zooms in to the back of her head, and the screen turns to black, match-cutting to the wedding scene, in which we see the back of her head, the camera panning to her left revealing Hadass's father, who stands very close to Anshel. The camera then pans to the right and dollies out behind Hadass's father, including Avigdor who faces Anshel, thus exposing that Anshel and Avigdor are looking at each other. Avigdor's look and nod to Anshel seem to encourage him to go ahead with the wedding, but when Anshel turns away from Avigdor, facing the camera in close-up, the song renders the line: "I'm not the bride but I'm the groom-to-be," indicating that the deep and meaningful exchange of looks that should be exchanged between the bride (Hadass) and the groom (Anshel) is exchanged between Avigdor and Anshel, conveying the feeling/notion that they are marrying each other. While on Yentl's part this might be an expression of a wish to marry Avigdor, on Avigdor's part it expresses the feelings he has for Anshel, and because of Yentl's disguise, the image, in compliance with the editing, ultimately conveys the notion of a gay marriage.

Likewise, when the crowd of men accompanying Anshel advances toward the canopy, the camera zooms in to a close-up on Anshel's face: He stops walking, looks backward to Avigdor, who is seen in medium shot in the background looking at Anshel. The camera then dollies out and we see the canopy, Hadass standing on the right, covered with a veil, Anshel uncovering her face for a moment and then quickly covering it again. While doing this he looks horrified, whereupon the editing takes us back to the tailor scene. The next cut to the marriage scene occurs when Yentl considers running away to a place no one would recognize her—the image of her terrified face in the fitting room is now out of focus, blurred, the editing transposing us again to the marriage scene through a match-cut (a dissolve) between her shining glasses and the flickering lights of candles in the dark held by the men escorting Anshel to the canopy in focus, while the lyrics of the song utter the words "where no one knows my face as a woman or a man." This, of course, is not an option, marking Yentl's distress in that she must decide what she is: man or woman (alluding to the castration fantasy). Yentl's mind, spinning with conflicting emotions, is expressed in the rhythm of the intercuts, which accelerates as the sequence progresses, and the constant motion in each scene, especially the dancing in circles in the wedding scene and the exchange of looks between Avigdor and Anshel. This whirl of intercuts between the two scenes produces an undefined mental space in terms of both gender (man/woman—the castration fantasy) and sexuality (the seduction fantasy), a space in which spectators are swirling as well.

Still in the wedding scene, after Yentl expresses her wish to run away she reminds herself that there is a reason not to, the song explaining: "There's someone I would miss/ and being near him is what this is all about." But then the camera dollies in to a medium close-up to reveal Avigdor's proximity to Anshel, Avigdor encircling Anshel with the rest of the men without taking his eyes off him, suggesting once more that the dance is celebrating a marriage between two men. This gay subtext, visually conveyed (as well as our knowledge that in fact it is a marriage between two *women*), reverberates in the song, now addressing Yentl's father and referring to Yentl marrying Hadass: "Papa dear, you dreamed of dancing at my wedding/ But something tells me that I'm right/ You wouldn't want to dance tonight!"

This confusion of gender and sexuality continues, and whatever separation of spaces as determined by Orthodox Judaism—between men/women, between gay/straight—collapses into that mental space established in between, or rather beyond, binary categories and norms. The confusion intensifies when we see Hadass in the wedding scene looking to the opposite side, presumably at Anshel, but then the eyeline match leads us to Yentl in the fitting room (a different space/scene), standing and rendered from a low-angle shot, emphasizing the perfect eyeline match, as the song continues: "He likes me—I like her/ And I've reasons to think she likes me." We then return to the wedding scene, where Avigdor is seen in the men's section trying to catch Hadass's eyes, her eyes continuing to search for Anshel's, the song explaining: "She keeps him—he keeps her/ I keep things as they were/ It's a perfect arrangement for three!"

As the crosscutting continues, we see Hadass on a chair carried by two men to the dancing area (reserved for men) while other guests lift Anshel's chair toward Hadass. The two, elevated over the crowd of men, finally face each other. While Anshel is swirling, surrounded by the dancing crowd circling him, we get a rapid montage of faces looking at Anshel on the chair, celebrating, Avigdor among them; the montage is interrupted by an intercut taking us back to the fitting room, where Yentl prays in despair, spinning around herself, the lyrics of the song concluding, "Tomorrow night . . . is now tonight!" Only then does the whirling of movement stop. Anshel's and Hadass's chairs in the wedding scene are lowered as they face each other from a close distance: The deed is done—a semiotic space has been consolidated for spectators in which all intelligibility, or experience, contingent on binarism is dissolved.

Even after the camera lingers in the wedding scene, the editing continues to reinforce the blending of spaces within the scene: While Anshel is sitting in the men's section looking at Hadass, Hadass is sitting in the section allocated for women; but then Hadass and Anshel's exchange of looks bridges these separate spaces. Moreover, the confusion and ambiguity do not end. Diegetic music begins to play, preparing for the traditional "handkerchief" dance, in which the bride holds one end of the handkerchief while the groom holds its other end so that they can dance without touching. But Anshel pulls away when he sees Avigdor about to leave with a woman he is consoling himself with to clear the way for Hadass's and Anshel's wedding night. When Anshel asks Avigdor why he is leaving, Avigdor hands him a small book saying: "A wedding gift for you, for both of you." The book, *The Holy Letter*, "written by one of the great Rabbis, Nachmonides (*Ha'Ramban*), five hundred years ago," instructs the husband in how to approach his wife on the wedding night, giving precedence to the woman's enjoyment. While facing Anshel, Avigdor reads: "Converse with her to put her mind at ease, speak words that arouse her to love, desire, and passion and words of reverence for God," which makes Anshel feel uneasy; in the next shot Avigdor puts his hand around Anshel's shoulders, draws him closer, and softly whispers in his ear (he knows the words by heart): "Never force her. Her mood must be as yours." Avigdor lifts his eyes as if intending to point Anshel in Hadass's direction, but a reverse shot of Hadass does not follow. He continues: "Win her with graciousness and seductiveness," whereupon Anshel turns his head toward Avigdor's cheek, the image conveying now a gay seduction.

It is then that we see Hadass from *both their* points of view, as if they were one, thus dissolving a possible reading of her image as "to-be-looked-at-ness" in terms of gender difference. If she is to be considered a fetish at all (in counterpoint with Yentl/Anshel, whose image resists such consideration all through), it would be in relation to both genders. Indeed, while dancing, Hadass returns a look to both Anshel and Avigdor—due to their proximity to each other they cannot be told apart, although we may assume Hadass is flirting with Anshel. The shot/reverse shot continues as Avigdor's words progress: "Be patient until her passion is aroused," which of course arouses Anshel/Yentl's desire for Avigdor, who keeps whispering in her ear: "Begin with love, and when her mood is ready, let her desire be satisfied first, her delight is what matters." The music and the dance end and Avigdor leaves Yentl more perplexed than ever, as these instructions can hardly help her on her wedding night with Hadass, although she seems very much aroused by them in relation to Avigdor. Moreover, through these instructions, Avigdor seems to be expressing a wish to be in Anshel's place, using Anshel as a proxy, while at the same time he almost makes love to him.

No doubt, narratively speaking, the way the tailor scene is intercut with the wedding scene reflects Yentl's panic in that she is going to marry a woman *tomorrow*, not leaving her any time to reflect on her "crazy" decision. Hence the generating of the castration[15] fantasy—as well as the seduction fantasy—placing Yentl in a position from which she will have to further confront questions pertaining to her gender and sexuality. However, the fluidity of space, created by incessant movement (that of the characters, of the camera, the accelerated rhythm created by the intercuts, and the dancing) and enhanced by song, is what characterizes the semiotic, and sustains the experience of feminine enjoyment in that it cannot fall under any definite category. It creates a bridge between all spaces involved (one of "blended voices"): the diegetic ones (private/public; men/women; gay/straight) and that shared by the protagonists and spectators.

In sum, this sequence leaves Yentl with several questions (addressed to the spectators as well): In terms of the castration fantasy—Am I a man or a woman ("I'm not the bride but I'm the groom to be")? In terms of the seduction fantasy, it becomes even more complicated—Who, or what, is the origin of my sexuality and desire? What ignites my sexual desire? How will I channel this whirl of emotions? The answer for Yentl is that they will be channeled to her love for the Talmud, which brings us to the primal scene fantasy (Whose desire am I a result of?) and to what is missing from Yentl's answer: She is the creation of her own desire, but only 90 percent; to complete the process (get to 100 percent), she needs to assimilate (fully own) her sexuality and womanhood into her love for the Talmud. For the spectators, this is a lesson in, as well as an experience of, the struggle for authenticity: For desire (which must be assumed as one's own) to be realized is a winding road, full of hurdles and fright, but nevertheless one that must be taken.

After the wedding, Avigdor comes to visit the couple and the "*ménage à trois*" is put to the test. It fails because Avigdor realizes that Hadass is in love with Anshel and he assumes Anshel feels the same, but Yentl wishes that Avigdor desire her in the same way he desires Hadass, as a woman. However, the marriage, enabled by Yentl's disguise, generates a process of discovery and self-expression for both Yentl and Hadass, paving the way to Yentl's acknowledgment of her womanhood as well as a happy marriage between Hadass and Avigdor. Anshel, who cannot consummate the marriage, "transgressing" yet another commandment (to procreate) introduces Hadass to the wonders of the Talmud (her basic transgression), channeling her attraction to Hadass to the exaltation she derives from study of the Talmud: "In an extraordinarily tender and erotic scene of instruction, the forbidden sexual energy is deflected into a mutual reading of the Talmud" (Garber 1997: 78). Yentl's desire to teach Hadass Talmud is inherent in the sexual attraction she feels toward Hadass's tenderness, kindness, and beauty—and vice versa, Hadass's sexual attraction to Anshel stems from Anshel's kindness, understanding, and sharing what he holds most near and dear to his heart, namely, studying the Talmud with a fellow student.

Fernley and Maloof (1985: 43–5) see in Hadass and Yentl's homoeroticism a reference to the basis for the sexual development of a girl in her relationship with her mother, the child's first object. In this light, homoeroticism between women fulfills the need to recreate the relationship with the mother, a need a man cannot fulfill. Thus, the relationship between Hadass and Yentl also incorporates a kind of mother-daughter relationship, especially given that Yentl was deprived of her own mother. What is particularly striking in this context is that the two do not fall into an imaginary unity that effaces difference; on the contrary, the homoerotic relation between Yentl and Hadass is replete with the same *Jewissance* as the relationship between Anshel and Avigdor. This is basically what ignites the fire for Yentl in her relationship with Hadass. After all, it is Hadass who ends up learning the Talmud and not Yentl sewing or cooking, and Hadass accepts it as a token of Anshel's love for her.

Before Anshel leaves for Lublin to meet Avigdor and tell him the truth, Hadass promises him that she will be studying during his absence—the key to a successful, unusual, and untraditional marriage—whereupon they declare love for each other, thus foregrounding the idea that love of the Talmud cannot be divorced from the feminine enjoyment. It is this process that brings Yentl to love herself as a woman. Yentl and Hadass's relationship thus seems to be an exchange of gifts that is not meant to alter their personalities, but add a meaningful dimension to their womanhood, mediated by studying the Talmud together and holding conversations that Hadass could never imagine would take place between husband and wife. Yentl teaches Hadass three important lessons: she has a mind of her own; wife and husband *can* be friends; and the Talmud, which ensures the first two, will also ensure a happy marriage. Hadass teaches Yentl what her mother never had a chance to: tenderness and the love of female companionship. But, most of all, she learns that all women can study the scriptures, which means she can be a woman scholar, possibly a teacher too.

In the eighth song ("Will Someone Ever Look at Me . . ."), Yentl expresses her wish that Avigdor look at her the way he looks at Hadass, while afraid that the way she (Yentl) looks at him might give her away. But again, this is not what Yentl's journey is all about. In the ninth song ("No Matter What Happens"), upon realizing she has been given the gift of love from Hadass ("What she's taught me/ Isn't written anywhere/ And I'm supposed to be the one/ Who's wise") she finally finds her voice as a woman—it is the voice of love. Although she wants to declare her love for Avigdor, pronouncing her need for him to touch her, it is the freedom to be herself that she cherishes most: "To see myself/ To free myself/ To be myself at last!" This brings her to the decision to change the state of things: "A voice deep inside/ Is getting stronger/ . . . It can't be the same anymore/ I promise it won't be the same/ Anymore!" And what does this inner voice tell her to do? Yentl's love for both Avigdor and Hadass makes it clear once again that the love story in the film is not a mere infatuation with either of the sexes, but an erotic, deep love, inseparable from the experience of reading the Talmud. This empowers her to pursue her dream (the end of her process)—learn the Talmud without a disguise. In the tenth song ("No Wonder" [reprise]), when Yentl is parting with Hadass before leaving for Lublin (to tell Avigdor the truth) Hadass becomes "the wonder of wonders/ No man can deny," fully grasping now what Avigdor sees in her: "So why would he change her?/ She's loving—she's tender—/ She's woman—/ So am I." After she confesses her love for Avigdor as a woman, realizing she now owns her enjoyment as a scholar and a desiring woman, she frees herself from both Avigdor and Hadass in pursuit of a place that will allow her to entwine her womanhood and sexuality into her Talmudic scholarship.

Avigdor's fury and sense of betrayal when Yentl reveals her true sex to him toward the end of the film arises not only from the fact that the homoeroticism added depth to his intimacy with Anshel, but also because he cannot conceive that such an experience, *Jewissance,* can stem from a relationship with a woman. Therefore, Yentl cannot accept his plan to marry her after he confesses that he loves her too, his rage subsiding and turning into tenderness—she understands that she will not be his equal, a fellow student, anymore. Consequently, she convinces him to take a statement to the Rabbi annulling the marriage on the grounds it was never consummated, an explanatory letter to Hadass, and then to marry Hadass.

In the final scene of the film, which takes place on a ship, Yentl again addresses her father in heaven (resonating her plea to him when she left her hometown as Anshel), as well as the whole universe,[16] only this time to tell him that she cannot be satisfied with just "a piece of sky." In the eleventh song ("A Piece of Sky"), her own father is thus associated with the great spiritual father, whom the film continually identifies with both lack and enjoyment, as reflected in the lyrics: "The more I live—the more I learn/ The more I learn—the more I realize/ The *less* I know." This is both the Father of the Law ("less") and a father of feminine enjoyment designing the subject in process, operating in the gap between the binarism of gender and sexual identities, in which a new consciousness and alternative lifestyles are made possible. Hence Yentl's answer to Avigdor's earlier question, "What more do you want?": "More!" The singing device (sealing her lips in public), resonating with the distinction made by Yentl and her father between God and the neighbors regarding the study of the Talmud, is finally broken in the diegesis. Thus, while sailing on a ship toward an unspecified destination (judging by its overall design, most likely America, thus providing an analogy to Streisand's launching her directorial career in Hollywood[17]) that will allow her to be a woman Talmudic scholar, no longer disguised as a man, Yentl's inner and outer worlds, signifying desire and feminine enjoyment, come together through her willingness to sing in public. First, we hear her song on the soundtrack (her lips still sealed) surrounded by the people on the ship (immigrants) below decks; but then, after ascending to the outside deck, she starts singing her way through the crowd toward the stern, now lip-syncing the words. No longer is her *body* severed from her voice, as it were, thus lending greater validity to the polyvocal nature of the Talmud through a woman's voice belonging to her body. This completes Yentl's process of self-creation—her subjectivization, assuming full ownership over her desire and feminine enjoyment. This transgressive self-creation through the musical numbers also challenges the conventions of the musical genre. As Fernley and Maloof (1985: 42) point out, there are no spectacle scenes in the film and Streisand is the only one who sings. They rightly see the unique use Streisand makes of the musical and the lyrics as undermining "any attempt to pin Yentl down." Barbra Streisand's stupendous voice, a major element of the semiotic in film, creates a sense of transcendence that indicates a plea addressed to "all our fathers" in heaven,[18] the people on the ship, and the audience.

Choice, change, and responsibility are born in a place of doubt, rather than of strict norms. Yentl establishes for Avigdor and Hadass, as well as for the spectators, a *signifying* space that Kristeva ([1979] 1995: 222) also applies to her discussion of third generation feminism, "a mental space that is at once corporeal and desirous." Within this space the notion of identity itself is challenged. Kristeva is referring here to the "mobility within individual and sexual identity, and not through a rejection of the other" ([1979] 1995). This *signifying* space is important "not only to counterbalance the mass-production and uniformity of the information age, but also to demystify the idea that the community of language is a universal, all-inclusive, and equalizing tool" (223). This is why a work of art, as well as the artistic experience that can highlight the diversity of identifications with it and the relativity of cultural and social existence producing a unique space of enjoyment for different spectators—*Yentl* for that matter—is not only effective and affective on a large scale, but also, to put it into Kristeva's words, "takes on the question of morality" ([1979] 1995). And it is precisely this question of ethics that we find so appealing in the kind of subjectivization offered by *Yentl*, as well as in many other gender-crossing films.

"It Ain't All She Ain't!": Against Fetishism (*Calamity Jane*)

In most gender-crossing films we find that the gender-crossing protagonists are characterized by feminine enjoyment, regardless of their signifier for the real. For Yentl, it is the love of Talmud; for Calamity Jane (the Wild West tomboy category) of the musical version, it is the love of riding freely in open spaces, sharpshooting, fighting Indians, and so on. Nobody will ever take this away from her. The mental and physical space created in *Yentl* already exists for Calamity (Doris Day)—in the liminality of the Wild West. Unlike Yentl, who must disguise herself to maintain her economy of feminine enjoyment, Calamity operates freely in this semiotic space that she fully owns, one usually occupied by men, while she constantly changes it from within. This semiotic space, like in *Yentl*, is enhanced by Calamity's songs and Doris Day's sweet and harmonious voice. Through Calamity's character, the film rescripts not only norms of gender and sexuality, but also those of the Western, deconstructing many of its myths. However, like in *Yentl*, Calamity's womanhood and sexuality are generated through a friendship with another woman, creating a striking gay subtext that Eric Savoy (1999: 173) delightfully refers to as "little closet on the prairie."

Be it protagonists who transition from a phallic to a feminine enjoyment, as we shall see in the case of *Some Like It Hot* (1959), or protagonists for whom the feminine enjoyment constitutes their starting point, it seems that the creation of a queer space in many cross-dressing and tomboy films is related to the period in which they were made. When homosexuality was either legally or normatively banned, the films thus circumvented the censorship of the time and appealed to gay audiences. This suggests that any such space bordering on the unfamiliar and unrecognizable must be *included* and allowed to make necessary changes, hence, the protagonists' sexual maturation in a queer space in *Calamity Jane*, alluding to the time the film was made (1953),[19] or in *Yentl*, alluding to the 1980s but still very relevant today in Orthodox societies. Over the years, the transition from a phallic economy to a non-phallic one has found other modes of expression, depicting mainly transgender characters.

Calamity Jane takes place during the late nineteenth century (like *Yentl*) in Deadwood, part of the Dakota Territory. Jane Canary, known by everyone as Calamity Jane, or Calam for short, is a sharpshooter who undertakes the task of protecting the town's inhabitants, particularly the stagecoach, from the marauding Sioux. Her best friend is gunman Wild Bill Hickok (Howard Keel), whom she confides in, although he is also somewhat of a rival as far as shooting skills and fearlessness are concerned. Calamity shows no signs of femininity. She is oblivious of normative gender differences, evinced by the fact that while thinking she is in love with a soldier (whose life she saves), Lieutenant Danny Gilmartin (Philip Carey), it never occurs to her to alter her appearance. As to Danny, he only sees her as one of the guys, not even remotely suspecting that she might have amorous feelings toward him. There is a dearth of women in the area, and as such, the proprietor of the Golden Garter, the local saloon, sends for actresses to perform for his male customers. When one of his attempts to bring in an actress goes awry, Calamity takes it upon herself to rectify the situation. The rest of the plot develops through a series of events that acquaint Calamity with her womanhood and real feelings—for a woman friend and for Bill.

A brief examination of *Calamity Jane* shows the relevancy of the distinction between the phallic economy and the feminine one and the latter's power to change norms from within. Through her relationship with and love for Katie (Allyn McLerie) Calamity discovers she loves Wild Bill Hickok and not Lieutenant Gilmartin, like she thought she did. Bill realizes that he loves her too, and we know that he will not present an impediment to what is most near and dear to her. In the last scene of the film (the double marriage), we still see Calamity hiding a gun in her wedding gown. But what is especially striking about this film is its way of suggesting that the gender-crossing character/image counterpoints, as well as deconstructs, the female as fetish.[20]

The gun, which in the Western represents the phallus in the sense that it is used as a symbol of "manhood" and bravery, is the first thing that is demystified and revealed as an ultimate fetish, signifying nothing except the phallic economy. Upon her return to Deadwood, Calamity is asked if anything exciting happened on her trip, whereupon she concocts a series of events about her bravery in fighting Indians. When her male friends dare question the truth of her story (her coachman indicates to them behind her back that they are highly exaggerated), she pulls out a rope and throws the lasso around the coachman's neck, thus putting an end to their sarcastic treatment of her. On the surface it is Calamity who is being ridiculed by a bunch of men, but in effect the main mystifying element of the Western, namely the white men's battles against the Indians (the antagonists of the Western), is deconstructed through demystification of the gun. In fact, attributing the gun to Calamity is one of the key elements through which she is constituted as an antithesis to the female character as fetish in narrative film.

The Golden Garter, naturally a place reserved for men (and prostitutes—in the classical Western), is characterized from the start as a space of phallic economy governed by fetishism. The men exchange and look at pictures of women imprinted on cards—sheer fetishes. The only woman who has access to the saloon is of course Calamity, who, when handed the picture of the ultimate fetish (proclaimed as such by Bill, in his own words), singer Adelaid Adams (Gale Robbins), her response is that Adelaid looks like a fat cow, indecently dressed. The fact that the men in the saloon look at Calamity differently (do not see her as fetish), as well as her own unique way of looking at gender difference, sets her apart from a fetishistic economy, as well as a phallic one. The function of the proprietor of the saloon bar, Henry Miller (Paul Harvey) is to procure live fetishes for his customers. He thus sends for what he assumes is a beautiful female performer to appear on the stage and entertain the men, which marks the beginning of a series of mistaken identities.

The name of the (male) performer is Francis Fryer (Dick Wesson), which sounds like "*Frances* Fryer." Hence the mistaken identity. Fearful of the men's reaction, Miller forces Francis to dress up in full fetishistic attire, including a curly red wig. Not surprisingly, Francis starts his performance by revealing one of his legs to the cheering crowd. The shot/reverse-shot editing used in classical cinema in relation to male characters looking at women is ridiculed and deconstructed here by two factors: First, Francis is very far from possessing the necessary attributes of a female fetish, which does not constitute an impediment on the men's part to treating her as one—the mere knowledge that she is a woman suffices; and second, Calamity is set apart from this fetishistic look through her reaction to what she sees. In the midst of the shot/reverse-shot series, when the scene cuts to Calamity and Bill, both staring at Francis, Calamity asks Bill if he sees anything peculiar, whereupon Bill answers that "She ain't very pretty" (a fact that does not keep Francis from continuing to draw cheers from the male crowd), to which Calamity responds: "It ain't all she ain't!"

When Francis's wig is sucked up by a trombone the masquerade comes to an end. However, this only serves as another incident of mistaken identity, which further develops the distinction between (Doris Day in the role of) Calamity and the image of woman as fetish. Disappointed and feeling cheated, the men in the saloon begin to storm out. Calamity, eager to put an end to the commotion and not really grasping what all the fuss is about, vows to get them the one woman they are all drooling over: singer Adelaid Adams, who is in Chicago. Bill laughs at the idea and tells Calamity that the night Adams steps on the stage, he will come to the opening dressed as a Sioux squaw lugging a papoose. But Calamity is determined to keep her promise and goes to Chicago. The stage Adelaid Adams performs on is a refined variation of the Golden Garter. While singing, she is wearing but a corset, white hose, and high-heel shoes (like in the pictures the men were drooling over in the Golden Garter, thus reinforcing her character as fetish). Calamity is standing very far from the stage, able to catch just a glimpse of her. After the show is over, we see Adelaid and her assistant, Katie, preparing for Adelaid's trip to Paris. After Adelaid leaves, Katie, whose dream is to be on stage, admired by audiences the way Adelaid is, puts on her costume and mimics her in front of the mirror. Her singing is clearly not as good as Adelaid's, which emphasizes the power of culture in manipulating women into wanting to be treated as fetishes. It is then that Calamity enters the room, mistaking Katie for Adelaid. At first, Katie tries to correct her, but then, after making sure that no one will recognize her in Deadwood, she goes along with it. Like Yentl, meeting another woman, in this case Katie, constitutes Calamity's awakening as both a woman and a sexual being. Looking at her, she exclaims in wonder that Katie is the most beautiful creature she has ever seen.

After arriving at Deadwood, Katie is recognized by Francis, which makes her lose the little confidence she had in passing as Adelaid. When she starts singing, Calamity says she did not sound that way in Chicago, and tells her to sing out, but Katie bursts into tears, admitting that she is not Adelaid Adams. The Golden Garter falls silent. Everyone present is on the verge of rioting, but Calamity fires a shot into the air and defends Katie. They allow Katie to carry on, and her performance wins them over. Obviously, it is not her singing that does so, but the thought that finally they have a real female performer to look at. On the balcony above, Bill Hickok, dressed as an Indian woman—one among many devices exposing the Western as a performance or masquerade—lassos Calamity and hangs her high and dry. Indeed, the Golden Garter emphasizes the performative aspect of the classical Western in that it condenses its demystification through one of its major tropes: the saloon.

Calamity takes Katie under her protective wing, much like a husband takes a wife to their new lodgings after marrying her. When Katie sees Calamity's shabby and dusty cabin, Calamity proposes returning her to town, but Katie insists that all the cabin needs is "a woman's touch." The two start to sing "A Woman's Touch," which becomes a sound bridge for a wonderful montage showing the transformation of both the cabin and Calamity, who cleans up—indeed, a "little closet on the prairie." The process of their growing love and friendship is further condensed at the end of the montage when the camera dollies in to the windowsill showing the image of a red flower blooming in a pot.

To attract Lieutenant Gilmartin, the man Calamity *thinks* she is madly in love with, she tries to dress, look, and act more like a lady. One day, Danny and Bill (who are both in love with Katie—Bill does not yet know he loves Calamity) pay a visit to Calamity's cabin. Katie manages to lure Bill out of the cabin for a few minutes; while alone with Danny, she tells him straight out that Calamity loves him and that she, Katie, is trying to stay away from him to keep her friendship. However, Danny tells Katie he is not interested in Calamity. But Katie insists that Calamity has changed and had a makeover, proving she will be accepted at a local ball the following weekend. When Calamity returns home after falling into a river while trying to cross it wearing a beautiful yellow dress—her dress, face, and hair are all smeared with mud—the attempt to make her into an object to be looked at by men fails. Even at the ball, when she appears in a ravishing pink gown, people wonder if it is really Calamity they see. All the men ask her to dance, but she still maintains her unfeminine walk, keeps her gun in the pocket of her coat, and is not afraid to use it when she finds out that Danny and Katie are in love. Mad with jealousy, she fires in the air. Is she jealous of Katie, or of Danny? Telling Bill that she did not bring Katie all the way from Chicago to Deadwood for Danny does not clarify the matter for us.

Calamity and Katie's feud culminates at the Golden Garter in a parodic variation of the classical gun fight between two men. Katie, doing a number with Francis on the stage, interrupts it when she spots Calamity, who warns her to leave town. Katie asks one of the men to lend her a gun and hollers to Calamity to hold up her glass. Calamity obeys, convinced Katie will miss it. Katie points the gun and fires, but then we hear a shot off-screen and see Calamity's glass breaking into pieces in her hand. The reverse shot shows Bill holding his gun and we understand it was he who hit the glass by firing his gun at the same moment as Katie fired hers. Everyone thinks it was Katie, including Calamity and Katie herself (who actually hit a barrel full of whiskey, the liquor pouring freely out of it), and they cheer her. Why does Bill intervene? It seems the gun has no place in Calamity and Katie's unique friendship, and Bill, probably unconsciously, is protecting it. It might also be that he is protecting his own territory—being the famous gunman that he is. That he literally acts here as a protector of women is highly unlikely because he cannot prevent the shooting itself, as his own occurs concurrently with Katie's. Thus, his intervention does not mean that a gun is not meant for a woman (because he does accept Calamity with a gun, even after he acknowledges her as a woman[21]), but that it has no place in Calamity's relationship with Katie.

Like *Yentl*, *Calamity Jane* creates a non-phallic space, evinced by its parody of fetishism in which sexuality and feminine enjoyment have no clear boundaries, cannot be pinned down, and is emphasized even in the quick manner the characters' feelings are transferred from one object to another. But the pairing-up of the foursome—Katie with Danny and Calamity with Bill—is not a choice made at random. The two pairs signify two different economies of enjoyment: the former, a phallic one, is associated with the beginning of a civilization (Danny is a captain in the army and Katie comes from the big city of Chicago); the latter, that of feminine enjoyment, is associated with liminality (the Wild West). However, the liminality of the Wild West here is transformed into a place governed by the semiotic (light, music, singing, dancing, rhythm, and motion). Deadwood, known for its lawlessness, where murder is common and punishment for murder not always fair and impartial, as we well know from Westerns (the town attained further notoriety for the murder of gunman Wild Bill Hickok in the second half of the nineteenth century), becomes in *Calamity Jane*, through its marriage to the musical, a utopic space (for both its protagonists and spectators) in which feminine enjoyment reigns supreme.

"Nobody's Perfect!": From the Phallic Space to the Feminine One (*Some Like It Hot* and *Victor Victoria*)

Another striking comparison, or distinction, between the phallic and non-phallic economies is portrayed in *Some Like It Hot*, in which feminine enjoyment "comes" to Jerry (Jack Lemmon), who never expected it and does not really know what to make of it. Fleeing the mob after witnessing an execution in 1929 Chicago (the days of Prohibition) compels the two male protagonists, Jerry and Joe (Tony Curtis), to leave the state disguised as two female players in an all-female big band going to Florida. Osgood Fielding III (Joe E. Brown) is a millionaire smitten with Daphne/Jerry, while Joe/Josephine falls in love with Sugar (Marilyn Monroe). To win her over, he pretends to be heir to the Shell Oil Company—the serious young millionaire Sugar has always dreamed about.[22] At the end of the film it looks like Jerry will have no choice but to succumb to Osgood's insistence to become his "wife."

This immortal comedy might be considered a quintessential example of how the experience of feminine enjoyment transcends the language pertaining to the norms of sexual difference and the heterosexuality associated with it (the dialogue was written by Wilder and I. A. L. Diamond), inscribing spectators (like *Yentl* and *Calamity Jane*) in a space in which the walls of binary classification of sexuality and gender tumble down for both Jerry and the spectators. Three sequences stand out in this respect, and in all of them the phallic enjoyment is juxtaposed with feminine enjoyment. In the first, two scenes occurring simultaneously intercut each other.[23] In one scene, after convincing Jerry to accept Osgood's invitation to a nightclub, Joe and Sugar are on Osgood's yacht where he is trying to woo her. In his disguise as a rich oil millionaire, he pretends to be the owner of the yacht and an incurable impotent. Shots from this scene alternate with shots from a nightclub scene, where Osgood and Daphne/Jerry are doing the tango. The second sequence is the scene that follows, occurring in the hotel room, in which Jerry announces to Joe his engagement to Osgood. The third is the last scene of the film, showing the two couples in a boat sailing to Osgood's yacht after Joe and Jerry are found out by the mob.

The editing device used in the parallel-editing sequence (alternating between shots of the yacht scene and the nightclub scene) transposing us from one scene to the other is the swish pan. This technique is a horizontal camera movement (pan) at a very rapid speed, usually used to suddenly shift our attention from one object to another situated in the *same* space/scene. The unusual use of the swish pan here (connecting as it were *two* spaces/scenes) conveys a double meaning/experience: first, that these are two distinct spaces—the scene in the yacht symbolizing the phallic economy, while the tango scene generating for both Jerry and the spectators the experience of feminine enjoyment; and second, Jerry's (as well as the spectators') *transition* (conveyed by the swish pan) from a phallic economy to that of feminine enjoyment. Although Joe does experience a different kind of pleasure by pretending to be an impotent millionaire, letting himself being seduced by Sugar (rather than be a seducer), nevertheless neither he nor we can forget for one minute that he is masquerading. Not so Jerry, whose feminine attire allows him to set himself free, a freedom achieved through the tango (dance and music, *the semiotic*—there is no dialogue in this scene). The image of Daphne/Jerry and Osgood doing the tango, upsetting its distinct gender roles—man leads, woman follows ("Daphne, you're leading again!")—generates for the spectators a gay subtext.[24] In fact, part of the dialogue in the yacht, which does not contain one ounce of truth, is applicable to the visuals in the nightclub (yet another function of the swish pan): an ecstatic Jerry giving in to the pace of the tango with Osgood. At first, he looks reluctant, but not for long: What seemed before like a gesture indulging his best friend (with whom he might be in love without knowing it), looks now like an enjoyment never experienced before. Joe's references to his (pretend) impotence, saying how women leave him cold (which as we know is a complete lie), about how "Mother Nature" can sometimes be cruel, might thus be attributed to the queer couple doing the tango, namely to the notion that in 1959 United States, being gay was indeed considered owning a cruel destiny. However, it is Jerry's ecstasy, reinforced by dance, that transposes to the spectator. According to Jennifer Wicke (1997: 369), the tango technique accurately expresses the gender swapping characterizing the sequence, but the tango also connotes passion. And, as mentioned before, it is the unusual use of the swish pan that transposes us from the world of the phallic to that of the non-phallic—an unexpected enjoyment, unexplainable, that makes no sense to Jerry, so much so that he seriously considers Osgood's proposal.

Indeed, when Joe returns from Osgood's yacht, he finds Jerry in ecstasy, lying in bed holding a pair of castanets (connoting both feminine and masculine tropes) and humming the tango melody, whereupon he tells Joe he is engaged. When Joe asks who the lucky girl is, he gleefully announces, "I am!" and is pleased to say that the wedding will be in June. When an astounded Joe tells him he cannot marry Osgood, Jerry wonders if he is too old, eventually acknowledging that there is a problem, none other than Osgood's mother, which he is not really concerned about because he does not smoke. When asked what they are going to do on their honeymoon, Jerry says they have already talked about it—Osgood prefers the Riviera, but Jerry would rather go to Niagara Falls. Clearly, the experience of feminine enjoyment, in which all connotative and linguistic meanings lose their grip on the ability to communicate, being taken over by the semiotic (Jerry moving around with his castanets, frantically humming the tango tune), continues to characterize this scene as well. When Joe finally manages to bring Jerry down to earth, stressing that he is a boy and there are "rules," "conventions" ("Guys don't marry guys!"), Jerry says, in a sorrowful and indignant tone, "I'm a boy, oh boy I'm a boy, I wish I was dead." Is Jerry forced to awaken from his experience of finally being the object of another man's desire, from being bisexual, from his enjoyment of being a woman, or from enjoying mere transvestism? There is no definitive answer to these questions, aside from the fact that every connotation behind the signifiers in the dialogue simply fly out the window for Jerry and the spectators alike. This scene shows how the experience of feminine enjoyment cannot comply with any intelligibility, category, or identity regulated in language by the norms of sexual/gender difference. For Jerry, it is indeed a one-time, short-lived experience precisely because it does not make any definitive sense to him. Nothing in the film suggests that Jerry might be in love or even slightly attracted to Osgood, so what is he getting off on then? It might be that the experience of finally being the object of desire rather than a perpetual, frustrated desiring subject (both Joe and Sugar are out of reach for him) generates the experience of feminine enjoyment, which is indeed a way out of the deadlock of desire, independent of any object.[25]

This dialogue technique in which signifiers are detached from their connotative meaning is reiterated in the boat scene ending the film. After Joe's short confession to Sugar that he is a liar and a cheat, the two kiss and disappear into the background (the phallic economy, or the fetish and the fetishist[26]); the camera then focuses on the queer couple. Now it is Jerry, forced to endure the burden of the norm, who tries to talk Osgood out of the marriage plan, but fails: Jerry says he cannot marry in Osgood's mother's dress because he is built differently—Osgood proposes to adjust it; Jerry says he is not a natural blonde—Osgood doesn't mind; Jerry confesses he is a chain smoker (Osgood's mother hates smoking), Osgood remains indifferent; Jerry says he has been living with a saxophone player for three years (thus expressing his unconscious attraction to Joe)—Osgood forgives him. After declaring that he cannot have children, to which Osgood proposes adoption, a disdainful Jerry takes off his wig stating, "You don't understand, I'm a man!" Osgood's reply is "Nobody's perfect," leaving Jerry in a state of bewilderment, which very often characterizes the experience of feminine enjoyment, much like experiencing poetic texts in which one can never arrive at a definite meaning. Here the open ending of the film (like in *Yentl*, emphasized by the trope of sailing) conveys the sense of freedom from norms. The journey toward self-creation for Jerry begins now.

Another example of a transition from phallic to feminine enjoyment is that of Marshal King (James Garner) in Blake Edwards's *Victor Victoria* (1982). We have chosen this example because of certain critiques[27] accusing the film of "compulsory heterosexuality," which in our opinion is to overlook the essentials. In an emblematic scene that takes place in a cabaret, gender and sexuality are condensed as a fluid experience, achieved through music and dance. The scene occurs after King finds out, much to his consolation, that the man he is in love with is a woman, who has been impersonating a gay man performing as a female singer (Julie Andrews). The dance performed on the cabaret stage is a spectacle of rapid movement performed by four men. The number starts with a medium shot from behind a curtain showing their appearance on stage: the first, the second, and so on moving slowly and sensually toward the center of the stage, dressed as women. The costume of each dancer is composed of a feminine and a masculine side (one covering the front of the body; the other its back). They first show the feminine side, two of them wearing women's dresses and masks (the masks covering the back of the head); the other two wearing wigs, women's dresses, and make-up. The camera then dollies out, and the long shot that follows shows the dancers turning around, revealing the other side of their bodies—in black tuxedos: again, the two facing the audience show their own faces, while the other two, with their backs to the audience, wear masks. They split and pair up in a dance, moving rapidly in circles, the rhythm accelerating to the point that it becomes impossible to distinguish the front of the body from the back. The camera changes positions and angles, alternating between shots of the dance and shots of the audience, thus creating more movement and difference. Then, the two pairs of lovers are seen, framed in one shot: One gay—Victoria's friend, Toddy (Robert Preston) and King's assistant, "Squash" (Alex Karras)—and one straight—King and Victoria, Victoria still in men's attire, not knowing yet that King has discovered she is a woman. The two pairs are sitting at a table, fascinated by the dance performed on stage, the space/experience of gender and sexual fluidity having already been established by the dance—for both the diegetic and non-diegetic audience. This marks King's transition from a phallic space to a semiotic one, replete with feminine enjoyment.

For a gay audience, the dance can clearly be experienced as a gay performance in drag. For a straight audience, it is the experience of fluidity and indistinguishability, as well as a parody of the classical heterosexual dance that pairs only straight couples, that legitimizes and gives credence to the gay couple sitting next to the straight one (at the beginning of the scene the gay couple is shown sitting at a separate table, although Victoria is in a manly attire, which visually renders two gay couples). The stage performance—a mise-en-abyme—in this scene epitomizes our analogy of the fluidity inherent in the techniques and aesthetics of gender-crossing films and that of gender and sexuality. If the marriage between the image and the body of the actor is the anchoring point of fantasy when viewing a film, here the constant and rapid visual flipping of the gender costumes in their capacity of expressing the bounds of sex, gender, sexuality, and identity impedes any such fixation, suggesting that all categories related to them belong to social forms of masquerade, the performative. Although we know that the dancers are all men, as do all present in the cabaret, the delight derived from the number is not conflated with this knowledge, but rather with the baffling visuals and the uncertainty of sexuality stemming from them, enhanced by the choreography of the dance and the music accompanying it. The enjoyment that the audience in the cabaret is experiencing is *enhanced* for the spectators by the different camera positions and editing: We get to see a different show than the diegetic audience: a more rhythmical, rapid, and baffling one.

In this musical comedy it is the protagonist's lover (King) who undergoes subjectivization. That this happens to him in his capacity as spectator says something about the effect of the semiotic queerness on spectatorship. In fact, King's whole process of subjectivization is rendered in a series of reaction shots at what he sees, starting with his compulsive heterosexuality being confronted with the discovery that the female performer mesmerizing his sight is a man.[28] King's battle with his straight manhood (there are ample examples) is meant to bring him to accept gay people as his peers, not just prove Victoria's sex. What drives him crazy is both the thought that he might be attracted to a man (which he *is*), and his entry into an unknown territory/space (queer spaces—cabaret and gay clubs) that is strange to him, one he cannot control, one that controls him. In the end, it is King who comes to occupy Victoria's and Toddy's space and not the other way around. We may assume that had it not been for this process of subjectivization, he would probably have fired his assistant when he discovered he was gay. The last scene of the film shows King at Victoria's side sitting by a table and enjoying Toddy's parody of "The Shady Dame from Seville," performed earlier in the film by Julie Andrews/Victor/Victoria. Preston's manly hoarse voice and repeated tumbles when missing the dance steps evince the knocking down of the walls of heteronormativity through music and dance, which King is finally able to rejoice in—drawing us into its queer space and leaving us there (like *Some Like It Hot*), rocking the foundations of our imaginary.

6

From "Inherent Transgression" to the Body as "Semiotic *Chōra*"

The Trans Body and Desire: Between Blocking and Creating a Semiotic Space

Western liberal societies no longer seem to have a problem accepting gay people, who have gradually been asserting their rights as equals. This means that the family structure is also undergoing meaningful changes that are reflected in the many narrative films openly representing gay relationships and love stories. In the production of feminine-enjoyment spaces, it thus makes no sense anymore to ascribe gay subtexts to gender-crossing films—hence, the loss of interest in cross-dressing and, to a large extent, the tomboy category.[1] The way has been paved for trans people to come into the spotlight. Such is *3 Generations* (Gaby Dellal 2015), in which teenager Ray (Elle Fanning) fights to be allowed to pursue his gender as a young man, supported by his mother (Naomi Watts) and lesbian grandmother (Susan Sarandon), while trying to convince his absent father that it is the right choice.

Trans films expose two prevalent phenomena. First, social intelligibility, language itself, is still very much contingent upon binary norms of sexuality and gender; second, certain norms, such as the opposition to gay marriages, the persistence of the definition of spaces according to gender and sexual identity, and so on shelter deviant modes of enjoyment that must be kept in the dark. Thus, trans characters who represent a space of feminine enjoyment are always a potential menace threatening to uncover someone's dark secrets. We use "feminine enjoyment" here, like elsewhere, to emphasize the notion of category (of sex, sexuality, and gender) subversion, as well as the notion of self-creation (the satisfaction of the drives; the realization of desire), which in many ways corresponds to the way Lacanian psychoanalyst

Patricia Gherovici (2017: 549) uses Lacan's notion of the *sinthome* in regard to trans persons:

> How productive was this neologism? The shift in terminology related the symptom to art, with sinthome defined as the creative knotting together of the registers of the Symbolic (language, speech), the Real (...*jouissance*, the distribution of pleasure in the body), and the Imaginary (images, meaning) whose interlocking sustain the subject's reality.... The symptom as *sinthome* is an invention that allows someone to live by providing an organization of *jouissance*. Identification with the *sinthome* occurs when one identifies with the particular form of their enjoyment, thereby deriving their selfhood.[2]

As Gherovici notes, Lacan coined the term *sinthome* in relation to James Joyce's writing style and artistic activity at large, while moving away from linguistics. In dismantling the relations between gender and language, the transgender imposes on language a kind of boundary expansion and enrichment, not unlike poetics, which transcends the intelligibility of language. However, trans characters expose also another phenomenon: Trans films often evince how their very visibility or appearance poses a menace not only to sexual and gender conformism but also to perverse modes of enjoyment (e.g., sexual harassment, violent sex against one's will, incest, and pedophilia) practised and thriving in secret, often condoned by "the Law." Slavoj Žižek (1994: 55) argues: "What 'holds together' a community most deeply is not so much identification with the Law that regulates the community's 'normal' everyday circuit, but rather *identification with a specific form of transgression of the Law, of the Law's suspension* (in psychoanalytic terms, with a specific forms of *enjoyment*)" (italics in the original).[3]

Public Law thus has a "shadowy double," an "obscene superego underside" (1994) often justified by codes of honor (most common in the military) through which individuals become part of a group ("one of us"), unable to resist its code, the code being "the specific form of *transgression* that pertains to this community" (1994, italics in the original). Be the specific form of transgression a code of honor or a deviant sexual behavior, the cohesive element of all such forms is obscene enjoyment, its manifestation carried out in secret (known only to the victims and the victimizers). It draws its power from what becomes, in fact, a (transgressive) code that must be followed by all the members of a group and all those identifying with it (like the police in so many instances in history), making it possible for the transgressors to freely practice and get away with it. Therefore, a space dominated by inherent transgression can neither conceptually nor physically contain a space of feminine enjoyment or any space that threatens to expose it. The #MeToo movement and the exposure of sexual abuse by clergymen in recent years have revealed the enormous pervasiveness of such codes that defy the Public Law to the point that they can no longer be kept in secret precisely because of their pervasiveness. Such transgressors must be held accountable.

The dramas portraying trans protagonists thus evince them as a source of panic for those who practice all types of sexual conduct in secret as inherent transgressions, obscene forms of enjoyment that harm others. In such contexts, the clash between the space occupied by the protagonists (governed by feminine enjoyment), a space that defies the persisting binary gaze of the law, and the space governed by obscene enjoyment constitutes a learning experience for the spectator in that it shows that the genuine desire to pursue a gender identity which upsets hegemonic norms, in fact, stands to unravel obscene manifestations of enjoyment sheltered by "the Law" itself.

For example, the practice of child abuse as an inherent transgression of the institution of the Catholic Church is wonderfully depicted in an Almodóvar film where we have a trans woman—*La mala educación* (*Bad Education*, 2004). In this film, the trans character (Francisco Boira) is directly linked to the ongoing abuse of young boys by various clergymen in Catholic boarding schools. Although the trans character here is not a representative of feminine enjoyment but a drug addict whose life has been ruined beyond repair by those who were meant to educate him, she is characterized as an emblem of the victimhood of the dark side of the church. She thus becomes a constant reminder of the ways young lives are destroyed by the obscenity of the clergy.[4] In such dramas it is this kind of exposure that constitutes the ethical aspect of the gender-crossing character: While for the trans characters the abuse has ruined their life, for the spectators it becomes an eye-opening experience. In other words, such films as well evince through trans characters that whatever their gender or sexuality might be, they do not hurt anyone, as opposed to obscene enjoyment, which does. Other films, like *Ma Vie en rose* (*My Life in Pink*, Alain Berliner 1997) and *Tomboy* (Céline Sciama 2011), concentrate on the dread striking parents and communities when faced with trans children.

In what follows, this chapter focuses on three films. The first two deal with transphobic violence, which we read as a manifestation of the dread striking communities whose lives are dominated by phallic economies that shelter obscene enjoyment, violence being one such form of enjoyment: Kimberly Peirce's *Boys Don't Cry* (1999), which is the first *narrative* film about a trans man (played by Hilary Swank, who won an Oscar for her performance), which dramatizes the real life story of Brandon Teena[5] and Sebastián Lelio's *Una mujer fantástica* (*A Fantastic Woman* 2017, Oscar winner for Best Foreign Language Film of 2018). Upon its release, the latter film provoked discussion about the plight of trans women in Latin America, about familial homophobia, and about the cinematic representation of transgender lives. In his review of the film, Tomás Dodds (2018: 2) writes:

A *Fantastic Woman* is also the story of the lack of public policies toward trans people. What happened to Mariana is less fiction than we would hope for. Despite strong trans movements since the early 1970s, today's trans community in Chile suffers high levels of discrimination. Almost 97% of trans people have been discriminated against by their families; in almost two years different courts proved nine cases of torture of trans inmates in jails; and 55.2% of Chilean trans people have tried to commit suicide.

Revisiting Kimberly Peirce's *Boys Don't Cry*, thus, is inevitable and necessary. Both films consider not only the narrative of gender transgression but also the cinematic forms crafted to tell such stories and to confront the violence and punishment meted out to transgender bodies. In each film, the trans protagonist is violated by patriarchal dynamics, in conflict with conventional masculinities and femininities and at odds with the law such that the latter offers them no protection and instead extends and intensifies the violence they face. In both films, the trans protagonists "leave" their own body at a moment of extreme danger (*Boys Don't Cry*) or distress (*Una mujer fantástica*), and they rewrite the codes of embodiment and experiences of love and subjectivity as a consequence. Eliza Steinbock (2017: 400) writes: "While feminist film theory raises the question of a trans character and viewing positions, queer film criticism historically has foregrounded the analysis of a transsexual person's portrayal in terms of sexual subversion." Steinbock refers to Laura Mulvey's problematic (temporary) trans identification theory (1981), thereupon contrasting it with Jack Halberstam's (2001, 2005) theorization of the trans gaze, namely how narrative film can use our adjustments to the classic Hollywood cinematic grammar—the shot/reverse shot—as key to the dismantling of sex/gender stability (Halberstam's test case is *Boys Don't Cry*).

We hope to have shown how spectators are inscribed in the cinematic space in ways that surpass the S/RS device (see also our analysis of *Being John Malkovich* below), the latter being just one of many techniques that draw us into the imaginary space of a film, and regardless of what is perceived as "identity"—whether gender or otherwise. Nikki Reitz's (2017: 1) assertion that "negative stereotypes can directly impact the judgement of one group of people on another" can certainly be upturned: Positive characterization of trans protagonists can directly affect audiences. However, the contention that only trans women and not cisgender men (Reitz 2017: 4), or vice versa, can adequately act in roles depicting trans characters is not one we can accept, given our theorization of the body-actor-character, particularly when it concerns the employment of stars.[6] Moreover, subjectivization relates to a change in intersubjective relations and one's subjectivity, not to one's identity, and it is this change that can produce new perspectives regarding the identity of another, including trans persons. Trans films that produce an experience of feminine enjoyment (through engagement with the trans protagonist's desire and inscription in the filmic space) stand to "rewrite" not only the portrayal of trans characters in films but also the debasing ways trans persons are treated in many societies.[7] And to generate an affect of revolt on the part of spectators, films cannot bypass the foregrounding of the treatment of gender subversion in certain societies. In *Boys Don't Cry* this foregrounding is achieved by coercing Brandon into femaleness, against his will and in the cruelest way imaginable; in *Una Mujer Fantástica*, by brutally denying Marina her right to mourn her lover *in public*, to occupy the same space as his "normal" family does.

In other words, we must not confuse the way narrative films employ gender norms and behavior to manipulate audiences into revolting against them with how these norms are used in public discourse (e.g., the media) to discredit gender subversion and reify heteronormativity.[8] Moreover, as previously noted, the space of violence is not the only one the two films emphasize; they produce a space of feminine enjoyment and encourage us to engage with it: In Brandon's case, the space that he creates for Lana (Chloë Sevigny) and himself defies binary categories of sexuality and gender, putting the emphasis on subjectivity; it forces us to consider gender in terms of desire, not identity, and not even performance. In the case of *Una mujer fantástica*, the protagonist's space represents the realization of desire, concomitant with renouncing/denouncing the dependence on the look of the Other, a theme fully explored in this film, and vicariously suggested in *Boys Don't Cry*—which is why we analyze the two films separately: What in the geographical and social milieu of *Boys Don't Cry* can never flourish becomes possible in *Una mujer fantástica*, starting with the fact that the protagonist does not hide the fact that she is a trans woman.

Indeed, we should distinguish between how and why the protagonists are treated the way they are in the diegeses of the films and the way they might be experienced by different audiences. In the diegesis of *Boys Don't Cry* Brandon is a passing man for the cis men and women he associates himself with (except for Lana who very quickly understands that he is different from the men she knows). And passing, as Leanne Dawson (2015: 206) suggests (and can be fully applied to Brandon), "is . . . used by transgender people as a strategy either to avoid negative attention or punishment for their supposed gender transgressions or out of a belief that they should be read externally in line with what they consider to be their internal gender identity." In the diegesis of *Una mujer fantástica* Marina is a trans woman (played by Daniela Vega, a trans woman—actress and singer). The realization of desire must be severed from the look, recognition, or acceptance of the Other, which characterizes Marina's journey, a process that Brandon never gets a chance to undergo. However, both films distinguish between the space occupied by the trans protagonist and the one regulated by rigid binary gender norms: In *Boys Don't Cry* the space of Brandon and Lana is counterpointed with that of the cis men; in *Una mujer fantástica*, the space in which the spectators are inscribed first takes on the form of a journey, both physically and mentally, and then, as the film progresses, Marina's own body becomes the space she inhabits. That both films generate (in us) an affect of revolt against the violence inflicted on the protagonists when denied their desire is the main strategy used to ally *our* desire with theirs. As Brenda Cooper (2002: 49) argues in relation to *Boys Don't Cry*, "The privileged subjectivities of heterosexuality and hegemonic masculinity are dismantled, while female masculinity and gender fluidity are privileged and normalized," thus demonstrating the film's "destabilizing" potential and "liberatory function."

Finally, the meta-cinematic fantasy *Being John Malkovich* (1999) reflexively shows how this becomes possible in cinema: By inscribing spectators in the Other's desire through the body of the actor and camera (in this film, the body of the actor is analogous to that of the camera), the film becomes a fantasmatic receptacle containing our desire, regardless of gender, sex, sexuality, or any other definitions assigned to the subject. The film is unique in having three protagonists who embody three different positions in relation to the Other's desire and who, therefore, use Malkovich's receptacle in different ways, leading to different consequences. These consequences usher spectators to prefer one use (signifying the pursuit of authenticity, love, and truth) rather than another (the pursuit of fame and narcissism, rendered as alienation).

"They Say I'm the Best Boyfriend They Ever Had": *Boys Don't Cry*

Brandon is a young trans man who clearly wants to pursue young women as a man. True, Brandon wants to be part of a phallic community, belong to the category of men; he is not interested in creating a category of his own. However, it is clear from the start that in his relationship with Lana Tisdel he offers her an experience of enjoyment that goes beyond the phallic economy, one that sweeps her off her feet. In addition, in the circles Brandon frequents neither trans persons nor any queer sexuality is condoned. As Dawson (2015: 209) notes, "Brandon must display poor, rural Midwestern masculinity to be accepted by local men; indeed, socio-economic position informs [his] masculinity for gender does not operate in isolation, but rather intersects with class, ethnicity and other aspects of identity." The film starts with a group of young men yelling "You fucking dyke," "You freak," who chase Brandon to a trailer where his cousin Lonny (Matt Mcgrath) shelters him. Even Lonny pins Brandon to the wall and asks him what is wrong with him, and then, after Brandon frees himself from his grasp, implores him to admit that he is not a boy but a "dyke." Realizing that Brandon's presence in his life poses a threat, Lonny evicts him from his trailer in Lincoln, Nebraska.

Brandon leaves Lincoln and ends up in Falls City, Nebraska, where, while in a bar, he is more than happy to defend the honor of a young woman, Candace (Alicia Goranson), who works there and is being harassed by an older man. Two friends of Candace, John Lotter (Peter Sarsgaard) and Tom Nissen (Brendan Sexton III), ex-convicts and violent psychopaths, save him from being beaten by the harasser. They recognize in Brandon's enjoyment of violent behavior a "brotherly" conduct making him worthy of becoming part of their group. Brandon then becomes romantically involved with their friend, Lana, but his brushes with the law prior to coming to Falls City catch up with him and he is placed in the women's section of the town's prison. Lana bails Brandon out and declares her love for him regardless of his gender. However, when John and Tom discover Brandon is not a cis man, they rape and later murder him.

Boys Don't Cry generated much debate about whom or what Brandon really was and why he was so brutally murdered.[9] In our opinion, the film suggests that Brandon's fatal mistake is that he thought his only choice, in order to be a real man, was to adopt exaggerated macho codes of behavior and place himself in situations and locations where, to be accepted, he felt he had to express this macho stereotype in the form of bar fights, smoking, drinking, foul language, idleness, chivalry, and violence. The first time we see Brandon enjoying this type of behavior, thinking it would facilitate his passing as a man, is when his cousin Lonny pins him to the wall, trying to make him see he lives a dangerous life; unlike Lonny, who seems terrified at what Brandon's hunters might do to him, Brandon seems rather pleased with the situation. This is when Lonny asks him "What's wrong with you?" As Brandon's modus operandi is picking up girls in bars, his formal "initiation" into this type of manhood by John and Tom occurs in a bar. John and Tom drive him to their place, where Brandon wakes up the next morning not knowing where he is, signifying his inability to recognize the reality around him—that he is now in a lethal space.

The code of codes of the male members of the group that Brandon joins is homophobia and transphobia; thus it is clear from the beginning that he cannot really be fully a part of it, that if or when the truth comes out, he will be doomed. In the spiritually and materially impoverished society of Falls City such codes reign supreme and abiding by them is tragically the only thing its cis men inhabitants can do. Betrayal of the codes thus becomes an unforgivable act. As Linda Dittmar (2002: 147–48) argues, "Brandon is . . . also murdered because of . . . the brutalizing and dysfunctional life in a small Midwestern farming community that is stranded . . . in the material and spiritual poverty of dead-end lives."

The first time Brandon realizes his friends' irrational violent behavior might put him in danger is shown in two consecutive scenes. In the first,

Lana and another girl need to go to work, and Candice asks Brandon to drive because John is too intoxicated. Having been provoked by a group of girls driving by, John presses Brandon to accelerate. Brandon seems to enjoy the race until a police car begins following them for speeding and John forces Brandon to take a gravel road. The dust raised by the car (covering the screen) becomes a metaphor for Brandon's blindness: He shouts, "I can't see!" and looks worried. The police car catches up with them, and although the policeman says he could run them all in, he only gives Brandon (who takes the blame for speeding upon himself) a ticket.[10] Relieved, they get in the car, but John yells at Brandon not to "pull that shit" again with him. A bewildered Brandon answers that John was the one who told him to race after the girls' car and accelerate when they spotted the police car, implying that he (John) is the one at fault, but John insists that Brandon "fucked up" and pulls everyone out of the car ("my car" when it is really Candace's), except for Lana. This inscribes him as someone who, as the leader of the group, has the power not only to usurp a space that does not belong to him and call it "my" (car, house, and so on) but also to exclude people from it as he pleases. Left behind, Brandon (slightly positioned in the foreground of the mise-en-scène) and Candace (in the background) look astounded by John's irrational and violent behavior, and Katie (Alison Folland), another friend who works with Lana, also in the background, exclaims, "Welcome to psycho land!" This mise-en-scène, Katie's remark, the darkness of the night, and the bare landscape suggest that Brandon is finally awakening to the danger that was lurking there all along, one he blinded himself to because of his haste in adopting a set of codes he really had nothing in common with. A few seconds later John reverses and Lana tells Katie to get in the car, "He's taking us to work." The scene that follows takes place after the car disappears into the darkness of the night, in the middle of nowhere. Tom, who remains with the girls and Brandon, says he has been told that John cannot control his impulses, and that he is the only one able to control him. It is at this point that Brandon realizes how different he is from them: Tom (who is somewhat of a pyromaniac—when he returns for Katie, John says that Tom set his own house on fire) lights a fire and asks Brandon to cut himself with a knife (something he and John used to do when incarcerated), but Brandon declines, admitting that he is a "pussy."

It is then that Brandon decides to go back to Lincoln and sort out his past problems with the law and finally appear in front of a judge, but he cannot endure being treated like a girl and as Lana has become his beacon of light (he left for Lincoln after their first kiss), he escapes back to Falls City. Lonny warns him that they hang queer people there, but all Brandon can think about is Lana, whom he says he intends to marry. He goes straight to her place of work. Lana is on the night shift and when she spots Brandon outside (she takes a break and opens the window of her upper story office to smoke a cigarette) she looks happy to see him. While she is standing by the window Brandon takes a picture of her with a Polaroid camera, illuminating her for a split second. This signifies that Lana indeed might be Brandon's hope for a new life; however, the darkness surrounding them forebodes a different fate (the Polaroid also suggests that happiness will not last).

After this scene they make love for the first time. Lana clearly experiences a kind of enjoyment unknown to her before. She realizes during their lovemaking that Brandon is not a cis man: When Brandon leans over her, she accidentally catches a glimpse of the cleavage showing above his bound breasts—Brandon remains fully dressed. Kindly, she reassures him that everything is fine, and falls in love with him. Their relationship establishes a space of feminine enjoyment, which Lana and Brandon seem to thrive in but have no name for.

From this scene on, the film distinguishes between two spaces: the one occupied by John and Tom and the one occupied by Brandon and Lana, in which we inscribe. Dawson (2015: 214) writes:

> The relationships between [Brandon] and [his] ... love interest ... [is] presented as somewhat removed from the power structures theorised by Foucault and foreground touch and feelings over sight and patriarchal logic.... Indeed, the cis men are fixated on categories and measurement, although their employment in manual labour, or lack thereof, and socioeconomic position diseempowers them, on a larger scale at least, and instead they aim to control their social circle, rather than society at large. It is clear, however, that such cis men, alongside medical examiners, police officers and immigration officials are invested in the medical gaze and the administrators of its validity.

The collision of Brandon and Lana's space and that of the cis men becomes but a matter of time. With every appearance of John and Tom on-screen, Brandon and Lana's space becomes more and more imperiled, and the apprehensive affect generated is more on the side of spectators than that of the lovers. Brandon is seen increasingly enjoying the company of women rather than that of his male friends, suggesting his abandonment of "John's" space. However, John is disconcerted by Lana's relationship with Brandon, whom he considers a "wuss." After the lovemaking scene, the girls give Brandon a birthday party at Lana's place, which John literally invades. Lana's mother (Jeannetta Arnette) rebukes his not having knocked on the door and so does an angry Lana when he enters her room. John tells Lana he does not understand what she sees in Brandon and that he is concerned about her; in fact, he feels betrayed by Lana severing herself from what he represents as a man, his codes of manhood. He resents that "his" territory has been taken over by a "little man," as he later calls Brandon in a two-shot of them while sitting on a sofa, warning him, "You have to remember one thing, that this is *my* house!" Lana's house is no more John's than

Candace's car is his; such appropriations of material things and space are meant to remind everyone that whoever dares to not abide by his codes will be deserving of severe punishment. Lana, whom the scene cuts to, to show her reaction, indeed has good reason to look worried, as are the spectators.

The scene that follows mirrors the one in which Brandon takes the picture of Lana in terms of mise-en-scène, but with John occupying Brandon's position, as if he has come to reclaim a space lost to him. We see John positioned under Lana's window, looking up at her while she is working. However, in the earlier scene with Brandon we have a dialogue between them: The low angle from which shots of Lana are rendered, simulating Brandon's point of view, and the high angle from which shots of Brandon are taken, rendering her point of view, suggest a real dialogue (rendered in shot/reverse shot), that they *see* each other, evinced also by the open window at the beginning of the scene, which later enables the dialogue. In contrast, in the scene featuring John, Lana is seen working behind a closed barred window, as if trapped by John's look—the shots rendered creating a sense of *tableau*, though they are supposed to simulate his point of view from below. This suggests that John is not really seeing Lana; he is not even looking at her most of the time—the camera shows him in a close-up shutting his eyes, which is to say that for John, Lana is but a fantasy, "imprisoned" in his mind as an object to be looked at. It also suggests that he is oblivious of boundaries (the window bars).

Feeling John's presence lurking in the dark and knowing how unpredictable and dangerous he is, Lana tells Brandon the next day that she has quit her job and suggests they move to Memphis, where Brandon will manage Lana's karaoke singing career—thus expressing her desire to get as far as possible from Falls City. Contrary to Lana, a still somewhat blind Brandon (who has found a job), insists they stay in Falls City and get their own trailer. Moreover, Brandon decides to sort out his trouble with the police, but when he arrives at the police station he is identified as Teena Brandon and put in jail in the women's section.

The scene showing Brandon behind bars writing a letter to Lonny is intercut with that of Candace going through his things and discovering his biological sex and birth name. This parallel editing conveys that Brandon's misdemeanors (the summons that Candace finds with Brandon's birth name) and his transgenderism (his tampons and jeans stained with menstrual blood) are entangled, that his so-called inclination to get in trouble with the law (which he believes, as expressed in the voice-over rendering the content of the letter to Lonny) is a direct outcome of his being the prisoner of a community that condemns his desire to be a man. Brandon is not confused about his desire, but in a society that puts people in jail for not conforming to local norms of gender, he must lie his way through life, sometimes even steal or cheat.

Enraged by the news about Brandon, John and Tom arrive at Lana's house with the intent to undress him. Lana tries to save Brandon from this humiliation by offering to take him into her room and do the check. When they are alone, she tells him that no such thing is necessary and after a short while exits the room and lies to everyone that he is a man—not only to save him but also because for her Brandon is the kind of man she desires and is happy with, as she repeatedly tells him every time he makes up a story about his "condition." John and Tom are not satisfied with Lana's statement and push Brandon into the bathroom, taking down his pants and underwear. John opens the door for Lana, who wants to come in to avert further escalation, but he forcibly holds her down and compels her to look at Brandon's genital area; she shields her eyes to avoid further shaming Brandon and implores John to leave him alone. That the camera shows us Brandon's genital area emphasizes not only Brandon's humiliation but also the idea that there is no essential connection between biology and gender, a notion that Lana seems to be the only one who understands and accepts.

After Lana screams at John and Tom to let Brandon go, the soundtrack goes silent; the camera, as if in a haze, shows a medium close-up of Brandon held down by John and Tom, whose faces only partly appear on-screen. The visuals become somewhat blurry and Brandon's expression turns inert, as if his soul has been sucked out of his body: He lifts his head slightly, the scene cutting to a shot showing Brandon, fully dressed, looking at what is happening to him.[11] Arguing that the film solicits viewer empathy through revulsion on the one hand and sympathy or empathy for the queer on the other, Dawson (2015: 215) relies on Halberstam's (2005: 77) claim that *Boys Don't Cry* gives mainstream viewers access to a "transgender gaze" even after Brandon's body has been brutally exposed; moreover, Dawson stresses that Halberstam's argument is based on queer temporality when stating that the film constructs this transgender gaze "'capable of seeing through the present to a future elsewhere,' helped by certain 'experimental moments in this otherwise brutally realistic film' in which the director creates 'slow-motion or double-speed time warps.'" The mise-en-scène shows Candace and Katie positioned in the foreground, one on each side of Brandon, and Brandon in the background, the composition forming a triangle (Figure 6.1); however, it is Brandon who appears foregrounded by a spotlight while the other two remain in the dark. Besides the adoption of "a transgender gaze," Brandon's splitting conveys an additional double meaning: First, as in many cases of sexual and mental abuse, Brandon's mind severs itself from his body to be able to endure the emotional and physical pain inflicted on him—in his experience John and Tom are stripping him of his manhood, forcing him and his female friends to see him as woman; second, this shot mirrors the previous one, in which Brandon appears held down by his two assailants. This mirroring suggests that his cis women friends would never have succumbed to such a form of cruelty (the positioning of Katie and Candace

FIGURE 6.1 Boys Don't Cry (*Kimberly Peirce 1999*).

in front of Brandon in the fantasized shot conveys a sense of Brandon being shielded by them), regardless of how cheated they feel at having discovered Brandon's birth sex. Indeed, in the scene in which Candace finds Brandon's summons she kneels to the ground and starts sobbing. She is saddened (she also liked Brandon as a man and wished she could find a husband like him), and then confused and somewhat lost, but would never assault Brandon for it—on the contrary, she shelters him after the rape.

That Brandon is a victim of delinquent codes of manhood is evinced in the shot that follows, connoting the Crucifixion (Figure 6.2): We see a broken Brandon, his knees bent forward, unable to stand on his feet, his genital area showing (his upper body remains covered by his t-shirt), held by John (on the right side of the frame) and Tom (on the left side), the composition thus creating the form of a cross; Brandon is once more spotlighted (some of the light also illuminates John's and Tom's faces)—all this appears in the background of the mise-en-scène, though the lighting is foregrounding Brandon's victimhood. In mid-ground, we see Lana from behind, kneeling in the dark, her position connoting an iconography of Mary Magdalene kneeling before or after Christ's death on the cross; in the foreground, the back silhouettes of Lana's mother (on the left) and Katie (on the right) create a closed frame, whereupon the scene cuts again to an imagined reaction-shot of Brandon to emphasize his realization that he has been a victim of twisted manhood. At this point, the film brings us back to reality: The soundtrack returns, and the assault continues for a short while, when Lana's mother kicks John and Tom out of her house.

What is so powerful and moving about this scene, especially the portions in which it leaves the realm of reality and enters that of the fantastic, is the

FIGURE 6.2 Boys Don't Cry (*Kimberly Peirce 1999*).

way it associates love with art. Brandon's conflation with Christ suggests love, not only victimhood, while the cinematic work (the interruption of sound, the mise-en-scène and composition connoting painting, the lighting, and the editing) suggests sublimation—not just the idea that the aesthetics of film has the power to render the most horrible of crimes by aestheticizing it, but rather the notion that *love*, like art, is a form of sublimation, as well as redemption. We engage with the love that Brandon and Lana feel for each other and recognize it as a redeeming force, though it cannot flourish in Falls City.

What facilitates Brandon's tragic murder is the fact that the local sheriff, rather than protecting Brandon and arresting John and Tom after the assault, is preoccupied with Brandon's gender "transgression." It is indeed tragic because the murder could have been averted had the local police performed its duty. That, like John and Tom, the sheriff suffers from homophobia and transphobia is quite clear; but might it not also be because his interest is to protect the "shadowy double" of "the Law"? In fact, are not homophobia, transphobia, and misogynism the shields that protect the obscene secrets of individuals or groups governed by brutal codes?

The scene in which Brandon reports the assault and rape to the local sheriff is intercut with that of the assault, this paralleling suggesting that the former is but a repetition of the latter, another form of abuse and dehumanization. It is one of the film's main strategies to ensure the spectators' alliance with Brandon. The sheriff starts by telling Brandon that it is surprising that his assailants did not finger him, because this is what men are expected to do to girls, and continues: "After you had your pants off, how were you positioned in the backseat? . . . You was on your back? Now, you say you're twenty-one and you never had sex before." This demonstration of cis-heteronormativity and transphobia is conveyed as a direct *assault* on Brandon: The intercut shows at this point Brandon being thrust down in the car by John and Tom, about to be raped. Melissa Rigney (2003–4: 9) rightly claims that the rape "fixes" and "normalizes" Brandon's body: "It is a graphic visual assertion of who is 'male' and who is 'female.'" But this is not in order to rewrite his identity as "a masculine lesbian," as Rigney (11) later asserts, but rather to condemn the mentality of a society dominated by cis men that cannot see beyond depraved "maleness"—and so, the sheriff continues: "When they had a spread of you and when they poked you, where'd they try to pop it in first?" All through these quoted lines the sheriff remains off-screen (the camera focuses on Brandon, the victim); we only hear his voice and coarse language—a ubiquitous voice echoing the ruthless crime committed, which, although occurring earlier in time, is depicted simultaneously. It becomes clear that rather than have the interest of the victim at heart the sheriff represents the same prejudice and ignorance that is effectively signing Brandon's death warrant. At this point the film chooses to show at length another portion of the rape's chronology. John and Tom take Brandon to Tom's house, warning him to keep silent about the rape or else they will kill him. Brandon promises not to say anything, adding, "It's all my fault" (reverberating with so many rape cases in which the victim is made to feel guilty).

He then goes into the bathroom, turns the water on, and escapes through the window. He goes to Lana's house, but her mother is reluctant to help. In the next scene we see Brandon examined by a female doctor or nurse, and the comparison between her treatment of Brandon and the sheriff's is inevitable: She is nice and gentle, reassuring and compassionate, approaching Brandon like any victim of such a heinous crime should be approached. The next shot takes us back to the last portion of the sheriff's interview (belonging to the parallel-editing sequence) and shows his face for the first time. He says: "Why do you run around with guys, bein' you're a girl yourself, why do you go around kissin' a girl?" which implies that there are strict codes of manhood (which the sheriff clearly enjoys implementing) that are not to be transgressed. Brandon tries to resist this line of interrogation, "I don't know what this has to do with what happened." But the sheriff insists that Brandon answer his questions. Brandon caves in, saying "I have a sexual identity crisis." Forced to repeat the sentence, he starts crying and seems crushed. The parallel editing thus shows, in addition to Brandon's repudiation of the space governed by obscene codes of manhood he no longer wishes to be associated with, how he is coerced into admitting he has a problem because he wishes to be a man, which he does not recognize as a problem. Spectators do not have to be trans or gay to revolt against such a misuse of the law.

Knowing that he cannot return to Lana's home because of her mother, Brandon goes to Candace's house. Shocked at the sight of his injuries, she takes him in. Brandon showers, tenderly touching his body (his face, neck, and shoulders are rendered in close-up; his thighs are photographed from behind), as if wishing he were able to protect it, soothe it (the camera evinces the delicate motion of the hands on the body), not fully grasping why it has been so viciously attacked. This scene symbolizes Brandon's desire to purge his body of all the manly signs/codes he once wished to be associated with or adopt, while the camera refuses to disclose those parts of the body attesting to his birth sex. This is further emphasized by this scene being paralleled with one that chronologically proceeds it, in which he makes a fire and burns the Polaroid photographs of him alone and with John and Tom. Meanwhile, Lana's mother tells John that the rape has been reported and asks him to come clean about it, but John and Tom deny the crime to her.

Lana goes to Candice's and finds a traumatized Brandon hidden in the shed near her house. Lana finally gets Brandon to let her make love to him, to feel what she has felt with him (in their second lovemaking scene Brandon is reluctant to let Lana touch his genitals, and she tells him that she wants him to share her experience). This scene might be read as lesbian lovemaking, but we consider it a denunciation on Brandon's part of what he has been taught so far about cisgender manhood.[12] Realizing that Lana accepts him as a trans man, Brandon comes clean to her about all his lies and they make plans to go to Lincoln. But it is too late. John and Tom (who have been summoned by the police) drive to Candace's house where they find Brandon: John shoots Brandon, and Tom, Candace, as Lana fights with them, begging them to stop. Tom stabs Brandon's lifeless body and tries to shoot Lana, but John stops him. John and Tom flee the scene while a crying Lana stays with Brandon's body. The next morning, Lana awakens next to Brandon's corpse, now connoting the *Pietà*. Her mother arrives and takes her away. The last scene shows Lana leaving Falls City, driving in her car by night, while a letter Brandon wrote to her is heard in his voice-over, professing his hopes and love for her. Lana seems somewhat pleased to leave behind the wasteland of Falls City, its darkness (most of the film's plot occurs at night or in darkness, showing only glimpses of light) symbolizing the danger looming over anyone who dares challenge the codes of its male community.

To recapitulate, *Boys Don't Cry* is about a trans man who in the diegesis passes as a cis man, which the film takes advantage of in that it problematizes every possible aspect of cis-heteronormativity, dismantling the relations between birth sex, gender, and sexuality, while using various strategies and cinematic language to engage spectators with Brandon and Lana's experience regarding both their non-phallic mode of enjoyment and revolt against the oppression and violence exerted on them. Handling Brandon's body as polymorphous—Brandon's desire is to be a man, but the film suggests that this desire has nothing to do with either birth sex or sexuality—offers cisgender spectators a chance to reflect on cis-heteronormativity. That the latter is equally implemented by two psychopaths and representatives of "law and order" instructs cisgender spectators that aberrant conduct is part and parcel of backwardness and power structures, not of transgender. Herein lies the ethics of subjectivization in this film.

"What Doesn't Kill You Makes You Stronger": The Polymorphous Body of *Una mujer fantástica*

Marco Posadas (2017: 647) writes: "Laverne Cox's words . . . addressing antitrans policies condense the transphobic conundrum as I see it in my clinical practice: 'This is not only about accessing public restrooms, but about public existence. It's about the right of trans people to exist in public spaces.'" This is the explicit theme of *Una mujer fantástica*; its implicit theme is the protagonist's process of subjectivization, with which we engage. Although Marina is a trans woman in the diegesis, and played by a trans-woman actress, the film deliberately abstains from hyperbolizing her femininity; on the contrary, the treatment of her body, not too different from Brandon's, solicits a polymorphous reading. It seems like this film picks up where *Boys Don't Cry* leaves off: it teaches us not only the same lesson (about the plague of power structures dominated by obscene cis-heteronormativity and transphobia), while promoting transgender human rights, but also how to renounce the dependence of being defined by the Other's look, even when the latter is a loving one.

Marina works as a waitress by day and a pop singer by night. Her elderly lover, Orlando (Francisco Reyes), probably also a father figure to her, has a stroke, causing him to fall down a staircase, dying in the process. Because of his injuries, Marina is suspected by doctors and the police of being involved in a violent relationship with him that might have caused his sudden death. In addition, she is immediately dispossessed of her dog, car, and the apartment she shared with Orlando by his sons and ex-wife and is forbidden from attending the funeral services. Like Brandon, whose sense of manhood in the beginning is contingent upon how other men (and women) see and define him, Marina's sense of womanhood depends on her lover's approving look and desire. However, rather than despair, she embarks on a journey through which she will have to renounce this dependence, while carving for herself, as well as the spectators, a space in which change occurs, accentuated by the motif of *flânerie*, which creates a sense of journey (both physical and inner/spiritual), and in which we have no choice but to partake, simply because continuing to view the film means accompanying Marina in her *flânerie*, as well as occupying the spaces she comes to occupy/conquer.

She finds a way to properly undergo a process of bereavement, after which she devotes herself to a career as an aria opera singer, turning her body into a vessel for her unique voice. Her body thus becomes a space of the sublimation associated with feminine enjoyment.

The film opens with a montage of the Iguazú Falls, which Orlando plans to take Marina to for her birthday. The falls are part of a huge nature reserve located half in Brazil and half in Argentina: a space that becomes a visual metaphor for a polymorphous gender. Moreover, some of the shots depict the Argentinian side of the "Devil's Throat" (the most overwhelming and forceful of all falls), with its changing aspects, ranges of colors, and powerful currents, which metaphorically implies that the protagonist as a trans woman is a "force of nature," a fantastic woman, not only because she has a tempestuous character but also because as a trans woman, she is an unsettling figure. The last shot of the opening sequence (the falls) dissolves into an image of a man (Orlando) lying motionless on his back on the stone bench of a sauna, the steam clouding the image, whose colors change from monochromatic red to blue. This image, portraying Orlando as a cadaver, foretells his actual death and establishes the notion that Orlando's dead body, its appropriation by Marina and her mourning process, will determine her attitude toward her own body and image, as well as toward her calling in life.

As long as Orlando is alive (a very short period of time in the plot, but a prolonged one in the story), Marina does not question her body, or her identity as a woman. Thus, when she is told by the doctor that Orlando is dead, she goes into the *ladies'* room and cries. Traumatized by Orlando's sudden passing, she leaves the hospital. But then Orlando's brother Gabo (Luis Gnecco) asks the police to bring Marina back to the hospital to investigate Orlando's bruises. Marina is asked to identify herself as Daniel, her birth name as printed on her identity card. From this scene onward, she crosses different spaces—feminine, masculine, gay, and straight—her image and the different ways it is reflected in mirrors and windows pointing to the *inner* transformation she undergoes regarding the way *she* sees her body and self, without Orlando's desirous approval.

As soon as Orlando dies, Marina incessantly finds herself in situations in which she is rejected and debased, chased out of the space she shared with Orlando, her visibility challenged and dented. Three scenes stand out in this respect. The first (rendered in dialogue) describes Marina's first encounter with Orlando's transphobic ex-wife, Sonia (Aline Küppenheim), when she is asked to return the car, and her first attempt to take part in Orlando's burial ceremonies, to say goodbye to him, is shunned; instead, she is offered money as "compensation," which she refuses to accept. Marina and Sonia meet in the parking lot of Sonia's building and Sonia says to her: "I have been wondering how you look for about a year, it's different face-to-face." Marina replies: "As you can see ma'am, flesh and bones," thus suggesting that it was not necessarily Marina's gender that attracted Orlando to her. Later, after inspecting the car, Sonia tells Marina how she and Orlando used to have a "normal" marriage and life, so when he came to her to explain things, she thought that it was a "perversion," adding that when she looks at Marina she does not know what she sees. She then pauses, her eyes scrutinizing Marina's body, and says: "A chimera, that's what I see."[13] When Marina expresses her wish to attend the wake, saying she knows how to be "discrete," Sonia forbids her to do so and demands that she stay away, emphasizing that it is her and her loved ones' duty to take care of all the funeral arrangements. She adds that she will not expose her young daughter to the sight of Marina. She remains indifferent to Marina's response that for her, Orlando was a loved one, and calls her "Daniel" to further demean her.

The second scene depicts a physical examination of Marina (to rule out the suspicion of an abusive relationship with Orlando). She is summoned to the police station, and when she tries to resist the exam, the police officer (a woman) in charge of her case threatens that her refusal might prompt the opening of a criminal investigation. Marina thus forces herself to agree to the examination. She overhears the doctor asking the officer how to approach her, given that her birth name is "Daniel"—as a man, or a woman? The policewoman, who is present all through the examination, instructs him to approach her as a woman, "Marina." Holding the camera in his hands, the doctor first asks her to uncover her upper body (she is dressed in a hospital gown), and we see her in a medium shot, slowly uncovering her shoulders and chest. The voice of the doctor is heard while his body remains off-screen (he says "Okay"). Then we see the doctor holding the camera, instructing her to raise her right arm. The shot that follows is a full one showing Marina with her right arm raised, the other covering her genital area with the gown. This is repeated with Marina's left arm. So far, all that is revealed both to the examiners and to the spectators is that Marina's body (her armpits included) is hairless and her breasts are not particularly augmented. But then, when asked to uncover her lower body, the scene cuts from her body to the doctor and the policewoman, and then again to her body, preserving Marina in a medium shot throughout, refusing to show the spectators what the officials see: Marina's genitals. What follows are two consecutive reaction shots of the doctor and the officer that intensify the sense of ambiguity of this scene, as their reactions are very difficult to read. This difficulty seems to have a double purpose: First it emphasizes that, despite the fact that this is the implementation of a formal procedure under the medical and judicial gazes (although they approach her quite considerately, in a professional manner), for Marina this is an invasion of her body, a violation she cannot condone, as suggested by her facial expression when she leaves the premises. Second, for the spectators, she remains an ambivalent, polymorphous figure: Her resistance to be defined by the judicial and medical gazes is translated by the film through the rendering of shots and editing into a body/text that resists a definitive reading/interpretation and engages the spectators with Marina's revolt.

This double resistance (on Marina's part, as well as the film's) is magnified in a scene that follows shortly after, in which she battles against a sudden gust of wind. Marina goes to her classical-music voice coach, who tells her he is only a "teacher for singing," and she affirms: "And you're not my psychologist" (nor my father, for that matter, or any other). She begins practising, at which point the scene cuts to Marina, alone on a sidewalk (her singing still accompanying the visuals in a sound bridge), a force of nature battling against another force of nature—a visual metaphor condensing her against-the-grain being, her resistance, as well as her determination to overcome all the blows inflicted upon her. Her singing on the soundtrack suggests that hers is an inner force, her unique form of expression that has nothing to do with gender, foreboding the creation of a mental space, one of feminine enjoyment inhabiting her body (Figure 6.3).

The third scene depicting the aggression inflicted on Marina is also the most violent. After being thrown out of the apartment she shared with Orlando by his son Bruno (Nicolás Saavedra) and dispossessed of her dog, Diabla, an infuriated Marina decides to attend the wake. She enters the church, but Sonia orders her out. Orlando's brother, Gabo, the only member of the family to show her empathy, follows her and tries to apologize, but Marina tells him that saying goodbye to Orlando is her basic human right. He agrees and she leaves. While walking, three of Orlando's sons follow her in a car and harass her, calling her a "fucking faggot," "monster," and other names. She tries to get away, but they keep chasing her, whereupon two of them get out of the car and force her in. In the car, they continue to call her names. Marina tries to resist, battling with them and asking about the dog, telling them their father would be ashamed of them. At this point they wrap her face with scotch tape, deforming it, while they keep mortifying and

FIGURE 6.3 Una mujer fantástica (A Fantastic Woman, *Sebastián Lelio 2017*).

FIGURE 6.4 Una mujer fantástica (A Fantastic Woman, Sebastián Lelio 2017).

terrorizing her: as they forcefully cover her mouth with the tape, they urge her to speak, knowing that she no longer can. The camera then zooms in to a medium close-up of her deformed face, as she breathes heavily (Figure 6.4).

After she is thrown out of the car, Marina sits down on a large piece of rock belonging to a dilapidated building. It is set against a wall on which there is a huge graffiti of a skeleton drawn in carbon, connoting a chimera—that which the men in the car have tried to turn Marina into, thus emphasizing the power of external/social forces on individual subjectivity (they succeed in making her feel like a monster). She manages to get up, still breathing heavily, leans against a nearby car, and looks at her distorted face as reflected in one of its windows. She removes the tape and walks away. The car represents here a phallic violent space that cannot contain Marina's polymorphous gender, which will find a space of its own. For now, the way the film inscribes us in Marina's desire is through her insistence that it is her human right to participate in the public spaces in which the funeral services take place, one she relentlessly fights to realize, despite how she feels (thus suggesting that it is the human right of any trans person to occupy public places), and through Marina's scenes of humiliation and abuse, against which we revolt.

After the abuse scene in the car, Marina is seen wandering the streets in a state of shock until nightfall, when she enters a gay club. She gets intimate with a man and performs fellatio on him (the camera does not disclose the act itself, only infers it), but it does not give her any pleasure. On the contrary, as she traverses the dance floor, its flickering lights form thin yellow stripes on her face alluding to those of the scotch tape that had bound it. This suggests that sex with a stranger only deepened her hurt and humiliation, that she must look for other ways to redeem herself. She stops and looks across the dance floor, where she "sees" Orlando looking back at her. She approaches the center of the floor and slowly starts dancing, as if in a trance.

In the next shot we see her in medium close-up wearing a different dress, a golden glittering gown; as the camera dollies out we perceive that the gown is only a large ornate golden and silvery cape covering her mundane denim dress, identical to the capes worn by a group of dancers surrounding her, their moves synchronized with hers, after which they lift her up, as befitting the star of a show. In the next shot she is seen floating in the air (no longer held by the dancers), the cape connoting the wings of an angel, her body progressing toward the camera, until her confident and glowing face (rendered in close-up, from a high angle) is seen looking directly at the camera, her clear image lit against the blurred, faded background. This scene evinces that at this point in her life Marina still needs to imagine Orlando's approving gaze to feel beautiful and glamorous. However, her soaring up toward the camera, looking directly into it (evinced by the beautiful face of the close-up—as opposed by her previously deformed face) suggests that she is willing to leave any physical space, even a queer one, in favor of a spiritual one; the way she looks into the camera reflects also the way cinema addresses spectators by inscribing us in its space, which is not a real space but an imaginary/fantasmatic one, recalling the scene in which Brandon leaves his body to gaze at his abuse. While Brandon forces us to look at his abuse through his eyes, Marina is directly appealing to our gaze by addressing the camera (Figure 6.5).

Though she decides not to go to the funeral service after all these experiences, Marina changes her mind after her attempt to find out if Orlando left her anything in his sauna locker. While at her sister's home, where she finds refuge, she looks at a locker key Orlando left with the number

FIGURE 6.5 Una mujer fant*á*stica (A Fantastic Woman, *Sebastián Lelio 2017*).

181 (a palindrome alluding to her ambiguous image) and says to herself, "What doesn't kill you makes you stronger." This marks the beginning of her change, her inner transformation. She first goes to a beauty salon to have her hair and nails done. Looking at her hands, she says to the manicurist that they look like those of an "orangutan." This insecurity about herself (who/what she is) is rendered in the scene that follows, in which two men holding a huge mirror cross her path; they stop as one of them says, "Wait, I have to adjust," and we see Marina looking at her wobbly reflection in the mirror (Figure 6.6). The men manage to take the mirror away, thus "erasing" her reflection.

However, after having a drink in a bar, Marina resumes her *flânerie*, her body again reflected in the windows of a block of storefronts as she strolls along the street, creating an image of a double accompanying her: The frame is split in two symmetrical parts, one showing Marina; the other, her reflection. However, although this suggests that she still feels torn inside, we infer from the proximity of the reflection accompanying the body in its continual motion that Marina has embarked on a journey that will bring her closer to herself, her true self, no longer dependent on the look/desire of the Other.

Shortly after, she goes to Orlando's health club, in which the space is gender divided. However, the thought of going directly to the men's area (where the lockers are) is difficult for her, and to reassure herself of her womanhood she first enters the women's section. After buying a ticket she undresses and wraps her body with a towel, like women do, from the armpits half-way to the knees. She looks around (the shots in the women's area are filtered with a blue shade—a color usually associated in gender terms with boys, thus pointing to the polysemy that Marina's gender

FIGURE 6.6 Una mujer fantástica (A Fantastic Woman, *Sebastián Lelio 2017*).

represents). Then, as she gathers her courage to go in the men's area, she ties her hair with a rubber band. The shot that follows shows the men's area from within, filtered in shades of red and yellow, emphasizing both polysemy and the act of transition between the spaces and Marina's mood or state of mind. When Marina enters, the towel now wrapped around her waist (like men do), her upper body uncovered, the filters change to blue, and as she walks through the lines of men sitting on benches they change again, to a shade of pink. She approaches a man who works there and asks where the lockers are. As she enters the locker area, the shades change to green. All these shades are reminiscent of the Iguazú Falls metaphor, they recall the shades of the Devil's Throat's falls, namely, that Marina is a force of nature and that nothing stands in her way. She approaches Orlando's locker and opens it: We see her face in close-up (rendered from the position of the locker), looking at what might be the contents of the locker; she breathes heavily and, disappointed and baffled, looks away. She leaves the premises, but the camera, positioned now in front of the lockers, slowly dollies in to Orlando's open locker, revealing a black emptiness, until this blackness covers the whole screen. The film leads us to expect that Marina would at least find an envelope in the locker with tickets to the Iguazú Falls: At the beginning of the film, after we see Orlando lying in the sauna, he tells Marina he cannot find the envelope with the tickets; instead, he gives her another envelope with a note he wrote, in which he makes a commitment to take her to "one of the natural wonders in the world." We thus assume that Orlando must have forgotten the tickets in his locker. However, all Marina and we see is black emptiness.

This abyss-like emptiness symbolizes Orlando's death, as well as the screen's lack. For Marina, the locker in which she expects to find a token of Orlando's love and reassuring look turns into a gaze (in the Lacanian sense) signifying the lack in the Other, as well as her own. In terms of spectatorship, the two-dimensional black space of the locker suggests the paradoxical, double nature of the screen: a two-dimensional empty rectangle (today's screens, like those of the televisions, tablets, computers, and smartphones on which we watch films, are *black* until turned on) that becomes a colorful receptacle able to contain everything and anything, drawing our bodies into its space through the desire of the protagonist and the body of the camera. The locker thus signifies a receptacle of Marina's desire and ours, in which an imaginary space (that of fantasy) is created, filled with objects. The emptiness of the locker thus suggests that the very anticipation that this space be filled (the realization of being inscribed in the Other's desire) must be dissolved for subjectivization to occur. This is the film's way of thrusting Marina out from Orlando's desire, and the spectators from her desire that she must have Orlando's reassuring look, but not from her desire to grieve her lover.

In the scene that follows, an adamant Marina is seen grabbing a cab to attend Orlando's funeral. She is stopped by one of Orlando's sons and Sonia, who, accompanied by Orlando's brother, are driving back from the funeral, which they tell her is over. Sonia and her son yell at her to get out of their way and leave them alone, calling her names, but Marina climbs on the car roof and starts tromping on it with force, shouting, "I want my dog!" She slides down on the front window, gluing her hands to it, a menacing expression on her face: Rather than feeling a victim, she now appears as someone who has learned to assert her basic human rights, as if "conquering" the space (car) in which she was severely attacked: a beginning of her realization that she is the only one who can satisfy her desire. In a later scene, we understand that her dog has been returned to her when we see her jogging with it, her sole physical reminder of Orlando.

After Orlando's family drives away, she stays on the premises, where in the distance she sees a man walking with his back to her. She follows him into the crematorium through a back door leading to its basement, along a spiral corridor. When the lights turn to red, Marina finds herself facing Orlando. At this point, the scene conveys a descent into Hell, recalling Orpheus's descent to Hades to reclaim his beloved dead Eurydice, but without gender playing a role: The role of Orpheus is assigned to Marina, a trans woman, and that of Eurydice to Orlando, a cis man. Like Orpheus, Marina is a musician (a singer), longing for her dead beloved. However, as we know from this myth, Orpheus fails to resurrect Eurydice because he looked at her before coming out to the light, which in the context of this scene alludes to Marina's dependency on Orlando's reassuring look, one she must now give up. A frightened Marina gives in to Orlando's passionate kiss when he pins her to a wall, a red light emanating from an electric device hanging on the wall illuminating them. For Marina, the descent into Hell symbolizes her attempt to try to keep Orlando alive and regain the sense of belonging he represented for her—hence her understanding, as well as the spectators', that she must let go of this fantasy and find the sense of belonging within herself.

Even though we may read this scene as Marina's hallucination, or just a dramatization of her longing, Orlando's spirit is embodied by an actor who is very much alive, thus generating an experience of the uncanny. This is emphasized by Marina's reaction to her bodily experience with Orlando: When he turns away, he leaves behind an incredulous Marina, touching her lips while gasping for air. The knowledge that the bodies of both actors are real and were there in front of the camera during the kiss, bearing in mind that in the film's diegesis Orlando is a dead body, registers his appearance here as a "living dead"—a dark shadow recalling that of Eurydice, who can only materialize when she comes into the light outside Hades, analogous to the projection light or any apparatus through which the film comes to life on the screen. As Laura Mulvey (2006: 36) puts it, "The inanimate images of the film strip not only come alive in projection, but are the ghostly images of the now-dead resurrected into the appearance of life."

In terms of the filmic experience, because any attempt to touch the material body of the actor is, of course, futile (it hits on the lack of the screen), the scene rather seems to convey the power of film in engaging the spectators with the dynamic of desire/fantasy: It is precisely the absence/shadow of the material body on screen (marking its lack) that draws our desire into the filmic space, but it is its fantasmatic nature that sustains it, affects us, and makes us part of the protagonist's experience in the film's space. Our awareness of the imaginary nature of film, on the contrary, does not diminish this affect and effect on us. Thus, the spectators remain engaged with Marina's desire to mourn her lover.

Marina continues to follow Orlando, who disappears behind a closed door. Unable to open it, she vehemently bangs on the door; a buzzer is heard, and the door opens. She finds herself in one of the rooms of the crematorium (another space of the "dead") where Orlando's body is about to be burned. She finally gets to see his corpse and mourn his death as she holds his hand, tears coming down her face—a considerable shift from the passionate kiss "they" shared in the previous scene. Marina then watches Orlando's body being slid into the crematory, its metal door closing. The camera dollies in toward its round-shaped aperture, recalling the camera's movement in the locker scene; we see the yellow flames incinerating the body, the sound from the ignition of the fire and the noise of the flames amplified—indeed, a hellish experience. Again, this is a paradoxical image: On the one hand, it signifies a final parting with a loved one; for Marina it is her chance to grieve for Orlando privately after being disowned from her right to grieve for him publicly. It thus becomes a place in which she comes to recognize her own space and the power it entails. In terms of spectatorship, on the other hand, the scene suggests once more the paradox of the cinematic experience: It is precisely the absence of the real bodies of actors that enables our entrance into the imaginary space of film, its fantasmatic bodies "igniting" and sustaining our desire, a space that belongs to the public sphere becoming our own private space. In gender-crossing films, this ability, or rather power, is used, like in all narrative films, to inscribe the spectators in the space occupied by the protagonists, in which their desire is carried out. However, unlike other narrative films, where subjectivization is concerned, these films do not thrust the spectators out of the primal scene of the film altogether, but only divert our engagement with desire and our inscription in the filmic space to a specific desire and space.

The round shape of the crematory aperture is echoed in a later scene. We first see Marina at home, photographed in profile lying naked on a sofa, her knees bent upward and her dog at her feet. In the next shot we see why her knees are bent: She is looking at her face in a round-shaped mirror that is placed between her thighs, covering her genital area. The shot, rendered from Marina's point of view, shows her bent knees held together to support the mirror, her reflected face looking back at her from between her legs as she stares down at the mirror, her hands placed flat on the sofa beside her thighs and the front of her dog's head on the left-hand side of the screen (Figure 6.7).

This composition, as in the scene in which she is photographed by the doctor, concealing her genital area (we are prevented from getting information on whether she has retained her male genitals or if she has had a full gender reassignment through surgery), defies any fixed or final definition of gender. That what both Marina and we see in place of her genital area is her face as reflected in the mirror implies that from now on it is Marina who will decide who and what she is, regardless of any definite gender identity. As her sense of belonging/not belonging has been contingent on others—Orlando, his family, and the authorities—now, after having lost Orlando, she looks inside her soul for solace. The round shape of the mirror recalling that of the crematory window (her last sight of Orlando) implies that having forever lost Orlando's reassuring look, from now on she must rely on and draw her strength from the way *she* sees herself. In meta-cinematic terms, the image of the face framed by the round-shaped mirror covering Marina's genital area alludes to the close-up of the face in film, suggesting that the face of the actor/character in a film is only a reflection, and that the space inhabited by the actor is genderless, or multi-gendered, in the sense that desire, fantasy, and feminine enjoyment have nothing to do with gender.

The last scene depicts Marina in concert, rejoicing in her voice. The scene presaging this change is the one mentioned above, in which Marina's voice coach tells her that he is but her teacher for singing, for lyrics, not salsa or merengue. Marina asks him, if he is neither her psychologist nor her father, what did she come for? She does not wait for his answer and adds, "Maybe for a little love?" The teacher, who does not seem to agree with this line of thinking, tells her that St. Francis did not ask to be given love or peace, but to become an "instrument of love," a channel of God's peace. Marina fondly puts her arms around him from behind while he sits by the piano, but in

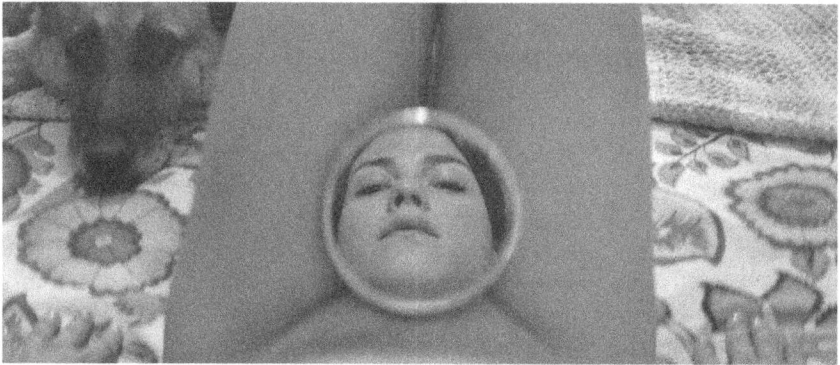

FIGURE 6.7 Una mujer fantástica (A Fantastic Woman, *Sebastián Lelio 2017*).

return, he suggests that she sing to him. Standing in front of him, she sings Vivaldi's aria "Sposa son disperzzata" (performed by Daniela Vega herself) in a beautiful falsetto/alto voice as he accompanies her on the piano. The song's lyrics tell the story of a wife's despair and pain for being ill-treated by a husband who does not return her love, echoing Marina's own feelings of hurt and pain: "I am a scorned wife/ Faithful, yet insulted . . . /And yet he is my heart." We mentioned before that this song continues in the scene that follows showing Marina trudging down a sidewalk into a wind so strong her body is almost parallel to the ground, fighting against it—a visual metaphor expressing her against-the-grain gender and characterization. But now, in retrospect, this scene adds another dimension: It evinces her resistance not only to her poor treatment by Orlando's family but also to the advice of her music teacher, to let her body become a vessel for God and love, that is, her talent, her extraordinary voice, rather than insisting she receive love from others.

Only in the final scene, at the opera, do we see Marina coming to terms with her voice coach's advice: dressed in an elegant dark velvet outfit resembling a man's tuxedo, her hair smoothly tied up (so far she has been seen dressed only in skirts and shirts, her hair loose), she sings the opening aria, "Ombra mai fu" (Never Was a Shade) from the opera *Serse* by Handel, an aria originally composed for a soprano castrato (in modern times performed by countertenor, contralto, or mezzo-soprano singers). In it, the King of Persia, Serse, expresses his gushing, loving gratitude to a plane tree for furnishing him with shade: "Tender and beautiful fronds/ Of my beloved plane tree/ Let Fate smile upon you/ May thunder, lightning, and storms/ Never disturb your dear peace." The camera slowly cranes in, showing Marina's face in close-up about to finish the aria: she first raises her face upward, as though she were indeed a vessel through which the music and lyrics come out, and then she slightly turns her head and closes her eyes, delighting in the music. The lyrics convey an unrealistic wish, that the tree endure all weather to be able to continue to furnish shade, thus expressing not just Marina's mourning for Orlando but also her unrealistic wish to be sheltered and protected by him forever. But as she sings the aria, Marina makes her peace with the thought that she no longer needs Orlando's protecting shade, becoming now a receptacle for her remarkable voice addressed to an audience. The feminine enjoyment Marina is now experiencing, as if in her own private space, is now shared by her audience in the concert hall. In terms of spectatorship, the scene symbolizes the way the space of the film is shared by its spectators: be it in a public or private place (especially in a public space, namely, a movie theater), film spectators tend to be oblivious of their surroundings (expressed in Marina's closing her eyes) while "contained" (immersed) in the filmic space.

In sum, Marina's process of subjectivization engages spectators with it via her *flânerie*, the affect of revolt it generates in us against the injustice she suffers, and finally, through the favorable change she undergoes regarding the treatment of her own body and self. In the end, her body becomes a receptacle not just for the feminine enjoyment she experiences, but an all-engaging space associated with a kind of love that is all-accepting and inclusive (associated with St. Francis's; in *Boys Don't Cry*, with Christ's). Like *Boys Don't Cry*, the film shows a treatment of dehumanization and rejection of the trans-body; it endorses the notion that gender identity, or any identity for that matter, as defined by the Other, is toxic for the subject, and places emphasis on the protagonist's polymorphous and polysemic body, drawing an analogy between the trans-body and the poetic text. By engaging us with Marina's desire to assert her human right to mourn her lover publicly, it calls for the allocation of trans spaces in the public domain. All these factors stand to change spectators' views of gender norms, transcending the boundaries of the screen, particularly when such norms are conflated with codes established or sustained by obscene enjoyment and transphobia.

The analogy between the polymorphous body and the polyvocality and polysemy of the film (as poetic text) is in keeping with Kristeva's analogy of body-text, through the notion of the semiotic *chōra*. In (narrative) cinema, this analogy includes also spectators, who are drawn into the filmic space through the eye-body of the actor/camera. We further explore this double binding in the meta-cinematic fantasy *Being John Malkovich*.

The Semiotic *Chōra*: Being or Using John Malkovich in *Being John Malkovich*

Craig Schwartz (John Cusack) is an unemployed, frustrated puppeteer married to Lotte (Cameron Diaz), who devotes all her attention to pets (especially Eliza, the chimpanzee) and pressures him to get a job. He is hired as a file clerk by Dr. Lester (Orson Bean) at LesterCorp, located in the strange low-ceiling offices on floor 7 ½ of the Mertin-Flemmer Building in New York City. He becomes infatuated with his coworker Maxine Lund (Catherine Keener), who does not return his affections. One day he discovers a small door hidden behind a filing cabinet that turns out to be a portal into the body of actor John Malkovich (John Malkovich). He goes through it, sliding along a tunnel, and for fifteen minutes he gets to see and sense whatever Malkovich does (Malkovich is engaged mostly with mundane activities).[14] He is then ejected into a ditch near the New Jersey Turnpike. He tells Maxine about the portal, and she sees the chance for financial gain in it. They place an advertisement for other people to enter the body of Malkovich (be someone else/a celebrity for fifteen minutes) for $200 a turn. Craig also tells Lotte about the portal, and after her first time in Malkovich's body she becomes obsessed with the experience. Having sensed and seen everything Malkovich is while taking a shower, she decides she must be a transsexual, but later abandons the idea. Lotte and Maxine discover they are attracted to each other, and Maxine agrees to make love to Lotte if and when Lotte is in Malkovich's body. She then seduces Malkovich; they go to his house and have sex while Lotte is indeed inside him. Rejected by Maxine, who is won over by Lotte, Craig binds and gags Lotte and locks her in a cage with her chimpanzee. He then enters Malkovich's body and tricks Maxine into believing that she is having sex with Lotte. Using his expert puppeteering skills, Craig discovers that he can enter the portal to control Malkovich's body and mind, causing the actor to feel like he is being possessed by someone else. After consulting with his friend, the actor Charlie Sheen, Malkovich trails Maxine to the Mertin-Flemmer building, discovers the portal and tries it, finding himself in a restaurant where everyone (men, women, and children alike) has his face and all they can say is "Malkovich." Ejected, he meets Craig by the turnpike and demands that the portal be closed, but Craig refuses. Meanwhile, Lotte escapes with the help of her chimpanzee, phones Maxine, and tells her that it was Craig who was having sex with her while inside Malkovich. But Maxine likes the idea that Craig can control Malkovich and again has sex with him, this time around fully aware that Craig is in his body, as well as "in control." Seeking help, Lotte finds Lester, who tells her he is Captain Mertin, the original founder of LesterCorp, and knows about the portal. Lester introduces Lotte to a group of elderly people who intend to use Malkovich as a host for prolonging their lifespans and maintaining their vitality. Any such host becomes ripe for lasting occupation, but not before the eve of his/her forty-fourth birthday (which explains why Lester has a room full of photographs documenting Malkovich's life from boyhood to adulthood, including his versatile professional life); when the host turns forty-four, the portal immediately moves on to its next host, an unborn child. If this brief window of ripeness is missed, entering the portal too late will result in being trapped forever within an unborn child. Thus, Lester's plan is to use Malkovich when ripe as the host for him and several of his friends. Lotte warns him that Craig currently has control of Malkovich.

Realizing that he can remain in Malkovich indefinitely and control his actions, Craig spends the next eight months in Malkovich's body, his personality/consciousness reflected now in Malkovich's physical appearance and in becoming a world-class puppeteer. Malkovich/Craig marries Maxine. She revels in their fame, but as her pregnancy advances (she becomes pregnant the first time she has sex with Malkovich, while Lotte is in his body), she starts to miss Lotte and distances herself from Malkovich/Craig. As Malkovich's forty-fourth birthday approaches, Lester, his friends, and Lotte kidnap Maxine. They all gather at the portal and phone Craig, threatening to kill her (which they do not intend to do) if he does not leave

Malkovich. Feeling betrayed and abandoned, Lotte attempts to kill Maxine anyway and chases her with a gun. Maxine escapes through the portal, Lotte after her and, because Malkovich's conscious mind is occupied by Craig, they are pushed into Malkovich's unconscious and witness several trauma-ridden scenes from his early childhood and adolescence.

After they are ejected, at the turnpike, Maxine, having snatched the gun, tells Lotte that she conceived when Lotte was inside Malkovich and she kept the child because it is "theirs." They reassure each other of their mutual love. Meanwhile, fearing for Maxine's life, Craig unwillingly leaves Malkovich's body, only to discover at the turnpike that Lotte and Maxine are together again. Lester and his friends enter Malkovich's portal. Craig enters the portal too, to regain control over Malkovich, but without knowing that he has missed the deadline. Seven years later, Malkovich, who looks like a physical fusion of himself and Lester, tells his friend Sheen about his plan to prolong their lives via Emily, Maxine's and "his" daughter, showing him a room with a wall covered with her photographs. As for Craig, he is now permanently trapped in Emily: Having lost the ability to control the body he occupies, he is now doomed to watch Emily's happy family through her eyes and begs her to no end to "look away."

We conclude our study with *Being John Malkovich* because it brings together the dialectic of desire/fantasy as discussed in the corpora of Chapters 1 through 4 and the notion and experience of feminine enjoyment as described in the corpus of Chapter 5. We included the film in our body-host category of the body-character-breach corpus in Chapter 1 (in which the body-character breach represents the wish to be able to fulfill the fantasy of being the Other) because all the characters in the film represent this fantasy and enjoy the short ride of being Malkovich. But Craig, rather than see what lessons he can learn from being someone else, decides to control and manipulate Malkovich, transforming him into his image and character while realizing his fantasies: to become a famous puppeteer and have Maxine. For persisting with this fantasy (he is unable to traverse it) and having missed the opportunity to undergo subjectivization, he is "punished" (like in Greek mythology) by being forever imprisoned in the Other's "unripe" body (Emily's) without being able to control it. We also included the film in the (fantastic) category of trans-body as part of the gender-crossing corpus in Chapter 5. This is because when Lotte is in Malkovich's body for the first time, she goes through a bodily experience knowing that it is not her own body, but someone else's belonging to a different gender. Hence her description of Malkovich as both male and female and later her conclusion that she must be a transsexual. Furthermore, the ability of film to render the unconscious (as discussed in Chapters 3 and 4) is alluded to in the film mostly through the scene in which Maxine is being chased by Lotte in Malkovich's unconscious. The whole portrayal of the film as a surreal fantasy attests to cinema's ability to render human subjectivity in general. Finally, *Being*

John Malkovich is a meta-cinematic film that focuses on the actor's body and persona, and the fantasies projected on it. As Lissa Weinstein and Banu Seckin (2008: 27) put it, Craig's "fusion with a live 'celebrity puppet' offers a solution to the dilemmas of being human—imperfection, vulnerability, and death." Moreover, like 8 ½ and *Mulholland Drive*, *Being John Malkovich* is a film that points to the operation of narrative film, while simultaneously undermining it.

The uniqueness of *Being John Malkovich* is the way it conflates Malkovich's *body* with a receptacle/space for all the characters who go through Malkovich's portal, as well as for all the spectators: (1) In terms of its basic characterization, his body is a non-gender, or rather an all-inclusive-gender receptacle (leading to the drives and the unconscious); (2) thus, the film's characters may experience and use it in different ways according to their subjective position in relation to the Other, as well as their willingness to change such positions; and (3) it is a metaphor for the interrelations between screen and spectator, as well as those of the main factors involved in the making of a film and its consumption (actors, director, producers, distributors, and so on). All these characterizations make the body of John Malkovich a perfect meta-cinematic example of the actor in cinema as a "semiotic *chōra*." However, like all other gender-crossing films, *Being John Malkovich* encourages the spectators to ally with one desire (Lotte's) rather than with another's, through its tackling of the notion of identity associated with fifteen minutes of fame and false appearances, as well as by designing a body-space that can be associated with the semiotic *chōra*. It thus offers an opportunity to reflect on what can make a subject happy. Herein lies the ethics of the film. Moreover, the film addresses all the rings of the "Borromean Knot," and their interrelations, evincing the importance of the real (satisfying desire in the real) in its relations to the imaginary and symbolic.

The main characteristics of the *chōra* are its constant motion and the fact that it is both matter and figurative—like the bodies of actors in film. In Plato's *Timaeus*, the *chōra* is a receptacle of becoming, associated with "the mother of the universe"; she contains all impressions and is stirred and informed by them, yet always maintains her own nature, never assuming a form of anything that enters her[15]—reverberating with the way an actor, as well as the filmic space, can contain many characters, as well as spectators, be stirred and informed by them (interpreted and experienced in various ways), and yet maintain the nature of film as imaginary. The association of the *chōra* with "the mother of the universe" (not the essential, biological one) is reflected in the physical characterization of the body of Malkovich: The aperture used to access this internal passage connotes the vagina, and this in turn leads to a long moist brown canal, connoting both the female cervix that leads to the uterus (birth) and the colon leading to the rectum (defecation). Birth and defecation are implied also in the abrupt way those who slide down this tunnel are ejected from it. That every character comes out of it with a different experience suggests a subjective trip replete with new possibilities (a "rebirth"), detoxification of fixations, of succumbing to external false identities and fame. As we shall see, such possibilities are contingent on recognizing our own desire, while renouncing our reliance on false identities. These likelihoods are not gender-connected but point to subjective positions and whether the subject is willing or not to undergo subjectivization. In Chapter 6, as in Chapter 5, subjectivization is thus associated with the material body as affected by the pulsations of the drive in its interactions with others, which stands to find its satisfaction in the creation of a semiotic space in which feminine enjoyment reigns supreme.

Plato's *chōra* has raised much debate over the years,[16] mostly in feminist readings of it, including severe criticism of Kristeva's appropriation of it.[17] On her revaluation of this appropriation, Maria Margaroni (2005: 82) argues that Kristeva's "introduction of the semiotic chora . . . marks her desire to move beyond the paradigm of a violent rupture that promotes a monolithic understanding of *logos* (relieved only by a feminized otherness outside it) and a metaphorics of gendered hierarchical op/positions (speech vs. silence, spirit vs. matter, time vs. space)." She continues to say that at the base of Kristeva's thinking "is the principle of this self-ordering, a materialist economy of the Beginning that permits Kristeva to displace all transcendental forms of origin (the Word, the divine nous, subjective will)" (2005). Whether or not Plato's characterization of the *chōra* points to a conflation with the mother's body (Derrida and Judith Butler argue that it does not, despite the analogy with "the mother" of all the universe) is beside the point; what matters are the drives in their first encounters with the body of the Other (usually, but not necessarily, the mother, starting with the birth experience)—an interrelation achieved through motion, rhythm, odor, sound, taste, and so on, which becomes the infant's space.

In *Being John Malkovich*, Malkovich's body provides and re-creates for his occupiers such a tactile space of motion, rhythm, odor, sound, and taste: Craig encounters it with the taste of coffee and toast when entering it for the first time while Malkovich is having his breakfast; Lotte with the tactile sensations when a naked Malkovich is taking a shower. It thus offers an encounter of one's drives with the tactility of the body of another. It is a genderless space insofar as it is all-inclusive (men, women, trans can enter it). However, for adults whose unconscious is a "metaphysical can of worms" (so referred to by Craig) replete with repressed traumatic and shameful memories or fantasies, to know how to take advantage of such a space (the semiotic)—that is, to undergo subjectivization (forsaking subjective structures or fantasies that render us unhappy)—takes a certain subjective structural flexibility in its relation to the Other. Which brings us to the question, why John Malkovich?

Scott Repass (2002: 30) quotes Jonze and scriptwriter Charlie Kaufman saying that as soon as they had a portal, it led directly to John Malkovich. According to Repass, this is because of the actor's enigmatic and ambivalent sexuality, his appearance as not quite "wholesome," an image intensified by the fact that Malkovich stays away from the public eye, never gives interviews, has no public relations agent, and so on. Daniel Shaw (2006: 116) makes a similar comment:

> The choice of John Malkovich was not an accidental one on the part of the writer and director. Malkovich is an enigmatic chameleon, both in his professional and in his personal life. As Kaufman described the eponymous actor . . . "there's something odd and completely unknowable about him. You never really know what's going on behind his eyes, so it becomes fascinating, and I think that works for this story."

As a public persona, Malkovich may be very difficult to know, but he is also difficult to pin down through his acting career (in both film and theater); until the making of *Being John Malkovich* he had acquired through films like *Dangerous Liaisons* (Stephen Frears 1988) and *The Portrait of a Lady* (Jane Campion 1996) on the one hand, and *The Object of Beauty* (Michael Lindsay-Hogg 1991) and *The Man in the Iron Mask* (Randall Wallace 1998), on the other, quite a versatile acting profile. Also noteworthy is *Mary Reilly* (Stephen Frears 1996), in which he plays the role of Dr. Jekyll/Mr. Hyde. According to Cynthia Baron (2002), Malkovich's screen persona is symptomatic to the end of the last millennium. Although binary categories are still dominant paradigms, she argues, the time has come to consider man's sexuality (not only that of women) as versatile, heterogeneous, and decentralized. It is in this sense that she regards Malkovich's sexuality as "queer." Malkovich's elusiveness/versatility is expressed in the film by various people he encounters (e.g., a taxi driver) who recognize him as an actor but cannot name any of his films, associating him with the character of a jewel thief. So, why, as Weinstein and Seckin put it, "the choice of Malkovich, an actor clearly cynical about his own celebrity . . . ?" Only to give "additional texture to a film that takes the malleability of public personas as its subject" (28)—as the two suggest? We regard all the elements that make Malkovich both elusive and versatile, as well as his "queerness," a perfect example of a body as semiotic *chōra*, able to contain everything and everyone that enters it.

The first depiction of being in the body of Malkovich (Craig's) is designed as an allusion to the opening sequence of Rouben Mamoulian's *Dr. Jekyll and Mr. Hyde* (1931).[18] To recall, this sequence includes an uninterrupted long take rendered from the protagonist's point of view: We do not see him, only what he sees, until he looks in a mirror reflecting his image. The same in *Being John Malkovich*: After Craig crawls down a dark stone-like murky passage, we see a light at the end of the tunnel and reach an oval-shaped frame through which we see the hands of a man at a breakfast table (someone is drinking coffee and eating toast) holding a newspaper. The rendering of the image through the oval shape, the rest of the frame remaining black, emphasizes the restriction of the POV shot (we see with Craig only what the person at the table is seeing. We also "hear sounds of bodily processes (chewing, swallowing . . .). The sounds are heard as if the audience were inside a sensory isolation chamber or a fantasy of the uterine environment" (Weinstein and Seckin 2008: 31–32). The man then clears the dishes before leaving the house to take a cab, checking his appearance in the mirror. It is then that Craig and we discover who the man is: actor John Malkovich. This allusion from *Dr. Jekyll and Mr. Hyde* (to which we return in our discussion of the film's reflexivity) emphasizes the idea that the body that we see in the mirror is not all there is: in *Dr. Jekyll and Mr. Hyde*, a respectable handsome-looking man, inside whom there is another "being" (his drives) he is not aware of; in *Being John Malkovich*, a body (Malkovich's) occupied by another body-mind, without Malkovich being aware of it. We have here two bodies and two minds, only one being aware of this strange situation. A similar shot is rendered in Lotte's first visit in Malkovich while he takes a shower and then dries himself, ending with Malkovich's reflection in the bathroom mirror. However, it is shorter, and we hear her thoughts/reactions to what she senses. For Lotte, seeing and *sensing* Malkovich washing his body is not a mundane act (like it might be for Malkovich), but a bodily experience that is more of an erotic/sexual nature, as she claims later, she had never felt before ("weird," "wet," "nice," "Ah, I feel sexy")—unlike Craig, who derives his enjoyment by controlling it, exploiting it.

Moreover, the notion of the split, as well as that of the mirror, suggests the dialectic of appearance (*semblance*) and truth. Dylan Evans ([1996] 2006), who traces Lacan's development of the use of the term *semblance*, notes that while in the early Lacan it was associated with the false appearances of the imaginary (i.e., narcissism, identity), in the later Lacan it is used to characterize general features of the symbolic and its relations to the other two orders (the imaginary and the real):

> Thus Lacan [in] his 1970–1 seminar . . . argues that TRUTH is not simply the opposite of appearance, but is in fact continuous with it: truth and appearance are like the two sides of a moebius strip, which are in fact only one. In the seminar of 1972–3, Lacan goes on to state that *objet petit a* is a "semblance of being" . . . , that love is addressed to a semblance . . . , and that *jouissance* is only evoked or elaborated on the basis of a semblance. (174, italics and caps in the original)

The long take in the allusion to *Dr. Jekyll and Mr. Hyde* is a kind of moebius strip, a semblance of being that can lead its characters either to truth or to appearance—depending on what they choose—emphasized by the camera movement.

The character representing the choice of truth is Lotte, whose initial thought after being in Malkovich is that she must go through a full gender reassignment. After her ejection from Malkovich, while driving to Lester's home (where they are invited for dinner) Lotte tells Craig that for the first time she knew who she was, like everything made sense. Craig contradicts her and says that she was not she but John Malkovich (who is but a *semblance*), and for the moment she seems pleased with this notion. At Lester's she discovers a room with the walls covered with Malkovich's photos from different periods. Back in the car, she asks Craig if he does not think it "weird" that Malkovich has a portal and what its significance might be. Craig, whose thoughts are constantly preoccupied with Maxine, fails to engage with Lotte's thoughts and she says she does not even care, adding, "It's kind of sexy" that he has a portal, "sort of like he's a vagina, it's sort of vaginal, like he has . . . a penis and a vagina. . . . It's sort of like Malkovich's feminine side . . . I like it." It is evident that it is difficult for her to put into words what she is experiencing. She stammers, pauses in between phrases, and when she finally has a revelation, she concludes that she must be a transsexual.

However, falling in love with Maxine (which for Lotte is her truth) makes her realize that love is more important than being a transsexual, that love disregards gender. *She* is willing to sleep with Maxine as a woman; it is Maxine who insists that they have sex only when Lotte is in Malkovich. Lotte, whose subjective structure is the most flexible, preserves her experience of feminine enjoyment every time she is in Malkovich, resulting even in the "impregnation" of her lover (you will remember that Maxine is impregnated while having sex with Lotte while in Malkovich's body), a fantasy (possible only in fantastic films) that points to Lotte's power to enact the changes she is going through in the miraculous space of feminine enjoyment. Unlike Craig, she is not interested in self-creation as manifested in a narcissistic union/fusion with the Other, but in her own happiness. Lotte does not have any interest in Malkovich's body as such, aside from what she experiences while inside him and is therefore so terribly hurt by Maxine's treachery. What she experienced as a new beginning with Maxine is crushed and betrayed when Maxine lets Lotte understand that her condition for making love to her is Lotte's being in Malkovich. As it turns out, Maxine is willing to use Malkovich's body for her own expediency, even to sleep with him when Craig is in his body (she despises Craig). Through Lotte's experience (hence her association with animals, which here represents drives and not instincts—the chimp has an unconscious), we come to understand the nature of the body as semiotic *chōra*. The way she uses Malkovich's body suggests that for her his body is a space of feminine enjoyment. Renouncing it means that this space has been internalized.

Unlike Lotte, Craig is incapable of experiencing feminine enjoyment, hence his misuse of the *chōra*, Malkovich's body. In his case, the mirror, which enables him (and us) to understand through whose eyes he sees what he sees the first time he is in Malkovich's body, is a metaphor for Craig's experience in Malkovich: being caught in a world of luring appearances and unsatisfied desire—endless alienation and distress—as opposed to Lotte, and later, Maxine. This is evident through the puppets and the way he changes them according to his fantasies, like when he creates the Maxine puppet, "whom he can make behave as he wishes the real Maxine would. He transforms the Heloise puppet, changing her dress and painting her toenails. . . . Craig's wishful denial is highlighted by contrast with the immediately ensuing scene, where Maxine tells him, 'You're not someone I could get interested in, Craig. You play with dolls'" (Weinstein and Seckin 2008: 31).

Rather than experiencing a space of feminine enjoyment, Craig uses Malkovich to promote his art in a narcissist way. Shaw quotes a portion of an interview with Charlie Kaufman, who wrote *Being John Malkovich*: "Well, you are inside someone else's skin, but Craig doesn't have the experience of being Malkovich, he has the experience of using Malkovich. He uses him to be with Maxine, and then he uses Malkovich's notoriety to get his own career going. *So, it's 'Using John Malkovich.'* Yeah, I'd say it's 'Using John Malkovich.' [laughs]" (Kaufman in Shaw 2006: 115, italics in the original).

Craig's narcissism derives from never having been recognized as an artist; hence his experience of alienation and despair. Weinstein and Seckin's argument that all the fantasies in the film are narcissistic and reflect the wish to achieve "serial immortality" (2008: 29; "serial immortality" is borrowed from Shaw [2006: 114]) applies only to Craig (and Maxine, up to a point). The people occupying Malkovich use his body for different purposes (except its transient visitors, who just want to experience their fifteen minutes of fame). The gap between Craig's artistic talent and his misery cannot be missed and is portrayed at the outset, as Weinstein and Seckin (2008: 27–28) describe when Craig's marionette seeks his image in the mirror:

> As the audience realizes that the puppeteer is an exact duplicate of his marionette, the marionette begins an elaborate and beautiful dance, tumbling through space in moves that defy gravity. The puppeteer's hands move frantically; he is sweating as if he has himself performed the physical feats carried out by his creation. The puppet collapses in despair, raises its hands to its face and weeps. The puppeteer hangs the marionette from the theatre's ceiling; its legs dangle, impotent, in space.

The more frustrated Craig is (as emphasized even by the title of the puppet's performance, "Dance of Despair and Disillusionment"), the more he sinks deep into the world of appearances, narcissism, and unsatisfied desire, as Dana Dragunoiu (2001–2: 1) notes about the first scene of the film: "This psychic split recalls Jacques Lacan's formulation of the human subject as divided between a narcissistic being (me) and a speaking subject (I), which fuels its attempts to validate its fictional unity of being by convincing the outside world to pronounce it authentic."

This is illustrated in a scene that takes place shortly after the beginning of the film. While sitting on a sofa reading a newspaper, Craig overhears a voice emanating from his television set (probably at the end of a news broadcast) announcing that "Puppeteer Derek Mantini thrilled onlookers as he performed *The Belle of Amherst*," Craig puts away the newspaper, while the voice continues, "with a sixty-foot Emily Dickinson puppet." The scene cuts to the television set where an enormous puppet is seen against a bridge as if floating in the air, dressed in a white gown reminiscent of Dickinson's period. She holds a book in her hand and recites Dickinson's famous "I'm Nobody! Who Are You?" (1861). The poem reads as follows:

> I'm Nobody! Who are you?
> Are you—Nobody—too?
> Then there's a pair of us!
> Don't tell! They'd advertise—you know!
> How dreary—to be—Somebody!
> How public—like a Frog—
> To tell your name—the living June—
> To an admiring Bog!
>
> (Dickinson 1960: 133)

The speaker in Dickinson's poem is clearly addressing the reader/s ("you"), thus making a pact with us in being "nobody," as opposed to those who insist on being "somebody." But Craig makes nothing of it. "Gimmicky bastard," he scoffs (referring to the famous artist) after hearing the first line of the poem, and starts philosophizing, while buffering the sound of the rest of the announcement. He says to Eliza, the chimp sitting next to him, "You don't know how lucky you are, being a monkey, because consciousness is a terrible curse, I think, I feel, I suffer." However, he does not pause to contemplate on why, for example, he suffers, beyond his envy of Mantini and frustration at not being recognized as an artist. This becomes evident when he says, "And all I ask in return is to do my work," while watching the puppeteer on the television screen doing *his* work in front of a mesmerized crowd.

Mantini's performance is a mise-en-abyme reflecting all the themes of *Being John Malkovich*. It contains various arts and medias: puppeteering; theater (the play about Dickinson's life, by William Luce); television (Luce is known for writing not only for the stage but for television as well); film, of course—the big screen containing the TV one (a frame within a frame—the reflexivity of the mise-en-abyme); and poetry. Not just any poem by

Dickinson, but this specific poem in which the "nobody"—the private, anonymous individual self—is juxtaposed with the somebodies who seek their self-worth outside, from the masses, whose recognition is compared to the croak of frogs in the bog. As Dragunoiu (2001–02: 15) notes, the poem offers an alternative to the chase after external recognition. In contrast to those who love to broadcast their own names, the speaker of the poem reaches out to someone like her to establish a relationship/partnership (what kind of liaison this might be—sexual or other—is left in the obscure) based on mutual trust (secrecy, it must not be told to anyone, lest it be advertised).

So, what we have here is the theme of truth/authenticity versus that of appearance and alienation as related to the world of fame and celebrity, the cult of which reigns supreme in the popular media, pushing people to cultivate an appealing yet false persona. Even if it lasts for fifteen minutes only, it becomes *everything*. Therefore, its counterpoint must be *nothing* and its subject nobody. But being Nobody seems to mean more than just shunning the fifteen minutes of fame or being wary of the dreariness of public opinion. It reverberates with Cordelia's "Nothing" in Shakespeare's *King Lear* (Act I, Scene I), in which she tells Lear that her love for him measures that of a daughter to her father, *nothing* more. An outraged (foolish) Lear will have to pay a high price to learn what that "nothing" means. It is, of course, associated with truth/authenticity, its specific content here being love. The homeomorphic moebius strip in *Being John Malkovich*, like in Lacan, has a continuous inverse function between two topological spaces: "misrecognition" and frustration (false identity and unsatisfied desire) and feminine enjoyment (authenticity and satisfaction). It is up to the subject to decide which space s/he will occupy. When Malkovich goes through his own portal, all he can see and hear is his head on other people (including children) uttering his name. It is the most uncanny scene in the film: With all its suggestive narcissism, it is a repelling rather than a luring one for Malkovich and spectators alike, one that conveys the film's anti-fetishism—rather than draw the spectators into the space of the scene, it is meant to put us off.

In our opinion, Craig's "Dance of Despair and Disillusionment" at the very beginning of the film, when at the end of its performance (at the sound of prerecorded applause) the marionette representing Craig notices its strings and smashes the mirror and furniture in the miniature theater, renders Craig's inability to break free, that is, he is controlled by his fixations. Thus, when he gets control of Malkovich, he again dances the "Dance of Despair and Disillusionment" (to gain Maxine's admiration), achieving fame and worldwide recognition while still in his body, which now looks like Craig's, with the human-size puppet performing in a ballet with real ballerinas. In all the renditions of Craig's "Dance of Despair and Disillusionment," the puppet is still in his image; in the latter case, it is a perfect enlarged duplication of the doll in the opening scene. Craig sees only himself in every other he meets (like Malkovich when he enters his own portal). It is no accident that he loses Maxine, for whom living with him becomes intolerable when he reaches the peak of his career.

In addition to his professional frustration, what keeps Craig a forever unsatisfied desiring subject is his futile pursuit of Maxine, which, again, results in a narcissistic, destructive fusion with the Other—if he cannot have her as himself, he will as Malkovich. Thus, in our opinion, what the film stresses is the dire consequences of circumventing the real. As Craig is caught in the dialectic between the imaginary (fantasy, narcissism) and the symbolic (desire), he fails to find his authenticity in the real (feminine enjoyment), using his amazing talent as puppeteer only for the sake of fame.[19]

As to Maxine, her aloofness, as well as physical attractivity, seem to suggest that up to a point, she incarnates *objet a:* She sets both Lotte's and Craig's desire in motion, and has no problem doing the same for Malkovich. She is both the object and the voice of desire. As Naomi Segal (2009: 166) puts it,

> In the intra-diegetic terms of the functions of desire, however, it is Maxine's. Maxine starts out as a glossy model type as ready with a put-down as a come-on. She bedazzles both Craig and Lotte, not only as the object of their lust but as possessing, seemingly without effort, the smooth surfaces their chaotic bodies lack. She wears close-fitting monochrome outfits, sits with her legs comfortably spread, smokes, leafing magazines, mobile phone in hand; she is always who and where she wants to be.

Segal rightly quotes Maxine's following lines in her capacity as the voice of desire:

> The way I see it, the world is divided into those who go after what they want and those who don't. The passionate ones, the ones who go after what they want, may not get what they want, but they remain vital, in touch with themselves, and when they lie on their deathbeds, they have few regrets. The ones who don't go after what they want. . . well, who gives a shit about them anyway? (2009)

However, Maxine's lines already imply that desire must be fulfilled in the real, as she herself will realize while living with someone she despises. As her pregnancy attests, the real cannot be disregarded anymore.

That the symbolic order (the realm of desire) is not the trajectory that provides the subject with either satisfaction or happiness is evinced by how language is treated through the characters of Dr. Lester and his "executive liaison," Floris (Mary Kay Place). Dr. Lester attests that he is not who he claims to be, namely that appearances (identity—the imaginary) are misleading, and that he has a speech impediment due to which no one understands what he is saying. He is probably feeling that language cannot express what he feels or is, while in fact all he says is intelligible. Floris, on the other hand, "misunderstands" everything she is told, twisting it around to serve her lusting after Craig. What is striking about both Floris and Lester is their discourse, replete with enjoyment (*significance*). Dragunoiu (2001–02: 4) notes, "this is a space fraught with unrequited sexual desire. Dr. Lester makes no secret about his lust for Floris ... Floris makes advances on Craig, and Craig becomes hopelessly smitten with his co-worker Maxine." This is true enough. However, Floris and Lester are like poets (adhering to their *syntome*): Floris's speaking impediment sounds more like rhyme ("yes," "chest," "suggest") and her language is that of metaphor (in the poetic sense): "Ooh, what magic those fingers could work on the right cabinet, mmm. Maybe you could alphabetize me. And don't forget, 'I' comes before 'U.'" So, what Lester and his group seek through "serial immortality" is to keep both desire and feminine enjoyment alive.

Malkovich *will* be affected by Lester's occupation of his body (at the end of the film he looks and acts like Lester) and up to a point, this is a misuse of his body, not unlike Craig's; however, what Lester cannot renounce is what almost two centuries ago he experienced as happiness in the space of floor 7 ½ which he designed for another in the name of love. We learn about the history of "this famous floor" from a video screened on a television set (also suggesting the film's meta-cinematic nature) Craig watches after he joins LesterCorp. The camera zooms in to the screen, showing the company's workers with their backs bent; then, another shot reveals a man and a woman in the corridor addressing both each other and the camera. The woman asks the man about the low ceilings and he recounts its history, rendered visually in a simulation of a flashback, starting "in the late 1800s" (which, of course, is the era of the advent of film), when James Mertin, an Irish ship captain (later in the film we learn that Lester "is" Mertin), came to New York and decided to erect an office building. One day, he received a visit from a little person he mistakes for a young girl, but she corrects him, "an adult lady of miniature proportions," complaining that "the world was not built with me in mind, doorknobs are too high, chairs are unwieldy, high-ceilinged rooms mock my stature. . . . Why cannot there be a place for me to work that's safe and comfortable?" Having heard her distress, Mertin decides to marry her and build a special floor designed for her unique stature: "Woman, your story moves me like no other. Me own sister was tiny and then died. Therefore, I shall make ye me wife. And I shall build a floor in my building, between the seventh and eighth which will be scaled down." As Lester explains to Craig, this "scaling down" is also a matter of economization, "Low Overhead, my boy! We pass the savings on the you." In our words, this means a re-economization of enjoyment, associated with love.

Two points are striking in this tale: The materiality of the building (made of stone and wood), signifying the real, and the notion that happiness must be found in the real and depends on adjusting the world to the exact, unique size of each subject. Lester translates the materiality of stone and wood into that of a body. This is what Captain Mertin understands when he meets his future wife: for her to be happy she needs to occupy an exact space in the real adjusted to her physical size and needs, and he provides one for her. In his search for a new body, unlike Craig, Lester is looking out for his friends, not just for himself; he wants them to experience the satisfaction he did/does. This is not the real in its brute traumatic sense, but in its sense of feminine enjoyment—that which allows the longevity of satisfaction. That this strange floor is the habitat of LesterCorp, as well as that the portal is situated in one of its offices, points to its characterization as a semiotic space cut out for the uniqueness of everyone. For Captain Mertin, sharing his wife's new habitat (reflected in that Lester decided to situate LesterCorp in it) must have been quite an effort, as evinced by all those who find themselves in the half floor having to walk cramped and bent over, but it constituted a satisfaction of desire for both him and his wife. True, having gone through the portal, Lester and his group do "erase" Malkovich (and forty-four years later will erase Emily), but if we accept the notion of the body-space as semiotic *chōra*, this unethical aspect would be constituted only in the way one uses it—not for sustaining a narcissistic experience, but the experience of feminine enjoyment. Unlike Craig, who coercively destroys Malkovich's acting career by bidding him to do only what he desires, obliterating Malkovich's consciousness for the sake of his own fame and recognition, Lester and his group do not seek fame, but the longevity of feminine enjoyment. At the end of the film we see a happy and vital Malkovich/Lester married to Floris, trying to ensure his and his friends' lasting joviality by preparing Emily as their future receptacle.

While Maxine remains indifferent to the video (she does not even watch it), Craig seems quite taken by it. The same with the discovery of the portal. The trouble is that rather than let himself *experience* (like Lotte), he keeps philosophizing about it, not unlike Kristeva's ([1974] 1984: 13) description of the philosophers of language, who are "embodiments of the Idea . . . nothing more than the thoughts of archivists, archeologists, and necrophiliacs. Fascinated by the remains of a process which is partly discursive, they substitute the fetish for what actually produced it." And so, when Lester tells Craig (in a café) once more (indeed, why does Lester insist on telling Craig about his salacious thoughts and sensations?) about the way he approaches women, "I am the love god Eros. . . . I intoxicate you, my spunk is, to you, manna from heaven," rather than wondering what makes Lester so vital, looking bored (probably not believing a word Lester is saying), Craig again excuses himself to pursue Maxine, who will never return his feelings. Not that Lester is necessarily the lecher he portrays himself to be, but his words, replete with (feminine) enjoyment (*signifiance* rather than significance), point to a world very different from Craig's, one that keeps escaping Craig. That Malkovich is not the only person to have a portal suggests that the body is a receptacle for human subjectivity: desire, fantasy, and enjoyment, the economy of their interrelations depending on each subject. "Being John Malkovich" thus also means "Using John Malkovich," and the film encourages the spectators to use its/our body like Lotte has used Malkovich's: At its end we see Lotte and Maxine as a happy couple raising their daughter, Emily, while Craig remains trapped in Emily's young consciousness, doomed to see what she sees, a forever desiring, unsatisfied and frustrated subject.

Being John Malkovich: A Meta-Film

We consider *Being John Malkovich* a meta-film,[20] starting with the fact that it is a fantasy, which points to the illusionary/imaginary nature of film as fantasy. When viewing a film, we do not have to imagine the filmic space or its characters, as they are meticulously designed and portrayed, given to us as ready-made objects, like John Malkovich is given to us in the film. However, that Malkovich's body represents the filmic space in which spectators are inscribed, "used" differently by its characters, suggests that although inscription in the filmic space is the same for all spectators, the way this inscription is used might differ from spectator to spectator depending on the position occupied in relation to the Other. Indeed, "being" suggests the phenomenological aspect of engagement with the imaginary space of film. *Being John Malkovich* seems to suggest how this engagement can be used by the film itself in favor of subjectivization. Unlike figurative painting or still photography, film is an art in motion: Through the work of the camera and editing it expands the boundaries of its frame, as well as those of our imaginary/imagination, inscribing us into its space, potentially causing spectators to "move," slide on a moebius strip, beginning with semblance (appearance) and ending with feminine enjoyment. As the subject/spectator in narrative film must have a fantasy to traverse it, film (as *objet a*) is a "*semblance* of being" evoking enjoyment, here evincing the importance of the ring of the real in the Borromean knot.

That *Being John Malkovich* goes against the grain in its non-fetishistic portrayal of protagonists, contrasting the "stunningly beautiful puppets . . . with its unattractive 'live' characters" (Weinstein and Seckin 2008: 28), is expressed mostly in Diaz's deconstruction of her glamorous stardom and her association with animals, which implies favoring the creation of an expanded world of imagination rather than a preordained inert fantasy. This also suggests that subjectivization may become an inherent component of the cinematic experience: While the body of Malkovich as semiotic *chōra* represents the space in which spectators are inscribed at large, the half floor (between two floors), indeed quite "weird" (a term Lotte tends to repeat), represents not only the notion that the filmic space lies somewhere *between* the imaginary and the real (appearance and truth), life and death, the screen and the spectator, but also, and most importantly, the uniqueness in which it is designed and manipulated to engage spectators with one desire rather than another's.

The first meta-cinematic rhetorical device of the film is the allusion to the opening sequence of Mamoulian's *Dr. Jekyll and Mr. Hyde* previously discussed, which conveys the uncanniness of the filmic space at the outset (its separate/split nature yet unified by one body, like Jekyll/Hyde). It infers the essence of film and is evinced by the oval shape for viewing, rendering the restriction of the characters, as well as ours, to Malkovich's point of view.[21] Its long take through which the film draws us into its space conveys the continuity between two separate spaces (that of the film and that of the spectator) through the merger of three points of view (of the protagonist, the camera, and the spectator) and bodies (of the protagonist, the camera, and the spectator), while only one eye-body is diegetic (the protagonist's in *Dr. Jekyll and Mr. Hyde;* Malkovich's in *Being John Malkovich*). The other two (camera and spectator) are in turn separate eye-bodies and spaces that come together only in the spectator's imaginary during the viewing of the film. The eye-body of the camera was present on the set; while filming the scene, the eye-body of the actor was not there (only that of the camera). Yet, the point of view take creates the illusion that what we see is rendered through the eyes of the protagonist. And because we are glued to this point of view, we "occupy" both positions: the one the camera occupied in the real and that of the protagonist (in the imaginary). This double occupancy is further emphasized by the camera movement, which simultaneously simulates that of the character/actor and draws us into the diegetic space, thus allying our eye-body with both the camera's and the protagonist's. It is in this sense that this uninterrupted camera movement reflects a moebius strip, a truth that is continuous with appearance, a *semblance* of being, film as *objet a* that evokes our enjoyment, as well as the love of cinema/film. Moreover, the point of view take, which in the diegesis allies Malkovich's eye-body with Craig's, suggests that it is the eye-body of the spectator, namely our subjectivity, through which the film comes alive. Film may render subjectivity (the unconscious), but it is the engagement of the unconscious of spectators that makes the film a unique experience of the narrative and the artistic.

The episode in which Lotte and Maxine go through Malkovich's portal and witness various scenes stored in his unconscious portrays this unique experience. The very first scene they occupy is in fact Malkovich's own primal scene: They are thrown into a bedroom where little Malkovich is looking at his parents having sex (their naked bodies are covered). A frightened Maxine wonders where they are, and Lotte responds: "We're in Malkovich's subconscious." The editing cuts from Maxine to the couple in the act (whom Maxine is watching without understanding what she sees) and then to the little boy (young Malkovich), inferring that he is a witness as well, that he is part of this space while watching the coitus. The cuts here suggest different spaces, yet the film renders the scene as one space shared by the performers of the sexual act and the spectators. That Maxine does not grasp where she is infers that the inscription of spectators into the structure of the filmic scene through its affinity with that of the primal scene occurs unconsciously. Spectators are inscribed in an uncanny (evinced by the little boy's presence and look) space (through the eye-body of the characters) without being aware of it. This inscription of eye-body occurring in the primal-scene space is "literalized" in the film by Maxine having sex with Lotte while in Malkovich's body, Lotte seeing and sensing what Malkovich is. This occurs as well by Craig having sex with Maxine while in Malkovich's body, which means that inscription in the structure of the primal scene in any case occurs while viewing a film without the spectator being aware of it and regardless of what the spectator (of whatever gender) might sense—pleasure/enjoyment or discomfort. What counts is that whatever it is that the spectator senses is enabled by this inscription. Indeed, the reflexivity of the bedroom scene tackles such inscription (like various scenes in the body-character-breach corpus): it emphasizes the boy's stupefaction and Maxine's feeling of estrangement. After clarifying where they are, she yells to her that this is the last thing she will ever see, which infers the primal scene's imprint in the human unconscious and the notion that once we watch a narrative film, we are (re)trapped in the primal-scene structure. The trip into Malkovich's unconscious also signifies the "unconscious" of the film (hidden meanings, subtexts, and enigmas, as well as the imprint of the unconscious of its makers).

The chase (Lotte is chasing Maxine with a gun) in this strange Asher's-maze space continues: Maxine is now in the locker area of Malkovich's high school. The guys are poking fun at him, calling him "Fag-o-vich!" (alluding to his unclear sexuality) while one of them is dragging his slender naked body (photographed from behind) through the mocking crowd. Maxine then escapes this space, descending a staircase while the off-screen voice of a little boy is heard, repeating "I'm bad; I'm bad" over and over (the super ego internalized). The cut takes us to little Malkovich, sitting hunched over in a rocking chair in the basement, dressed in a suit (like an adult). Then we see Maxine crawling through corridors and more unfamiliar spaces, arriving at an iron barrier through which she sees Malkovich sniffing female underpants, possibly pointing to the "perverse" nature of narrative film in that it inscribes us in its space through the primal scene.

This characterization of the unconscious (rendering the traumatic and shameful—the repressed) in flux, not differentiating between spaces or times, refers not only to cinema's ability to render ("enter") the unconscious but also to the way film blurs various boundaries between the real and the imaginary, as well as those of time and space. The unattainable real (the actors in front of the camera) becomes imaginary when viewed by the spectators; past becomes present—what happens in a film unfolds in front of our eyes as a "here" and "now"; and the three different filmic spaces as defined above merge into one (shared) space, which is the in-between space of cinema—the half floor between seven (might *seven* refer to cinema as the seventh art?) and eight (an allusion to Fellini's *8 ½*?), an all-inclusive weird and queer space. This is why Maxine, who is being chased by an armed and screaming Lotte ("I'm gonna kill you!"), must break through the barrier and *enter* the space (a bathroom) in which Malkovich revels in sniffing the woman's panties, while Malkovich himself, as in all the other scenes of this uncanny trip, remains oblivious of Maxine's presence, or Lotte's for that matter, as if he were not there: What enables the "entrance" of the spectator into the filmic space through the primal scene (its gate, portal) is precisely the fact that the actor is not there on the screen; the actor cannot see the spectator, only the latter can watch the former (film's voyeurism).

The scene that follows shows a college-age Malkovich sitting on a sofa next to a young woman who tells him, "You're creepy," then cuts to a scene occurring in a school bus, the children calling young Malkovich "Little Johnny Malk-o-pee!" A mortified Malkovich is revealed, again hunched over, in one of the back seats, his arms holding his about-to-collapse body, alone and ashamed for having wet himself. Strangely enough, it is after this trip down Malkovich's unconscious that Lotte and Maxine are reunited. Maxine tells Lotte that she is "the father" or "another mother" (it does not really matter) of her baby because it was conceived while Lotte was in Malkovich's body. Appeased, Lotte says in a warm voice, "So, we're parents? Together?" and Maxine, smiling, replies, "Yeah." These last words infer that the creators of the film may be its *auteurs* but "parenthood" (bearing and giving life to a film) occurs in a strange space shared by their creation (the film and what it contains), creators, and spectators. This space is, of course, genderless, containing various subjectivities—as the whole sequence suggests, subjectivity/the unconscious (desire, fantasy, and enjoyment) has not much to do with gender. That said, the fact that Lotte, as well as her union with Maxine, represents feminine enjoyment, does imply, like *Boys Don't Cry*, that women are more receptive to it and, moreover, that the filmic space as described here can be manipulated in a way that engages the spectators' desire with that of specific characters: In all the other films analyzed in Chapters 5 and 6, our desire is so manipulated as to engage with Lotte's desire (and later with the love between her and Maxine).

As a meta-cinematic film, *Being John Malkovich*, like *8 ½* and *Mulholland Drive*, alludes also to other aspects of filmmaking in which spectators are not involved but nevertheless are affected by directing and production decisions made before and during the filming. Three factors seem to be crucial in this respect: the director (in this case, scriptwriter Kaufman is no less the film's *auteur* than Jonze is);[22] the actor; and the producer/s, publicity agents, or distributors. Craig represents the director. That his art is puppeteering infers that everything, including the actors, certainly those in leading roles, is designed according to his artistic vision: We see Craig first pulling the strings of a puppet designed in his own image; then the same puppet is acting out Craig's fantasy about Maxine with a puppet in her image; and finally, a human-sized puppet in his own image is dancing with human ballerinas. But most of all, we see Malkovich as a puppet animated (by Craig) from inside his own "flesh and blood" body. So, the actor may constitute the body-space for the spectators, but the one calling the shots is the director. One evening after eight months of controlling Malkovich and reveling in his narcissistic experience, Craig/Malkovich watches a documentary on television, the narrator asserting that it is about how Malkovich reinvented puppeteering, "the man above the strings," the television screen now showing a still of Malkovich holding the strings of the little Craig marionette. When the narrator announces that Malkovich's rise to fame brought about a renaissance in puppeteering, the documentary shows a portion of "Malkovich's Puppetry Master Class": An irritated Malkovich, holding his head with his hands, says to one of his students: "No, no, no! What are you doing?" The student replies that he is making the puppet weep, but Malkovich insists: "You're making him weep but you yourself are not weeping. Don't ever fuck with the audience, until the puppet becomes an extension of you, it's a novelty act." Then he adeptly shows him how to do it.

This master class in puppeteering in the documentary is, of course, a mise-en-abyme alluding to a master class in acting, stressing that the director is the one breathing life into his actors, from whom he demands the same. Moreover, Malkovich's transition from acting to puppeteering in the film points to the decision of many actors (including Malkovich himself) to switch to directing. In one of the documentary's interviews, prior to the master-class scene actor/director Sean Penn says: "If there's anything that upsets me about it, it's feeling like if I move into it too quickly, I'll be . . . deemed an imitator." This implies that an actor who wants to transition to directing must feel "ripe" for it (suggested also by the ripe consciousness of the body to be occupied), and that a true director is an *auteur*, not just an imitator. The puppeteering here is then a metaphor for the work of the director, and Jonze is probably already planning his next meta-cinematic project together with the other *auteur* of the film, Kaufman—*Adaptation* (2002), a film on the authorship of the scriptwriter within the film industry.[23]

What makes filmmakers (great) *auteurs* is their own unique artistic vision, a uniqueness that we also associate with feminine enjoyment. And Jonze's vision in his collaboration with Kaufman is a "weird," uncanny one. Their actors are always made to look unattractive and slovenly—quite the opposite of stars; their mise-en-scènes carry a sense of gloominess evinced by the films' palette: murky, brownish, greenish, and other dark colors associated with the unconscious (from whence *auteurs* draw their material). In *Being John Malkovich*, even the chimp is traumatized by a scene from her past—a parody directed at the Jonze-Kaufman authorship. In the scene that depicts Lotte's captivity in the chimp's cage, a flashback of the ape takes us to a past occurrence in her life when her parents were brutally attacked by men and killed, leaving Eliza an orphan. This scene, parodic as it may be, alludes to the *auteurs* being "prisoners" of *their* unconscious (from where artistic creation derives its powers) and vision, yet releasing others from their "prisons" (Eliza releases Lotte).

That said, the director has no film, or rather, his vision in narrative cinema cannot come to life, without actors: Craig has no existence without his puppets. It is a must no director can circumvent. Craig's occupation of Malkovich's body thus infers a kind of symbiosis that cannot be dissolved during filming. Therefore, the body of the actor is also a receptacle for the director's subjectivity during production. This symbiosis is dissolved only at the end of production: Both actor and director are set free to proceed with their next project. However, this will only mean symbiosis anew. We might read the choice of Malkovich, who also does theater, in this respect as a wish on the part of the film director not to simultaneously occupy the same stage (the setting) his actor does. This sheds light on the actors' position/experience as well. While filming, they only see themselves and the director (and, of course, other people involved in production), not necessarily the other actors, and certainly not the audience. A dialogue between two characters occupying the same diegetic (imaginary) space rendered in a shot/reverse shot, though evincing a *dialog* in the diegesis, may nevertheless be shot in two different spaces, the actors involved never having met; the editing will do the job. This is both a narcissistic and an alienating experience.

Conversely, the actor in theater always shares a stage with other actors and their audiences are there, in front of them. Might this be why Malkovich, like many other cinema actors, does theater as well? The dialogue with other characters/actors that is missing from the filmic set, as well as from the interaction between actor and spectator during the projection of the film, is very much alive in theater between the actors on the stage and between them and their audiences (each time a different one, with different, instant feedback). So, what for spectators in cinema becomes an intimate space into which we are drawn, for directors and actors of film seems like an alienating one. Their recognition and fame come later, through stardom, prizes, and so on. Hence, Jonze's refusal to maintain his actors' quality of stardom, which, as mentioned before comes through particularly in Diaz's portrayal, would have weakened the sense of alienation.

The only one of the three protagonists of the film who wears white and who Jonze does not deliberately make unattractive is Maxine, who represents the producer and all kinds of agents involved in preproduction. We mentioned above that when the video depicting the history of the half floor is screened on the television monitor, Maxine remains indifferent and looks away. But when Craig tells her about Malkovich's portal, she immediately sees the profit in it, which is the producer's role. She assumes responsibility for advertising it, making sure that as many visitors/spectators as possible come in to enjoy the ride, exploiting Malkovich for her own gain. This is also emphasized by her seduction of Malkovich (the way producers "seduce" their actors, sometimes even forcefully) and then creating a world of fame for Craig when she discovers he can control Malkovich, as well as her reveling in his success (she becomes his agent), connoting a parasite. The sequence portraying Craig and Maxine in the spotlight recalls endless premieres and parties representing the dazzling life of Hollywood. As Weinstein and Seckin (2008: 31) note, "Maxine's aloofness and sense of entitlement breed an uninhibited, predatory relationship toward those around her. Her tangential relationship to reality is tersely expressed in a statement to Craig that 'truth is for suckers.'" That Maxine starts to miss Lotte (she has a doll in her image) as her pregnancy advances throws a vivid light onto the hollow life of glitzy Hollywood: The art of filmmaking is not to be confused with it.

In conclusion, bearing in mind that the semiotic *chōra* is the space in which change occurs, constituting a potential force for the changing of norms and regulations within the symbolic, *Being John Malkovich* as a meta-cinematic film suggests that cinema as a narrative and art form possesses such a potential due to its ability to exploit the spectators' inscription in the filmic space by allying our desire with those who, rather than remaining trapped in narcissism and alienation, choose to pursue true fulfillment. Experiencing this stands to produce a change in *the spectators*' imaginary, the way we see and look at things.

In the films analyzed in Chapters 1 to 4, subjectivization regarding both the protagonists and the spectators consisted in renouncing the position of being inscribed in the Other's desire, which for spectators entailed either being thrust out of the primal scene/the filmic space or not being allowed to access it altogether due to certain aesthetic and rhetorical devices (e.g., *The Conversation* [1974]). In Chapters 5 and 6 we have a different rhetorical device: Rather than thrusting us of the primal scene structure, the films use our inscription in their space to differentiate between the desire of the protagonists (with which we engage) and those who threaten its fulfillment. But because we remain inscribed in the filmic space throughout, we get to *experience* both. In comedies, as in the drama *Yentl*, the filmic space in which we are inscribed is also the space in which the protagonist realizes her desire; hence engagement with her desire goes hand in hand with inscription in the filmic space/primal scene. However, in dramas like *Boys Don't Cry* and *Una mujer fantástica*, in which the protagonists' desire is counterpointed with that of the antagonists, whose actions are supposed to devastate the spectators, it is precisely the fact that we *remain* inscribed in the filmic space throughout the film that we get to experience the devastating actions of the antagonists. Hence the separation between the antagonists' desire and the protagonists, with which we engage, as well as the difference in our experience of the space occupied by the antagonists (horror) from that occupied by the protagonists (feminine enjoyment, the semiotic). Similarly, in *Being John Malkovich* the film allies our desire with those who take the path of feminine enjoyment: it shows us that their journey pays off.

APPENDIX

Body-Character-Breach Taxonomy

1. **Body switch.** Of all the body-character-breach categories, this is the most salient. It comprises mostly comedies. As explained in the example of John Woo's action drama *Face/Off*, in this category we have the co-presence of two swapped bodies, each containing two opposite characters (good/evil; young/old; female/male; married/single; active/passive; and so on). In addition to having to struggle with a situation in which a character inhabits a body that is not theirs, which is required from us within a particular fantastic situation, we are constantly required to cross-compare between the characters. The 1976 version of *Freaky Friday* (directed by Gary Nelson), in which a mother and her daughter swap bodies, generated, in addition to two remakes, a subgenre of body-switch comedies in the late 1980s. For example, in *Like Father Like Son* (Rod Daniel 1987), the characters of the father (Dudley Moore) and the son (Kirk Cameron) switch bodies; in *Dream a Little Dream* (Marc Rocco 1989), during an experiment that goes wrong, the consciousness of an elderly dream researcher (Jason Robards) is transferred to the body of a teenager (Corey Feldman).[1] In *The Change-Up* (David Dobkin 2011), a married man (Jason Bateman) with two kids and a loving wife and a single man (Ryan Reynolds) in his sexual prime swap bodies. Body-switch comedies also include a variety of coming-of-age films centering on gender.

2. **Reincarnation.** Here we are compelled to bear in mind that a deceased character occupies the body of another in the present. The oppositions (young/old; white/black; male/female) are thus manifested in a new body (actor) playing another, very different (dead) character. In *Chances Are* (Emile Ardolino 1989), we have to imagine that Louie Jeffries (Chris McDonald) has switched his (dead) body with that of Alex Finch (Robert Downey Jr.). Other examples of reincarnation are *All of Me* (Carl Reiner 1984) and *Down to Earth* (Chris Weitz and Paul Weitz 2001). *Birth* (Jonathan Glazer 2004) uses the reincarnation genre to make us believe that

Cameron Bright, who plays the character of ten-year-old Sean, is in fact Anna's (Nicole Kidman) late husband. In contrast to the body of the ten-year-old boy, we are required to imagine a sexually mature grown man. Bright's gloomy acting stands in direct opposition to his baby face and undeveloped young body.

3. **Body transformation.** Here we have one character whose body has been radically transformed and is therefore played by *two different actors*. As in the body-switch category, here too the oppositions (old/young; female/male; refined/common; fat/thin) are manifested in the perceptual contradiction between body and character, with the exception that here we have only one character. In *Big* (Penny Marshall 1988), after the disappearance from the screen of the young actor (David Moscow) who plays twelve-year-old Josh, we are left with Josh's character inhabiting the body of a young man, played by Tom Hanks. Our perception of the body of actor Tom Hanks is contradicted by his acting, which simulates the behavior and gestures of a twelve-year-old. In *17 Again* (Burr Steers 2009), we have a reversed situation. Thirty-seven-year-old Mike O'Donnell (Matthew Perry), whose life failed to meet his expectations, goes back to being seventeen (played by Zac Efron) and gets the chance to rescript it. These films relate the body transformation to age. *La piel que habito* (*The Skin I live In*, Pedro Almodóvar 2011) relates it to sex and gender: a male character, Vicente (Jan Cornet), is transformed into Vera Cruz (Elena Anaya) after having been subjected to a male-to-female gender reassignment surgery. A variation of this category is to be found in *Fight Club* (David Fincher 1999), which deals with a mental transformation. Here we supposedly have *two* characters (Jack and Tyler) played by two actors (Edward Norton and Brad Pitt). At the end of the film, they turn out to be one character (Jack/Norton) who has undergone a psychic transformation. The oppositions are manifested by the co-presence of the two actors throughout the film. The perceptual crisis indeed arises at the end when we realize that what we have seen is one split character, Jack/Norton, and that Tyler/Pitt is but a figment of his imagination. Hence, we are obliged to retroactively modify our impressions and perceptions.

Other variations of this category may be found in films where only one actress plays a character whose transformation is achieved by makeup, clothes, and so on, like *Vertigo* (Alfred Hitchcock 1958), and *Shallow Hal* (Bobby Farrelly and Peter Farrelly 2001). In *Transamerica* (Duncan Tucker 2005) and in *La ley del deseo* (*Law of Desire*, Pedro Almodóvar 1987), the oppositions are manifested in one female actress (Felicity Huffman and Carmen Maura respectively) playing trans women, whereby we have to imagine that the image of the female actress, whose femininity is hyperbolized, was a man who transitioned into a woman.

4. **Multiple-body character.** Here the main character is played by one or more actors (one character, multiple bodies). The oppositions are manifested in the difference between the physique and attributes (sensual/apathetic, old/young, black/white, tall/short, male/female, and so on) of the actors who play the main character. In *Every Day* (Michael Sucsy 2018), based on the 2012 novel of the same name by David Levithan, sixteen-year-old Rhiannon (Angourie Rice) falls in love with a traveling soul ("A") who wakes up each morning in a different body (including that of Rhiannon, the only one "A" decides not to control), man or woman, each time played by a different actor of different age, size, race, and so on. The following are three counter-cinema examples: In *Cet obscure objet du désir* (*That Obscure Object of Desire*, Luis Buñuel 1977), the female part is played by two actresses; in *Palindromes* (Todd Solondz 2004) thirteen-year-old Aviva is played by seven actresses of different age and race; and in *I'm Not There* (Todd Haynes 2007) American singer Bob Dylan is played by six actors/stars of different age, sex, and race.

   A variation of this category comprises films in which one actor plays more than one character. In *La Strategia del Ragno* (*The Spider's Stratagem*, Bernardo Bertolucci 1972), the characters of the son and father are played by the same actor (Giulio Brogi) and bear the same name (Athos Magnani).[2] In *Dr. Strangelove* (Stanley Kubrick 1964), Peter Sellers plays three different characters. In David Lynch's *Lost Highway* (1997) and *Mulholland Drive* (2001), both known for their use of the dream/fantasy structure, we have one actress playing two different characters. Classical/mainstream and *auteurs'* films have also shown a fascination with one actor playing different characters: from Charles Chaplin playing two polar characters in *The Great Dictator* (Chaplin 1940) to Alec Guinness playing eight different characters in *Kind Hearts and Coronets* (Robert Hamer 1949) and Peter Sellers playing three different characters in *The Mouse That Roared* (Jack Arnold 1959).

5. **Body host.** This category is epitomized by *Being John Malkovich* (Spike Jonze 1999), in which one actor-body (John Malkovich) is occupied alternately by three different characters: Craig Schwartz played by John Cusack, Maxine Lund by Catherine Keener, and Lotte Schwartz by Cameron Diaz.[3] When Malkovich's body is taken over by Craig/Cusack, we struggle with having to disregard Malkovich's physique and persona and attribute his behavior,

physical changes, gesticulations, and so on, to another character. The oppositions here address sex (male/female), gender (femininity/masculinity), fame/lack of recognition, and sexual orientation (straight/gay). In *The Host* (Andrew Niccol 2013), Saoirse Ronan plays the resistance fighter Melanie, whose body is forced to host an invading alien named Wanda. Wanda is a gentle and peace-seeking creature (outside Melanie's body she resembles a jellyfish) who becomes aware of the agony her kind inflicts on human beings who are forced to host them. For most of the film, Melanie, who has no control over her body, is represented by Ronan's voice (with an echo effect) in Wanda's thoughts. Thus, the body hosts two characters in conflict: aggressive fighter Melanie and the nonaggressive Wanda.

6. **Bodiless characters** (see Chapter 1). Broadly, we can divide this group, some of them analyzed in the first chapter, into three subcategories (not including films in which a character/protagonist is temporarily missing from the diegesis, for example, *Laura* [Otto Preminger 1944]):

   a. Films in which we have a character who is not personified by an actor, for example, Hitchcock's *Rebecca* (1940) and *Psycho* (1960), as well as *Monsieur Klein* (*Mr. Klein*, Joseph Losey 1976). In *Psycho*, Norman's mother's voice is heard to indicate her omnipresence. Only at the end of the film do we learn that Norman (Anthony Perkins) killed her years ago, used his taxidermy skills to preserve her body in the cellar, and proceeded to wear her clothes and talk in her voice. In *Monsieur Klein*, Robert Klein (Alain Delon), a Jew in 1942 Paris, is sought by the police. He is never seen in a frontal or close shot. These films evince the imaginary nature of the unity of body-actor-character, hence of cinema.

   b. Films in which a character is invented in the diegesis while the protagonist, as well as other characters in the film, is unaware of its fictional nature. A salient example is "Mr. Kaplan" in *North by Northwest* (Alfred Hitchcock 1959), which, like *Rebecca*, puts the emphasis on *objet a* as the cause of desire—an emptiness that sets the plot in motion, namely both the protagonist's and the spectators' desire.[4]

   c. Films in which we do not see the actor but hear his/her voice, as their character is not a subject, like in *2001: A Space Odyssey* (Stanley Kubrick 1968) and *Her* (Spike Jonze 2013). These films put the emphasis on voice and on gaze being the two partial objects most relevant to film. In representing the split subject, they also represent cinema's own split nature, namely that the unity between sound and image, or any other coherence in film, is an illusion.

Gender-Crossing Taxonomy

1. **The cross-dresser.** Cross-dressing was the largest gender-crossing category in narrative film until the late 1990s, not only in comedies but also in dramas. It comprises five salient characteristics:
   a. Many of the protagonists (male or female) are performers (e.g., actors, musicians, comedians), which enhances the notion of self-creation and gender as performance.
   b. The protagonist faces a certain difficulty, jeopardy, or other existential misfortune (unemployment, the need to avoid life endangerment, and so on), due to which s/he is forced to disguise as the opposite gender as well as adopt a whole set of mannerisms, gesticulation, and comportment.
   c. All the other characters in the films are kept in the dark until the end, when the protagonists reveal their "true" gender, usually after falling in love with a character of the opposite sex.[5]
   d. The act of becoming a cross-dresser is sometimes displayed in detail.
   e. Queer subtexts: These open a space of homoeroticism, homo-lesbianism, bisexuality, and other configurations of sexuality, as well as gender, none of which has the upper hand.

   That cross-dressing is most popular in comedies seems to be due to the anarchistic and subversive nature of comedy, always expressing freedom—from norms, conventions, ideology, stagnation, and so on. Cross-dressing comedies follow a long tradition of mistaken identities, masquerade, carnival, and disguise in plays and novels. Charlie Chaplin was the first to engage with this tradition on the screen in three films: *The Masquerader* (1914), *A Woman* (1915), and *Behind the Screen* (1916). Salient examples include *Queen Christina* (Rouben Mamoulian 1933), *Some Like It Hot* (Billy Wilder 1959), *Tootsie* (Sydney Pollack 1982), *Victor Victoria* (Blake Edwards 1982),[6] and *Yentl* (Barbra Streisand 1983).

2. **The tomboy.** The tomboy is one category among others in J. Jack Halberstam's (1998: 5–9, 187–93, 267–70, 298–9) comprehensive cultural study of "female masculinity." In most cases, Halberstam argues, early boyish behavior in girls (when it is not exaggerated)

is condoned, even deemed natural, as it is associated with the kind of freedom encouraged by society and culture. However, when this kind of overt identification with manhood continues after latency into adolescence and later, it becomes as alarming as its opposite phenomenon (what we might call "male femininity"). The characteristics of the tomboy in cinema are that she is motherless (sometimes an orphan, which emphasizes the notion of autogenesis), wears boyish or masculine attire, is adventurous, has "bad" manners, and, above all, has a strong will. All these are associated with a love of freedom leading to a unique form of autogenesis, which is why the tomboy usually operates in liminal spaces not yet "tamed" by culture in which laws are not applied or have gone bankrupt, where different codes rule, usually associated with men. A salient example is the Wild West heroine: Her character has fascinated both filmmakers and audiences in dramas and in musicals, as well as in television series, mostly based on real but mythologized women of the Wild West (i.e., Calamity Jane and Annie Oakley).[7] The following are but three examples of films in which the protagonists are young women who have conquered territories reserved for men, moving and riding freely in them and sharpshooting, re-scripting the Western genre: the two versions of Annie Oakley (*Annie Oakley*, George Stevens 1935, starring Barbara Stanwyck and the musical comedy *Annie Get Your Gun*, George Sidney 1950, starring Betty Hutton), and the musical comedy *Calamity Jane* (David Butler 1953, starring Doris Day).

3. **The transvestite.** Narrative cinema, especially Hollywood, has shown little interest in male characters who put on women's lingerie or full attire just because it constitutes their special mode of erotic pleasure (what characterizes the transvestite). A particularly interesting figure is the serial transvestite killer who dresses in female clothes ("gets into mother's skin"), usually when he feels sexually aroused by a woman, which generates the urge to kill that woman. *Psycho* and *Dressed to Kill* (Brian De Palma 1980) are salient examples. These films, in which the transvestite killer (a psychotic) takes Mother's place in the real, point to the coveting of this place not only in the mother's capacity to give birth but also as the one deemed as the source of all creation.[8]

This idea is emphasized in the hybrid horror musical (based on a musical stage production of 1973) parodying both the story of Frankenstein and the myth of Dracula, *The Rocky Horror Picture Show* (Jim Sharman 1975), which became a cult movie through its musical numbers and episodic structure. In Mary Shelley's book, Frankenstein sets out to create humans because he cannot accept the loss of his mother (signifying castration) and the deadlock of desire (he ends up creating a monster). *Rocky* suggests that such a loss can be endured in a space replete with the kind of enjoyment (feminine enjoyment) that provides a solution to the lack experienced in desire by breaking free from normative sexuality, song, and dance (creativity, movement, and imagination), which has been captivating audiences for decades: during its screening, the viewers sing, dance, and dress up as different characters from the film.[9]

The French *Une nouvelle amie* (*The New Girlfriend*, François Ozon 2015) marks a refreshing appearance of a transvestite character.[10] Claire, a married young woman (Anaïs Demonstier), develops a romantic relationship with her deceased best friend's husband, David (Romain Duris), after she discovers that he prefers and enjoys wearing women's clothing. Claire helps him achieve a full look of a woman, "Virginia," leaves her husband, and moves in with David/Virginia and the baby. For Claire, falling in love with Virginia constitutes a transition from the phallic enjoyment to the feminine enjoyment, one she never experienced with her husband, although we might also claim that she has found a way to cheat death in that Virginia personifies both a man and her dead friend, a kind of taking the lost object's place in the real. But then, is not lasting satisfaction (allied with feminine enjoyment) a way of overcoming the primordial loss?

4. **Trans protagonists.** In this category, we include transgender characters who wish to be associated with the opposite sex/gender either by passing or openly, before or after hormonal and other treatments, and pre- or postoperative transsexuals (who have achieved a full sex and gender reassignment). In narrative cinema we find mostly trans women. In 1970 two narrative films dealing with trans women were made in the United States: *The Christine Jorgensen Story* (dir. Irving Rapper)—a realist adaptation of the true story of the famous Swedish trans women who became a media star in the United States—and *Myra Breckinridge* (dir. Michael Sarne)—a self-reflexive fantasy satire freely adapted from a Gore Vidal novel. While the first film is mainly concerned with the heroine's process of achieving a final and coherent identity—that of a heterosexual woman—the latter presents a figure (played by Raquel Welch) whose sex reassignment serves as a device enhancing the idea that sexuality has no coherent ties to either sex or gender (it thus deals with subjectivity, although in an inept manner).[11] Films or television dramas featuring trans protagonists usually tackle the notions of identity versus subjectivity.

Over the years, the trans phenomena seems to have been embraced by mainstream narrative cinema, inspired to a large extent by Spanish *auteur* Pedro Almodóvar, whose films are replete with trans characters, the ambivalence of sex and gender (always addressing subjectivity—not identity) paralleled with the abundance of intertextuality referring to film, art in general, music, and literature. This parallel suggests the notion of (self-)creation out of what already exists in culture in new and challenging hybrid forms. To name but a few of his films in which trans characters personify this notion, although they are not always the protagonists: *La ley del deseo* (1987), *Todo sobre mi madre* (*All About My Mother* 1999), and *La piel que habito* (2011).[12]

More recent examples are *The Danish Girl* (Tom Hooper 2015), based on the 2000 novel by the same name by David Ebershoff, and *Una mujer fantástica* (*A Fantastic Woman*, Sebastián Lelio 2017), in which the protagonist is played by Daniela Vega, a trans woman (see Chapter 6).

5. **Trans-body.** We borrow this term and notion from Chris Straayer (1996: 70–4) for films that rely on the cross-dressing "formula except that they portray a 'genuine' sexual transformation rather than gender disguise. They epitomize both the potential and the danger of the collapse of gender and sexuality" (70). Straayer's examples are all comedies, for example, *A Florida Enchantment* (Sidney Drew 1914), *Turnabout* (Hal Roach 1940), and *Switch* (Blake Edwards 1991), evincing a kind of enjoyment that we associate with the feminine one. Like many of the body-switch comedies, these films occur through some kind of spell or wish that comes true, "remarkable for the way they literalize in the image a gender inversion theory of homosexuality that collapses homosexuality with transsexualism via the notion of 'a woman in a man's body' or vice versa" (71).[13] Trans-body exists also in fantastic dramas, in which the sex change simply occurs without any sort of magic or wish on the part of the protagonist, such as Sally Potter's adaptation of Virginia Woolf's *Orlando: A Biography* (1928), *Orlando* (1992). An unusual variation of trans-body is *Being John Malkovich* (1999), which we also included in our body-host category in Chapter 1. As the film is a meta-cinematic one, wrapping-up our model of spectatorship, we devote a lengthy analysis to it in Chapter 6.

6. **The drag queen.** Drag queens have appeared in narrative cinema usually as gay male performers (but they can also be trans characters, or just transvestites).[14] As defined by Esther Newton's (1972: 106–11) seminal book on drag queens and camp,[15] they

are characterized by three main attributes: inaptness; theatricality, and humor. Elizabeth Kaminski and Verta Taylor (2008: 49–54) argue that drag performances have played a crucial role in the constitution and legitimization of a collective gay identity in America. They established a bridge between straight audiences and gay communities, and moreover, the willingness of drag queens to identify themselves in public as openly gay people was an inspiration to join forces with gay liberation. In narrative films, drag queens play a similar role: their campy humor; flamboyant numbers; sense of inaptness; self-awareness; parodic impersonations of cultural icons; an amazing ability to overcome any hardships through comicality, including self-mockery; and artistic and theatrical expression have played a decisive role not only in popularizing the films themselves but also in mitigating fears and resentment on the part of straight communities and movie lovers and solidifying a dialogue between communities with different sexual orientations. Moreover, drag queens are considered to see beyond, to be soulful healers much like therapists.[16] All these are expressed in films like *The Adventures of Priscilla, Queen of the Desert* (Stephan Elliott 1994, which includes musical numbers), *To Wong Foo, Thanks for Everything! Julie Newmar* (Beeban Kidron 1995), and *Flawless* (Joel Schumacher 1999). The first two films each feature three drag queens; in the latter one we have one drag queen aspiring to be a trans woman who manages to win over her fiercest enemy. Walt Koonz (Robert De Niro) is a grumbling homophobic police officer who suffers a debilitating stroke and is assigned to a rehabilitation program that includes speech therapy with the drag queen next door, Rusty (Philip Seymour Hoffman). Their bumpy relationship gradually develops into a firm and true friendship, during which Waltz mellows, becoming appreciative of the life of queer people and the need to protect them against prejudice and violence. Rusty is not a professional speech therapist (she can give music lessons), but the fact that she does help Waltz on more than ameliorating his speech emphasizes the drag queen's unusual skill as a therapist ("queen of hearts") who uses the "talking cure"—jokes, puns, sexual innuendoes, and so on—to mend people's prejudices, as well as overcome her own suffering. Moreover, Walt's acceptance of his blemished manhood and seeing how Rusty copes with his misfortunes enables him to recognize and accept true love.

NOTES

Introduction

1 Which is what attracted theoreticians of film and fantasy to consider spectatorship in terms of using film as a setting for scripting the spectator's own desire.
2 See Odeya Kohen-Raz and Sandra Meiri (2017), and Meiri and Kohen-Raz (2017).

Chapter 1

1 Such a possibility has been addressed by films like *Simone* (Andrew Niccol, 2002) and *Kennes Ha'atidanim* (*The Congress*, Ari Folman, 2013). In the *Twilight Saga: Breaking Dawn, Part 2* (Bill Condon, 2012), the couple's baby is a CG baby; her unnaturalness though complies with her being a vampire. On the uncanniness of human-like characters in digital cinema, see, for example, John Belton (2017).
2 A similar technique, known as "found footage" has been popularized during the last two decades in a fairly small subgenre of horror films.
3 Some experimental narrative films, like *Enter the Void* (Gaspar Noé, 2009), have adopted the idea of adhering the camera to subjective shots throughout the film, minimizing frontal appearances of their protagonist but without restricting the camera to actual point-of-view shots.
4 For a full analysis of this point-of-view sequence, see Eric Austin Thomas (2015).
5 Tactile and haptic theories have proved otherwise. Notwithstanding these theories, in our view, sight and sound are a precondition for other senses to be involved in the cinematic experience.
6 Unlike theories of realism that regarded film's technological advancements as helping representation and verisimilitude, or postmodernist theories claiming that it is precisely these advancements that have destroyed any possibility of believing in the precedence of the referent, we claim that 3-D, for example, like other cinematic technologies before it, have all been compensating for the lack on the screen.

7   *Birdman* (Alejandro González Iñárritu, 2014), for example, shows us exactly what the cinema can do that the theater cannot—enter the space of the stage, with the camera, and show us details of the actors that are impossible to see otherwise.

8   See, for example, Jacques Lacan ([1959–60] 1997: 67–8) and Chapters 3 and 4 here.

9   An example of this is the unusual documentary *Poslednata Lineika na Sofia* (*Sofia's Last Ambulance*, Llan Metev, 2012), photographed entirely from the inside of an ambulance. The camera work focuses closely, using mostly medium shots, on the emotions of the paramedic crew, without ever showing the patients. Another example is *Caché* (*Hidden*, Michael Haneke, 2005), in which the tapes recording the façade of the protagonists' house at length are shot from the point of view of an outsider's camera we never get to see.

10 John Fletcher (1995: 346) writes, "Rebecca is a name without a body, while the female protagonist ... who is the spectator's chief point of narrative identification for the first three quarters of the film, is never named in her own right."

11 In Modleski's (2016) feminist reading of the film, the wrong answer to this question is tied up with the impossibility of separating from the "mother," because the protagonist, whose Electra complex is at the heart of the film, ends up in her mother's clutches again as a result of directing her desire to her husband (the father figure), asking herself what he wants. Our point is that in the fundamental relationship with the enigmatic desire of the Other, there is never a "right" answer.

12 See Raymond Bellour ([1975] 2000).

13 Exemplified by the restaurant scene in *Vertigo* (similar to the strategy used in the auction scene of *North by Northwest*), in which Scottie sees "Madeleine" for the first time: "Twice in the scene we see shots of Madeleine that cannot be taken from Scottie's subjective position, although this is precisely what seems most logical and is also what Hitchcock interpreters tend to assume. Each of these shots is followed by actual shots from Scottie's point of view" (Elsaesser and Hagener 2010: 105). On Slavoj Žižek's notion of the cinematic suture, see Žižek (2001: 12–68).

14 Donna Kornhaber (2017: 6) claims that similarly to the failed attempt to "incorporate the posthuman into our already known systems," there is also a failure of representation, "failure of cinematic visual culture itself. Just as the film opens in its final act to a vision of the posthuman that finally leaves all known markers of the human behind, so too does it gesture dimly to an as yet unknowable postcinema that will ultimately be born of the catastrophe of representation that is still to come."

15 See James L. Hodge's (2014–15) argument on the spectator's "ubiquity" in *Her*. On Johansson's voice as an "acousmêtre" enhancing this ubiquity, see 66–8.

16 See Jean Epstein ([1921] 1977: 9).

17 This film was also the inspiration for Pedro Almodóvar's *La piel que habito* (2011). On this intertextuality, see Darren Waldron and Ros Murray (2014).

18 No one understood this better than Hitchcock, when in *Psycho* (1960), for example, he manipulates the spectator into complying with Norman's desire that Marion's car be already swallowed by the swamp. No matter how many times we have seen the film (so we know that Norman himself murdered Marion and not his mother), it still works.

19 On the decline of the studio system see, for example, Thomas Schatz (1988, 411–92).

20 Of course, cinema's ability to create a "here and now" renders it a medium best equipped not to just represent historical events but also comment on them, change our perspective on past events, and create collective memory.

21 Eastwood's film is exceptional in that its actors (Alek Skarlatos, Anthony Sadler, and Spencer Stone) who play the three protagonists in their adult lives are the real persons on whose experiences the fictional film is based. It thus simulates a documentary re-enactment (incorporating real footage at its end), blurring the boundaries between the documentary footage at the end of the film and all the other staged scenes of the film, in which *actors* who we recognize from other films play supporting roles.

Chapter 2

1 The two characters, claims Robert Hanke (1999), display both violence and sensitivity, the dynamics of masculinity exhibited in the cinema of John Woo.

2 On romance being a stumbling block of trans films, see Traci B. Abbott (2013).

3 In French—*la Chose*.

4 See Sigmund Freud's "Analysis of a Phobia in a Five-Year-Old Boy" ([1909] 1955).

5 The excess in relation to bodies in film has been addressed by many, especially in relation to genre and gender. See, for example, Linda Williams (1991). Her article brings the two together by exploring the "perverse" pleasure spectators derive from watching three excessive "body genres" (pornography, horror, and melodrama) and by assigning to each one a primal fantasy.

6 These are the three basic subjective clinical structures (positions) in relation to the lack in the Other (castration, the symbolic): the first, the neurotic (hysteric and obsessional neurotic), is characterized by repression; the second, the perverse, by disavowal; and the third, the psychotic, by foreclosure. The difference between hysteric and the obsessional neurotics is in the kind of question they raise. The hysteric's question (more common of women) addresses his or her sex ("What am I—man or woman?"), whereas the obsessional neurotic (more common of men)—the contingency of existence ("To be or not to be?"). See Chapter 2 here (on Hamlet) and Chapter 5 on the three primal fantasies and gender-crossing protagonists.

7 Indeed, what is the secret charm of psychotic characters like Hannibal Lecter (*The Silence of the Lambs*, Jonathan Demme 1991) and Norman Bates or of all the perverse characters in Almodóvar's films?
8 On the real as that which determines the realization of desire, see Chapters 5 and 6.
9 This is how literally any *body* might become the object of one's realized/literalized fantasy, such as in situations of incest, when the symbolic law of incest interdiction ceases to function.
10 Unlike other body-character-breach films, in which the spectators are confronted with the real of the body, in *Shallow Hal*, this confrontation is experienced by Hal alone. For us, Rosemary's obese body is a symbolized body, part of her characterization.
11 Discussions of the uncanny or the double function of Madeleine/Judy in *Vertigo* are quite ample. See, for example, Vincent L. Barnett (2007), Elisabeth Bronfen (1993), Glen O. Gabbard (1998), Joyce Huntjens (2003), and Modleski (2016: 94).
12 See Žižek's (1991: 83–7) discussion of how the sublime object loses its power of fascination for the subject.
13 This is the scene Hitchcock refers to in his interview with Truffaut; see quote in Chapter 1.
14 The language Buñuel chooses for the film is French, but he dubs both actresses with a third voice. Similarly, he dubs Rey with Michel Piccoli's voice to make it sound like a more authentic French. Hence, Mateo, which is how he is called by Conchita in the film, is referred to as "Mathieu" in many reviews and subtitling.
15 See George Wilson and Sam Shpall's (2012) analysis of the many twists and misleads in *Fight Club*.

Chapter 3

1 See Nathalie Bondil-Poupard (2001: 157).
2 As Lesley Brill (2002) puts it in reference to *Spellbound*, "Psychoanalysis is a sister to cinema rather than a rival."
3 Although Freud ([1907] 1959: 8) thought dreams in life were too complex to be represented in cinema, he nevertheless compared the dreamers in life with artists/creators.
4 See Freud ([1899] 1997), especially Chapter 6, "The Dream-Work."
5 On homoerotic psychoanalytic readings of Hitchcock's films, see D. A. Miller's (1990) analysis of *Rope* (1948) and Robert J. Corber's (1991) study on homosexuality and political allegory in *Strangers on a Train* (1951). On *Spellbound*, see David Greven's (2017) queer reading of the film, in which he deems the dream a manifestation of homosexual panic (e.g., the masked man as bearing the secret of the forbidden fantasy).

6 Oedipus in Sophocles' play *Oedipus Rex*, who insists on remaining true to his conviction that his adoptive parents are his biological ones by trying to avoid fulfilling the Oracle's prophecy that he is destined to sleep with his mother and kill his father, flees Corinth for the city of Thebes, where he ends up doing just that with his real mother and father.

7 On this change, see Royal Brown (1980).

8 According to Robert Eberwein (1984: 35), we can detect reenactments of early childhood experiences in the symbolic imagery of films depicting dreams.

9 Gilbert Gabriel (2011: 64–8) shows how the soundtrack in Ballantine's dream sequence emphasizes and mirrors the shift from reality to the hypnotic state, the surreal atmosphere and the dreamer's disturbed senses of dislocation, confusion, and shock, for example, wide pitch sounds, dynamic ranges, "fluctuation" (unsteady rapid vibrato), and the dominance of the theremin, "that produces an 'other-worldly sound.'"

10 See Paul Gansky's (2013) comparison between the two films in terms of props and materials.

11 On the analogy of the two characters, see Andrew Britton ([1986] 2008).

12 See Bondil-Poupard (2001: 301).

13 In Britton's ([1986] 2008: 187) analysis, the wheel symbolizes the vagina, in the sense that "with the death of the father, the mother is now sexually available to the dreamer." In contrast, William F. Van Wert (1979: 44–45) claims that if the wings mean an uplifting salvation for Ballantyne, the "bent and limp" wheel, symbolizing the genitalia, "must be dropped."

14 See Donald Spoto (1983: 277). James Bigwood (1991: 35) claims that although Bergman's account was highly exaggerated, the dream sequence nevertheless had been "certainly forty or fifty seconds longer than it finally wound up." Bondil-Poupard (2001) also elaborates on these portions, all pointing to Ballantyne's fear of sexual relations with Constance, but she reads them as part of a Freudian parody.

15 Britton ([1986] 2008: 185–6) ascribes the constancy in the name "Constance" to women in general.

16 On the cinematic dream in *Spellbound* as a trauma experienced by the spectators as well, see E. Ann Kaplan (2005).

17 Harry's passive, infant-like characterization, according to Dennis Turner (1985: 18–19), reflects the position of spectators, who can do nothing except view the film.

18 Coppola (in Johnson 1977: 132) said that in Harry's portrayal he used repetition as a new mode of characterization "instead of just a classic playwright's way of giving you a little background and unveil traits and show you the contradictions. I'm just showing you the same moment over and over. I'm using *repetition instead of* exposition" (italics in the original).

19 Waldemar Zusman (1998: 254–5) distinctly links Harry's parricide fantasy and unresolved Oedipal complex to his reclusiveness, a connection that we also suggest through our focus on guilt.

20 Norman K. Denzin (1992: 141) writes, "Always in the service of others, Harry now learns that the voyeur's eye points in two directions, inward to self and outward to the other. Harry has become the other who bugs himself."
21 See Freud ([1918] 1955).
22 Harry's surname is Caul (i.e., fetal membrane—which suggests his regressive state), whose homophone is "call" (as in to make a call, suggestive of his profession). The distinction between the two meanings can be made only if written or in context, the kind of distinction Harry never seems to make.
23 Catherine Zimmer (2015: 19) claims that sound is the dominant element in the film in that "the smooth unfolding of the images" is dependent on the "audio surveillance."
24 For a discussion of the overhearing, or "hearing awry," in the film, see David Copenhafer (2018).
25 For a full account of the intertextual relations between *The Conversation* and *Blow-Up*, see Turner (1985: 8–11). For a comparative study on surveillance and ethics in *The Conversation* and *Rear Window*, see Anders Albrechtslund (2008).
26 Or as Turner (1985: 8) puts it, the audience follows the "threads" of the detective plot to its core but ends with a false interpretation. Thus, "the result is not the security of solution, but the threat of *mise-en-abyme*" (italics in the original).
27 Thomas Docherty (1993: 218–19) sees the opening sequence of the movie as mise-en-abyme.

Chapter 4

1 Interestingly enough, counter-cinema does not refrain from casting female stars. Besides Claudia Cardinale in *8½*, we might mention here the casting of Brigitte Bardot in Jean-Luc Godard's *Le Mépris* (1963), also a meta-cinematic film dealing with the film industry that problematizes, inter alia, the engagement with films via stars à la Bardot.
2 It is well known, for example, that for the role of Scarlett O'Hara in *Gone with the Wind* (1939) numerous actresses and stars of the time were screen tested, until it was felt that Vivien Leigh was "the one." Indeed, the film owes much of its success to its casting. That the role of Rhett Butler was "meant" for Clark Gable was without dispute, but the studio invested much effort into finding its perfect match for Scarlett. The point is that ever since then it has become impossible to separate her from the one chosen to play the role.
3 The animated characters are unable to speak, hence the need to employ actors' voices. In recent years one of the ways of increasing the value of digital animation feature films has been recruiting stars or well-known actors whose audiences may recognize them through their voices.

4   See Metz ([1977] 1982), esp. 138–42, but in the context of comparing film and dream also 101–19. The example is taken from the notes of Alfred Guzzetti, the translator (143n6).

5   One explanation for the difficulty of describing a dream in words lies, according to Silvano Arieti (1976: 54–5), in endoceptual memory, which is the central component of the dream: "The endospatial memory is beyond the cognitive stage of the imagination, for it produces nothing similar to the sensory perception, it cannot be easily identified, and is impossible to translate into words. This memory remains at the preverbal level, and although it has emotional power, it does not expand into a clear emotional feeling."

6   On the projection of subjectivity into Bazin's notion of objectivity, see Philip Rosen (2011: 116n13). Rosen rightly notes that the word "complex" in the original French appears in scare quotes.

7   Metz ([1968] 1991: 232) also discusses at length the extratextual mirroring of Fellini's creative process as a director. This is an additional layer of the structure seen in the film, what Metz referred to as "construction en abyme" (228).

8   Elaborating on this subject, Fellini notes, "The result was the story of a director who must begin a film but cannot remember the plot and continues to oscillate between two planes: reality and imagination" (Angelo Solmi [1962] 1967: 168; cited also in Wheeler Winston Dixon 2017). The relationship between the diegetic characters in the film and the film within the film see below reflects that between the extra-diegetic and the diegetic characters (i.e., Fellini/Guido).

9   In his analysis of the film's narrative structure and narration, Edward Branigan (1978) challenges this view by showing that the chaotic time, space, and structure are part of a more symmetrical text, hence closer to the classical text paradigm.

10 As Ed Cameron (2015: 112) rightly claims, the fundamental split in Guido's subjectivity between the affectionate and the sensual is "represented throughout the film in the division between the women in [his] life: Mother/Luisa on the affectionate side and Saraghina/Carla on the sensual side."

11 On Fellini's intentions and use of Cardinale in his intersection of reality (his life as an artist, filmmaking) and film (8½), see Donald P. Costello's (1981: 4–11) comprehensive analysis.

12 On the versions promulgated by Fellini regarding creating a legend of himself through his "autobiographical" films (in interviews given over the years, for example, in 1965, 1976, 1985), see John C. Stubbs (2002: 130n7). See also John Baxter (1993), who provides detailed synopses of most of Fellini's films and delves into background material concerning the development of the screenplays, casting and selection of the crew. However, much of the data provided cannot be severed from the notion that runs the gamut of this book: Fellini's self-promulgated "myth." This notion comes forth also in *Fellini on Fellini* (1976), as well as in Hollis Alpert (1986), although to a lesser degree (see especially Chapter 13, on the production of *8½*). See as well Charlotte

Chandler's (2001) book of interviews with Fellini, especially the three chapters, "Dreams are the Only Reality" (3–4), "A Legend and the Small Screen" (189–203) and "Daymares and Nightdreams" (189–217); and Damian Pettigrew's (2003) book titled *Fellini, I'm a Born Liar: A Fellini Lexicon* (the same title of his documentary, *Fellini, je suis un grand menteur*, 2002). Worth looking at for the theme of memory in Fellini is the book edited by Valentina Cordelli, Riccardo Costantini, and Luca Giuliani (2003).

13 On Fellini's auteurism, see Stubbs (2015), especially his chapters "Fellini, Jung and Dreams" (37–69) and "Autobiography and Fellini's Portrait of the Artist" (105–35). The latter chapter appeared as an article in *Cinema Journal* (2002), from which we quote. It explores *8½* as a meta-film demonstrating Fellini's four-stage creative process (as defined by Henri Poincaré): preparation, incubation, *Eureka!* moment, and verification. On the creative process in relation to psychology in Fellini, see Renzo Canestrari (2011). on Fellini's *oeuvre*, see Peter Bondanella (1992); Bondanella and Cristina Degli-Esposti (1993); Frank Burke (1996); Cordelli, Costantini and Giuliani (2003); Marguerite R. Waller (2002). On the contextualization of Fellini's work into that of his contemporaries, see Manuela Gieri (1995); on Fellini's literary collaborations and sources of inspiration, see also Federico Pacchioni (2014).

14 The book, edited by Tullio Kezich and Vittorio Boarini renders Fellini's drawings of his dreams and the written texts accompanying them.

15 According to Cameron (2015: 105), Fellini highlights the "conventional nature" of extra-diegetic expectations (as classical narrative does), but (unlike classical narrative) "draws attention to that which causes desire at the expense of that which might satisfy desire. By doing so, Fellini's film forces spectators to traverse the fantastic expectations of cinematic narrative and confront the drive of cinema as an end in itself, thereby also highlighting the psychoanalytic distinction between desire and drive." This contention is of course true, except for the cast. The sublimation of the drive through artistic creation, "which aims at the [Lacanian] Real precisely at the point where the Real cannot be reduced to reality," (104) might be the theme of the film; however, we maintain that what sustains the spectators' engagement with Fellini's film is the satisfaction of (the spectators') desire through the cast as fantasy objects.

16 See Costello (1981: 4–6).

17 In this respect, not casting an important character (like in the bodiless-character films, discussed in Chapter 1) means resisting this kind of transgression.

18 The metaphor Fellini uses for his film is a sculpture, one that he can break into pieces in order "to examine the pieces one by one" (quoted in Costello 1981: 3).

19 Because *Mulholland Drive* has an incoherent, confusing structure, it has had ample interpretations. According to some, it is a mystery that refuses to be solved (Owen Gleiberman 2001; Jennifer A. Hudson 2004; Glen Kenny 2001; Jean Tang 2001; Kenneth Turan 2001), or it can be understood as situations relating to each other through repetition and variation instead of causality (András Bálint Kovács 2007, 167–70). Others have argued that the coherence

of the film is revealed through the perspective of the dream (Walter Chaw and Bill Chambers 2001; Katherine N. Hayles and Nicholas Gessler 2004; Phillip Lopate 2001; Amy Taubin 2001), which also explains its surrealist techniques (Michael Pattison 2013; Clint Stivers 2014). Jay R. Lentzner and Donald R. Ross (2005: 102) note that even those interpreting the film this way claim the dream is too convoluted to follow. Robert Sinnerbrink (2013: 80) describes it as "a complex reflection on cinematic narrative conventions that renders unstable any straightforward linear interpretation." Stephen N. Docarmo (2009: 658) further states that "even if we accept the reading above [dream], much in the film remains resolutely irrealist, refusing to 'add up.'" For a comprehensive analysis of the dream see also David Andrews (2004).

20 "Winkie's" alludes to "wink," which in the meta-cinematic context refers to the entire complexity of vision—the illusion of movement and that of the continuity created by the editing mechanism. On the many cinematic allusion reflecting the classical Hollywood filmmaking before the dissolution of the big studios, see Roger F. Cook (2011: 374–5). According to Cook, the mental world of the protagonist, as destroyed by the Hollywood Dream Factory, reflects the power mainstream film narrative wields against women by immersing them in its fantasy world, and thus binding them to a spectral collective guilt. On the dream as fantasy see also Franklin Ridgway (2006) and René Thoreau Bruckner (2008). On lesbian fantasy specifically, see Heather Love (2004).

21 Recalling the split in Dorian Gray's character in Oscar Wilde's novel *The Portrait of Dorian Gray* (1890).

22 According to Jennifer McMahon (2011: 113–14) this exemplifies what existentialist philosopher Jean-Paul Sartre deems "bad faith" regarding both the character and the narrative.

23 McMahon (120) connects the seductive femme-fatal allure of Rita with the ambivalence Diane feels toward Camilla: "She is her beloved but also her betrayer, thus Diane loves her and at the same time loathes her."

24 For a close reading of the audition scene, see George Toles (2004).

25 Vernon Shetley (2006: 117) thoroughly analyzes the echoing of *Vertigo* in *Mulholland Drive*—like guilt, amnesia, replication of the object of desire—but at the same time shows that the latter is an ambivalent revision of the former, as it "multiplies [*Vertigo*'s] complications and dissolves its fixed points," like masculine and feminine, voyeur and object (124). Moreover, according to Shetley, Lynch restores, explores, and exposes what Hitchcock had repressed, especially regarding the Hispanic past of California and feminine sexuality and homosexuality (126–7). While both films reflect on the cinema as a medium that might bring about brutal consequences, Hitchcock "offers a grimly disillusioned vision" that Lynch does not by involving the viewer as an accomplice in the brutal power Scottie imposes on his object of desire (127–28). As we hope we have shown in our analysis of *Vertigo* in Chapter 2, Hitchcock only does so up to a point.

26 Here Lentzner and Ross again interpret Diane's contradictory desire as affirming her wish to compensate herself for childhood wounds and repair her relationship with her narcissistic mother.

27 There is a somewhat sadistic side to Camilla. It might be that this is Diane's experience of her, but either way her sadism reflects the "cruelty" of the exclusion from the primal scene. On Camilla's sadism (and her reference to the "femme fatale"), see Ridgway (2006: 5–6); on this as a projection on Diane's part, see 11–12.

28 Tony Hughes-d'Aeth (2013: 28–9) connects the primal scene to the inversion of fantasy/reality, as evinced in these two scenes: "The audition [in the dream] works in direct parallel with the scene at the party, on the other side of the blue box, in which Dianne watches on, seething, as Adam proposes to Rita, his newly chosen 'leading lady'" (30).

29 Tarja Laine (2009: 331) refers to this "game" of names as "the relationship between naming and existing." Ronie Parciack (2011: 79–80) claims that the instability of names in the film is an epitome for the fluidity of characters in Lynch's movies. Moreover, Parciack wonders if death is even possible in a world of "fluid characters," which, of course suggests the actors' immortality on the screen.

30 In his discussion of dream/reality, Geoff Klock (2017: 54) claims that there are three levels of "dreaming" in the movie, the major one being the affair and separation of Diane and her neighbor, the same one who appears to get her things back. For Klock, the last part of the film, which we identify as "reality," is thus just as Hollywood-like as Diane's fantasies: "Watts [i.e., Diane] fantasizes that her affair was not with the plain neighbor but with a beautiful actress."

31 See also Robert A. Rushing (2010), who sees the Silencio scene as an example of anamorphosis, mostly in contemporary films, a sudden shift that requires from the observer or spectator a change of perspective; according to Allister Mactaggart (2010: 61, 63), the mechanical gap in the apparatus produces a split "between authenticity and artifice . . . between absorption and distance in the spectator," and, in Lacanian terms, the lack in the symbolic; Laine (2009: 335) sees this scene not only as part of the misleading logic of the film, but also as a betrayal of what she calls "affective agreement," as it "tricks the spectator by privileging the proprioceptive bodily system over the exteroceptive and cognitive, thereby insisting that the spectator acquire a broken mode of apprehending the film." On the blue box as a symbol of void, but also as a space of fantasy in the sense of Freud's "screen memories," see Debra Shostak (2008: 3–4, 16–17).

32 According to Katherine M. Reed (2016: 18) the Silencio scene epitomizes "the reality of the entire plot to this point: what is real and what is illusion?" and like the characters, the viewers "are invited to rethink what they have accepted as fact"; it is the door through which we are led to the "other" side—the reality of the second part of the film.

33 "The blue box operates visually as the conduit between the two worlds. Like the parents' bedroom door for a child, the box simultaneously contains the 'other' world of primal fantasy . . . and yet opens up to its infinitely unknowable space of longing. Lynch is positioning love at this juncture" (Hughes-d'Aeth 2013: 29).

34 For Greg Olson (2008: 579), "The blue-lit entrance to Club Silencio admitted Diane (as Betty) to a space in which she metaphorically saw her own death racing toward her."
35 This final word, Justus Nieland (2012: 95) writes, shows *Mulholland Drive*'s fascination and self-exploration of the cinematic experience as part of the fundamental question "What is Cinema?"
36 See also Martha P. Nochimson (2013: 116–17).
37 In his comparison of Betty/Watts, Toles (2004: 11) writes: "While Naomi Watts is still busy delineating, on one level, Betty's potentially life-altering audition, her acting speaks to and encloses another woman's tragedy (a woman we haven't, at this point in the narrative, officially met)." A. H. Denham and F. D. Worrell (2013: 22) claim that "there is something very contrived about Betty's character, as bad fiction is contrived. The viewer knows, and is meant to know, that Watts is play-acting when we watch Betty. We are meant to be aware that everything Betty says is scripted, preordained by an idealized paradigm that lacks the texture, substance, and complexity of real life . . . Betty is an exaggeration, a hyperbole of the imagination."
38 See also also Zina Giannopoulou (2013) and Shostak (2008).
39 Herein lies the force of advertisement as well. See Roland Barthes ([1964] 1977).
40 For an intertextual reading of *Mulholland Drive*, see Ebrahim Barzegar (2014).
41 Regarding the dominance of illusion in the noir style, see also McMahon (2011), James Naremore (2008), and Shostak (2008).
42 See Jennifer M. Barker's (2008) reading of the film as a spectacle of synaesthesia. The way seeing (and hearing) involves other senses in the viewing of film, although not the focus of our book, is nevertheless a major concern. In the Club Silencio scene, it might be our invocatory drive that engages other senses (sight might even be secondary here), certainly arousing a shivering affect, and not only in its uncanny sense (the latter is achieved through the interrelation of sound and sight). See also Zachary Tavlin (2013) on affect.

Chapter 5

1 On the history of cross-dressing in comedies, see John Phillips (2006: 51–84).
2 Castration, the lack, enables the subject to maintain the belief or fantasy that there is the One who is not accessible (the ideal of no boundaries and limitations lives on). In this sense, Lacan's notion regarding the phallus as fetish (the signifier of lack) is in keeping with Freud's ([1913] 1958) descriptions of replacements of the slain primordial father in *Totem and Taboo*. Tribes, groups, and categories are created and coalesced around the idea of the missing One (e.g., "one for all and all for one").
3 See Jacqueline Rose's (1982: 52) mention of the Holy Scriptures as a source of Saint Theresa's enjoyment because she cannot derive a definite meaning from the text.

4 What cannot find representation in the unconscious—associated with the real.
5 See Bruce Fink ([1995] 1997: 98–121) and Lacan ([1972–3] 1999: 78–89).
6 For a comprehensive survey of this history, see Vern L. Bullough and Bonnie Bullough (1993, especially 145–73).
7 The basic compendium of Jewish law and thought; its tractates comprise mainly the discussions collectively known as the *Gemara*, whose purpose is to elucidate the germinal statements of law (the *Mishnah*); however, it is assembled in a quite associative way, and the debates and interpretations on specific subjects do not distinguish between the theological (e.g., the nature of God) and the trivial, leaving many subjects unresolved and open to further interpretations, *ad infinitum*. See the scene in which Yentl explains to Hadass what the Talmud is all about.
8 A yeshiva is an institute for men only where religious texts are studied, primarily the Talmud and the Torah (the first five books—Pentateuch—of the Old Testament) during daily lectures or classes. Working in pairs uniquely characterizes the yeshiva learning style.
9 An interview in which Jacques Derrida answers questions about sexual difference, femininity, and feminism.
10 Michele Aaron (2000a, b) targets the analogy the film—and Streisand herself—creates between same-sex attraction and "Jewishness."
11 For a general, multireligious presentation of this transition, see Guy G. Stroumsa ([2005] 2009).
12 According to Marjorie Garber (1997: 80), Yentl's cross-dressing also marks such category crises as the oppression of the Jews in Eastern Europe and the need to emigrate, discrimination of female Jewish artists in Hollywood, "and ... women in the producer's role—the role so often occupied by Jewish *men*" (italics in the original). In this context, the cross-dressing "is a compelling illustration of what I take to be the power of the transvestite in literature and culture." To this, we might add Streisand's acknowledgment of the value of self-fulfillment through semiotic elements, such as her singing, a career that made her want "more"—acting and, finally, directing.
13 "Musical tradition in *ḥazzanut* means a melodic pattern to be followed, the choice of a specific tetrachord or other scale, which is representative of a certain mood, or a stock of motives to be arranged and rearranged in changing melodic structures. Among the special features of East Ashkenazi *ḥazzanut* was its emotional power, which was stressed by the early writers" ("Cantorial Music," *Encyclopaedia Judaica* 2007).
14 According to Jewish law, when a husband dies it is the moral obligation of his brother to marry the widow. Since Avigdor is declared unfit to marry Hadass and considers Anshel his brother, he is determined to apply this law to solve his problem (remain close to both Hadass and Anshel).
15 On the fitting scene in relevance to castration see also Garber (1997: 80).
16 Again, Streisand seems also to be addressing the audience—to endorse her admirable ambition to write, direct, and produce the film as well as star in it—to establish her own voice, authorship.

17 The scene carries a sense of the history of cinema in that it alludes to the waves of European directors and professionals in the art of cinema who immigrated to America, where they found a new home (Hollywood). This is a reminder that what made Hollywood great is not only its phallic economy—the similar way in which all the big studios, dominated by men, operated—but also the uniqueness that each actor or *auteur* brought to the industry.
18 Streisand dedicated the film to her father, who died when she was one year old.
19 On *Calamity Jane*'s transformation as a key element, see also Tamar Jeffers McDonald (2007).
20 This might explain why women love this film—they are fed up with looking at themselves as fetishes, to-be-looked-at objects alone. In her fascinating (ethnographic) investigation of the place of female movie stars in the lives of female spectators, Jackie Stacey (1994: 81) quotes a letter received from a Doris Day fan (Veronica Millen): "I saw *Calamity Jane* 88 times. . . . My favourite star of all times, even now, is Doris Day."
21 At the end of the film, when he discovers Calamity is still carrying a gun on the way to their honeymoon, he takes it away from her, but only because a gun has no place on a honeymoon. There is much in the film that attests to Bill's acceptance of and love for Calamity for what she is.
22 In this disguise Joe imitates Cary Grant's accent: "And where did you get this phony accent? Nobody talks like that!"—he is asked by Jerry in one of the scenes.
23 See also Chris Straayer's (1996: 61–4) interpretation of these scenes.
24 The gay subtext is enhanced if we adopt the idea that Osgood knows that he is in fact pursuing a man. There is much in the film that supports this interpretation (e.g., the fact that none of his marriages lasted, the way he keeps up his grin, and of course, the fact that he does not care about Jerry's confession ["I'm a man"] at the end of the film). See also Ed Sikov (1994: 146).
25 On the dynamic of desire in the film, see Raúl A. Galoppe (2003).
26 As Anette Kuhn (1987: 712) observes, when Jerry and Joe, and thereafter Sugar, arrive at the train station, they first appear visually on the screen as fetishes (shot from behind, in a close-up rendering their legs in high-heel shoes). However, while the shot of the two disguised men is rendered from the camera's point of view, the ones of Sugar are rendered from that of the two men. That said, the scene distinguishes between Joe's reaction (pleasure), and Jerry's, which is one of discomfort. He is concerned about them not being able to do a "jello on springs" walk like Sugar, totally oblivious of the pleasure Joe derives from gazing at her behind. This distinction, in our opinion, indicates an awareness of the treatment of female actresses like Monroe as fetishes, also suggesting its performtive aspect.
27 See, for example, Straayer (1996: 64–9).
28 In our opinion, Andrews's appearance as "man" is much more attractive and sexier than that as a "woman" (Would King even have looked at Victoria the way she looked before deciding to disguise?). What mesmerizes King is

precisely the moment when the female performer takes off her wig, revealing that she is a handsome "man."

Chapter 6

1 In *L'Animale* (Katharina Mückstein 2018), Mati (Sophie Stockinger) is a teenaged tomboy preparing for her final high school exams before leaving for a university in Vienna to study veterinary medicine (her mother's profession). She spends most of her time hanging out with an all-male motorbike gang (she always wins), and is closest to Sebi (Jack Hofer), the son of a local farmer, who asks her to be more than friends. But Mati falls in love with Carla (Julia Franz Richter). As a result, Sebi and the motorbike gang start persecuting her, first by humiliating her, then by coercing her into vandalizing the supermarket where Carla works, and finally by smashing the window of Carla's house when she and Carla are seen sleeping in an embrace. Although for spectators it is clear from the start that Mati is a lesbian, in the diegesis, in the rural society she lives, she must hide her sexual preferences (her father is a closeted homosexual). She is accepted as tomboy but not as a lesbian.
2 Patricia Gherovici's essay is one of many in the 2017 *TSQ* dossier (4, 3-4) dedicated to trans and psychoanalysis, explaining how Lacanian psychoanalysis can be read and used to/for the benefit of trans persons.
3 See also Žižek (1997: 18–27, 54–60).
4 For a further reading on aspects of the body, trauma, and history in the film see Victor Fan (2012) and Julián Daniel Gutiérrez-Albilla (2013).
5 Worth noting is the documentary *The Brandon Teena Story* (Susan Muska and Gréta Olafsdóttir 1998).
6 On the impact of paratextuality regarding trans films, see Andre Cavalcante (2013).
7 Notwithstanding those examples chosen by Lucy J. Miller (2017), that all trans films played by cisgender actors are made for a cisgender audience, therefore unsympathetic to trans characters, recalls the notion that cross-dressing films by cisgender filmmakers in the past were made for cisgender audiences only, therefore unsympathetic to gay audiences, a claim we hope we have managed to debunk. On how cinematic grammar implicates cisgenderism, see Laura Copier and Eliza Steinbock (2018). Particularly engaging is Steinbock's (2009) analogy between transsexual bodies and cinematic language ("somatechnics"), through which transsexuality might be read.
8 See John M. Sloop (2000), who names *Boys Don't Cry* as just another manifestation of how public discourses concerning cases such as the Brandon Teena narrative work to stabilize sex, to reiterate sexual norms, rather than to encourage or explore gender fluidity.
9 See, for example, the dossier published in *Screen* (Aaron 2001; Jack J. Halberstam 2001; Julianne Pidduck 2001; Patricia White 2001; Jennifer

Devere Brody 2002), and a more recent account of the phenomena of "passing" in the film (Leanne Dawson 2015). See also the documentary *Gendernauts: A Journey through Shifting Identities* (Monika Treut 1999), in which one of the characters raises the question about Brandon's sexual and gender identity.

10 Jennifer Esposito (2003) analyzes this scene, along with other "border-crossing" actions on Brandon's part, as a performance of white masculinity.

11 This is how, according to Halberstam (2001: 294), the film forces "spectators to adopt, if only for a short time, Brandon's gaze, a transgender gaze."

12 Arguing that the film reinscribes the normative nature of white masculinity by showcasing Brandon Teena's failed performance as a performance while allowing the "biological men" to just "be" men, Esposito (2003), also claims that the film categorizes Brandon as "lesbian," and we, as viewers of the film, are interpellated as border patrols and help in the lesbianizing of Brandon. Notwithstanding the one scene to which this might apply, the rest of the film does not seem to support this contention; on the contrary, it makes clear Brandon's desire to be a man and love a woman as a man, decrying all demeaning labels that address Brandon as a "dyke"—because in his surroundings the desire to be a man cannot be condoned, let alone contained. The debate on the Brandon Teena has expanded its boundaries to the question of race as well (why the character of DeVine was excluded from the film)—see C. Riley Snorton (2017: 177–243).

13 Chimera is, in Greek mythology, a monster composed of the parts of more than one animal.

14 See Jeff Guinn and Douglas Perry (2005) who, based on Andy Warhol's proclamation that everyone will be world famous for fifteen minutes, explore the consequences of short-period fame as experienced by one-hit-wonder artists, short-career professional sports athletes, political figures, reality television celebrities, and others.

15 See Plato (2008: 38–48).

16 On an elaborated discussion of the *chōra* in Plato's *Timaeus*, see, for example, Emanuela Bianchi (2006); Derrida ([1987/1993] 1995); Elizabeth Grosz (1994); and Luce Irigaray ([1974] 1985).

17 See Judith Butler (1993: 27–56).

18 See Chapter 1.

19 Artists need public recognition for their art, but this must be achieved through a unique artistic vision expressing the artist's authenticity, and not for the sake of fame per se.

20 See also Martin Kley (2007), who explores the meta-cinematic aspect of the film through the use of puppeteering, which symbolizes and allegorizes stardom and spectatorship and the relationship between the two.

21 The oval shape recalls both early cinema, especially the iris, and the way photographs in the period of Robert Louis Stevenson (the author of *The Strange Case of Dr. Jekyll and Mr. Hyde*) used to "frame" the human portrait

in a bright oval shape, obscuring the rest of the photograph. The year the novel was published (1886) marks the period of the first experiments that led to the advent of film (see, for example, James Monaco [1981: 20–7]).

22 For a comprehensive study on Jonze's body of work (including musical video clips and commercials) see James Annesley (2013). On Kaufman's scriptwriting, see Chris Dzialo (2009).

23 Worth noting is how Kaufman transitioned as *auteur* to directing as well (*Synecdoche, New York*, 2008; *Anomalisa*, 2015).

Appendix

1 Although this film does not require that we do a cross-comparison, we nevertheless must imagine that teenager Bobby/Feldman is in fact the elderly Coleman/Robards, who is striving to look and behave like (the real) Bobby/Feldman. These endeavors include an appropriation of some of Michael Jackson's 1980s persona characteristics.

2 Bertolucci is known for his Freudian inclination and recurrent theme of the role of individual subjectivity and early traumas in the shaping of history. Here he uses the uncanny motif of the double to impregnate the film with a nightmarish quality. For example, in the flashbacks, the father is depicted as young as his son, looking identical, since both characters are played by the same actor. This might have seemed less uncanny (the flashbacks depict the father in his youthful years) had it not been for the fact that all the other characters in the flashbacks (the father's associates) are played by the same actors as well, with no attempt to make them appear younger.

3 Worth noting is the extent to which Diaz is stripped of her star persona for her role in this film.

4 On the objects in Hitchcock's films, see, for example, Mladen Dolar (1992) and Slavoj Žižek (1992).

5 This is one of the reasons why some scholars consider cross-dressing in classical and mainstream cinema devoid of any real political power. See, for example, Butler (1993: 125–8), Bert Cardullo (1995), Kuhn (1987), and Daniel Lieberfeld (1998). We oppose such approaches, rather favoring those who argue that the queer subtexts (see, for example, Straayer 1996) provide grounds enough for the subversion of social and cultural norms pertaining to gender and sexuality, or Garber's (1997: 8–9; 67–92) approach, which maintains that cross-dressers find their erotic pleasure in the very act of putting on garments and accessories of the opposite sex, namely transvestism. This notion is evident in scenes portraying the whole process of the makeover.

6 A remake of the German *Viktor und Viktoria* (Reinhold Schünzel 1933).

7 For a comprehensive genealogy until the late 1980s, see Pam Cook (1988). See also Yvonne Tasker (1998: 52–3).

8 See Sandra Meiri (2011) and Chapter 4 in this book.

9 On the cult status of *The Rocky Horror Picture Show*, see Patrick T. Kinkade and Michael A. Katovich (1992), and Gaylyn Studlar (1989).

10 For a review on the film's representation of transwoman, see Julia Dettke (2016) and Maria San Filippo (2016).

11 On the transgressive pleasures the film provides, also due to this "unclarity," see David Scott Diffrient (2013).

12 In *La piel que habito*, the sex change is imposed on the protagonist through a brutal coercive process (by a psychotic surgeon), but its outcome is a beautiful and artistic woman who in the end is worthy of her mother's recognition. See also Zachary Price (2015) and Cath Davies (2017).

13 Worth noting is also the category of "trans-sex casting" (Straayer 1996: 74–8). The quintessential example is of course Divine, the drag queen, in John Waters' films such as *Pink Flamingos* (1972), *Female Trouble* (1974), and *Hairspray* (1988). In the cinematic remake of *Hairspray* (Adam Shankman 2007) John Travolta plays the role of the mother.

14 To this date no narrative films have been made on drag kings. On the history and culture of this phenomenon, see Halberstam and Del Lagrace Volcano (1999).

15 On camp, see also Leo Bersani (1978: 208); in relation to camp and subjectivity, he thinks the only way camp parody can be eroticized is through the outbursts of hatred characterizing the performer's parody—surely a form of feminine enjoyment, in the service of a defense mechanism; Caryl Flinn (1995: 61; camp as defamiliarization—this idea comes through much earlier in Susan Sontag [1964]); and Moe Meyer (1994; camp as queer parody).

16 See the documentary *Queens of Heart: Community Therapists in Drag* (Jan Haaken 2006).

REFERENCES

3 Generations (2015), [Film] dir. Gaby Dellal, USA: Big Beach Films, InFilm Productions and IM Global.
8½ (1963), [Film] dir. Federico Fellini, Italy/France: Cineriz and Francinex.
The 15:17 to Paris (2018), [Film] dir. Clint Eastwood, USA: Malpaso Productions and Village Roadshow Pictures.
17 Again (2009), [Film] dir. Burr Steers, USA: Offspring Entertainment.
2001: A Space Odyssey (1968), [Film] dir. Stanley Kubrick, UK/USA: Stanley Kubrick Productions and MGM.
2010: The Year We Make Contact (1984), [Film] dir. Peter Hyams, USA: MGM.
Aaron, Michele. (2000a), "Hardly Chazans: *Yentl* and the Singing Jew," in Bill Marshall and Robynn Stilwell (eds.), *Musicals: Hollywood and Beyond*, 125-31, Exeter: Intellect Books.
Aaron, Michele. (2000b), "The Queer Jew and Cinema: From Yidl to Yentl and Back and Beyond," *Jewish Culture and History*, 3 (1): 23-44.
Aaron, Michele. (2001), "Pass/Fail," *Screen*, 42 (1): 92-6.
Abbott, Traci B. (2013), "The Trans/Romance Dilemma in *Transamerica* and Other Films," *The Journal of American Culture*, 36 (1): 32-41.
Adaptation (2002), [Film] dir. Spike Jonze, USA: Good Machine, Intermedia and Propaganda Films.
The Adventures of Priscilla, Queen of the Desert (1994), [Film] dir. Stephan Elliott, Australia: Latent Image Productions and Specific Films.
A. I. Artificial Intelligence (2001), [Film] dir. Steven Spielberg, USA: Amblin Entertainment and Stanley Kubrick Productions.
Albert Nobbs (2011), [Film] dir. Rodrigo García, UK/Ireland/France/USA: Mockingbird Pictures, Trillium Productions, Parallel Film Productions, Morrison Films and WestEnd Films.
Albrechtslund, Anders (2008), "Surveillance and Ethics in Film: *Rear Window* and *The Conversation*," *Journal of Criminal Justice and Popular Culture*, 15 (2): 129-44.
All of Me (1984), [Film] dir. Carl Reiner, USA: Kings Road Entertainment.
Alpert, Hollis. (1986), *Fellini: A Life*, New York: Simon and Schuster.
Althusser, Louis. ([1970] 1971), "Ideology and Ideological State Apparatuses," in *"Lenin and Philosophy" and Other Essays*, trans. Ben Brewster, 127-86, New York: Monthly Review Press.
American Sniper (2014), [Film] dir. Clint Eastwood, USA: Mad Chance, Joint Effort and Malpaso Productions.
Andrews, David. (2004), "An Oneiric Fugue: The Various Logics of *Mulholland Drive*," *Journal of Film and Video*, 56 (1): 25-40.

Angelucci, Gianfranco, and Liliana Betti. (1974), *Il Film "Amarcord" di Federico Fellini*, Bologna: Cappelli.
L'Animale (2018), [Film] dir. Katharina Mückstein, Austria: Nikolaus Geyrhalter Filmproduktion and La Banda Film.
Annesley, James. (2013), "Being Spike Jonze: Intertextuality and Convergence in Film, Music Video and Advertising," *New Cinemas: Journal of Contemporary Film*, 11 (1): 23-37.
Annie Get Your Gun (1950), [Film] dir. George Sidney, USA: MGM.
Annie Oakley (1935), [Film] dir. George Stevens, USA: RKO Radio Pictures.
Anomalisa (2015), [Film] dir. Charlie Kaufman and Duke Johnson, USA: HanWay Films, Starburns Industries and Snoot Films.
Arieti, Silvano. (1976), *Creativity: The Magic Synthesis*, New York: Basic Books.
The Ballad of Little Jo (1993), [Film] dir. Maggie Greenwald, USA: Joco AND PolyGram Filmed Entertainment.
Bankier van het Verzet [*The Resistance Banker*] (2018), [Film] dir. Joram Lürsen, The Netherlands: NL Film, Mollywood and Nanook Entertainment.
Barker, Jennifer M. (2008), "Out of Sync, Out of Sight: Synaesthesia and Film Spectacle," *Paragraph*, 31 (2): 236-51.
Barnett, Vincent L. (2007), "Dualling for Judy: The Concept of the Double in the Films of Kim Novak," *Film History*, 19 (1): 86-101.
Baron, Cynthia. (2002), "Buying John Malkovich: Queering and Consuming Millennial Masculinity," *Velvet Light Trap*, 49: 18-38.
Barthes, Roland. ([1964] 1977), "Rhetoric of the Image," in Stephen Heath (ed. and trans.), *Image Music Text*, 32-51, London: Fontana Press.
Barthes, Roland. ([1980] 1981), *Camera Lucida: Reflections on Photography*, trans. Richard Howard, New York: Hill and Wang.
Barzegar, Ebrahim. (2014), "*Mulholland Drive*: An Intertextual Reading," *CINEJ Cinema Journal*, 4 (1): 63-78.
Baudry, Jean-Louis. ([1970] 1985), "Effects of the Basic Cinematographic Apparatus," in Bill Nichols (ed.), *Movies and Methods: An Anthology*, 531-42, Berkeley, Los Angeles and London: University of California Press.
Baxter, John. (1993), *Fellini: The Biography*, New York: St. Martin's Press.
Bazin, André. ([1945] 2005), "The Ontology of the Photographic Image," in Hugh Gray (trans.), *What Is Cinema*, vol. 1, 9-16, Berkeley, Los Angeles and London: University of California Press.
Behind the Screen (1916), [Film] dir. Charlie Chaplin, USA: Lone Star Corporation.
Being John Malkovich (1999), [Film] dir. Spike Jonze, USA: Gramercy Pictures, Propaganda Films and Single Cell Pictures.
Bellour, Raymond. ([1975] 2000), "Symbolic Blockage (on *North by Northwest*)," trans. Mary Quaintance, in Constance Penley (ed.), *The Analysis of Film*, 77-192, Bloomington and Indianapolis: Indiana University Press.
Belton, John. (2017), "The Uncanny Nature of the Cinematic Image," *New Review of Film and Television Studies*, 15 (4): 400-4.
Benjamin, Walter. ([1936] 1968), "The Work of Art in the Age of Mechanical Reproduction," in Hannah Arendt (ed.) and Harry Zorn (trans.), *Illuminations: Essays and Reflections*, 217-52, New York: Schocken Books.
Bersani, Leo. (1978), *A Future for Astyanax: Character and Desire in Literature*, London: Marion Boyars.

Bianchi, Emanuela. (2006), "Receptacle/*Chōra*: Figuring the Errant Feminine in Plato's *Timaeus*," *Hypatia*, 21 (4): 124-46.
Big (1988), [Film] dir. Penny Marshall, USA: Gracie Films and 20th Century Fox.
Bigwood, James. (1991), "Solving a *Spellbound* Puzzle," *American Cinematographer*, 72 (6): 34-40.
Birdman or (The Unexpected Virtue of Ignorance) (2014), [Film] dir. Alejandro González Iñárritu, USA: New Regency Pictures, M Productions and Le Grisbi.
The Birds (1963), [Film] dir. Alfred Hitchcock, USA: Alfred J. Hitchcock Productions.
Birth (2004), [Film] dir. Jonathan Glazer, UK/France/Germany/USA: Lou Yi Inc. and Academy Films.
The Birth of a Nation (1915), [Film] dir. D. W. Griffith, USA: David W. Griffith Corp. and Epoch Producing Corporation.
The Blind Side (2009), [Film] dir. John Lee Hancock, USA: Alcon Entertainment.
Blow-Up (1966), [Film] dir. Michelangelo Antonioni, UK/Italy/USA: MGM and Bridge Films.
Bohemian Rhapsody (2018), [Film] dir. Bryan Singer, UK/USA: GK Films, New Regency Pictures, Queen Films and Tribeca Productions.
Bondanella, Peter. (1992), *The Cinema of Federico Fellini*, Princeton, NJ: Princeton University Press.
Bondanella, Peter, and Degli-Esposti, Cristina (eds.). (1993), *Perspectives on Federico Fellini*, New York: G. K. Hall.
Bondil-Poupard, Nathalie. (2001), "Such Stuff as Dreams are Made On: Hitchcock and Dalí, Surrealism and Oneiricism," in Guy Cogeval and Dominique Païni (eds.), *Hitchcock and Art: Fatal Coincidences*, 155-73, Mazzotta, France: Centre Pompidou.
Bonitzer, Pascal. (1992), "Hitchcockian Suspense," in Slavoj Žižek (ed.), *Everything You Wanted to Know about Lacan but Were Afraid to Ask Hitchcock*, 15-30, London: Verso.
Boyarin, Daniel. (1997), *Unheroic Conduct: The Rise of Heterosexuality and the Invention of the Jewish Man*, Berkeley, Los Angeles and London: University of California Press.
Boyhood (2014), [Film] dir. Richard Linklater, USA: IFC Productions, Detour Film Production and Cinetic Media.
Boys Don't Cry (1999), [Film] dir. Kimberly Peirce, USA: Hart-Sharp Entertainment, IFC Films and Killer Films.
The Brandon Teena Story (1998), [Film] dir. Susan Muska and Gréta Olafsdóttir, USA: Bless Bless Productions.
Branigan, Edward. (1978), "Subjectivity under Siege: from Fellini's *8½* to Oshima's *The Story of a Man who Left His Will on Film*," *Screen*, 19 (1): 7-40.
Brill, Lesley. (2002), "*Spellbound*: Love and Psychoanalysis," in *Criterion Collection* edition of *Spellbound*, September 23.
Britton, Andrew. ([1986] 2008), "Alfred Hitchcock's *Spellbound*: Text and Countertext," in Barry Keith Grant (ed.), *Britton on Film: The Complete Film Criticism of Andrew Britton*, 175-93, Detroit, MI: Wayne State University Press.
Brody, Jennifer Devere. (2002), "Boys Do Cry: Screening History's White Lies," *Screen*, 43 (1): 91-6.

Bronfen, Elisabeth. (1993), "Risky Resemblances: On Repetition, Mourning, and Representation," in Sarah Webster Goodwin and Elisabeth Bronfen (eds.), *Death and Representation*, 103–29, Baltimore, MD: Johns Hopkins University Press.

Brook, Clodagh. (2007), "Borderlines: 8½, *Sogni d'oro* and the Real-Dream Continuum," *Forum Italicum*, 41 (1): 111–26.

Brown, Royal. (1980), "Hitchcock's *Spellbound*: Jung Versus Freud," *Film/Psychology Review*, 4 (1): 35–58.

Bullough, Vern L. and Bonnie Bullough. (1993), *Crossdressing, Sex and Gender*, Philadelphia: University of Pennsylvania Press.

Burke, Frank. (1996), *Fellini's Films: From Postwar to Postmodern*, New York: Twayne Publishers.

Butler, Judith. (1993), *Bodies That Matter: On the Discursive Limits of "Sex,"* London and New York: Routledge.

Caché [Hidden] (2005), [Film] dir. Michael Haneke, France/Austria/Germany/Italy: Les Films du Losange and Wega Film.

Calamity Jane (1953), [Film] dir. David Butler, USA: Warner Bros.

Cameron, Ed. (2015), "From Symptom to Sublimation: Fellini's 8½ and the Circuit of Art Cinema," *Italica*, 92 (1): 102–20.

Canestrari, Renzo. (2011), "Arte e psicologia: riflessioni sull'itinerario artistico di Federico Fellini, creatività e passaggio dell'età di mezzo," *Rivista di estetica*, 48: 55–64.

"Cantorial Music," *Encyclopaedia Judaica* 2007. http://id.loc.gov/authorities/genre Forms/gf2017026151.html (accessed December 30, 2018).

Cardullo, Bert. (1995), "The Dream Structure of *Some Like It Hot*," *Etudes Anglaises*, 48 (2): 193–7.

Carroll, Nöel. ([1985] 1996), "The Power of Movies," in *Theorizing the Moving Image*, 78–93, New York: Cambridge University Press.

Cavalcante, Andre. (2013), "Centering Transgender Identity via the Textual Periphery: *TransAmerica* and the 'Double Work' of Paratexts," *Critical Studies in Media Communication*, 30 (2): 85–101.

Cet obscure objet du désir [That Obscure Object of Desire] (1977), [Film] dir. Luis Buñuel, France/Spain: Greenwich Film Productions, Les Films Galaxie and InCine.

Chances Are (1989), [Film] dir. Emile Ardolino, USA: Lobell/Bergman Productions.

Chandler, Charlotte. (2001), *I, Fellini*, New York: Cooper Square Press.

The Change-Up (2011), [Film] dir. David Dobkin, USA: Original Film and Big Kid Pictures.

Chaw, Walter and Bill Chambers. (2001), "*Mulholland Drive*," *Film Freak Central DVD Review*. https://www.filmfreakcentral.net/ffc/2012/05/mulholland-driv e.html (accessed December 30, 2018).

Un Chien Andalou [An Andalusian Dog] (1929), [Film] dir. Luis Buñuel with Salvador Dalí, France.

Chion, Michel. ([1982] 1999), *The Voice in Cinema*, trans. Claudia Gorbman, New York: Columbia University Press.

The Christine Jorgensen Story (1970), [Film] dir. Irving Rapper, USA: Edward Small Productions.

The Conversation (1974), [Film] dir. Francis Ford Coppola, USA: The Directors Company, The Coppola Company and American Zoetrope.

Cook, Pam. (1988), "Women," in Edward Bascombe (ed.), *The BFI Companion to the Western*, 240-3, New York: Atheneum.

Cook, Roger F. (2011), "Hollywood Narrative and the Play of Fantasy: David Lynch's *Mulholland Drive*," *Quarterly Review of Film and Video*, 28 (5): 369-81.

Cooper, Brenda. (2002), "*Boys Don't Cry* and Female Masculinity: Reclaiming a Life & Dismantling the Politics of Normative Heterosexuality," *Critical Studies in Media Communication*, 19 (1): 44-63.

Cop Land (1997), [Film] dir. James Mangold, USA: Woods Entertainment and Across the River Productions.

Copenhafer, David. (2018), "Overhearing (in) *Touch of Evil* and *The Conversation*: From 'Real Time' Surveillance to Its Recording," *Sound Studies: An Interdisciplinary Journal*, 4 (1): 2-18.

Copier, Laura, and Eliza Steinbock. (2018), "On Not Really Being There: Trans Presence/Absence in *Dallas Buyers Club*," *Feminist Media Studies* 18 (5): 923-41.

Copjec, Joan. (1994), *Read My Desire: Lacan against the Historicists*, Cambridge, MA: MIT Press.

Corber, Robert J. (1991), "Reconstructing Homosexuality: Hitchcock and the Homoerotics of Spectatorial Pleasure," *Discourse*, 13 (2): 58-82.

Cordelli, Valentina, Riccardo Costantini, and Luca Giuliani (eds.). (2003), *La invenzioni della memoria: Il cinema di Federico Fellini*, Udine, Italy: Centro espressioni cinematografiche.

Costello, Donald P. (1981), "Layers of Reality: 8½ as Spiritual Autobiography," *Notre Dame English Journal*, 13 (2): 1-12.

Cowie, Elizabeth. (1997), "Fantasia," in *Representing the Woman: Cinema and Psychoanalysis*, 123-65, London: Macmillan Press.

Dällenbach, Lucien. ([1977] 1989), *The Mirror in the Text*, trans. Jeremy Whiteley and Emma Hughes, Chicago: The University of Chicago Press.

Dangerous Liaisons (1988), [Film] dir. Stephen Frears, USA/UK: Lorimar Film Entertainment and NFH Productions.

The Danish Girl (2015), [Film] dir. Tom Hooper, UK/USA/Germany/Denmark: Working Title, Pretty Pictures, Artemis Productions and Shelter Prod.

Davies, Cath. (2017), "What Lies Beneath: Fabric and Embodiment in Almodovar's *The Skin I Live in*," Film, *Fashion & Consumption*, 6 (1): 65-79

Dawson, Leanne. (2015), "Passing and Policing: Controlling Compassion, Bodies and Boundaries in *Boys Don't Cry* and *Unveiled/Fremde Haut*," *Studies in European Cinema*, 12 (3): 205-28.

Dayan, Daniel. (1974). "The Tutor-Code of Classical Cinema," *Film Quarterly*, 28 (1): 22-31.

De Lauretis, Teresa. (1994), *The Practice of Love: Lesbian Sexuality and Perverse Desire*, Bloomington and Indianapolis: Indiana University Press.

Deleuze, Gilles. ([1985] 1989), *Cinema 2: The Time-Image*, trans. Hugh Tomlinson and Barbara Habberjam, Minneapolis: University of Minnesota Press.

Denby, David. (1974), "Stolen Privacy: Coppola's *The Conversation*," *Sight & Sound*, 43 (3): 131-3.

Denham, A. H. and F. D. Worrell. (2013), "Identity and Agency in *Mulholland Drive*," in Zina Giannopoulou (ed.), *Mulholland Drive*, 8–37, London and New York: Routledge.
Denzin, Norman K. (1992), "*The Conversation*," *Symbolic Interaction*, 15 (2): 135–50.
Derrida, Jacques. ([1987/1993] 1995), "Khôra," in Thomas Dutoit (ed.), *On the Name*, trans. Ian McLeod, 89–127, Stanford, CA: Stanford University Press.
Derrida, Jacques and Christie V. McDonald. (1982), "Interview: Choreographies," *Diacritics*, 12 (2): 66–76.
Dettke, Julia. (2016), "Seeing Is Being: Transfer, Transformation, and the Spectatorship of Transgender Mobility in François Ozon's *The New Girlfriend*," *Transfers*, 6 (2): 142–5.
Dickinson, Emily. (1960), "(Poem 288)," in Thomas H. Johnson (ed), *The Complete Poems of Emily Dickinson 1850–1870*, 133, Boston, MA: Little, Brown and Company.
Diffrient, David Scott. (2013), "'Hard to Handle': Camp Criticism, Trash-Film Reception, and the Transgressive Pleasures of *Myra Breckinridge*," *Cinema Journal*, 52 (2): 46–70.
Dittmar, Linda. (2002), "Performing Gender in *Boys Don't Cry*," in Frances Gateward and Murray Pomerance (eds.), *Sugar Spice and Everything Nice: Cinemas of Girlhood*, 145–62, Detroit, MI: Wayne State University Press.
Dixon, Wheeler Winston. (2017), "A Fantastic, Enchanted Ballet: Federico Fellini's *8½* (1963)," *Senses of Cinema*, 82, January. http://sensesofcinema.com/2017/cteq/8-%C2%BD-federico-fellini/ (accessed December 30, 2018).
Doane, Mary Ann. (1980), "The Voice in the Cinema: The Articulation of Body and Space," *Yale French Studies*, 60: 33–50.
Doane, Mary Ann. (2003), "The Close-Up: Scale and Detail in the Cinema," *Differences*, 14 (3): 89–111.
Docarmo, Stephen N. (2009), "Postmodernist Quietism in Polanski's *Chinatown* and Lynch's *Mulholland Drive*," *The Journal of Popular Culture*, 42 (4): 646–62.
Docherty, Thomas. (1993), "The Space of Narrative," *Tropismes*, 6: 209–23.
Dodds, Tomás. (2018), "*Una Mujer Fantástica*," *Journal of Homosexuality*. https://doi.org/10.1080/00918369.2018.1539580 (accessed April 30, 2019).
Dolar, Mladen. (1992), "Hitchcock's Objects," in Slavoj Žižek (ed.), *Everything You Always Wanted to Know about Lacan (But Were Afraid to Ask Hitchcock)*, 31–46, New York: Verso.
Down to Earth (2001), [Film] dir. Chris Weitz and Paul Weitz, USA: Village Roadshow Pictures.
Dr. Jekyll and Mr. Hyde (1931), [Film] dir. Rouben Mamoulian, USA: Paramount Pictures.
Dragunoiu, Dana. (2001–2), "Psychoanalysis, Film Theory, and the Case of *Being John Malkovich*," *Film Criticism*, 26 (2): 1–18.
Dream a Little Dream (1989), [Film] dir. Marc Rocco, USA: Lightning Pictures.
Dressed to Kill (1980), [Film] dir. Brian De Palma, USA: Filmways Pictures and Cinema 77 Films.
Dr. Strangelove or: How I Learned to Stop Worrying and Love the Bomb (1964), [Film] dir. Stanley Kubrick, USA/UK: Hawk Films.

Durgnat, Raymond. (1974), *The Strange Case of Alfred Hitchcock, or the Plain Man's Hitchcock*, Cambridge, MA: MIT Press.
Dyer, Richard. (1986), *Heavenly Bodies: Film Stars and Society*, New York: St. Martin's Press.
Dzialo, Chris. (2009), "'Frustrated Time' Narration: The Screenplays of Charlie Kaufman," in Warren Buckland (ed.), *Puzzle Films: Complex Storytelling in Contemporary Cinema*, 107-28, Chichester, West Sussex: Wiley Blackwell.
Eberwein, Robert. (1984), *Film and the Dream Screen: A Sleep and a Forgetting*, Princeton, NJ: Princeton University Press.
Elsaesser, Thomas and Malte Hagener. (2010), *Film Theory: An Introduction through the Senses*, London and New York: Routledge.
Enter the Void (2009), [Film] dir. Gaspar Noé, France/Germany/Italy/Canada/Japan: Fidélité Films, Wild Bunch and BUF.
Epstein, Jean. ([1921] 1977), "Magnification and Other Writings," trans. Stuart Liebman, *October*, 3: 9-25.
Esposito, Jennifer. (2003), "The Performance of White Masculinity in *Boys Don't Cry*: Identity, Desire, (Mis)Recognition," *Cultural Studies ↔ Critical Methodologies*, 3 (2): 229-41.
Evans, Dylan. ([1996] 2006), *An Introductory Dictionary of Lacanian Psychoanalysis*, London and New York: Routledge.
Evans, Peter W. (1995), *The Films of Luis Buñuel: Subjectivity and Desire*, Oxford: Clarendon Press.
Every Day (2018), [Film] dir. Michael Sucsy, USA: Likely Story and FilmWave.
Face/Off (1997), [Film] dir. John Woo, USA: Paramount Pictures, Touchstone Pictures and Permut Presentations.
Fan, Victor. (2012), "Redressing the Inaccessible through the Re-inscribed Body: *In a Year with 13 Moons* and Almodóvar's *Bad Education*," in Brigitte Peucker (ed.), *A Companion to Rainer Werner Fassbinder*, 118-41, Malden, MA and Oxford: Blackwell Publishing.
Felicia's Journey (1999), [Film] dir. Atom Egoyan, Canada/UK: Alliance Atlantis Communications, Icon Entertainment International, Icon Productions, Marquis Films Ltd., Screenventures XLIII and The Movie Network (TMN).
Fellini, Federico. (1976), *Fellini on Fellini*, eds. Anna Keel and Christian Strich, and trans. Isabelle Quigley, New York: Delacourt Press/Seymour Lawrence.
Fellini, Federico. (2008), *Federico Fellini: The Book of Dreams*, eds. Tullio Kezich and Vittorio Boarini, trans. Aaron Maines and David Stanton, New York: Rizzoli. http://www.premiere
Fellini, je suis un grand menteur [*Fellini, I'm a Born Liar*] (2002), [Film] dir. Damian Pettigrew, France/Italy/UK: Arte, Portrait & Cie, Tele+, and Dream Film.
Female Trouble (1974), [Film] dir. John Waters, USA: Dreamland.
Fernley, Allison and Paula Maloof. (1985), "*Yentl*," *Film Quarterly*, 38 (3): 38-46.
Fight Club (1999), [Film] dir. David Fincher, USA: Fox 2000 Pictures, Regency Enterprises and Linson Films.
Fink, Bruce. ([1995] 1997), *The Lacanian Subject: Between Language and Jouissance*, Princeton, NJ: Princeton University Press.
Flawless (1999), [Film] dir. Joel Schumacher, USA: Tribeca Productions.

Fletcher, John. (1995), "Primal Scenes and the Female Gothic: *Rebecca* and *Gaslight*," *Screen*, 36 (4): 341–70
Flinn, Caryl. (1995), "The Deaths of Camp," *Camera Obscura*, 35: 53–84.
A Florida Enchantment (1914), [Film] dir. Sidney Drew, USA: Vitagraph Company of America.
Freaky Friday (1976), [Film] dir. Gary Nelson, USA: Walt Disney Pictures.
Freaky Friday (2003), [Film] dir. Mark S. Waters, USA: Casual Friday Productions, Gunn Films and Walt Disney Pictures.
Freud, Sigmund. ([1909] 1955), "Analysis of a Phobia in a Five-Year-Old Boy," in James Strachey (ed. and trans.), *The Standard Edition of the Complete Psychological Works of Sigmund Freud, Volume X (1909): Two Case Histories ("Little Hans" and the "Rat Man")*, 1–150, London: The Hogarth Press and the Institute of Psychoanalysis.
Freud, Sigmund. ([1918] 1955), "From the History of an Infantile Neurosis," in James Strachey (ed. and trans.), *The Standard Edition of the Complete Psychological Works of Sigmund Freud, Volume XVII (1917–1919): An Infantile Neurosis and Other Works*, 1–124, London: The Hogarth Press and the Institute of Psychoanalysis.
Freud, Sigmund. ([1919] 1955a), "A Child Is Being Beaten: A Contribution to the Study of the Origin of Sexual Perversions," in James Strachey (ed. and trans.), *The Standard Edition of the Complete Psychological Works of Sigmund Freud, Volume XVII (1917–1919): An Infantile Neurosis and Other Works*, 175–204, London: The Hogarth Press and the Institute of Psychoanalysis.
Freud, Sigmund. ([1919] 1955b), "The 'Uncanny,'" in James Strachey (ed. and trans.), *The Standard Edition of the Complete Psychological Works of Sigmund Freud, Volume XVII (1917–1919): An Infantile Neurosis and Other Works*, 217–56, London: The Hogarth Press and the Institute of Psychoanalysis.
Freud, Sigmund. ([1913] 1958), "Totem and Taboo: Some Points of Agreement between the Mental Lives of Savages and Neurotics," in James Strachey (ed. and trans.), *The Standard Edition of the Complete Psychological Works of Sigmund Freud, Volume XIII (1913–1914): Totem and Taboo and Other Works*, 1–161, London: The Hogarth Press and the Institute of Psychoanalysis.
Freud, Sigmund. ([1907] 1959), "Delusions and Dreams in Jensen's *Gradiva*," in James Strachey (ed. and trans.), *The Standard Edition of the Complete Psychological Works of Sigmund Freud, Volume IX (1906–1908): Jensen's "Gradiva" and Other Works*, 1–96, London: The Hogarth Press and the Institute of Psychoanalysis.
Freud, Sigmund. ([1908] 1959), "'Civilized' Sexual Morality and Modern Nervous Illness," in James Strachey (ed. and trans.), *The Standard Edition of the Complete Psychological Works of Sigmund Freud, Volume IX (1906–1908): Jensen's "Gradiva" and Other Works*, 177–204, London: The Hogarth Press and the Institute of Psychoanalysis.
Freud, Sigmund. ([1923] 1961), "The Ego and the Id," in James Strachey (ed. and trans.), *The Standard Edition of the Complete Psychological Works of Sigmund Freud, Volume XIX (1923–1925): The Ego and the Id and Other Works*, 1–66, London: The Hogarth Press and the Institute of Psychoanalysis.
Freud, Sigmund. ([1924] 1961), "The Dissolution of the Oedipus Complex," in James Strachey (ed. and trans.), *The Standard Edition of the Complete*

Psychological Works of Sigmund Freud, Volume XIX (1923-1925): The Ego and the Id and Other Works, 171-80, London: The Hogarth Press and the Institute of Psychoanalysis.

Freud, Sigmund. ([1927] 1961), "Fetishism," in James Strachey (ed. and trans.), *The Standard Edition of the Complete Psychological Works of Sigmund Freud, Volume XXI (1927-1931): The Future of an Illusion, Civilization and its Discontents, and Other Works*, 147-58, London: The Hogarth Press and the Institute of Psychoanalysis.

Freud, Sigmund. ([1899] 1997), *The Interpretation of Dreams*, trans. A. A. Brill, London: Wordsworth Editions.

Friedberg, Anne. (1990), "An Unheimlich Maneuver between Psychoanalysis and the Cinema: *Secrets of a Soul* (1926)," in Eric Rentschler (ed.), *The Films of G. W. Pabst: An Extraterritorial Cinema*, 41-51, New Brunswick, NJ and London: Rutgers University Press.

Fuller, Graham. (2001), "Babes in Babylon," *Sight & Sound*, December: 14-17.

Gabbard, Glen O. (1998), "*Vertigo*: Female Objectification, Male Desire, and Object Loss," *Psychoanalytic Inquiry*, 18 (2): 161-7.

Gabriel, Gilbert. (2011), "Altered States, Altered Sounds: An Investigation of how 'Subjective States' are Signified by the Soundtrack in Narrative Fiction Cinema," PhD diss., Centre for Language and Communication Research, Cardiff University.

Galoppe, Raúl A. (2003), "From *Some Like It Hot* to Lacan's Sexuation Theory: "Imperfect" Explorations of Sex, Gender and Desire," in Peter Schulman and Frederick Alfred Lubich (eds.), *The Marketing of Eros: Performance, Sexuality, Consumer Culture*, 38-50, Essen, Germany: Die Blaue Eule.

Gansky, Paul. (2013), "Severed Objects: Spellbound, Archives, Exhibitions, and Film's Material History," *Film History*, 25 (3): 126-48.

Garber, Marjorie. (1997), *Vested Interests: Cross-Dressing and Cultural Anxiety*, London and New York: Routledge.

Geheimnisse Einer Seele [*Secrets of a Soul*] (1926), [Film] dir. G. W. Pabst, Germany: Neumann-Filmproduktion.

Gendernauts: A Journey through Shifting Identities (1999), [Film] dir. Monika Treut, USA/Germany: Hyena Films.

Gherovici, Patricia. (2017), "Depathologizing Trans: From Symptom to Sinthome," *TSQ Transgender Studies Quarterly*, 3-4 (4): 534-55.

Giannopoulou, Zina. (2013), "*Mulholland Drive* and Cinematic Reflexivity," in Zina Giannopoulou (ed.), *Mulholland Drive*, 53-74, London and New York: Routledge.

Gieri, Manuela. (1995), *Contemporary Italian Filmmaking: Strategies of Subversion—Pirandello, Fellini, Scola and the Directors of the New Generation*, Toronto, Buffalo and London: University of Toronto Press.

Gilda (1946), [Film] dir. Charles Vidor, USA: Columbia Pictures Corporation.

Giulietta degli Spiriti [*Juliet of the Spirits*] (1965), [Film] dir. Federico Fellini, Italy/France: Rizzoli Film and Francoriz Production.

The Glass Castle (2017), [Film] dir. Destin Daniel Cretton, USA: Netter Productions.

Gleiberman, Owen. (2001), "*Mulholland Drive*," *Entertainment Weekly*, October 19. http://www.ew.com/ew/article/0,,253984,00.html (accessed December 30, 2018).

Gone With the Wind (1939), [Film] dir. Victor Fleming, USA: Selznick International Pictures and MGM.
The Great Dictator (1940), [Film] dir. Charlie Chaplin, USA: Charles Chaplin Productions and One Production Company.
Greven, David. (2017), "Mirrors without Images: *Spellbound*," in *Intimate Violence: Hitchcock, Sex, and Queer Theory*, 81–112, Oxford: Oxford University Press.
Grosz, Elizabeth. (1994), "Women, Chora, Dwelling," *ANY: Architecture New York*, 4: 22–7.
Guinn, Jeff and Douglas Perry. (2005), *The Sixteenth Minute: Life in the Aftermath of Fame*, New York: Tarcher.
Gutiérrez-Albilla, Julián Daniel. (2013), "Scratching the Past on the Surface of the Skin: Embodied Intersubjectivity, Prosthetic Memory, and Witnessing in Almodóvar's *La mala educación*," in Marvin D'Lugo and Kathleen M. Vernon (eds.), *A Companion to Pedro Almodóvar*, 322–44, Malden, MA and Oxford: Blackwell Publishing.
Hairspray (1988), [Film] dir. John Waters, USA: Palace Pictures.
Hairspray (2007), [Film] dir. Adam Shankman, USA: Ingenious Media and Zadan/Meron Productions.
Halberstam, J. Jack. (1998), *Female Masculinity*, Durham and London: Duke University Press.
Halberstam, J. Jack. (2001), "The Transgender Gaze in *Boys Don't Cry*," *Screen*, 42 (3): 294–8.
Halberstam, J. Jack. (2005), *In a Queer Time and Place: Transgender Bodies, Subcultural Lives*, New York: New York University Press
Halberstam, J. Jack and Del LaGrace Volcano. (1999), *The Drag King Book*, London: Serpent's Tail.
Hanke, Robert. (1999), "John Woo's Cinema of Hyperkinetic Violence: From *A Better Tomorrow* to *Face/Off*," *Film Criticism*, 24 (1): 39–59.
Hayles, Katherine N. and Nicholas Gessler. (2004), "The Slipstream of Mixed Reality: Unstable Ontologies and Semiotic Markers in *The Thirteenth Floor*, *Dark City*, and *Mulholland Drive*," *PMLA*, 119 (3): 482–99.
Her (2013), [Film] dir. Spike Jonze, USA: Annapurna Pictures.
Hodge, James J. (2014–15), "Gifts of Ubiquity," *Film Criticism*, 39 (2): 53–78.
Hoffmann, E. T. A. ([1816] 1969), "The Sandman," in Leonard J. Kent and Elizabeth C. Knight (eds. and trans.), *Tales of E. T. A. Hoffmann*, 93–125, Chicago: The University of Chicago Press.
The Host (2013), [Film] dir. Andrew Niccol, USA: Chockstone Pictures and Nick Wechsler Productions.
Hudson, Jennifer A. (2004), "'No Hay Banda, and Yet We Hear a Band': David Lynch's Reversal of Coherence in *Mulholland Drive*," *Journal of Film and Video*, 56 (1): 17–24.
Hughes-D'Aeth, Tony. (2013), "Psychoanalysis and the Scene of Love: *Lars and the Real Girl*, *In the Mood for Love*, and *Mulholland Drive*," *Film and History: An Interdisciplinary Journal of Film and Television Studies*, 43 (2): 17–33.
Huntjens, Joyce. (2003), "*Vertigo*: A Vertiginous Gap in Reality and a Woman Who doesn't Exist," *Image [&] Narrative: Online Magazine of the Visual Narrative*,

5, January. http://www.imageandnarrative.be/inarchive/uncanny/joycehuntjens.htm (accessed December 30, 2018).

I'm Not There (2007), [Film] dir. Todd Haynes, USA/Germany: Endgame Entertainment, Killer Films, John Goldwyn Productions and John Wells Productions.

Intolerance: Love's Struggle throughout the Ages (1916), [Film] dir. D. W. Griffith's, USA: Triangle Film Corporation and Wark Producing.

Irigaray, Luce. ([1974] 1985), "Plato's Hystera," in Gillian C. Gill (trans.), *Speculum of the Other Woman*, 243–364, Ithaca, NY and London: Cornell University Press.

Jeffers McDonald, Tamar. (2007), "Carrying Concealed Weapons: Gendered Makeover in *Calamity Jane*," *Journal of Popular Film & Television*, 34 (4): 179–87.

Jefferson, Ann. (1983), "'Mise-en-Abyme' and the Prophetic in Narrative," *Style* 17 (2): 196–208.

Johnson, Robert K. (1977), "A Conversation in Private," in *Francis Ford Coppola*, 127–44, Boston: Twayne Publishers.

Jones, Ernest. ([1949] 1976), *Hamlet and Oedipus*, New York: W. W. Norton & Company.

Kaminski, Elizabeth and Verta Taylor. (2008), "'We're Not Just Lip-Synching Up Here': Music and Collective Identity in Drag Performances," in Jo Reger, Daniel J. Meyers and Rachel L. Einwohner (eds.), *Identity Work in Social Movements*, 47–76, Minneapolis: University of Minnesota Press.

Kaplan, E. Ann Ann. (2005), "Melodrama and Trauma: Displacement in Hitchcock's *Spellbound*," in *Trauma Culture: The Politics of Terror and Loss in Media and Literature*, 66–86, New Brunswick, NJ and London: Rutgers University Press.

Kennes Ha'atidanim [*The Congress*] (2013), [Film] dir. Ari Folman, Israel/Germany/Poland/Luxembourg/Belgium/France/USA: Bridgit Folman Film Gang and Pandora Filmproduktion.

Kenny, Glenn. (2001). "*Mulholland Drive*," *Premiere the Movie Magazine*, October 12.

Kind Hearts and Coronets (1949), [Film] dir. Robert Hamer, UK: Ealing Studios and Michael Balcon Productions.

King, Barry. (1991), "Articulating Stardom," in Christine Gledhill (ed.), *Stardom: Industry of Desire*, 169–82, London and New York: Routledge.

Kinkade, Patrick T. and Michael A. Katovich. (1992), "Toward a Sociology of Cult Films: Reading *Rocky Horror*," *The Sociological Quarterly*, 33 (2): 191–209.

Kley, Martin. (2007), "German Romanticism Goes to Hollywood: Heinrich von Kleist's *On the Puppet Theater* and *Being John Malkovich*," *South Central Review*, 24 (3): 23–35.

Klock, Geoff. (2017), "'Goodnight, Sweet Betty': Levels of Illusion in *Mulholland Drive* and *Hamlet*," *Quarterly Review of Film and Video*, 34 (1), 50–65.

Kohen-Raz, Odeya and Sandra Meiri. (2018), "Revisiting Metz: Bodiless-Character Films and the Dynamic of Desire/Fantasy in Narrative Cinema," *New Review of Film and Television Studies*, 16 (1): 62–80.

Kornhaber, Donna. (2017), "From Posthuman to Postcinema: Crises of Subjecthood and Representation in *Her*," *Cinema Journal*, 56 (4): 3–25.

Kovács, András Bálint. (2007), "Things that Come after Another," *New Review of Film and Television Studies*, 5 (2): 157–71.
Kracauer, Siegfried. ([1960] 1997), *Theory of Film: The Redemption of Physical Reality*, Princeton, NJ: Princeton University Press.
Der Krieger und die Kaiserin [*The Princess and the Warrior*] (2000), [Film] dir. Tom Tykwer, Germany: X-Filme Creative Pool and Westdeutscher Rundfunk (WDR).
Kristeva, Julia. ([1974] 1984), *Revolution in Poetic Language*, trans. Margaret Waller, New York: Columbia University Press.
Kristeva, Julia. ([1979] 1995), "Women's Time," in Ross Guberman (trans.), *New Maladies of the Soul*, 201–24, New York: Columbia University Press.
Kristeva, Julia. ([1997–8] 2002), *Intimate Revolt: The Powers and Limits of Psychoanalysis*, trans. Jeanine Herman, New York: Columbia University Press.
Kuhn, Annette. (1987), "Sexual Disguise and Cinema," in *The Power of the Image: Essays on Representation and Sexuality*, 48–73, London and New York: Routledge.
Lacan, Jacques. ([1959] 1977), "Desire and the Interpretation of Desire in *Hamlet*," *Yale French Studies*, 55/56: 11–52.
Lacan, Jacques. ([1956–7] 1994), *Le séminaire de Jacques Lacan, Livre IV: La relation d'objet et les structures freudiennes*, Paris: Publication interne de l'Association freudienne internationale.
Lacan, Jacques. ([1959–60] 1997), *The Seminar of Jacques Lacan, Book VII: The Ethics of Psychoanalysis*, ed. Jacques-Alain Miller and trans. Dennis Porter, New York and London: W. W. Norton & Company.
Lacan, Jacques. ([1964] 1998), *The Seminar of Jacques Lacan, Book XI: The Four Fundamental Concepts of Psychoanalysis*, ed. Jacques-Alain Miller and trans. Alan Sheridan, New York and London: W. W. Norton & Company.
Lacan, Jacques. ([1972–3] 1999), *The Seminar of Jacques Lacan, Book XX: On Feminine Sexuality, The Limits of Love and Knowledge, 1972–1973, Encore*, ed. Jacques-Alain Miller and trans. Bruce Fink, New York and London: W. W. Norton & Company.
Lacan, Jacques. ([1949/1966] 2006), "The Mirror Stage as Formative of the Function of the I as Revealed in Psychoanalytic Experience," in Bruce Fink (trans.), *Écrits*, 75–81, New York and London: W. W. Norton & Company.
Lacan, Jacques. ([1958/1966] 2006), "The Significance of the Phallus," in Bruce Fink (trans.), *Écrits*, 575–84, New York and London: W. W. Norton & Company.
Lacan, Jacques. ([1960/1966] 2006), "The Subversion of the Subject and the Dialectic of Desire in the Freudian Unconscious," in Bruce Fink (trans.), *Écrits*, 671–702, New York and London: W. W. Norton & Company.
Lacan, Jacques. ([1962–3] 2014), *The Seminar of Jacques Lacan, Book X: Anxiety*, ed. Jacques-Alain Miller and trans. A. Rea Price, New York: Polity Press.
Lady in the Lake (1947), [Film] dir. Robert Montgomery, USA: MGM.
Laine, Tarja. (2009), "Affective Telepathy, or the Intuition of the Heart: *Persona* with *Mulholland Drive*," *New Review of Film and Television Studies*, 7 (3): 325–38
Lalechet al hamayim [*Walk on Water*] (2004), [Film] dir. Eytan Fox, Israel: Lama Productions and United King Films.

Landsberg, Alison. (2004), *Prosthetic Memory*, New York: Columbia University Press.
Laplanche, Jean and Jean-Bertrand Pontalis. ([1967] 1973), *The Language of Psychoanalysis*, trans. Donald Nicholson-Smith, New York: W. W. Norton & Company.
Laplanche, Jean and Jean-Bertrand Pontalis. ([1964] 1986), "Fantasy and the Origins of Sexuality," in Victor Burgin, James Donald and Cora Kaplan (eds.), *Formations of Fantasy*, 5–34, London and New York: Routledge.
Laura (1944), [Film] dir. Otto Preminger, USA: Twentieth Century Fox.
Lentzner, Jay R. and Donald R. Ross. (2005), "The Dream That Blister Sleep: Latent Content and Cinematic Form in *Mulholland Drive*," *American Imago*, 62 (1): 101–23.
Letter to Jane: An Investigation about a Still (1972), [Film] dir. Jean-Luc Godard and Jean-Pierre Gorin, France: Sonimage.
La ley del deseo [*Law of Desire*] (1987), [Film] dir. Pedro Almodóvar, Spain: El Deseo and Laurenfilm.
Lieberfeld, Daniel. (1998), "Keeping the Characters Straight: Comedy and Identity in *Some Like It Hot*," *Journal of Popular Film & Television*, 23 (3): 128–35.
The Life and Death of Peter Sellers (2004), [Film] dir. Stephen Hopkins, USA/UK: HBO Films, BBC Films, Company Pictures and De Mann Entertainment.
Like Father Like Son (1987), [Film] dir. Rod Daniel, USA: Imagine Films Entertainment.
Lopate, Phillip. (2001), "Welcome to L.A.: *Muhlolland Drive*," *Film Comment*, September–October: 44–50.
Lost Highway (1997), [Film] dir. David Lynch, USA/France: CiBy 2000, Asymmetrical Productions and Lost Highway Productions LLC.
Love, Heather. (2004), "Spectacular Failure: The Figure of the Lesbian in *Mulholland Drive*," *New Literary History*, 35 (1): 117–32.
Loving (2016), [Film] dir. Jeff Nichols, USA/UK: Raindog Films and Big Beach Films.
Lukacher, Ned. (1986), *Primal Scenes: Literature, Philosophy, Psychoanalysis*, Ithaca, NY and London: Cornell University Press.
Ma Vie en rose [*My Life in Pink*] (1997), [Film] dir. Alain Berliner, Belgium/France: Canal+, Eurimages, CNC and TF1 Films Production.
MacTaggart, Allister. (2010), *The Film Paintings of David Lynch: Challenging Film Theory*, Bristol, UK: Intellect.
La mala educación [*Bad Education*] (2004), [Film] dir. Pedro Almodóvar, Spain: El Deseo, Canal+ España and Televisión Española.
Maltby, Richard. (1995), *Hollywood Cinema*, Malden, MA and Oxford: Blackwell Publishing.
The Man in the Iron Mask (1998), [Film] dir. Randall Wallace, USA/France: United Artists.
The Man Who Wasn't There (2001), [Film] dir. Joel and Ethan Coen, USA/UK: Working Title Films, Gramercy Pictures, Good Machine, Mike Zoss Productions and Constantin Film.
Manlove, Clifford T. (2007), "Visual 'Drive' and Cinematic Narrative: Reading Gaze Theory in Lacan, Hitchcock, and Mulvey," *Cinema Journal*, 46 (3): 83–108.

Margaroni, Maria. (2005), "The Lost Foundation: Kristeva's Semiotic Chōra and Its Ambiguous Legacy," *Hypatia*, 20 (1): 78–98.
Mary Reilly (1996), [Film] dir. Stephen Frears, UK/USA: NFH Productions.
The Masquerader (1914), [Film] dir. Charlie Chaplin, USA: Keystone Film Company.
Mayne, Judith. (1993), "Star-Gazing," in *Cinema and Spectatorship*, 123–41, London and New York: Routledge.
McGowan, Todd. (2004), "Lost in Mulholland Drive: Navigating David Lynch's Panegyric to Hollywood," *Cinema Journal*, 43 (2): 67–89.
McGowan, Todd. (2007a), *The Impossible David Lynch*, New York: Columbia University Press.
McGowan, Todd. (2007b), *The Real Gaze: Film Theory after Lacan*, New York: State University of New York Press.
McGowan, Todd. (2015), *Psychoanalytic Film Theory and "The Rules of the Game,"* New York and London: Bloomsbury Academic.
McMahon, Jennifer. (2011), "City of Dreams: Bad Faith in *Mulholland Dr.*," in William J. Devlin and Shai Biderman (eds.), *The Philosophy of David Lynch*, 113–26, Lexington, KY: University Press of Kentucky.
Meiri, Sandra. (2011), "The (Po)Et(h)ics of Horror: The Transvestite Killer Revisited," in Boaz Hagin, Sandra Meiri, Raz Yosef and Anat Zanger (eds.), *Just Images: Ethics and the Cinematic*, 192–211, Newcastle upon Tyne: Cambridge Scholars Publishing.
Meiri, Sandra and Odeya Kohen-Raz. (2017), "Mainstream Body-Character Breach Films and Subjectivization," *The International Journal of Psychoanalysis*, 98 (1): 201–17.
Le Mépris [*Contempt*] (1963), [Film] dir. Jean-Luc Godard, France/Italy: Rome Paris Films, Les Films Concordia and Compagnia Cinematografica Champion.
Metz, Christian. ([1975] 1976), "The Fiction Film and Its Spectator: A Metapsychological Study," trans. Alfred Guzzetti, *New Literary History*, 8 (1): 75–105.
Metz, Christian. (1980), "Aural Objects," *Yale French Studies*, 60: 30–40.
Metz, Christian. ([1977] 1982), *The Imaginary Signifier: Psychoanalysis and Cinema*, trans. Celia Britton, Annwyl Williams, Ben Brewster and Alfred Guzzetti, Bloomington and Indianapolis: Indiana University Press.
Metz, Christian. ([1968] 1991), *Film Language: A Semiotics of Cinema*, trans. Michael Taylor, Chicago: The University of Chicago Press.
Meyer, Moe. (1994), "Reclaiming the Discourse of Camp," in *The Politics and Poetics of Camp*, 1–22, London and New York: Routledge.
Michael Jackson: Searching for Neverland. (2017), [Film] dir. Dianne Houston, USA: Lifetime and Silver Screen Pictures.
Miller, D. A. (1990), "Anal *Rope*," *Representations*, 32: 114–33.
Miller, Lucy J. (2017), "Fear and the Cisgender Audience: Transgender Representation and Audience Identification in Sleepaway Camp," *The Spectator*, 37 (2): 40–7.
Modleski, Tania. (2016), *The Women Who Knew Too Much: Hitchcock and Feminist Theory*, London and New York: Routledge.
Monaco, James. (1981), *How to Read a Film: The Art, Technology, History and Theory of Film and Media*, Oxford and New York: Oxford University Press.

Monsieur Klein [*Mr. Klein*]. (1976), [Film] dir. Joseph Losey, France/Italy: Lira Films, Adel Productions, Nova Films and Mondial Televisione Film.
The Mouse That Roared (1959), [Film] dir. Jack Arnold, UK: Highroad Productions and Columbia Pictures Corporation.
Una mujer fantástica [*A Fantastic Woman*] (2017), [Film] dir. Sebastián Lelio, Chile/Germany/USA/Spain: Muchas Gracias, Komplizen Film, Participant Media and Setembro Cine.
Mulholland Drive (2001), [Film] dir. David Lynch, USA/France: Les Films Alain Sarde, Asymmetrical Productions, Babbo Inc., Canal+ and The Picture Factory.
Mulvey, Laura. (1975), "Visual Pleasure and Narrative Cinema," *Screen*, 16 (3): 6–18.
Mulvey, Laura. (1981), "Afterthoughts on 'Visual Pleasure and Narrative Cinema' inspired by King Vidor's *Duel in the Sun* (1946)," *Framework: The Journal of Cinema and Media*, 15/17: 12–15.
Mulvey, Laura. (2006), *Death 24x a Second: Stillness and the Moving Image*, London: Reaktion Books.
Myra Breckinridge (1970), [Film] dir. Michael Sarne, USA: Twentieth Century Fox.
Naremore, James. (2008), "Noir in the Twenty-First Century," in *More than Night: Film Noir in Its Contexts*, 278–310, Berkeley, Los Angeles and London: University of California Press.
Newton, Esther. (1972), *Mother Camp: Female Impersonators in America*, Chicago: The University of Chicago Press.
Nieland, Justus. (2012), *David Lynch*, Urbana: University of Illinois Press.
Nochimson, Martha P. (2002), "*Mulholland Drive*," *Film Quarterly*, 56 (1): 37–45.
Nochimson, Martha P. (2013), "*Mulholland Dr.*: An Improbable Girl in a Probable World," in *David Lynch Swerves: Uncertainty from Lost Highway to Inland Empire*, 89–121, Austin: University of Texas Press.
North by Northwest (1959), [Film] dir. Alfred Hitchcock, USA: MGM.
Une nouvelle amie [*The New Girlfriend*] (2015), [Film] dir. François Ozon, France: Mandarin Films, Mars Films and France 2 Cinéma.
The Object of Beauty (1991), [Film] dir. Michael Lindsay-Hogg, UK/USA: Avenue Pictures, BBC and Winston Films.
Olson, Greg. (2008), *David Lynch: Beautiful Dark*, Lanham, MD: The Scarecrow Press.
Orlando (1992), [Film] dir. Sally Potter, UK/Russia/France/Italy/The Netherlands: Adventure Pictures, Lenfilm Studio, Mikado Film, Rio and Sigma Film Productions.
Pacchioni, Federico. (2014), *Inspiring Fellini: Literary Collaborations Behind the Scenes*, Toronto, Buffalo and London: University of Toronto Press.
Palindromes (2004), [Film] dir. Todd Solondz, USA: Extra Large Pictures.
Parciack, Ronie. (2011), "The World as Illusion: Rediscovering *Mulholland Dr.* and *Lost Highway* through Indian Philosophy," in William J. Devlin and Shai Biderman (eds.), *The Philosophy of David Lynch*, 77–92. Lexington, KY: University Press of Kentucky.
Pattison, Michael. (2013), "In Dreams and Imagination: Surrealist Values in *Mulholland Dr.* and *Inland Empire*," *Senses of Cinema*, 66, March. http://sensesofcinema.com/2013/feature-articles/in-dreams-and-imagination-surrealist-values-in-mulholland-dr-and-inland-empire/ (accessed December 30, 2018).

Perlmutter, Ruth. (2005), "Memories, Dreams, Screens," *Quarterly Review of Film and Video*, 22 (2): 125–34.
The Pervert's Guide to Cinema (2006), [Film] dir. Sophie Fiennes, UK/Austria/The Netherlands: Amoeba Film, Kasander Film Company, Lone Star Productions and Mischief Films.
Pettigrew, Damian. (2003), *I'm a Born Liar: A Fellini Lexicon*, New York: Harry N. Abrams.
Phillips, John. (2006), *Transgender on Screen*, New York: Palgrave Macmillan.
Pidduck, Julianne. (2001), "Risk and Queer Spectatorship," *Screen*, 42 (1): 97–102.
La piel que habito [*The Skin I Live In*] (2011), [Film] dir. Pedro Almodóvar, Spain: El Deseo, Canal+ España and Televisión Española.
Pink Flamingos (1972), [Film] dir. John Waters, USA: Dreamland.
Plato. 2008, "Timaeus," in *Timaeus and Critias*, trans. Robin Waterfield, 1–100, Oxford: Oxford University Press.
The Portrait of a Lady (1996), [Film] dir. Jane Campion, UK/USA: Polygram Filmed Entertainment and Propaganda Films.
Posadas, Marco. (2017), "Psychoanalysis and Psychoanalytic Theory as Tools to Increase Trans Visibility," *TSQ: Transgender Studies Quarterly*, 4 (3–4): 647–53.
Poslednata lineika na Sofia [*Sofia's Last Ambulance*] (2012), [Film] dir. Llian Metev, Bulgaria/Germany/Croatia: Sutor Kolonko and Nukleus Film.
Price, Zachary. (2015), "Skin Gazing: Queer Bodies in Almodóvar's *The Skin I Live In*," *Horror Studies*, 6 (2): 305–17.
Psycho (1960), [Film] dir. Alfred Hitchcock, USA: Shamley Productions.
Queen Christina (1933), [Film] dir. Rouben Mamoulian, USA: MGM.
Queens of Heart: Community Therapists in Drag (2006), [Film] dir. Jan Haaken, USA: Kwamba Productions and Portland State University.
Ratner, Megan. (2001), "Notes on *The Conversation* (Francis Ford Coppola, 1974)," *Senses of Cinema*, 13, April. http://sensesofcinema.com/2001/70s-us-cinema/conversation/ (accessed December 30, 2018).
Rear Window (1954), [Film] dir. Alfred Hitchcock, USA: Patron inc.
Rebecca (1940), [Film] dir. Alfred Hitchcock, USA: Selznick International Pictures.
Reed, Katherine M. (2016), "'We Cannot Content Ourselves with Remaining Spectators': Musical Performance, Audience Interaction, and Nostalgia in the Films of David Lynch," *Music and the Moving Image*, 9 (1): 3–22.
Reitz, Nikki. (2017), "The Representation of Trans Women in Film and Television," *Cinesthesia*, 7 (1): 1–7.
Repass, Scott. (2002), "*Being John Malkovich* Review," *Film Quarterly*, 56 (1): 29–36.
Ridgway, Franklin. (2006), "'You Came Back!' or Mulholland Treib," *Post Script: Essays in Film and the Humanities*, 26 (1): 43–61.
Rigney, Melissa. (2003–4), "Brandon Goes to Hollywood: *Boys Don't Cry* and the Transgender Body in Film," *Film Criticism*, 28 (2): 4–23.
The Rocky Horror Picture Show (1975), [Film] dir. Jim Sharman, UK/USA: Twentieth Century Fox and Michael White Productions.
Romeo and Juliet (1968), [Film] dir. Franco Zeffirelli, UK/Italy: BHE Films, Verona Produzione and Dino de Laurentiis Cinematografica.
Rope (1948), [Film] dir. Alfred Hitchcock, USA: Transatlantic Pictures.

Rose, Jacqueline. (1982), "Introduction II," in Juliet Mitchel and Jacqueline Rose (eds.), *Feminine Sexuality: Jacques Lacan and the école freudienne*, 27–57, New York and London: W. W. Norton & Company.

Rosen, Philip. (2011), "Belief in Bazin," in Dudley Andrew (ed.), *Opening Bazin: Postwar Film Theory and Its Afterlife*, 107–18, Oxford: Oxford University Press.

Roustang, François. (1983), *Psychoanalysis Never Lets Go*, trans. Ned Lukacher, Baltimore, MD: Johns Hopkins University Press.

Rushing, Robert A. (2010), "Blink: The Material Real in *Cache*, *Mulholland Dr.* and *Doctor Who*," *Post Script: Essays in Film and the Humanities*, 30 (1): 21–34.

Rushton, Richard. (2004), "The Psychoanalytic Structure of Trauma: *Spellbound*," *Journal for Cultural Research*, 8 (3): 371–84.

Simone (2002), [Film] dir. Andrew Niccol, USA: Niccol Films.

San Filippo, Maria. (2016), "Female Trouble: Representing Transwomen in *The Danish Girl* and *The New Girlfriend*," *Journal of Bisexuality*, 16 (3): 403–7.

Savoy, Eric. (1999), "'That Ain't All She Ain't': Doris Day and Queer Performativity," in Ellis Hanson (ed.), *Out Takes: Essays on Queer Theory and Film*, 151–82, Durham and London: Duke University Press.

Schatz, Thomas. (1988), *The Genius of the System: Hollywood Filmmaking in the Studio Era*, New York: Pantheon Books.

Schindler's List (1993), [Film] dir. Steven Spielberg, USA: Amblin Entertainment.

Segal, Naomi. (2009), *Consensuality: Didier Anzieu, Gender and the Sense of Touch*, Amsterdam: Radopi.

Shallow Hal (2001), [Film] dir. Bobby Farrelly and Peter Farrelly, USA/Germany: Conundrum Entertainment and Shallow Hal Filmproduktion GmbH & Co. KG.

Shaw, Daniel. (2006), "On Being Philosophical and *Being John Malkovich*," *Journal of Aesthetics and Art Criticism*, 64 (1): 111–18.

Shetley, Vernon. (2006), "The Presence of the Past: *Mulholland Drive* against *Vertigo*," *Raritan*, 25 (3): 112–28.

Shostak, Debra. (2008), "Dancing in Hollywood's Blue Box: Genre and Screen Memories in *Mulholland Drive*," *Post Script: Essays in Film and the Humanities*, 28 (1): 3–21.

Sikov, Ed. (1994), *Laughing Hysterically: American Screen Comedies of the 1950s*, New York: Columbia University Press.

The Silence of the Lambs (1991), [Film] dir. Jonathan Demme, USA: Strong Heart/ Demme Production and Orion Pictures

Sinnerbrink, Robert. (2013), "Silencio: *Mulholland Drive* as Cinematic Romanticism," in Zina Giannopoulou (ed.), *Mulholland Drive*, 75–96, London and New York: Routledge.

Sloop, John M. (2000), "Disciplining the Transgendered: Brandon Teena, Public Representation, and Normativity," *Western Journal of Communication*, 62 (2): 165–89.

Smoke (1995), [Film] dir. Wayne Wang, USA/Germany/Japan: NDF, Euro Space and Smoke Productions.

Smultronstallet [*Wild Strawberries*] (1957), [Film] dir. Ingmar Bergman, Sweden: Svensk Filmindustri.

Snorton, Riley C. (2017), *Black on Both Sides: A Racial History of Trans Identity*, Minneapolis: The University of Minnesota Press.
Sobchack, Vivian. (1994), "Phenomenology and the Film Experience," in Linda Williams (ed.), *Viewing Positions: Ways of Seeing Film*, 36–58, New Brunswick, NJ and London: Rutgers University Press.
Solmi, Angelo. ([1962] 1967), *Fellini*, trans. Elizabeth Greenwood, London: Merlin Press.
Some Like It Hot (1959), [Film] dir. Billy Wilder, USA: Ashton Productions and The Mirisch Corporation.
Sontag, Susan. (1964), "Notes on 'Camp,'" in *Against Interpretation*, 275–92, New York: Anchor Books.
Spellbound (1945), [Film] dir. Alfred Hitchcock, USA: Selznick International Pictures and Vanguard Films.
Spoto, Donald. (1983), *The Dark Side of Genius: The Life of Alfred Hitchcock*, Boston, MA: Little, Brown and Company.
Stacey, Jackie. (1994), *Star Gazing: Hollywood Cinema and Female Spectatorship*, London and New York: Routledge.
Stam, Robert. (1983), "Hitchcock and Buñuel: Desire and the Law," *Studies in the Literary Imagination*, 16 (1): 7–27.
Steinbock, Eliza. (2009), "Speaking Transsexuality in the Cinematic Tongue," in Nikki Sullivan and Samantha Murray (eds.), *Somatechnics: Queering the Technologisation of Bodies*, 127–52, Farnham, UK: Ashgate Publishing.
Steinbock, Eliza. (2017), "Towards Trans Cinema," in Kristin Lené Hole, Dijana Jelača, E. Ann Kaplan and Patrice Petro (eds.), *The Routledge Companion to Cinema and Gender*, 395–406, London and New York: Routledge.
Stivers, Clint. (2014), "The Perils of Fantasy: Memory and Desire in David Lynch's *Mulholland Drive*," *Senses of Cinema*, 71, June. http://sensesofcinema.com/2014/feature-articles/the-perils-of-fantasy-memory-and-desire-in-david-lynchs-mulholland-drive/ (accessed December 30, 2018).
Straayer, Chris. (1996), "Redressing the 'Natural': The Temporary Transvestite Film," in *Deviant Eyes, Deviant Bodies: Sexual Re-orientations in Film and Video*, 42–78, New York: Columbia University Press.
Strangers on a Train (1951), [Film] dir. Alfred Hitchcock, USA: Warner Bros.
La Strategia del ragno [The Spider's Stratagem] (1972), [Film] dir. Bernardo Bertolucci, Italy: RAI Radiotelevisione Italiana and Red Film.
Stroumsa, Guy G. ([2005] 2009), "Transformations of Ritual," in Susan Emanuel (trans.), *The End of Sacrifice: Religious Transformations in Late Antiquity*, 56–83, Chicago: The University of Chicago Press.
Stubbs, John C. (2002), "Fellini's Portrait of the Artist as Creative Problem Solver," *Cinema Journal*, 41 (4): 116–31.
Stubbs, John C. (2015), *Federico Fellini as Auteur: Seven Aspects of His Films*, Carbondale: Southern Illinois University Press.
Studlar, Gaylyn. (1989), "Midnight S/excess: Cult Configurations of 'Femininity' and the Perverse," *Journal of Popular Film & Television*, 17 (1): 2–14.
Sunset Boulevard (1950), [Film] dir. Billy Wilder, USA: Paramount Pictures.
Switch (1991), [Film] dir. Blake Edwards, USA: Beco Films, Cinema Plus and HBO.
Synecdoche, New York (2008), [Film] dir. Charlie Kaufman, USA: Sidney Kimmel Entertainment.

Tang, Jean. (2001), "All You Have to Do Is Dream," *Salon*, November 7, 2001. https://www.salon.com/2001/11/07/mulholland_dream/ (accessed December 30, 2018).
Tasker, Yvonne. (1998), *Working Girls: Gender and Sexuality in Popular Cinema*, London and New York: Routledge.
Taubin, Amy. (2001), "In Dreams: *Mulholland Drive*," *Film Comment*, September-October: 50-4.
Tavlin, Zachary. (2013), "Singers, Psychos, and the Blues Reading Affect and the Virtual Beyond the Cinematic Subject," *Pennsylvania Literary Journal*, 5 (3): 86-106.
Thomas, Eric Austin. (2015), "Camera Grammar: First-Person Point of View and the Divided 'I' in Rouben Mamoulian's 1931 *Dr. Jekyll and Mr. Hyde*," *Quarterly Review of Film and Video*, 32 (7): 660-6.
Thoreau Bruckner, René. (2008), "Lost Time: Blunt Head Trauma and Accident-Driven Cinema," *Discourse*, 30 (3): 373-400.
To Wong Foo, Thanks for Everything! Julie Newmar (1995), [Film] dir. Beeban Kidron, USA: Amblin Entertainment.
Todo sobre mi madre [All about My Mother] (1999), [Film] dir. Pedro Almodóvar, Spain/France: El Deseo, Renn Productions and France 2 Cinéma.
Toles, George. (2004), "Auditioning Betty in *Mulholland Drive*," *Film Quarterly*, 58 (1): 2-13.
Tomboy (2011), [Film] dir. Céline Sciama, France: Hold Up Films, Arte France Cinéma and Lilies Films.
Tootsie (1982), [Film] dir. Sidney Pollack, USA: Mirage Enterprises and Punch Productions.
Transamerica (2005), [Film] dir. Duncan Tucker, USA: Belladonna Productions.
Treveri Gennari, Daniela. (2013), "Blessed Cinema: State and Catholic Censorship in Postwar Italy," in Daniel Biltereyst and Roel Vande Winkel (eds.), *Silencing Cinema: Film Censorship Around the World*, 255-71, New York: Palgrave Macmillan.
Truffaut, François. ([1966] 1984), *Hitchcock*, New York: Simon and Schuster.
Turan, Kenneth. (2001), "The Twists Along Mulholland," *The Los Angeles Times*, October 12: F21.
Turnabout (1940), [Film] dir. Hal Roach, USA: Hal Roach Studios.
Turner, Dennis. (1985), "The Subject of *The Conversation*," *Cinema Journal*, Summer: 4-22.
Twilight Saga: Breaking Dawn, Part 2 (2012), [Film] dir. Bill Condon, USA: Sunswept Entertainment and Temple Hill Entertainment.
Van Wert, William F. (1979), "Compositional Psychoanalysis: Circles and Straight Lines in *Spellbound*," *Film Criticism*, 3 (3): 41-7.
Vertigo (1958), [Film] dir. Alfred Hitchcock, USA: Alfred J. Hitchcock Productions.
Victor Victoria (1982), [Film] dir. Blake Edwards, USA: MGM and Pinewood Studios.
Viktor und Viktoria (1933), [Film] dir. Reinhold Schünzel, Germany: Universum Film (UFA).
Waldron, Darren and Ros Murray. (2014), "Troubling Transformations: Pedro Almodóvar's *La piel que habito/The Skin I Live In* (2011) and Its Reception," *Transnational Cinemas*, 5 (1): 57-71.

Waller, Marguerite R. (2002), "Introduction," in Frank Burke and Marguerite R. Waller (eds.), *Federico Fellini: Contemporary Perspectives*, 3–25, Toronto, Buffalo and London: University of Toronto Press.

Watson, William Van. (2002), "Fellini and Lacan: The Womb, and the Retying of the Umbilical," in Frank Burke and Marguerite R. Waller (eds.), *Federico Fellini: Contemporary Perspectives*, 65–91, Toronto, Buffalo and London: University of Toronto Press.

Weinstein, Lissa and Banu Seckin. (2008), "The Perverse Cosmos of *Being John Malkovich*: Forms and Transformations of Narcissism in a Celebrity Culture," *Projections*, 2 (1): 27–44.

White, Patricia. (2001), "Girls Still Cry," *Screen*, 42 (2): 217–21.

Wicke, Jennifer. (1997), "Double-Cross-Dressing: The Politics of a Genre," *Annals of Scholarship: An International Quarterly in the Humanities and Social Sciences*, 11 (4): 359–77.

Williams, Linda. (1981), *Figures of Desire: A Theory and Analysis of Surrealist Film*, Berkeley, Los Angeles and London: University of California Press.

Williams, Linda. (1991), "Film Bodies: Gender, Genre and Excess," *Film Quarterly*, 44 (4): 2–13.

Wilson, George and Sam Shpall. (2012), "Unraveling the Twists of *Fight Club*," in Thomas Wartenburg (ed.), *Fight Club: Philosophers on Film*, 78–111, London and New York: Routledge.

Wollen, Peter. (1972), "Godard and Counter Cinema: *Vent D'Est*," *Afterimage*, 4: 6–17.

A Woman (1915), [Film] dir. Charlie Chaplin, USA: The Essanay Film Manufacturing Company.

Yentl (1983), [Film] dir. Barbra Streisand, USA/UK: Ladbroke, Barwood Films and United Artists.

Les yeux sans visage [*Eyes without a Face*] (1960), [Film] dir. Georges Franju, France/Italy: Champs-Élysées Productions and Lux Film.

Zimmer, Catherine. (2015), *Surveillance Cinema*, New York: New York University Press.

Žižek, Slavoj. (1991), *Looking Awry: An Introduction to Jacques Lacan through Popular Culture*, Cambridge, MA: MIT Press.

Žižek, Slavoj. (1992), "Alfred Hitchcock, or, the Form and Its Historical Mediation," in Slavoj Žižek (ed.), *Everything You Always Wanted to Know about Lacan (But Were Afraid to Ask Hitchcock)*, 1–12, New York: Verso.

Žižek, Slavoj. (1994), *The Metastases of Enjoyment: Six Essays on Women and Causality*, London and New York: Verso.

Žižek, Slavoj. (1997), *The Plague of Fantasies*, London: Verso.

Žižek, Slavoj. (2001), *The Fright of Real Tears: Krzysztof Kieslowski between Theory and Post-theory*, London: BFI Publishing.

Zusman, Waldemar. (1998), "*The Conversation*: Psychic Reality, Neutrality, and Reaction Formation," *Psychoanalytic Inquiry*, 18 (2): 251–6.

INDEX

Aaron, Michele 271 n.10, 273–4 n.9
Abbott, Traci B. 262 n.2
acousmêtre 43–4, 261 n.15
Adaptation 247, see also Jonze, Spike; Kaufman, Charlie
The Adventures of Priscilla, Queen of the Desert 259, see also Elliott, Stephan
A. I. Artificial Intelligence 43, see also Spielberg, Steven
Albert Nobbs 173, see also García, Rodrigo
Albrechtslund, Anders 265 n.25
All of Me 251, see also Reiner, Carl
Almodóvar, Pedro
　La ley del deseo (Law of Desire) 252–3, 258
　La mala educación (Bad Education) 204
　La piel que habito (The Skin I live In) 79–80, 252, 258, 262 n.17, 276 n.12
　Todo sobre mi madre (All about My Mother) 258
Alpert, Hollis 266–7 n.12
Althusser, Louis 17
American Sniper 57, see also Eastwood, Clint
Anamorphosis 269 n.31
Andrews, David 267–8 n.19
Angelucci, Gianfranco 136
Annesley, James 275 n.22
Annie Get Your Gun 256, see also Sidney, George
Annie Oakley 256, see also Stevens, George
Anomalisa 275 n.23, see also Kaufman, Charlie

Antonioni, Michelangelo
　Blow-Up 117–18, 265 n.25
Ardolino, Emile
　Chances Are 63, 251
Arieti, Silvano 266 n.5
Arnold, Jack
　The Mouse That Roared 253
Auteur 13–14, 19, 20, 33, 60, 66, 79, 129, 136, 159, 163, 246–8, 253, 258, 267 n.13, 272 n.17, 275 n.23

Bálasz, Béla 48
The Ballad of Little Jo 173, see also Greenwald, Maggie
Bankier van het Verzet (The Resistance Banker) 57, see also Lürsen, Joram
Barker, Jennifer M. 270 n.42
Barnett, Vincent L. 263 n.11
Baron, Cynthia 234
Barthes, Roland 56, 157, 270 n.39
Barzegar, Ebrahim 270 n.40
Bashevis Singer, Isaac 174
Baudry, Jean-Louis 17
Baxter, John 266–7 n.12
Bazin, André 118, 127–8, 266 n.6
Beckett, Samuel 144–5
Behind the Screen 255, see also Chaplin, Charlie
Being John Malkovich 16, 205, 207, 229–50, 253–4, 258, 274 n.20, 275 n.22, 275 n.23, see also Jonze, Spike; Kaufman, Charlie
Bellour, Raymond 18, 261 n.12
Belton, John 260 n.1
Benjamin, Walter 55

INDEX

Bergman, Ingmar
  Smultronstallet (*Wild Strawberries*) 89
Berliner, Alain
  Ma Vie en rose (*My Life in Pink*) 204
Bersani, Leo 276 n.15
Bertolucci, Bernardo
  La Strategia del Ragno (*The Spider's Stratagem*) 253, 275 n.2
Betti, Liliana 136
Bianchi, Emanuela 274 n.16
Big 11, 63, 252, *see also* Marshall, Penny
Bigwood, James 264 n.14
Birdman or (*The Unexpected Virtue of Ignorance*) 261 n.7, *see also* Iñárritu, Alejandro González
The Birds 68, *see also* Hitchcock, Alfred
Birth 63–4, 251–2, *see also* Glazer, Jonathan
The Birth of a Nation 52, *see also* Griffith, D. W.
The Blind Side 57, *see also* Hancock, John Lee
Blow-Up 117–18, 265 n.25, *see also* Antonioni, Michelangelo
Boarini, Vittorio 136, 267 n.14
body-character-breach films
  bodiless character 6, 9–10, 11, 33–46, 50, 61–2, 71, 254–5, 267 n.17
  body host 6, 11, 16, 61–2, 230–1, 253–4, 258
  body-switch 6, 11, 59, 61–2, 71, 72–3, 74, 251, 258
  body transformation 6, 11, 15, 61–2, 71–3, 79–80, 172, 252–3
  multiple-body character 6, 11, 61–2, 77–8, 253
  reincarnation 6, 11, 61–2, 63–4, 71, 251–2
body genre 68, 262 n.5
Bohemian Rhapsody 57, *see also* Singer, Bryan
Bondanella, Peter 267 n.13
Bondil-Poupard, Nathalie 263 n.1, 264 n.12, n.14
Bonitzer, Pascal 48, 53
Boyarin, Daniel 175–6, 177, 181
Boyhood 57, *see also* Linklater, Richard
Boys Don't Cry 15–16, 204–17, 229, 246, 249, 273 n.8, 273–4 n.9, 274 n.10–12, *see also* Peirce, Kimberly
The Brandon Teena Story 273 n.5, *see also* Muska, Susan, and Gréta Olafsdóttir
Branigan, Edward 266 n.9
Brill, Lesley 263 n.2
Britton, Andrew 102–3, 264 n.11, n.13, n.15
Brody, Jennifer Devere 273–4 n.9
Bronfen, Elisabeth 263 n.11
Brook, Clodagh 135
Brown, Royal 264 n.7
Bullough, Bonnie, and Vern L. Bullough 271 n.6
Buñuel, Luis
  Cet obscure objet du désir (*That Obscure Object of Desire*) 11, 69, 77–8, 79, 80, 253, 263 n.14
  Un Chien Andalou (*An Andalusian Dog*) 99–100, 105
Burke, Frank 267 n.13
Butler, David
  Calamity Jane 14, 191–6, 256, 272 n.19–21
Butler, Judith 233, 274 n.17, 275 n.5

Caché (*Hidden*) 261 n.9, *see also* Haneke, Michael
Calamity Jane 14, 191–6, 256, 272 n.19–21, *see also* Butler, David
Cameron, Ed 266 n.10, 267 n.15, 276 n.15
camp 72, 258–9
Campion, Jane
  The Portrait of a Lady 234
Canestrari, Renzo 267 n.13
Cardullo, Bert 275 n.5

Carroll, Nöel   24
Cavalcante, Andre   273 n.6
Cet obscure object du désir (*That Obscure Object of Desire*)   11, 69, 77–8, 79, 80, 253, 263 n.14 *see also* Buñuel, Luis
Chambers, Bill   267–8 n.19
Chances Are   63, 251, *see also* Ardolino, Emile
Chandler, Charlotte   266–7 n.12
Chandler, Raymond   26
The Change-Up   251, *see also* Dobkin, David
Chaplin, Charlie
  Behind the Screen   255
  The Great Dictator   253
  The Masquerader   255
  A Woman   255
Chaw, Walter   267–8 n.19
Chion, Michel   43–4
chōra   16, 173, 178, 232–7, 242–4, 274 n.15–17, *see also* Kristeva, Julia; Plato
The Christine Jorgensen Story   257, *see also* Rapper, Irving
Claire, René   56
Coen, Joel, and Ethan Coen
  The Man Who Wasn't There   89
Condon, Bill
  Twilight Saga: Breaking Dawn, Part 2   260 n.1
The Conversation   12, 16, 87, 88, 90, 92, 106–21, 249, 264 n.17–19, 265 n.20, n.22–7, *see also* Coppola, Francis Ford
Cook, Pam   275 n.7
Cook, Roger F.   268 n.20
Cooper, Brenda   207
Copenhafer, David   265 n.24
Copier, Laura   273 n.7
Copjec, Joan   19
Cop Land   89, *see also* Mangold, James
Coppola, Francis Ford
  The Conversation   12, 16, 87, 88, 90, 92, 106–21, 249, 264 n.17–19, 265 n.20, n.22–7
Corber, Robert J.   263 n.5

Cordelli, Valentina   266–7 n.12, 267 n.13
corporeality   2, 23, 26, 46, 61, 191
Costantini, Riccardo   266–7 n.12, 267 n.13
Costello, Donald P.   266 n.11, 267 n.16, n.18
counter-cinema   6, 7, 13, 18, 19, 20, 37, 42, 50, 54–5, 60, 61, 69, 77, 120, 253, 265 n.1
Cowie, Elizabeth   18
Cretton, Destin Daniel
  The Glass Castle   57

Dalí, Salvador   99–102
Dällenbach, Lucien   124, 144–5, 164
Dangerous Liaisons   234, *see also* Frears, Stephen
Daniel, Rod
  Like Father Like Son   251
The Danish Girl   258, *see also* Hooper, Tom
Davies, Cath   276 n12
Dawson, Leanne   206, 207, 210, 212, 273–4 n.9
Dayan, Daniel   17, 41
Degli-Esposti, Cristina   267 n.13
De Lauretis, Teresa   18, 69
Deleuze, Gilles   20, 48
Dellal, Gaby
  3 Generations   202
Demme, Jonathan
  The Silence of the Lambs   263 n.7
Denby, David   115
Denham, A. H.   270 n.37
Denzin, Norman K.   265 n.20
De Palma, Brian
  Dressed to Kill   256
Der Krieger und die Kaiserin (*The Princess and the Warrior*)   89, *see also* Tykwer, Tom
Derrida, Jacques   175, 233, 271 n.9, 274 n.16
Dettke, Julia   276 n.10
Dickinson, Emily   238–9
Diffrient, David Scott   276 n.11
Dittmar, Linda   208
Dixon, Wheeler Winston   266 n.8

INDEX

Doane, Mary Ann   44, 47–8, 52
Dobkin, David
   The Change-Up   251
Docarmo, Stephen N.   267–8 n.19
Docherty, Thomas   265 n.27
Dodds, Tomás   204–5
Dolar, Mladen   275 n.4
Down to Earth   251, see also Weitz, Chris, and Paul Weitz
Dracula   256
Dragunoiu, Dana   237–8, 239, 241
dream
   and cinema   3–4, 7, 12, 14, 17–18, 30–2, 55–6, 62, 64, 87–91, 266 n.4
   in *The Conversation*   106–21
   in *8½ (Otto e mezzo)*   122–4, 128–45, 151, 157, 158, 160–4
   as mise-en-abyme   11–14, 91, 104, 119–20, 154–64
   in *Mulholland Drive*   122–4, 145–64, 253, 267–8 n.19–20, 269 n.28, n.30
   in psychoanalysis   3–4, 17–18, 64, 87–91, 263 n.3–4, 264 n.8, 266 n.5 see also Freud, Sigmund
   in *Spellbound*   92–105, 263 n.5, 264 n.8–9, n.13–16
Dream a Little Dream   251, see also Rocco, Marc
Dressed to Kill   256, see also De Palma, Brian
Drew, Sidney
   A Florida Enchantment   258
Dr. Jekyll and Mr. Hyde   26–7, 234–5, 244, 274–5 n.21, see also Mamoulian, Rouben
Dr. Strangelove or: How I Learned to Stop Worrying and Love the Bomb   253, see also Kubrick, Stanley
Durgnat, Raymond   34
Dyer, Richard   54
Dzialo, Chris   275 n.22

Eastwood, Clint
   The 15:17 to Paris   57, 262 n.21
   American Sniper   57
Eberwein, Robert   264 n.8

Edwards, Blake
   Switch   258
   Victor Victoria   199–201, 255, 272–3 n.28, 275 n.6
Egoyan, Atom
   Felicia's Journey   89
8½ (Otto e mezzo)   13, 16, 89, 118, 122–3, 128–45, 146, 151, 157, 158, 160–1, 162, 163–4, 232, 246, 265 n.1, 266–7 n.7–18, see also Fellini, Federico
Elliott, Stephan
   The Adventures of Priscilla, Queen of the Desert   259
Elsaesser, Thomas   41–2, 261 n.13
Enter the Void   33, 260 n.3, see also Noé, Gaspar
Epstein, Jean   47, 261 n.16
Esposito, Jennifer   274 n.10, n.12
Evans, Dylan   235
Evans, Peter W.   77–8
Every Day   61, 253, see also Sucsy, Michael

Face/Off   11, 59–60, 66–9, 74, 251, 262 n.1, see also Woo, John
Fan, Victor   273 n.4
fantasmatic space   3, 5, 12, 32–3, 41, 50, 55, 62, 75, 80, 83, 104, 105, 162, 222, 226
Farrelly, Bobby, and Peter Farrelly
   Shallow Hal   11, 71–3, 74–5, 77, 252, 263 n.10
Felicia's Journey   89, see also Egoyan, Atom
Fellini, Federico
   8½ (Otto e mezzo)   13, 16, 89, 118, 122–3, 128–45, 146, 151, 157, 158, 160–1, 162, 163–4, 232, 246, 265 n.1, 266–7 n.7–18
   Giulietta degli Spiriti (Juliet of the Spirits)   89
Fellini, je suis un grand menteur (Fellini, I'm a Born Liar)   266–7 n.12, see also Pettigrew, Damian
Female Trouble   276 n.13, see also Waters, John

feminine enjoyment 8, 14–16, 19, 167–73, 174, 176–9, 183, 187, 189, 190, 191–2, 196–200, 202, 203–4, 206, 210, 218, 220, 227, 228–9, 231, 233, 236–7, 239, 240, 241, 242–3, 246, 247, 250, 257, 258, 276 n.15
feminine structure 8, 171
Fernley, Allison 182, 188, 190
fetish, fetishism 10, 15, 28–9, 30, 34, 46, 65–6, 70, 71, 75–6, 117, 154, 171, 187, 192–4, 196, 198, 239, 242, 243, 270 n.2, 272 n.20, n.26
Fiennes, Sophie
The Pervert's Guide to Cinema 28
The 15:17 to Paris 57, 262 n.21, see also Eastwood, Clint
Fight Club 80–1, 252, 263 n.15, see also Fincher, David
Fincher, David
Fight Club 80–1, 252, 263 n.15
Fink, Bruce 1, 7, 169–70, 171, 173, 271 n.5
Flawless 259, see also Schumacher, Joel
Fleming, Victor
Gone with the Wind 58, 265 n.2
Fletcher, John 261 n.10
Flinn, Caryl 276 n.15
A Florida Enchantment 258, see also Drew, Sidney
Folman, Ari
Kennes Ha'atidanim (The Congress) 260 n.1
Foucault, Michel 19, 210
Fox, Eytan
Lalechet al hamayim (Walk on Water) 89
Franju, George
Les yeux sans visage (The Eyes without a Face) 10–11, 48–51, 66, 68, 69, 79, 80, 262 n.17
Frankenstein 51, 256–7
Freaky Friday (1976) 251, see also Nelson, Gary
Freaky Friday (2003) 11, 62, 63, see also Waters, Mark S.

Frears, Stephen
Dangerous Liaisons 234
Mary Reilly 234
Freud, Sigmund
daydream 3, 4, 17, 64, 89, 90, 263 n.3–4, 264 n.14, 269 n.31
see also dream
invocatory drive 9, 10, 25, 27, 42, 43, 44, 70, 117, 270 n.42
and Lacan 3, 32, 65, 87, 270 n.2
Oedipal structure, Oedipus complex 3, 4, 12, 32, 34, 38, 39, 64, 65, 74, 82, 88, 90, 119, 121, 128, 134, 264 n.6, n.19
pleasure principle 168, 169, 203, 256
scopic drive 9, 10, 25, 27, 30, 42, 43, 44, 70, 117
superego 87–8, 203
uncanny 7, 43–4, 45, 46, 73–4, 75, 225, 239, 245, 263 n.11, 275 n.2
Friedberg, Anne 89
Fuller, Graham 156, 163

Gabbard, Glen O. 263 n.11
Gabriel, Gilbert 264 n.9
Galoppe, Raúl A. 272 n.25
Gansky, Paul 264 n.10
Garber, Marjorie 188, 271 n.12, n.15, 275 n.5
García, Rodrigo
Albert Nobbs 173
gaze
cinema gaze 35, 36, 41, 42, 43–4, 45, 48, 52, 53, 70, 103, 104, 105, 117
and Lacan 25, 43–4, 45, 48, 53, 105, 204, 224, 254 see also Lacan
spectator's gaze 36, 70, 222
transgender gaze 205, 212, 222, 274 n.11
Geheimnisse Einer Seele (Secrets of a Soul) 89, 90, see also Pabst, G. W.
gender-crossing film

the cross-dresser 7, 14, 167, 171, 173, 178, 192, 202, 255, 258, 270 n.1, 271 n.12, 273 n.7, 275 n.5
the drag queen 7, 14, 167, 200, 258–9, 276 n.13–16
the tomboy 7, 14, 167, 171, 191, 192, 202, 255–6, 272 n.19, 273 n.1
the trans-body 7, 14, 16, 71, 79, 80, 167, 202, 205, 217–18, 229, 231, 258, 273 n.7
the trans protagonist 7, 14, 15–16, 64, 167, 172, 192, 202–6, 207, 217, 225, 229, 231, 236, 252–3, 257–8, 262 n.2, 273 n.7, 276 n.10
the transvestite 7, 14, 72, 167, 256–7, 258, 271 n.12, 275 n.5
Gendernauts: A Journey through Shifting Identities 273–4 n.9, *see also* Treut, Monika
Gessler, Nicholas 267–8 n.19
Gherovici, Patricia 203, 273 n.2
Giannopoulou, Zina 270 n.38
Gieri, Manuela 267 n.13
Gilda 146, *see also* Vidor, Charles
Giuliani, Luca 266–7 n.12, 267 n.13
Giulietta degli Spiriti (Juliet of the Spirits) 89, *see also* Fellini, Federico
The Glass Castle 57, *see also* Cretton, Destin Daniel
Glazer, Jonathan
  Birth 63–4, 251–2
Gleiberman, Owen 267 n.19
Godard, Jean-Luc
  Le Mépris (Contempt) 54, 265 n.1
  Letter to Jane: An Investigation about a Still 54
Gone with the Wind 58, 265 n.2, *see also* Fleming, Victor
Gorin, Jean-Pierre
  Letter to Jane: An Investigation about a Still 54
The Great Dictator 253, *see also* Chaplin, Charlie

Greenwald, Maggie
  The Ballad of Little Jo 173
Greven, David 263 n.5
Griffith, D. W.
  The Birth of a Nation 52
  Intolerance: Love's Struggle throughout the Ages 52
Grosz, Elizabeth 274 n.16
Guinn, Jeff 274 n.14
Gutiérrez-Albilla, Julián Daniel 273 n.4
Guzzetti, Alfred 266 n.4

Haaken, Jan
  Queens of Heart: Community Therapists in Drag 276 n.16
Hagener, Malte 41–2, 261 n.13
Hairspray (1988) 276 n.13, *see also* Waters, John
Hairspray (2007) 276 n.13, *see also* Shankman, Adam
Halberstam, J. Jack 255–6, 273 n.9, 274 n.11, 276 n.14
Hamer, Robert
  Kind Hearts and Coronets 253
Hancock, John Lee
  The Blind Side 57
Haneke, Michael
  Caché (Hidden) 261 n.9
Hanke, Robert 262 n.1
Harry Potter 56–7
Hayles, Katherine N. 267–8 n.19
Haynes, Todd
  I'm Not There 61, 253
Heath, Stephen 54
Her 9–10, 10–11, 42, 44–6, 50–1, 71, 254–5, 261 n.14–15, *see also* Jonze, Spike
Hitchcock, Alfred
  The Birds 68
  North by Northwest 9, 37–42, 71, 75, 254, 261 n.13
  Psycho 68, 152, 153, 154, 254, 256, 262 n.18
  Rear Window 117–18, 120, 265 n.25
  Rebecca 9, 10–11, 33–7, 38, 39, 40, 41, 46, 50, 71, 76, 254, 261 n.10–11

Rope 263 n.5
Spellbound 12, 88, 89, 90, 92–105, 114, 121, 151, 263 n.2, n.5, 264 n.6–16
Strangers on a Train 263 n.5
Vertigo 11, 29–30, 73–7, 79, 153–4, 252, 261 n.13, 263 n.11, 268 n.25
Hodge, James J. 261 n.15
Hoffmann, E. T. A. 74
Hooper, Tom
  The Danish Girl 258
Hopkins, Stephen
  The Life and Death of Peter Sellers 57
The Host 254, see also Niccol, Andrew
Houston, Dianne
  Michael Jackson: Searching for Neverland 57
Hudson, Jennifer A. 267 n.19
Hughes-D'Aeth, Tony 269 n.28, n.33
Huntjens, Joyce 263 n.11
Hyams, Peter
  2010: The Year We Make Contact 43

the imaginary
  in *Being John Malkovich* 232, 240, 243–4, 245–6, 248, 249
  in cinema, of the spectator 3–4, 5, 10–12, 17, 27, 28, 31, 32–3, 42, 46, 47, 55, 56, 57, 58, 62, 70–1, 72, 124, 126, 127, 201, 205, 222, 224, 226, 244, 245–6, 249
  in *The conversation* 111, 114, 116, 117, 118, 120, 121
  in *8½ (Otto e mezzo)* 123, 135, 136, 142, 143
  in *Her* 44, 45, 46, 71
  in Lacan 5, 8, 16, 17, 25, 32, 65–6, 68, 82, 88, 168, 171, 203, 235
  in *Les yeux sans visage (The Eyes without a Face)* 50, 51
  in *Mulholland Drive* 123, 145, 161
  in *Spellbound* 88, 95, 104

I'm Not There 61, 253, see also Haynes, Todd
Iñárritu, Alejandro González
  Birdman or (The Unexpected Virtue of Ignorance) 261 n.7
Intolerance: Love's Struggle throughout the Ages 52, see also Griffith, D. W.
Irigaray, Luce 274 n.16

Jackson, Michael 57, 275 n.1
"James Bond" 56, 126
Jeffers McDonald, Tamar 272 n.19
Jefferson, Ann 120
Johnson, Robert K. 114, 115, 117, 118, 264 n.18
Jones, Ernest 82
Jonze, Spike
  Adaptation 247
  Being John Malkovich 16, 205, 207, 229–50, 253–4, 258, 274 n.20, 275 n.22, 275 n.23
  Her 9–10, 10–11, 42, 44–6, 50–1, 71, 254–5, 261 n.14–15

Kaminski, Elizabeth 259
Kaplan, E. Ann. 264 n.16
Katovich, Michael A. 276 n.9
Kaufman, Charlie
  Adaptation 247
  Anomalisa 275 n.23
  Being John Malkovich 16, 205, 207, 229–50, 253–4, 258, 274 n.20, 275 n.22, 275 n.23
  Synecdoche, New York 275 n.23
Kennes Ha'atidanim (The Congress) 260 n.1, see also Folman, Ari
Kenny, Glen 267 n.19
Kezich, Tullio 136, 267 n.14
Kidron, Beeban
  To Wong Foo, Thanks for Everything! Julie Newmar 259
Kind Hearts and Coronets 253, see also Hamer, Robert
King, Barry 53–4
Kinkade, Patrick T. 276 n.9
Kley, Martin 274 n.20
Klock, Geoff 269 n.30

Kohen-Raz, Odeya   260 n.2
Kornhaber, Donna   261 n.14
Kovács, András Bálint   267 n.19
Kracauer, Siegfried   47, 51–2, 55–6
Kristeva, Julia   8, 14, 16, 81–2, 172–3, 179, 181, 191, 229, 233, 242
Kubrick, Stanley
   Dr. Strangelove or: How I Learned to Stop Worrying and Love the Bomb   253
   2001: A Space Odyssey   9, 42–4, 254–5
Kuhn, Annette   272 n.26, 275 n.5

Lacan, Jacques, *see also* Freud, Sigmund; gaze; subjectivity; the Imaginary; the real; the symbolic
   castration   2, 4, 6, 7, 8, 14, 19, 20, 24, 25, 51, 58, 64, 65, 70, 71, 72, 74–5, 88, 104, 119, 128, 168, 169, 170, 171, 176, 177, 185, 187, 257, 262 n.6, 270 n.2, 271 n.15
   das Ding   65, 66, 169, 176
   extimacy   7–8
   jouissance   7, 8, 167, 168, 169–70, 203, 235
   mirror stage   17
   objet a/objet petit a   5, 8–9, 11, 13–4, 25, 30, 32, 35, 36, 39, 40, 58, 65, 66, 235, 240, 243, 244, 254
   signifier   8, 65, 66, 69, 82, 155, 168, 169–70, 171, 173, 174, 270 n.2
   the traumatic   9, 10, 11, 12, 19, 44, 45, 55, 56, 64, 65, 66, 67, 68, 69, 70, 74, 75–6, 79, 83, 111, 112, 114, 117, 154, 155, 163, 233, 242, 245
   voice (as partial object)   10, 25, 42–5, 71
Lady in the Lake   9, 26, 27, 32–3, *see also* Montgomery, Robert
Laine, Tarja   269 n.29, n.31
Lalechet al hamayim (*Walk on Water*)   89, *see also* Fox, Eytan

La ley del deseo (*Law of Desire*)   252–3, 258, *see also* Almodóvar, Pedro
La mala educación (*Bad Education*)   204, *see also* Almodóvar, Pedro
Landsberg, Alison   57
L'Animale   273 n.1, *see also* Mückstein, Katharina
La piel que habito (*The Skin I live In*)   79–80, 252, 258, 262 n.17, 276 n.12, *see also* Almodóvar, Pedro
Laplanche, Jean   4, 18, 64, 88–9
La Strategia del Ragno (*The Spider's Stratagem*)   253, 275 n.2, *see also* Bertolucci, Bernardo
Laura   254, *see also* Preminger, Otto
Lelio, Sebastián
   Una mujer fantástica   16, 204–5, 206–7, 217–29, 249–50, 258
Le Mépris (*Contempt*)   54, 265 n.1, *see also* Godard, Jean-Luc
Lentzner, Jay R.   145, 150, 153, 162, 267–8 n.19, 268 n.26
Les yeux sans visage (*The Eyes without a Face*)   10–11, 48–51, 66, 68, 69, 79, 80, 262 n.17, *see also* Franju, George
Letter to Jane: An Investigation about a Still   54, *see also* Godard, Jean-Luc; Gorin, Jean-Pierre
Lieberfeld, Daniel   275 n.5
The Life and Death of Peter Sellers   57, *see also* Hopkins, Stephen
Like Father Like Son   251, *see also* Daniel, Rod
Lindsay-Hogg, Michael
   The Object of Beauty   234
Linklater, Richard
   Boyhood   57
Lopate, Phillip   267–8 n.19
Losey, Joseph
   Monsieur Klein (*Mr. Klein*)   254
Lost Highway   253, *see also* Lynch, David
Love, Heather   268 n.20

Loving 57, see also Nichols, Jeff
Lukacher, Ned 108, 115
Lürsen, Joram
  Bankier van het Verzet (*The Resistance Banker*) 57
Lynch, David
  Lost Highway 253
  Mulholland Drive 13, 16, 89, 122–3, 128, 145–64, 232, 246, 253, 267–70 n.19–42

McDonald, Christie V. 175
McGowan, Todd 19, 24–5, 53, 155
McMahon, Jennifer 268 n.22–3, 270 n.41
MacTaggart, Allister 269 n.31
Magritte, René 100
Maloof, Paula 182, 188, 190
Maltby, Richard 58
Mamoulian, Rouben
  Dr. Jekyll and Mr. Hyde 26–7, 234–5, 244, 274–5 n.21
  Queen Christina 255
Mangold, James
  Cop Land 89
The Man in the Iron Mask 234, see also Wallace, Randall
Manlove, Clifford T. 75
The Man Who Wasn't There 89, see also Coen, Joel, and Ethan Coen
Margaroni, Maria 233
Marshall, Penny
  Big 11, 63, 252
Mary Reilly 234, see also Frears, Stephen
masculine structure 8, 170–1, 198
The Masquerader 255, see also Chaplin, Charlie
Ma Vie en rose (*My Life in Pink*) 204, see also Berliner, Alain
Mayne, Judith 54
Meiri, Sandra 260 n.2, 275 n.8
Metev, Llan
  Poslednata Lineika na Sofia (*Sofia's Last Ambulance*) 261 n.9
Metz, Christian 3, 17, 24, 27–9, 30, 44, 55–6, 58, 77, 90, 124, 126, 127, 128, 161, 266 n.4, n.7

Meyer, Moe 276 n.15
Michael Jackson: Searching for Neverland 57, see also Houston, Dianne
Miller, D. A. 263 n.5
Miller, Lucy J. 273 n.7
mise-en-abyme
  in *Being John Malkovich* 238, 247
  in cinema 11–13, 14, 91
  in *The conversation* 119–20, 265 n.26–7
  in *8½* (*Otto e mezzo*) 129, 136–45
  in *Mulholland Drive* 154–64
  in *Rebecca* 33
  in *Spellbound* 104
  textual *mise-en-abyme* 13, 14, 124, 129, 141–2, 143, 144, 154, 162, 164
  in *Victor Victoria* 200
Modleski, Tania 34, 35, 36, 261 n.11, 263 n.11
Monaco, James 274–5 n.21
Monsieur Klein (*Mr. Klein*) 254, see also Losey, Joseph
Montgomery, Robert
  Lady in the Lake 9, 26, 27, 32–3
The Mouse That Roared 253, see also Arnold, Jack
Mückstein, Katharina
  L'Animale 273 n.1
Mulholland Drive 13, 16, 89, 122–3, 128, 145–64, 232, 246, 253, 267–70 n.19–42, see also Lynch, David
Mulvey, Laura 18, 205, 226
Murray, Ros 262 n.17
Muska, Susan, and Gréta Olafsdóttir
  The Brandon Teena Story 273 n.5
Myra Breckinridge 257, see also Sarne, Michael

Naremore, James 270 n.41
Nelson, Gary
  Freaky Friday (1976) 251
Newton, Esther 258–9

Niccol, Andrew
  The Host 254
  Simone 260 n.1
Nichols, Jeff
  Loving 57
Nieland, Justus 270 n.35
Nochimson, Martha P. 156, 157, 159, 161, 162–3, 270 n.36
Noé, Gaspar
  Enter the Void 33, 260 n.3
North by Northwest 9, 37–42, 71, 75, 254, 261 n.13, see also Hitchcock, Alfred

The Object of Beauty 234, see also Lindsay-Hogg, Michael
Olson, Greg 270 n.34
Orlando 258, see also Potter, Sally
Ozon, François
  Une nouvelle amie (*The New Girlfriend*) 257, 276 n.10

Pabst, G. W.
  Geheimnisse Einer Seele (*Secrets of a Soul*) 89, 90
Pacchioni, Federico 267 n.13
Palindromes 61, 253, see also Solondz, Todd
Parciack, Ronie 269 n.29
Pasolini, Pier Paolo 118
Pattison, Michael 267–8 n.19
Peirce, Kimberly
  Boys Don't Cry 15–16, 204–17, 229, 246, 249, 273 n.8, 273–4 n.9, 274 n.10–12
Perlmutter, Ruth 163
Perry, Douglas 274 n.14
The Pervert's Guide to Cinema 28, see also Fiennes, Sophie
Pettigrew, Damian
  Fellini, je suis un grand menteur (*Fellini, I'm a Born Liar*) 266–7 n.12
Phillips, John 270 n.1
photogénie 9, 47, 51–2
Pidduck, Julianne 273 n.9
Pink Flamingos 276 n.13, see also Waters, John

Plato 173, 232, 233, 274 n.15–16
Pollack, Sidney
  Tootsie 255
Pontalis, Jean-Bertrand 4, 18, 64, 88–9
The Portrait of a Lady 234, see also Campion, Jane
Posadas, Marco 217
Poslednata Lineika na Sofia (*Sofia's Last Ambulance*) 261 n.9, see also Metev, Llan
Potter, Sally
  Orlando 258
Preminger, Otto
  Laura 254
Price, Zachary 276 n.12
primal scene 4–5, 18, 32, 38, 64, 99, 104, 108–9, 111, 113, 117, 119
prosthetic memory 57
Psycho 68, 152, 153, 154, 254, 256, 262 n.18, see also Hitchcock, Alfred
Pudovkin, Vsevolod 56

Queen Christina 255, see also Mamoulian, Rouben
Queens of Heart: Community Therapists in Drag 276 n.16, see also Haaken, Jan

Rapper, Irving
  The Christine Jorgensen Story 257
Ratner, Megan 113
the real
  in *Being John Malkovich* 232, 235, 237, 240, 241–2, 243–4, 245
  of the body 65–9, 71–4, 263 n.10
  in *8½* (*Otto e mezzo*) 136, 145, 267 n.15
  in *Her* 42, 44, 45
  in Lacan 8, 12, 16, 19, 168, 170, 171, 173, 203, 235, 246, 257, 263 n.8, 271 n.4
  in *La piel que habito* (*The Skin I live In*) 79
  in *Les yeux sans visage* (*The Eyes without a Face*) 11, 79
  in *Mulholland Drive* 153, 154
  in *Spellbound* 102–3

in *Vertigo* 75, 76
in *Yentl* 174, 176, 191
Rear Window 117, 118, 120, 265 n.25, *see also* Hitchcock, Alfred
Rebecca 9, 10–11, 33–7, 38, 39, 40, 41, 46, 50, 71, 76, 254, 261 n.10–11, *see also* Hitchcock, Alfred
Reed, Katherine M. 269 n.32
Reiner, Carl
  All of Me 251
Reitz, Nikki 205
Repass, Scott 234
Ridgway, Franklin 268 n.20, 269 n.27
Rigney, Melissa 215
Roach, Hal
  Turnabout 258
Rocco, Marc
  Dream a Little Dream 251
The Rocky Horror Picture Show 256–7, 276 n.9, *see also* Sharman, Jim
the semiotic
  in *Being John Malkovich* 16, 229–43, 243–4, 249, 250
  in *Calamity Jane* 191, 196
  in cinema 14, 15, 16, 229
  in Kristeva 8, 172–3, 229
  in *Victor Victoria* 200
  in *Yentl* 174, 176, 177, 178, 179, 186, 187, 190, 271 n.12
Romeo and Juliet 51, *see also* Zeffirelli, Franco
Rope 263 n.5, *see also* Hitchcock, Alfred
Rose, Jacqueline 270 n.3
Rosen, Philip 266 n.6
Ross, Donald R. 145, 150, 153, 162, 267–8 n.19, 268 n.26
Roustang, François 115
Rushing, Robert A. 269 n.31
Rushton, Richard 95

San Filippo, Maria 276 n.10
Sarne, Michael
  Myra Breckinridge 257
Sartre, Jean-Paul 126, 268 n.22
Savoy, Eric 191
Schatz, Thomas 262 n.19
Schindler's List 57, *see also* Spielberg, Steven
Schumacher, Joel
  Flawless 259
Schünzel, Reinhold
  Viktor und Viktoria 275 n.6
Sciama, Céline
  Tomboy 204
Seckin, Banu 232, 234, 235, 237, 243, 249
Segal, Naomi 240
17 Again 252, *see also* Steers, Burr
Shakespeare, William
  Hamlet 91
  King Lear 239
  Romeo and Juliet 51
Shallow Hal 11, 71–3, 74–5, 77, 252, 263 n.10, *see also* Farrelly, Bobby, and Peter Farrelly
Shankman, Adam
  Hairspray (2007) 276 n.13
Sharman, Jim
  The Rocky Horror Picture Show 256–7, 276 n.9
Shaw, Daniel 234, 237
Shelley, Mary 51, 256–7
Shetley, Vernon 268 n.25
Shostak, Debra 269 n.31, 270 n.38, n.41
Shpall, Sam 263 n.15
Sidney, George
  Annie Get Your Gun 256
Sikov, Ed 272 n.24
The Silence of the Lambs 263 n.7, *see also* Demme, Jonathan
Simone 260 n.1, *see also* Niccol, Andrew
Singer, Bryan
  Bohemian Rhapsody 57
Sinnerbrink, Robert 267–8 n.19
Sloop, John M. 273 n.8
Smoke 125–7, *see also* Wang, Wayne
Smultronstallet (*Wild Strawberries*) 89, *see also* Bergman, Ingmar
Snorton, Riley C. 274 n.12
Sobchack, Vivian 4, 31

Solmi, Angelo   266 n.8
Solondz, Todd
  Palindromes   61, 253
Some Like It Hot   14–15, 191–2,
  196–9, 201, 255, 272 n.22–6,
  see also Wilder, Billy
Sontag, Susan   276 n.15
Sophocles   264
Spellbound   12, 88, 89, 90, 92–105,
  114, 121, 151, 263 n.2, n.5,
  264 n.6–16, *see also* Dalí,
  Salvador; Hitchcock, Alfred
Spielberg, Steven
  A. I. Artificial Intelligence   43
  Schindler's List   57
Spoto, Donald   264 n.14
Stacey, Jackie   54, 272 n.20
Stam, Robert   77
Star, star system, stardom   7, 10, 36,
  46, 51–2, 53–5, 57–8, 61, 78,
  123, 141, 142, 145, 146, 151,
  162, 163–4, 205, 243, 247, 248,
  253, 272 n.20, 274 n.20, 275 n.3
Steers, Burr
  17 Again   252
Steinbock, Eliza   205, 273 n.7
Stevens, George
  Annie Oakley   256
Stevenson, Robert Louis   274–5 n.21
Stivers, Clint   267–8 n.19
Straayer, Chris   258, 272 n.23, n.27,
  275 n.5, 276 n.13
Strangers on a Train   263 n.5, *see also*
  Hitchcock, Alfred
Streisand, Barbra
  Yentl   14–15, 173–91, 192, 194,
    196, 199, 249, 255, 271 n.7–16,
    272 n.17–18
Stroumsa, Guy G.   271 n.11
Stubbs, John C.   136, 266 n.12,
  267 n.13
Studlar, Gaylyn   276 n.9
Subjecthood   69, 70, 71, 78
subjectivity
  and body (characters/
    spectators)   10, 11, 12, 20, 23,
    26, 27, 33, 42, 43, 44, 46, 47,
    48, 49, 63, 67, 68, 70, 71, 79,
    275 n.2

and dream (dreaming character)
  88, 90–1, 95, 100, 115–16, 117,
  118, 120, 266 n.6, n.10
and gender-crossing   171, 205,
  206, 221, 231, 243, 244, 246,
  248, 257–8, 276 n.15
and Lacan   7–8, 71
subjectivization
  and dream   12, 102, 103, 105,
    115, 119–21
  and gender   8, 14, 167–8, 170,
    171, 173, 190, 191, 200, 205,
    217, 224, 228, 231, 233, 243
  and the meta-cinematic   13, 16,
    123, 142, 143, 157, 161
  process of   1–2, 5–8, 11, 12, 13,
    14, 16, 58, 69–83, 87, 91, 92,
    167–8, 170, 171, 173
Sucsy, Michael
  Every Day   61, 253
Sunset Boulevard   54, 163, *see also*
  Wilder, Billie
suture   35, 41–2, 261 n.13
Switch   258, *see also* Edwards,
  Blake
the symbolic
  in *Being John Malkivich*   232, 235,
    240, 249
  in *The Conversation*   114, 116,
    118–19
  and dreams   12, 14, 88, 90–1, 95,
    104–5, 264 n.8
  in *Face/Off*   67, 68, 69
  and gender   15, 16, 18, 168, 169,
    172–3, 176, 203
  in Hitchcock   38, 39, 40, 42, 74,
    76, 95, 104–5
  in Lacan   2, 8, 12, 17, 65–6, 70,
    71, 72, 82, 104–5, 203, 235,
    262 n.6
  in *Mulholland Drive*   154, 155,
    164, 269 n.31
  in *Spellbound*   95, 104–5
Synecdoche, New York   275 n.23,
  see also Kaufman, Charlie

tactility   28, 233, 260 n.5
Tang, Jean   267 n.19
Tasker, Yvonne   275 n.7

Taubin, Amy   267–8 n.19
Tavlin, Zachary   270 n.42
Taylor, Verta   259
Thomas, Eric Austin   260 n.4
Thoreau Bruckner, René   268 n.20
3 Generations   202, see also Dellal, Gaby
Todo sobre mi madre (All About My Mother)   258, see also Almodóvar, Pedro
Toles, George   158, 268 n.24, 270 n.37
Tomboy   204, see also Sciama, Céline
Tootsie   255, see also Pollack, Sidney
To Wong Foo, Thanks for Everything! Julie Newmar   259, see also Kidron, Beeban
Transamerica   64, 252–3, see also Tucker, Duncan
Treut, Monika
  Gendernauts: A Journey through Shifting Identities   273–4 n.9
Treveri Gennari, Daniela   141
Truffaut, François   29, 263 n.13
Tucker, Duncan
  Transamerica   64, 252–3
Turan, Kenneth   267 n.19
Turnabout   258, see also Roach, Hal
Turner, Dennis   264 n.17, 265 n.25–6
Twilight Saga: Breaking Dawn, Part 2   260 n.1, see also Condon, Bill
2001: A Space Odyssey   9, 42–4, 254–5, see also Kubrick, Stanley
2010: The Year We Make Contact   43, see also Hyams, Peter
Tykwer, Tom
  Der Krieger und die Kaiserin (The Princess and the Warrior)   89

Un Chien Andalou (An Andalusian Dog)   99–100, 105, see also Buñuel, Luis; Dalí, Salvador
Una mujer fantástica   16, 204–5, 206–7, 217–29, 249–50, 258, see also Lelio, Sebastián
Une nouvelle amie (The New Girlfriend)   257, 276 n.10, see also Ozon, François

Van Wert, William F.   264 n.13
Vertigo   11, 29–30, 73–7, 79, 153–4, 252, 261 n.13, 263 n.11, 268 n.25, see also Hitchcock, Alfred
Victor Victoria   199–201, 255, 272–3 n.28, 275 n.6, see also Edwards, Blake
Vidor, Charles
  Gilda   146
Viktor und Viktoria   275 n.6, see also Schünzel, Reinhold
Volcano, Del LaGrace   276 n.14
Voyeurism   27–8, 30, 32, 246, 265 n.20, 268 n.25

Waldron, Darren   262 n.17
Wallace, Randall
  The Man in the Iron Mask   234
Waller, Marguerite R.   267 n.13
Wang, Wayne
  Smoke   125–7
Warhol, Andy   274 n.14
Waters, John
  Female Trouble   276 n.13
  Hairspray (1988)   276 n.13
  Pink Flamingos   276 n.13
Waters, Mark S.
  Freaky Friday (2003)   11, 62, 63
Watson, William Van   136
Weinstein, Lissa   232, 234, 235, 237, 243, 249
Weitz, Chris, and Paul Weitz
  Down to Earth   251
White, Patricia   273 n.9
Wicke, Jennifer   197–8
Wilde, Oscar   268 n.21
Wilder, Billy
  Some Like it Hot   14–15, 191–2, 196–9, 201, 255, 272 n.22–6
  Sunset Boulevard   54, 163
Williams, Linda   78, 262 n.5
Wilson, George   263 n.15
Wollen, Peter   54–5
A Woman   255, see also Chaplin, Charlie
Woo, John
  Face/Off   11, 59–60, 66–9, 74, 251, 262 n.1

Woolf, Virginia 258
Worrell, F. D. 270 n.37

Yentl 14–15, 173–91, 192, 194, 196, 199, 249, 255, 271 n.7–16, 272 n.17–18, *see also* Streisand, Barbra

Zeffirelli, Franco
   Romeo and Juliet 51
Zimmer, Catherine 265 n.23
Žižek, Slavoj 15, 19, 28, 41–2, 87, 203, 261 n.13, 263 n.12, 273 n.3, 275 n.4
Zusman, Waldemar 264 n.19

www.ingramcontent.com/pod-product-compliance
Lightning Source LLC
Chambersburg PA
CBHW070016010526
44117CB00011B/1591